The Collected Works of Edith Stein

XI

The Collected Works
of

EDITH STEIN

Saint Teresa Benedicta of the Cross
Discalced Carmelite
1891-1942

Edited by
Dr. L. Gelber
and
Romaeus Leuven, O.C.D.

Volume Eleven

ICS Publications
Institute of Carmelite Studies
Washington, D.C.
2009

EDITH STEIN

The Collected Works of Edith Stein
Volume Eleven

Potency and Act

Studies Toward a Philosophy of Being

**Edited by
Dr. L. Gelber
and
Romaeus Leuven, O.C.D.**

**Introduction
by Hans Rainer Sepp**

Translated by Walter Redmond

ICS Publications
Institute of Carmelite Studies
Washington, D.C.
2009

Library of Congress Cataloging-in-Publication Data
Stein, Edith, Saint, 1891-1942.
   [Potenz und Akt. English]
Potency and act : studies toward a philosophy of being / edited .....by
L. Gelber and Romaeus Leuven ; introduction by Hans Rainer Sepp ;
translated by Walter Redmond.
         p. cm. -- (The collected works of Edith Stein ; v. 11)
   Includes bibliographical references and index.
   ISBN 978-0-935216-48-6 (alk. paper)
   1. Ontology. 2. Act (Philosophy) I. Gelber, Lucy. II. Leuven,
   Romaeus. III.
Title.
   B3332.S672 E54 1986 vol. 11
   [BD313]
   111--dc22
                                        2008054592

{v}   **Table of Contents**

Translator's Note

Potency and Act is the second of three works in which St. Theresa Benedicta of the Cross set out explicitly to relate the phenomenology of her teacher Edmund Husserl and the scholasticism of St. Thomas Aquinas.[1] She saw this project as her "proper mission," her "life's task."[2] She not only "contrasted" the two philosophies but "fused" them into her own "philosophical system," a search for perennial philosophy, "something beyond ages and peoples common to all who honestly seek the truth."[3]

Her philosophical development, though quite consistent, clearly falls into two phases: first phenomenology and then a synthesis of

---

[1]   Cf. author's preface, *Finite and Eternal Being, The Collected Works of Edith Stein*, vol. 9, Institute of Carmelite Studies Publications (hereafter cited as CWES followed by the volume number), pp. xxvii-xxviii. She tells us in her foreword to *Potency and Act* that while her "philosophical thinking was formed by Edmund Husserl, [she] has in recent years found a home in Aquinas's thought world. She now feels an inner need to allow the two ways of doing philosophy... to come to resolution within herself" p. 3 (also footnote).

[2]   This mission was "critically comparing" the two philosophies (Letter to Finke, January 6, 1931; cf. German Editor's Introduction, xiii) and she linked her "life's task" to *Potency and Act* (letter 135, to Conrad-Martius) wherein she examined "all the questions of principle between Thomas and Husserl" (letter to Finke, May 6, 1931; cf. xiv) and "endeavored to get from scholasticism to phenomenology and vice versa" (letter 135; cf. xviii).

[3]   *Verschmelzung* as well as *Gegenüberstellung* or *Auseindersetzung*. In her preface to *Finite and Eternal Being*, she says that the two "philosophical worlds that met within her understanding demanded critical comparison", and that her "personal concern was to seek the meaning of being and strive to fuse medieval thought with the lively thought of today." *Potency and Act*, she said, "grows into my 'philosophical system,' which of course is a give-and-take *between* Thomas and Husserl" (letter of March 9, 1932 to Ingarden). The final quote is from her preface to *Finite and Eternal Being*, p. xxviii (cf. German editor's introduction to *Potency and Act*, p. xxiii).

scholasticism and phenomenology. The second stage dates from 1925, when, after becoming a Catholic (1922), she began to study St. Thomas in earnest and to translate his *De Veritate* into German (published 1931-3, 1935). The first of the three works was a "conversation" between Husserl and Aquinas that later (1929) appeared as an article in the journal of phenomenology.[4] The second was the present work, *Potency and Act*, written in 1931 but published for the first time in 1998. The third was her major work, *Finite and Eternal Being*, written around 1935 and also published posthumously, in 1950.[5]

The content of *Potency and Act* differs from *Finite and Eternal Being*, not least in its "modal" approach to the study of being.[6] Her treatment of possible worlds and of form prescribing possibilities relates not only to phenomenological themes but to recent developments in logical semantics. Her contribution to the philosophy of religion is, of course, central in her work. We reach God, she says, not only through faith and contemplation but "by thinking," using "logical reasoning" both from the world without (as in St. Thomas's "five ways") and from the world within ("the way of St. Augustine") when

---

[4]   The article: *Jahrbuch für Philosophie und phänomenologische Forschung* (*Festschrift* in honor of Husserl); the manuscript: *Erkenntnis und Glaube* (vol. 15 of *Edith Steins Werke*, Herder) 1993. Both versions appear in opposing columns in *Knowledge and Faith*, translation of *Erkenntnis und Glaube* by W. Redmond, CWESviii, 2000.

[5]   *Endliches und ewiges Sein* (vol. 2 of *Edith Steins Werke*, Herder); English translation by Kurt Reinhardt, *Finite and Eternal Being*, CWESix, 2002.

[6]   Of *Finite and Eternal Being* she says in her preface (see xxviii): "A quite new version has come about; only a few pages have been taken from [*Potency and Act*] (the beginning of the first part). The starting point of the Thomistic doctrine of act and potency was kept— but only as a starting point. The question of being now stands in the center." Potency and act relate the "ultimate questions of being" and "lead at once into the heart of Thomistic philosophy" (*Potency and Act*, 5 and *Finite and Eternal Being*, p. 1). "Potentiality" means "possibility" as well as "level of being (154; cf. 104 and 110). On possibility in Husserl and Aquinas, see also *Knowledge and Faith*, pp. 62, 36-37.

we see the need for being that upholds our own— moreover, God's existence is a "purely formal conclusion."[7] Her many searching analyses are suggestive in their own right; for example, on human freedom and temporality, on self-knowledge and individuality, on eschatology and the "naught."[8] She also brings science into her discussion; with the help of a theory of taxonomical categories as both content and descent, she "fits evolution," where things change over time, "into the scholastic world view," with its static view of form.[9]

St. Theresa Benedicta generally follows St. Thomas; indeed, his concept of the analogy of being between God and creatures runs through her entire work. Yet she abandons his teaching on several basic points. Human identity is an important example. Individual things, she says, are of two kinds: those that are instantiations of a general "whatness" through their matter (Thomas's position, which she restricts to creatures below man) and persons, who have their own "thisness" (she uses John Duns Scotus's term *"haecceitas"*). Each human person is "unique in kind... each of us is our own species— the claim Thomas made for the angels."[10] She also differs from Thomas on "divine ideas," and she uses "matter" and "spirit" in the broader sense that matter characterizes all created things, even the soul, while "objective spirit" underpins our intellectual knowledge of material things.

She also takes issue with Husserl, most strikingly in her "Excursus on Transcendental Idealism" (360-378) wherein she defends "naive" realism against his "idealistic interpretation" of his own epistemology. And she stresses the Thomistic account of knowledge acquisition

---

7   Arguments for God's existence: 19-23, 217; from immanence: 20-21, 374; formal approach: 52, 8. Her remarks on atheism may reveal something about her personal struggles (217, 21, 217).

8   Freedom: 129, 254-5, 345ff; temporality: 9ff, 190-1 201ff, 219-20; "nothing": 110, 212ff; eschatology: 200-218.

9   283.

10   395

where the active role of the of the understanding (the "agent intellect") is subservient to its passive receptivity (the "possible intellect").[11] She is also responding to Martin Heidegger's *Being and Time*, and "the strong impression the book made on her," she says in her foreword, "may linger in the present work."[12]

The English text

St. Theresa Benedicta's expressions often have a scholastic as well as a phenomenological background. For example, *Sein* ("being") often reflects Latin *"esse,"* and *seiend* ("be-ing" with a hyphen) Latin *"ens."*[13] Some terms such as "transcendental," have quite different meanings in scholastic and phenomenological contexts.

Menschliches Sein appears as "human being" (the being that characterizes human beings). *Leben* is rendered as "life" or "living" ("spiritual life" does not have a specifically religious sense). I translate *Gemüt* as "emotion" and "sense appetite" not only because "emotion" is a usual translation of the word in a phenomenological context but especially because St. Theresa Benedicta uses it in the context of the Thomistic doctrine of the sense appetite (parallel to the will and linked to concepts of depth and value); nevertheless the word plays a broader role in her philosophy.[14]

---

[11]   Cf. *Knowledge and Faith*, pp. 45-6.

[12]   4.

[13]   28, etc. *Seiend* is used substantively ("a be-ing") and as a participle (e.g., 58). "Existent" translates *existierendes* (117). *Wesen* has two senses: "essence" or "be-ing" (cf. 247 and 269). I have consulted the Latin-German glossary St. Theresa Benedicta appended to her translation of St. Thomas's *Quaestiones disputatae de veritate*.

[14]   Cf. Dorion Cairns, *Guide for Translating Husserl* (The Hague, Nijhoff, 1973), p. 62. *Gemüt* joined to *Wille*, 190, 224 (and note).

I supply German terms in brackets, especially when St. Theresa Benedicta draws attention to an expression or when one English word corresponds to several German ones. The context usually determines when "spirit" and "mind" should be used for *Geist*, but often the word could be translated either way.[15] Where necessary I distinguish "body" (*Körper*) and "living body" (*Leib*).

"Material" has two quite different (and somewhat opposed) senses when it corresponds to *materiell* or *material*. The noun *Materie* and the adjective *materiell* refer to matter as what receives content and is paired with "form" as what gives content (this is the scholastic usage). For Theresa Benedicta, however, not all matter is physical or "space-filling" since all created things are material in some sense. *Stoff* is also translated as "matter" (or "piece" or "item" of matter). On the other hand, the adjective *material* means having "fullness" (or content) in contrast to the "formal," which is what is "filled."

I have supplied headings and often divided sentences and paragraphs. Non-English expressions are italicized as well as a few ordinary words used technically (e.g., "the *what*" and "the *how*"). When St. Theresa Benedicta stresses a Latin word that would already be italicized, I also underline it (for example, <u>*agens*</u>). When I supply a German term of which she emphasizes a part, I underline that part (<u>*Er*</u>-*kennen*). I add translations of Latin or Greek terms in brackets. The lists of works and of persons mentioned by St. Theresa Benedicta are the German editor's; the other indices are mine. Curly brackets {...} indicate page numbers of the German edition; angle brackets <...> enclose the German editor's additions and square brackets [...] my own. I wish especially to thank Mrs. Margareta Svjagintsev for her help and encouragement.

---

15 St. Theresa Benedicta insists that although "spirit" means more than mind ("intellect," 168), ordinary and philosophical usage tends to equate them (255; cf. 256).

{xi} # German Editor's Introduction

Potency and Act (*Potenz und Akt*), Edith Stein's phenomenologi-cal interpretation of the foundations of the philosophy of St. Thomas Aquinas, appears in print here for the first time. She wrote it in 1931 as the thesis with which she sought to qualify as a lecturer at the University of Freiburg. The work signals a twofold transition in her life. In her external life it marks the end of her association with the university. Internally it represents the merger of two philosophies which was prompted by her desire for system and is the result of the efforts of many years to portray the basic framework of St. Thomas's philosophy from a phenomenological perspective. At the same time it is the starting point for a more comprehensive work that she was to undertake a few years later, *Eternal and Finite Being*. But *Potency and Act* is more than a page in her biography and bibliography; it can quite well stand on its own and its topic and method are of fundamen-tal interest. We shall first comment on the origin of the work, then on its content, and finally on the transmission and formation of the text.

History of the work

In the summer of 1925 Edith Stein had been teaching for two years in the school of the Dominican Sisters in Speyer when she began work on a project she already had in mind: to master the philosophy of Thomas Aquinas.[16] It is important to note that the idea of relating {xii}

---

16   Cf. Stein's letter to Roman Ingarden of 8, 8,1925: "I recently began to study the *Quaestiones disputatae*, St. Thomas Aquinas's principal work on philosophy." (E. Stein, *Briefe an Roman Ingarden 1917-1938*, *Edith Steins Werke*, vol. 14 (heareafter cited as ESW follwed by the volume number), Freiburg, Basel, Vienna, 1991, Letter 88, pp. 159-160.) Similarly also in her letter to Fritz Kaufmann 13.9, 1925 (E. Stein, *Selbstbildnis in Briefe/ Zweiter Teil, 1934-1942* <ESWix>, Druten, Freiburg, Basel, and Vienna, 1977, supplement to part one, letter 38a, p. 185).

Thomism to phenomenology had guided her project from the start.[17] Her resolve to make the fundamentals of Aquinas's philosophy her own coincided with her return to phenomenology, which she had eschewed along with all philosophical and scholarly activity since her conversion in 1922. Her translation of St. Thomas's *Quaestiones disputate de veritate*, which she was beginning at this time,[18] also aimed from the start at a confrontation between Thomism and phenomenology. The first fruit of her project was "Husserls Phänomenologie und die Philosophie des hl. Thomas v. Aquino," an article which appeared in 1929 in the *Festschrift* of the phenomenology journal honoring Husserl on his seventieth birthday.[19]

From 1930 Stein linked her program of relating phenomenology to Thomism to another bid for a teaching position, this time in the University of Freiburg.[20] An external incentive for seeking a univer-

---

[17]   "And what will come of it I cannot now foresee: whether a translation (which does not yet exist) with notes or a treatise on Thomistic theory of knowledge and methodology, either by itself, or compared with phenomenological theory and method, or something else again (Letter 122, op. cit., p. 197).

[18]   On November 1, 1928, Stein mentions to Ingarden that she had gotten as far as the twenty-ninth question (Letter 122, op. cit., p. 197).

[19]   *Jahrbuch für Philosophie und phänomenologische Forschung*, supplementary issue, Halle a. d. Saale, 1929, pp. 315-338. Stein wrote the first version of this article in dialogue form: "Was ist Philosophie? Ein Gespräch zwischen Edmund Husserl und Thomas von Aquino," first published in *Erkenntnis und Glaube* (ESWxv), Freiburg, Basel, and Vienna, 1993, pp. 19-48. [Both versions printed in facing columns in *Knowledge and Faith*, CWESviii.]

[20]   H. Ott reconstructed her attempt in "Edith Stein (1891-1942) in Freiburg" (in *Freiburger Diözesan-Archiv*, 107 <1987>, pp. 253-274, especially pp. 264-273); see also Ott's additional remarks in his "Edith Stein und Freiburg," in R. L. Fetz, M. Rath and P. Schulz (ed.) *Studien zur Philosophie von Edith Stein. Internationales Edith Stein - Symposion*, Eichstätt, 1991 (*Phänomenologische Forschungen*, vols. 26-27.), Freiburg and Munich, 1993, pp. 107-139, especially 129ff. Her previous attempt to obtain an appointment at the University of Göttingen had failed.

sity position may have come from Heinrich Finke, professor emeritus of History in the University of Freiburg and president of the Görres-Gesellschaft. From their first meeting in 1929 he had advised her "not to bury her talent."[21] Edith Stein now turned to him for advice at the beginning of January, 1931. There was at the time the prospect of an appointment to a "Prussian Pedagogical Academy," but it was clear, as she wrote {xiii} Finke on January 6, that if she accepted she "would have to teach psychology, and once again I would lack the freedom for what seems to be my proper mission: critically comparing scholastic and recent philosophy." She goes on, "so if a university career were possible, I would decidedly prefer it, and if there were some hope in Freiburg I would like this best for several reasons."[22]

On January 24 and 25 she traveled to Freiburg where she met with Finke as well as with Martin Heidegger and Martin Honecker, who were representing the chair of philosophy at the University; she also paid Husserl a visit. Finke a few days before had sounded out the possibility of her receiving a stipend as a lecturer, and at the time this was likely through the Catholic Women's' League or the Görres-Gesellschaft.[23] Heidegger, according to Stein,[24] kept an open mind about her application but deferred to Honecker, who had precedence as chair for "Catholic appointments" of the Concordat.[25] Honecker, "cool at first," at last declared himself ready to handle the application process.[26]

---

[21] Cf. Stein's Letter to Finke of 6.1, 1931 (quoted by Ott, op. cit., p. 266).

[22] Letter to Finke of 6.1, 1931, quoted by H. Ott, op. cit.

[23] Cf. Fink's correspondence with Maria Schlüter-Hermkes, chair of the Catholic Womens' League, quoted by H. Ott, op. cit., pp. 267 and 270.

[24] Cf. Stein's letters of 26.1, 1931 to Finke, in H. Ott, op. cit., pp. 268f) and to Sister Adelgundis Jaegerschmid (ESWviii, letter 85 pp. 83f [*Edith Stein/ Self Portrait in Letters*, tr. Josephine Koeppel, O.C.D., CWESv, pp. 83f).

[25] According to Stein in her letter to Sister Adelgundis (Letter 85, op. cit., p. 84 [CWESv, p. 84]).

[26] Ibid.

After this favorable development,[27] Edith Stein decided to start at once on her application thesis, *Potency and Act*. From her correspondence with Sister Adelgundis Jaegerschmid we know the exact day she began work: January 27, 1931, two days after getting back from Freiburg.[28] In the same letter she mentioned that over the next six weeks "a rather bulky manuscript has materialized"[29]— surprising enough when we consider that she was still teaching at the time as well as correcting the galley proofs of the first volume of her translation of St. Thomas. Nevertheless she had already decided to ask for a leave of absence and this {xiv} she did before Easter of 1931. She went to stay in her mother's home in Breslau to be able to work undisturbed.

Although the work itself very soon became a priority,[30] Edith Stein did not lose sight of its purposes. The offer of a professorship in the Pedadogical Academy which was to be founded was postponed, since owing to the economic crisis funds were lacking for establishing such institutions,[31] but by early 1931 she considered withdrawing her application even should this offer materialize.[32] At the same time she was prepared to go on working for a longer time: "I'll not finish soon, however, since I must first go over in my mind all the questions of

---

[27] Looking back on her visit to Husserl and his wife at the end of her stay in Freiburg, Stein writes to Sister Adelgundis, "there was great surprise and joy in the Husserl home over the outcome" (ibid.).

[28] Letter of 28, 4, 1931 to Sr. Adelgundis (ESWviii, letter 89, pp. 86f [CWESv, pp. 86f]).

[29] Op. cit., p. 86 [CWESv, p. 86].

[30] In the same letter to Sr. Adelgundis she writes: "once I had begun the work, it immediately became more important to me than any other purpose it might serve" (ibid.)

[31] Cf. Stein's letter of 14, 6, 1931 to Roman Ingarden (ESWxiv, Letter 149, p. 223).

[32] Cf. her letters to Sr. Adelgundis on 28, 4, 1931 (op. cit.), and to Heinrich Fink on 6, 5, 1931 (in H. Ott, op. cit., p. 271).

principle between Thomas and Husserl."[33]

Her manuscript was nonetheless completed in late summer of that same year, 1931, and typed in September.[34] Copies must have been sent at once to Husserl, Honecker and Heidegger by the end of October when Stein again left Breslau.[35] On November 29 she wrote Roman Ingarden from Freiburg, where she had been staying in the convent of St. Lioba in Freiburg-Günterstal since the middle of the month to clarify her employment situation, that her application had been "rejected due to the general economic situation,"

> that is, both referees said that in view of my previous accomplishments I am qualified to lecture, but advised me against applying formally since my application could not be accepted in the School or in the Ministry.[36]

"In view of her previous accomplishments" can be interpreted to mean that {xv} Honecker, who had been proposed as the principal referee, still had not read Stein's work, at least completely, at the time of Stein's inquiry,[37] and that both professors recognized that the candidate, to judge from her scholarship already in evidence, was ready for

---

33 Letter of 6, 5, 1931 to Finke, in H. Ott, op. cit. See also her words to Fritz Kaufmann, letter of 14, 6, 1931: "I have been at home since Easter, busy with a large work that mushrooms unpredictably under my hands because I have so many years to work through" (ESWix, Letter 93a, p. 187 [CWESv, p. 91]), and to Sr. Adelgundis, letter of 28, 6, 1931: "<my work> has already grown into a monster and gives no sign of coming to an end. I want to keep at it until autumn, without interruption if possible." (ESWviii, Letter 95, p. 92f [CWESv, p. 95]).

34 Stein signed the foreword in the typewritten copy of her manuscript: "Breslau, September, 1931."

35 Cf. Stein's letter of 9, 3, 1932 to Ingarden (ESWxiv, Letter 152, p. 227).

36 ESWxiv, Letter 150, p. 224.

37 Tallying with this is the fact that Honecker —to judge by his separate

a lectureship, but advised her against applying in view of the desolate economic situation.[38]

Stein's other plans also fell through. The founding of the Pedagogical Academy was suspended for lack of funds. By early summer in 1931 a position in the University of Breslau had opened up, but this possibility, too, failed to materialize.[39] She received her appointment in the German Institute of Scientific Pedagogy in Münster in March 1, 1932. In the summer of that year Honecker, as we gather from her reply to him on July 8, 1932, advised her to apply to the University of Münster. In this letter she writes: "Here, too, I think there would be problems— especially now," meaning because

---

notes on *Potency and Act* which have been preserved— had only read a good fourth of the work (Honecker's notes were published by H. Ott, "Die Randnotizen Martin Honeckers zur Habilitationsschrift 'Potenz und Akt' <Martin Honecker's marginal notes on the application thesis *Potency and Act*>" in R. L. Fetz, M. Rath and P. Schulz (ed.) *Studien zur Philosophie von Edith Stein*, op. cit., pp. 140-145). After it was clear that Stein had accepted the rejection, Honecker no longer needed to study the whole work. — Evidently Heidegger was more interested in the substance of the work; Stein stresses this in two letters to Ingarden: "...he kept my work to read and the other day spoke with me about it for over two hours in a very pleasant and fruitful way, so I am really thankful to him" (letter of 25, 12, 1931, Letter 151, p. 225; see also letter 152, p. 227.).

[38]   "Although Honecker did not know me at all, he took great pains. He labored —in vain!— to obtain a stipend as a lecturer for me from the Ministry, discussed it for hours with me and with Husserl.... Heidegger was perfectly kind although he saw the matter as hopeless. He said that a year ago there would have been no problem." (Stein's Letter of 25. 12, 1931 to Ingarden, ESWxiv, Letter 151, p. 225). — It remains moot whether matters of substance also had something to do with Honecker's rejection; it is relevant, as H. Ott remarks, that Honecker's notes on *Potency and Act* are all negative ("Die Randnotizen Martin Honeckers," op. cit., p. 140).

[39]   Cf. Stein's letter of 28, 6, 1931 to Sr. Adelgundis (ESWviii, Letter 95, p. 92 [CWESv, p. 95]). — In connection with this plan, she would have been working on *Einführung in die Philosophie* [introduction to philosophy] (ESWxiii, Freiburg, Basel, and Vienna, 1991), which went back to the time of her assistantship to Husserl (cf. the editor's remarks, pp. 12f).

of the {xvi} continuing tight economic situation. Moreover, her new commitments in the Institute of Scientific Pedagogy pushed her plans for a university appointment into the background.

Stein's failure to gain a position in Freiburg temporarily removed her motive for continuing to work on *Potency and Act*. Shortly after her arrival in Münster she confessed to Ingarden that the manuscript would have to be "thoroughly gone over for publication."[40] This remark at least shows her general intention to publish it. Her teaching duties in the Institute in Münster hardly gave her any time to work on the manuscript. But she was able to put the work to use in her course during the Winter semester of 1932-1933. On November 11, 1932 she wrote to Ingarden:

> After returning here a year ago, I got back to work on Act and Potency for the first time: (1) to find out what still needed rewriting —answer: a large amount— and (2) to see how I could use it in my lectures (on the structure of the human person) —answer: in all sorts of ways—, but it all has to be rethought and reshaped, so this is taking most of my time. And since other things are going on at the same time, there is little likelihood that I shall soon get around to working through the work systematically.[41]

Edith Stein had once again spent the summer vacation with her family in Breslau. From there she went to Paris at the beginning of September to take part in the meeting of the *Société Thomiste* on phenomenology and Thomism on September 12, and went back to Münster in the middle of the month. Her second lecture course

---

[40]   Letter 152 of 9, 3, 1932, ESWxiv, p. 227.

[41]   ESWxiv, Letter 154, p. 230.

at Münster, "The Structure of the Human Person,"[42] did give her a chance to get back to *Potency and Act*, but course preparation, her immediate purpose, soon came first. However, at this time she may have received a new incentive to go ahead and prepare for publication the writing which had failed to win her a university position. For, at the end of the winter semester of 1932-1933, work on her wide-ranging lecture course and her return to the manuscript of *Potency and Act* awoke a need to take stock of her accomplishments to date and to identify her life's philosophical {xvii} mission. She at once sought a confidant who would help her gain clarity on the issue, and she hoped that this person would be Hedwig Conrad-Martius.[43] However, adverse circumstances precluded the discussion in the end; still, the letters they exchanged thereafter should have substantially influenced her resolve to continue working on *Potency and Act*.[44]

Edith Stein's obvious motive in turning to Conrad-Martius in this matter was the latter's review of Heidegger's *Being and Time* which had appeared in the *Deutsche Zeitschrift* in 1933.[45] She expected that Conrad-Martius might well be able to "discern the immanent teleology

---

[42]   Published in ESWxvi, Freiburg, Basel, and Vienna, 1994.

[43]   Hedwig Conrad-Martius and her husband Theodor Conrad belonged to the circle of Husserl's students in Göttingen. Conrad-Martius was Edith Stein's godmother at her baptism on January 1, 1922 in Bergzabern, where the Conrad's lived at the time. Conrad-Martius's memoirs (published in Edith Stein/ *Briefe an Hedwig Conrad-Martius* <letters to Hedwig Conrad-Martius>, Munich, 1960, pp. 61-83) as well as Stein's extant letters to her document their friendship.

[44]   By and large only letters by Edith Stein have been preserved. Conrad-Martius published Stein's letters to her in 1960 in a small volume (*Edith Stein/ Briefe an Hedwig Conrad-Martius*, op. cit.). They were included in ESWviii and ix.

[45]   Reprinted in H. Conrad-Martius/ *Schriften zur Philosophie* [writings on philosophy], vol. 1, edited by E. Avé-Lallemant, Munich, 1963, pp. 185-193. Stein was quite impressed by Heidegger's *Sein und Zeit*; all the more need, she felt, for distinguishing her position from his (cf. her forewords to

in my writings much better than I could myself," as Stein wrote to her on February 24, 1933, "in just the way you were able to write about Heidegger and Hartmann."[46] Conrad-Martius, as Stein wished, should "one day examine" her works with this purpose.

> You are, of course, familiar with my earlier writings. Then we could also consider including the small *Festschrift* article {xviii} and possibly the work on *Akt und Potenz* that I wrote in the summer of 1931. True, it is in no way in a condition ready for publication and I believe I've made headway in some points this winter; but at least you would see in it the attempt to get from scholasticism to phenomenology and vice versa.[47]

In this letter Stein gives us a first reason why she desired to be clear about the philosophical mission of her life: all her writings were leading up to "laying the foundations of education." A few weeks

---

Potency and Act, below p. 5, and to *Endliches und ewiges Sein/ Versuch eines Aufstiegs zum Sinn des Seins* <ESWii, Freiburg, Basel, and Vienna, third edition, 1986, p. xvi>. This need became more apparent as she realized that her attempt to examine Thomism from the phenomenological perspective was leading her to a comprehensive thematization of the question of being. Her coming to terms with Heidegger eventually appeared as an appendix in *Finite and Eternal Being* (her "Martin Heideggers Existentialphilosophie [Martin Heidegger's existential philosophy]," written in the summer of 1936 was planned as a second appendix to *Finite and Eternal Being*, the first being "Seelenburg [the interior castle]"; both appendices appeared in ESWvi: *Person und Welt/ Beitrag zum christlichen Wahrheitsstreben* [person and world/ contribution to the Christian search for truth], Louvain and Freiburg, 1962, pp. 39-68 (appendix i) and pp. 69-135 (appendix ii)).

46   ESWviii, letter 135, pp. 130f. [CWESv, p. 134] —Conrad-Martius wrote a critical analysis of N. Hartmann's position in her article "Bemerkungen über Metaphysik und ihre methodische Stelle [comments on metaphysics and its methodological position]" (*Philosophische Hefte*, 3 <1932/1933>; reprinted in Conrad-Martius, *Schriften zur Philosophie*, vol. 1, op. cit., pp. 49-88).

47   Letter 135, op. cit., 131 [CWESv, p. 134].

before the National Socialist takeover Stein was still working at the Institute of Scientific Pedagogy and at the time saw her further task in relation to her work there. But a few lines further on she frankly admitted her real need.

> Yes, so if you want to undertake to ascertain for your godchild the meaning of her life's task, I shall be glad to send you this monstrous opus <*Potency and Act*>, obviously for your severe criticism — for a *radical* critique, for I have often asked myself whether in fact, I am not overreaching my own capabilities in the philosophical work I have undertaken.[48]

Stein had another reason, directly connected with *Potency and Act*, for asking Conrad-Martius for her criticism. In chapter six of this work Stein had referred in detail to Conrad-Martius's *Metaphysische Gespräche* [metaphysical discourses].[49] Stein seemed to be least satisfied with this part of her own work, as she had repeated again and again in her letter of February 24, 1933 (where she speaks of the "impossible critical analysis of the *Metaphysische Gespräche*")[50] and in her following letters.[51] She not only seeks Conrad-Martius's judgment on this matter but also asks her to send her more recent writings.[52] Conrad-Martius's reaction to Stein's request must have

---

[48]   Op. cit., p. 132.

[49]   Halle, 1921.

[50]   SFWviii, Letter 135, p. 131.

[51]   Cf. Stein's letters to Conrad-Martius of 15, 12, 1934 (ESWix, Letter 189, p. 25) and of 21, 5, 1935 (ESWix, Letter 201, p. 37).

[52]   Thus Stein asks for her "L'existence, la substantialité de l'âme [existence, the substantiality of the soul]" (*Recherches philosophiques*, 2 <1932-933>, pp. 149-181) as well as for her manuscript "Grundformen des Seins/ Stoff und Geist [basic forms of being/ matter and spirit]," which was a first draft of Conrad-Martius's later book *Das Sein* [being] (Munich, 1957) (cf. Letter

been basically favorable, as we can gather from Stein's reply to her on March 23, 1933,[53] though Conrad-Martius did say she had little time, for Stein writes her on April 5.

> Since I'm packing just now, {xix} I shall send you the paper anyhow. But you should feel free to put it aside until you have enough time for it and can promise yourself some gain from it for your own use.[54]

Stein's external life was changing completely at this time. Because of the National Socialists takeover, she did not see any possibility of remaining employed as a Jew at a state institution, as was the Institute of Scientific Pedagogy. She forestalled her dismissal by asking to be relieved of her duties herself.[55] On July 14 she wished to leave Münster and enter the Carmelite convent in Cologne-Lindenthal, as she told the Conrad's at the end of June.[56] We also read in this letter: "Therefore you can understand that I am no longer that interested in my manuscript <*Potency and Act*>."[57]

A year and a half later —by which time, in October of 1933, Edith Stein had entered the Carmelite community in Cologne as a pos-

---

135); she also asked for her little work *Die "Seele" der Pflanze* [the "soul" of plants] (Breslau, 1934; cf. letter 189 [CWESv, p. 207]).

[53] ESWviii, Letter 138, p. 134 [CWESv, pp. 137f].

[54] ESWviii, Letter 139, p. 134 [CWESv, p. 138].

[55] Stein wrote her nephew Gordon on 4, 8, 1933: "It was my free decision to leave." (Letter in the Carmelite convent in Cologne) — On 7, 5, 1933 she wrote Elly Dursy: "I do not believe, however, in any return to the Institute nor, for that matter, in any possibility of a teaching career in Germany." (ESWviii, Letter 141, p. 137. [CWESv, p. 141]).

[56] FM Cf. Stein's letter to Conrad-Martius around the end of June, 1933 (ESWviii, Letter 146, p. 142 [CWESv, p. 147]).

[57] Ibid.

tulant— she wrote to Conrad-Martius, who in the meantime obviously had the opportunity to study Stein's writing.

> I am very grateful that you occupy yourself with *Akt und Potenz*.... I would appreciate very much knowing whether you consider it worth publishing and spending as much time on it as revision would still require.[58]

For the situation had changed after the community learned that Edith Stein could be expected to continue her scholarly work: "Mother Subprioress <Sr. Teresa Renata> is very eager for me to prepare it for publication."[59]

The final incentive to get back to work on *"Potency and Act"* came from Stein's ecclesiastical superior who some months later, after the middle of May, 1935, visited her with this instruction. She writes Conrad-Martius again on May 21.

> For the past few days our Father Provincial <Theodor Rauch> was here with us and he has given me the task of preparing *Akt und Potenz* for publication. Of course I took it out at once and have begun {xx} to review it.[60]

And she says once again: "Obviously your opinion would be most valuable." Yet Stein knew that Conrad-Martius had to struggle with health problems during those months, and so she adds: "But I do not want to bother you with that now that you are not feeling well."

---

[58]   Letter of 15, 12, 1934 (ESWix, Letter 189, p. 25 [CWESv, p]. 194).

[59]   Ibid.

[60]   ESWix, Letter 201, p. 37 [CWESv, p. 206]; see also Stein's letter of 14, 6, 1935 to Elly Dursy (ESWix, Letter 202, p. 39 [CWESv, pp. 207f]) and Stein's remark in the foreword to *Finite and Eternal Being* (ESWii, p. xiii).

Nevertheless, Conrad-Martius did send Stein the more recent works that she had asked for and deemed necessary for revising her manuscript.

In the following weeks Edith Stein devoted herself energetically to rewriting *Potency and Act*. She still writes Conrad-Martius on May 21: "At first I found little that needed to be changed. But I know well that the last parts will need much revision."[61] — and she writes to her again seven weeks later, on July 9: "I was stuck in the first part of my manuscript.... Probably not much of my manuscript will remain, for I now find it quite inadequate. So not reading it saved you time."[62] During these seven weeks her resolve to forego the revision of *Potency and Act* and start all over must have matured. The result of this new beginning is her main work, *Finite and Eternal Being*.[63] The bulk of this new work must have been finished by the end of the summer of 1935.[64]

There is a fragmentary foreword to *Potency and Act* dating from May 20, 1935 that Stein wrote right after receiving the Provincial's instruction, when she obviously still intended to revise it for publication.[65] Here is the text {xxi} (the beginning has not been preserved):

---

61   ESWxi, Letter 201, p. 37 [CWESv, p. 207]. Conrad-Martius also answered immediately: "I am so very sorry that I cannot now give you the criticism of "Akt und Potenz" that you have been requesting for so long. At present it is impossible for me to work, even just to read." Letter of 23, 5, 1935, in the Cologne convent).

62   ESWix, Letter 205, pp. 42 [CWESv, p. 212].

63   In the summer of 1937 Stein wrote Ingarden after a long interval: "I quite soon gave up the project <referring to *Potency and Act*> and have begun to write anew." (ESWxiv, Letter 160, p. 238.)

64   Stein wrote Ruth Kantorowicz, who typed the handwritten manuscript, on 12, 9, 1935: "It's not the whole of it— a little more than thirty pages will follow." (ESWix, Letter 211, p. 48 [CWESv, p. 217]).

65   This foreword was published in E. Stein *Erkenntnis und Glaube* (ESWxv), pp. 63f. The editors of this volume erroneously attributed it to the later work *Finite and Eternal Being*. [Cf. *Knowledge and Faith*, p. 81.]

These inquiries can offer but a very modest contribution to this task. This was clear to me when I wrote them four years ago and it is still clearer today when in obedience to my superiors I take them up again to go over them again for publication.

Edmund Husserl formed my philosophical thinking. In his school I had gained the maturity to do independent work before coming to know the thought world of St. Thomas Aquinas. While translating his *Quaestiones de Veritate*,[66] I became so absorbed by his thought world that an inner clash between it and the phenomenological way of philosophizing was inevitable. A first expression of this confrontation —hardly more than a study program— was a modest contribution to the *Festschrift* for Husserls seventieth birthday.[67]

The following studies represent a second, broader and deeper, endeavor. They set out from some basic Thomistic concepts without claiming to give a complete account of the Thomistic system or take a definitive stance on it. I lack the essential basis of a comprehensive knowledge of medieval philosophy essential for such an undertaking. The outward circumstances of my life have never allowed me to fill this large gap in my philosophical formation. I could make up for it only as far as my other professional duties at the time permitted. Hence all I can do now is show how far I have gotten in coping with the great questions of being with my two sets of tools: the medieval and the modern way of thinking. Perhaps it will help others to advance further.

Sister Teresia Benedicta a Cruce, O.C.D.

Carmelite Convent

Cologne-Lindenthal, 20, v, 1935

Philosophy

[Aim]

Potency and Act is divided into six chapters. The first begins to clarify the concepts of "potency" and "act." The second and third treat the questions from the formally ontological and materially [*material*] ontological viewpoints respectively. The remaining three chapters continue the materially ontological inquiry, defining material [*materiell*] being in the fourth and spiritual being in the fifth. The final sixth chapter discusses the finite be-ing as a "matter formed at several levels." {xxii} Here the inquiry turns to the structure of the world of fact wherein the material [*material*] has already received shape, is always "formed." The high point of the work is clearly chapters five and six (together they make up over two thirds of the work). Each contributes to Edith Stein's basic theme: the person (chapter five, especially section 8e) and man (chapter six, section 23).[68]

The work as a whole, as Stein writes in her foreword, aims at "gaining access to an understanding of St. Thomas Aquinas's method" (see below, p. 1). As a phenomenologist she knew that everything objective must be accessed appropriately so that it can show itself as what it is. And this is obviously one of her compelling reasons for studying Aquinas's philosophy against a phenomenological back-

---

[66]   <Stein's note>: *Untersuchungen über die Wahrheit*, Borgmeyer and Breslau, two volumes, vol. 1, 1931, vol. 2, 1932, plus Latin-German glossary, 1935 <new edition in ESWiii and iv>.

[67]   <Stein's note> "Husserls Phänomenologie und die Philosophie des hl. Thomas von Aquino" (op. cit.).

[68]   Many parallels to this set of topics also appear in Stein's course in Münster in the winter semester of 1932-1933, "Der Aufbau der menschlichen Person [the structure of the human person]" (ESWxvi, op. cit.); she used *Potency and Act* to prepare this work. The course focuses on human being to provide an outline of an anthropology as a foundation for education.

ground. Her phenomenological query thus aims at tracing Aquinas's "apocryphal" method, as it were, "the method he uses in practice, albeit we shall not get an explicit account of it from him" (p. 2). For Stein, however, this project does not involve, as we might think, reconstructing Thomas's method from a list of his theses.[69] Method is not an end in itself for Stein the phenomenologist; *things [Sachen]* are ever her focus. And this means that the methodical understanding of Aquinas's philosophy, a pressing need for her, rests upon a phenomenological analysis of things and their interconnections as Aquinas conceived them. Thus at the end of her foreword she announces that she is doing "an objective analysis of basic Thomistic concepts" (p. 3).

If her analysis is successful, she accomplishes three things. (1) The phenomenological method as she practices it, by identifying a network of things, confirms by another route the objective system behind Thomistic thinking. (2) At the same {xxiii} time the phenomenological approach proves to be a legitimate and fruitful way to deal with traditional questions in the context of recent philosophy. (3) Her approach convincingly shows that the phenomenology of today and the scholasticism of the past can communicate over the centuries— with a view to a *"philosophia perennis* [perennial philosophy]." This perennial philosophy is certainly Edith Stein's ultimate aim, her real concern, that drove her ever since she, as a phenomenologist, began to confront Thomism.[70]

---

[69]   Stein had already contrasted "phenomenological and scholastic methods" in the long sixth section of her article in Husserl's *Festschrift* ("Husserls Phänomenologie und die Philosophie des hl. Thomas v. Aquino, op. cit., pp. 329-338 [*Knowledge and Faith*, pp. 38-63].

[70]   Stein wrote Ingarden that *Potency and Act* "develops the problems only from Thomas's standpoint and then grows into my 'philosophy system'— which, of course, is a give-and-take *between* Thomas and Husserl." (ESWxiv, Letter 152 of 9, 3, 1932, p. 226)

[Overview]

Here we can but point to the great objective arc the design of her work describes. She begins her ascent —intended to be an *objective* penetration into Thomas's basic concepts (I, 1)— by briefly listing the matters she will treat. She notes here that "the contrast between potency and act" not only leads us "at once into the heart of Thomistic philosophy," but also relates "to the ultimate questions of being" (p. 5). Hence the being motif in Stein's later work *Finite and Eternal Being* is already prominent in *Potency and Act*, although it passes later into the background. In accord with Thomas Aquinas's teaching, she is already viewing the structure of being here —in respect to potency and act— as *defined by an analogy relation*, that is, by the analogy between the divine being and the being of creatures. Her discussion of Thomas's basic conceptual system seeks to take the notion of the *analogia entis* [analogy of being] into account from the start: nothing can "*be said of God and creatures in the same*" —but, precisely, *in an analogous*— "*sense*"— in other words, in virtue of this ontic analogy relation, philosophic discourse about God is possible in just this relational structure (see chapter 1, section 1 below).[71]

Even an inquiry aiming at things requires a previous justification of the method it will follow. So it is not surprising that Stein, after marking out the problems she will treat, inserts a reflection on her method between the other two sections of the first chapter. This second section begins with the definition of "*ontology*" as the procedure {xxiv} that ultimately focuses on being (p. 9). Here she is anticipating a later theme: that it is of great importance to take "formal distinctions

---

[71]   Cf. the work of Klaus Hedwig on this point, "Edith Stein und die analogia entis [Edith Stein and the *analogia entis*" in R. L. Fetz, M. Rath and P. Schulz (editors), *Studien zur Philosophie von Edith* Stein, op. cit., pp. 320-352.

of being" "in a purely ontological sense," apart from any entities interpreted theologically.

Husserl also uses both formally and materially ontological (or "regional-ontological") analyses. But the results of both, he insisted, are but "connecting motifs" serving to show, in a transcendental-phenomenological clarification that leads further on, that these results are "produced formations [*Leistungsgebilde*]" of a transcendental subjectivity that constitutes them. Edith Stein does not take this route. Like most of Husserl's students at Göttingen, she rejects the assumption of an absolute transcendental subjectivity— not however without granting some warrant to a constituting subjectivity. This implies that she shares —again, up to a certain point— the modern idea that shifts the Archimedean fulcrum for interpreting the world into subjectivity.

So it may appear odd in view of her purpose — which is to analyze objectively basic concepts of scholastic philosophy— that she chooses Cartesian doubt (but referring to the Augustinian and Husserlian versions) as her methodological starting point (p. 9). This is no mere bow to the philosophical spirit of the times, but tallies with the basic phenomenological question: "how is this or that given to me?" It will become apparent in the course of her work that reference to the subject means more for her than merely reflecting on how something is given to us, but includes a need for constitutive analyses.

Stein, like Husserl, calls for a "reflection on origins" (p. 15), an unbiased interpretation of Descartes' "*cogito ergo sum.*" But her understanding of the original certainty of being expressed in the principle "I am and am aware of this being" (the "sheer fact of being," p. 12) is quite unlike Husserl's. For Stein, our findings on the activity of the subject as it acts give us no reason to bracket out the question of the being of this act with reference to its immanent occurrence as an act. Rather, the act's very being, its "actuality," unveils *ex negativo* [by contrast] in its temporality, in its constant transition from potentiality to actuality, the "idea of pure being" (p. 10) that is not subject to such temporality.

So the result of considering origins for Stein is already quite different than for Husserl. While Husserl is led thereby to uncover the absolute immanent sphere of transcendental subjectivity, Stein takes the constituting role of subjectivity as a reason for showing {xxv} that this subjectivity has need of and relies upon something that it itself is not. The *fact* that subjectivity constitutes — and this means "brings about [*zeitigen*]"— time and is "fallen" points to something nontemporal; the fact that subjectivity is ever constituting *something* points to something such that it is not one with the immanent being of this subjectivity. Thus Stein concludes that from the sphere of immanence we must distinguish the transcendent sphere that "heralds itself" in the sphere of immanence without coinciding with it. And from both spheres we must further distinguish the sphere of "pure being" (which is "transcendent" in a second sense) (p.20).[72] The discipline that would embrace the meaning of being in all spheres is formal ontology.

Thus it is that for Edith Stein formal ontology is no longer prior to nor does it fit into transcendental phenomenology as Husserl supposed; rather they are related reciprocally. For her, too, formal ontology is referred to transcendental philosophy insofar as the latter is competent to inquire not only into the relation between the immanent and transcendent spheres (cf. p. 24) but also into the constitution of formal-ontological entities. Conversely, transcendental philosophy relies on formal ontology not only because its task is to determine, in conjunction with material ontology, the meaning of the being of immanence, but because the general clarification of the basic concepts of ontology is proper to it (p. 26).

---

[72]   From this starting point Stein develops a critique of transcendental-phenomenological idealism (cf. pp. 360 378 and our comments below).

The formal-ontological analysis Stein carries out in the second chapter treats *aliquid* (object), *quod quid est* (what), and *esse* (being) as basic ontological concepts. The (formal) determination of how being —departing from the formal— "fulfills" itself still falls to formal ontology. The being of concrete individuals contrasts with basic ontological concepts such as the "empty forms" of highest generality (others would be, for example, form, matter, genus, species, and individual *as such*). Empty forms are "needful"; they need to be "filled out" in concrete individuals. The being of "material ideas," of the species of lower and higher generality —the latter Stein calls "ideal objects."— is located between empty form and concrete individual. She describes the species in this middle area as a "formed fullness" that "can still enter other forms" (p. 44). As a structural element of an individual they have needful being; they need individuals for their actualization (in this sense they are forms). But their objective content are "in themselves" (hence fullness). {xxvi}

In regard to potency and act the formal analysis leads to the conclusion that whatever is not selfsufficient [*selbständig*] (all forms, everything general, all parts) is potential and that only a selfsufficient be-ing —"only a perfectly simple whole"— can be absolutely actual; that is, an individual wherein all basic forms coincide, "the be-ing absolutely" (p. 52). Both the *actus purus* of absolutely actual being and the potential being of all empty forms contrast with the be-ing that shares in both actual and potential being; such is the being of concrete individuals. At the same time the formal mode of the being of becoming (form and matter shape individual being concretely) contrasts with the absolutely actual. Formal analysis must leave open the question whether the being of ideal objects has a share in the actual as well as in the potential.

The third chapter bridges the formally ontological and the materially ontological inquiries. In the former study, Stein points out, "matter [*Materie*]" was already used in two senses, parallel to the two senses of "form"; it meant first, that wherein the empty forms receive fulfillment (in the species or, by means of them, in the concrete individual), and second, matter [*Stoff*] that receives form as it becomes. The succession of possible formings, she says, refers back to an unformed matter, *prima materia* [prime matter], which for Thomas Aquinas is pure potency, since it is receptive of all species of natural things and itself receives actual being only by taking in species. Analogously to this formal concept of matter as the purely potential in the context of natural philosophy, the material inquiry will also demonstrate, in the case of the *soul*, that is, of immanent being, an inner principle of form and an empty, formal concept of matter.

This transition chapter brings in another important concept: the basic material category of *spirit*. When subjectivity is no longer considered from the viewpoint of being-there-by-itself —as it was in the introductory chapter on method, which viewed the areas of transcendence from the viewpoint of the relation of the there-by-itself of immanence—, being that is conscious of itself differs from being that not only is conscious of itself but is so in the mode of being-there-for-itself. Stein calls the latter "immanent being" and the former "spirit." The immanent being of finite subjects is spiritual being insofar as it is conscious of itself. Their being is at the same time "less" than spirit as such, since in this mode it is also there-by-itself, and "more" insofar as it is not only a subject of self-consciousness but shows on account of its sensibility a "first transcendence" in its immanence (p. 100).

The third chapter has brought {xxvii} the analysis to the point where it is important to clarify the relationship of spirit and matter. This is done in chapters four and five, wherein material definitions are given of matter and spirit respectively. If matter, the "utmost in potentiality" (p.104), becomes actualized by receiving species, then the absolutely actual, as the absolutely spiritual, ultimately calls its opposite, matter, into being, since the species, as the ideal objects themselves, belong to the absolutely spiritual.

These reflections in the fourth chapter bring Stein to answer the question she left pending at the end of the second on the location of the being of ideal objects in respect to the relationship of potency and act. Ideal objects, as they belong to the absolutely actual, themselves stand in actual being; they are affected by God's active potency, which is not opposed to act, of calling things into existence as well as by the passive potency of things to be able to pass from nonbeing to being. Ideal objects are thus distinguished from the lower concrete species to which purely actual being is not proper, inasmuch as these species harbor in themselves elements of the contingent that are located not in ideal but in real being. Consequently the concrete material thing presupposes first ideas (objective spirit), second matter, and third the (subjective) spirit of creatures, relating ideas to matter. Questions about the knowability of the material as well as about the ontological location of living matter between spirit and matter remain open at this point and so call for a material analysis of spirit.

Chapter five turns to this task. Stein formulates her conclusions with the aid of the connecting motifs, the basic ontological concepts of *object*, *what*, and *being*.

(1) As an *object*, spirit as such is subdivided into subjective and objective spirit as well as into what is inherent in the subjective spirit as its forms and species. Subjective spirit is what is from itself and for itself. In contrast, the narrower definition —being-there-by-its-self— marks the intentional, immanent element of spiritual self-reference already discussed. And it is this element, Stein claims, broadening her account, that makes the subjective spirit a person. By the further element of being through itself, the one infinite divine person to which this element is proper is distinguished from the many possible finite persons.

Objective spirit implies idea-structures or ideas that are built into matter ("works"). If idealities inhere in the subjective spirit and hence are not objectively {xxviii} opposed to it, then we have here the third basic type of spirit: the forms and species of the subjective spirit. There may be a reciprocal relationship between the first and third basic types: objective ideas can be subjectively appropriated as intuiting and thinking functions and they can in turn be objectified as such functions.

(2) The *what* that fills these forms is characterized in general as "being illumined." In the case of a person the *what* is the *core* indicating its individual being, numerically and qualitatively unique. The forms of intuition and thought comprising the third of the three basic types mentioned above belong to this core. In the course of a man's life the potentiality of the core can be unfolded in this way or that, thus determining his character. The *what* of the second basic type (the ideas and works of persons) comprises the meaningful content of all real and possible things.

(3) As for spiritual *being*, the highest mode of being —as actual, conscious life (*actus purus* [pure act])— marks a boundary for finite persons to which they approach in diverse grades of being. The being of spiritual objects on the other hand lacks selfsufficiency but is bound in its being to persons, receiving its being in creaturely acts.

In the final sixth chapter Stein gives us the expected definition of the soul in relation to body and spirit. The soul, she says, is the "form of the body and the act of its potency" (p. 352). Unlike animals, man is not at the mercy of the reactions of his body, but can behave toward them up to a certain point by checking or affirming them. "Formed" in this way, the body is "the scene of what goes on in the soul and the organ for engaging the world outside" (ibid.). Insofar as the content of spiritual acts —unlike sense-data— does not involve an attachment to the body, the soul, which can actualize the spiritual, becomes a "purely spiritual substance" (p. 354).

This substance of the soul's actual life forms itself with the help of accidental forms, the species of successive acts: the *species sensibiles* [sensible species] and *species intelligibiles* [intelligible species]. Stein especially stresses that the *species sensibilis* is no mere sense datum, but a *sensibile* [what can be sensed] that is always already formed intuitively and intellectually in perception, memory, and imagination through the work of the understanding; it is "at bottom a *species sensibilis-intelligibilis* [sensible-intelligible species]" (p. 379). The *species intelligibilis* —as the form of a thing or of an act— is accessible through abstraction, when it is regarded apart from sensible matter and the form is brought into focus. The species then shows itself to be the "noematic-ontic form of the thing" and, correlatively, "the form of the act, the noetic form" (p. 379).

Chapter six deals {xxix} in detail with Hedwig Conrad-Martius's *Metaphysische Gespräche* [metaphysical discourses]. Stein especially criticizes the central notion of the work: that the human being possesses a double being and a corresponding "twofold birth." Man

is begotten and formed from the quality-giving bottomless primal grounds of nature, yet at the same time is he born from the "spirit"— hence he issues personally from below and from above.[73]

.

Stein doubts that man, as a free personal I, proceeds from God in any way different from other creatures. Her view is that man —*like any created thing*— has a being "from above," as he is set outside the divine being, as well as a being "from below," as he is bound into nature. Since nature, too, even though it is on its own, originates in matter actualized by the divine spirit, for Stein the origin of all being also points ultimately "above" to God's creating act. Only because man shares in spiritual being and is thereby

---

[73]   Cf. H. Conrad-Martius, *Metaphysische Gespräche*, op. cit., p. 234.

given an analogy with divine being that sets him apart from all nonpersonal creatures, he is "from above" in a way different from all nonpersonal creatures.

And "in virtue of this higher being, this personally spiritual being, a 'being born of spirit' (a life of grace) is possible for him." (P. 410)

[Transcendental idealism]

The discussion of the *species sensibilis* gives Stein the opportunity to include a remarkable "excursus on transcendental idealism" (pp. 360-378). For, she writes, the interpretation of the intellectual formation of the *sensibile* is "the point where 'idealism' and 'realism' part company" (p. 360). Stein is thinking in particular of the idealistic interpretation that Husserl gives his own theory of the transcendental constitution of the objective world. The excursus also shows why for Stein a transcendental-constitutive inquiry is possible that is both necessary —as it is for Husserl— yet eschews an idealistic interpretation. Hence it is not surprising that Stein calls for the application of the phenomenological reduction insofar as "it is actually admissible" (ibid.).

The initial question for her is the same as for Husserl: "how are we to understand that the sequences of acts constituting the thing ascribes to the world of things a being independent from the sequences themselves?" (p. 365) Now, Stein does not think Husserl's solution is adequate; for her, the objective being of the world of experience does not result from the data of perception motivating in the subject acts "that set before it a world of objects having the phenomenal character of selfsufficiency of being" (p. 372). From the premise "the world as it appears {xxx} to us... depends upon subjects of our own kind," it does not at all follow for Stein that the world's being "is identical to such appearing." On the contrary, she does not rule out "that another way to know the world is conceivable" (p.376).

She sees phenomenal evidence for this other way to know the world not only negatively in the realization that the appearance of the data of perception remains "a completely irrational fact" (ibid.) for purely immanent reflection, but positively in the insight that finite subjectivity in itself refers to what is *other* than the subjectivity itself, for in knowing, acting, and undergoing, subjectivity goes beyond itself into the world of things. Moreover subjectivity, as not being through itself but "placed into existence," refers "to a *principle* in the sense of what is original and unconditioned," and hence goes beyond itself toward something "wherein it itself has the reason for its being" (p. 374).[74] Hence she stresses the same factor of the needful being of subjective existence that she already brought in at the beginning as an argument against assuming an "absolute" subject.

---

[74]   This conveys the outlines of Stein's position on phenomenological philosophy. An inquiry of transcendental philosophy into the constitution question is located in a comprehensive ontology working with a phenomenological method (the method of a science of essence). In a way Stein thereby "inverts" Husserl's philosophical-scientific construction. As we mentioned, he fits ontological inquiry into that of transcendental philosophy (Husserl writes Stein on July 17, 1931 that universal ontology, too, "can do most valuable work, which I can to fit into my transcendental phenomenology <letter in the convent in Cologne>). In her *Festschrift* article Stein even uses Husserl's word for this "inversion": "shift of sign [of headings, *Vorzeichenänderung*]." "Thus all questions at bottom come down to questions about being, and all areas of philosophy become parts of a great ontology or metaphysics.... Husserl's 'transcendental phenomenology'... *is* this general ontology, with a radical shift of sign...." ("Husserls Phänomenologie und die Philosophie des hl. Thomas v. Aquino," op. cit., p. 325f [*Knowledge and Faith*, pp. 30-31].) This switch of headings does away with the prevalence of transcendental philosophy as an expression of Husserl's transcendental-phenomenological idealism.

Stein's position on the problem of idealism and realism —not opting for one or the other but correlating them to one other—[75] already lays the foundation in her project for the claim that a phenomenological approach can be applied to scholastic thought, or for that matter to a Christian worldview:

> Thus our inquiry {xxxi} into the functions of the intentional life of the spirit does not oblige us to abandon that view of the being of things as interpreted in the creation account and church teaching.

At the same time she emphasizes that this inquiry has a critical, clarifying function, if indeed it

> shows that much that naïve belief in experience takes as absolute is relative to a particular sensible-intelligible structure of the experiencing individuals (p. 377).

[Potency and Act and *Finite and Eternal Being]*

Our overview of *Potency and Act* suggests a basically plausible explanation why Edith Stein, as she was revising her work, decided to begin anew and take a quite different approach to the same problem

---

[75] Hanna-Barbara Gerl-Falkovitz expressed this vividly apropos Stein's *Einführung in die Philosophie* [introduction to philosophy]: for Stein, "therefore, there are two absolute areas: nature and consciousness, *neither of which is derivable from the other*" (Afterword to ESWxiii, p. 272). I would only add that for Stein the sphere of consciousness does not ultimately represent any absolute being (but a "relatively absolute" being, if we may use this paradoxical expression), *without* the {xxxi} second part of her statement losing any of its validity. We cannot pursue here Stein's conception of the complex relationship of subjectivity and reality based on this interpretation.

of interpreting the *analogia entis* phenomenologically. Her critique of both transcendental idealism and Conrad-Martius's *Metaphysische Gespräche* revealed that we can discern in man's free personal being a referring relation that puts him in touch with something spiritual, absolute and infinite, in touch with *actus purus*. In this novel metaphysical interpretation, supported by phenomenology, of the traditional *analogia entis*, the aim will be to trace the referring relation, in the phenomenological-ontological manner, by ascending from finite being to infinite being— and this is exactly what she does in *Finite and Eternal Being*.

In this later work her procedure will include several approaches to reach the "meaning of being" (cf. *Finite and Eternal Being*, chapter vi), and potency and act will only be one aspect (chapter ii),[76] and it is brought in on the same level as the analysis of essential and real being (chapter iii), essence, substance, form, and matter (chapter iv), and the transcendentals (chapter v). The last two chapters of *Finite and Eternal Being* treat how, in accordance with the *analogia entis*, infinite being *appears* in the finite, "is imitated" in it (chapter vii), and how individual human being {xxxii} should be conceived against the background of the meaning of particularity as such— this, too, is a final condition for show the *analogia entis* between the human and divine spirit (chapter viii). Thus in *Finite and Eternal Being* Stein came much closer to her goal of clarifying the question of being than she was able to do in *Potency and Act*.

---

[76]   Cf. Stein's remark in the forward to *Finite and Eternal Being* (ESWii, p. xiii): "A quite new version has come about; only a few pages have been taken from the old one (the beginning of the first part). The starting point of the Thomistic doctrine of act and potency was kept— but only as a starting point. The question of being now stands in the center. The comparative critique of Thomistic and phenomenological thought will ensue in the actual treatment of this question."

In regard to the way she finally chose to handle her material in *Finite and Eternal Being*, besides rearranging her topics and reorganizing her method, she made external changes: she no longer departs from Thomas's *Quaestiones disputatae* but from his early work *De ente et essentia*, and she also makes particular reference to Aristotle. Her intent critically to compare Thomism and phenomenology remained unchanged.

So what significance is left to *Potency and Act*? Did *Finite and Eternal Being* make it obsolete? We have already suggested that this is not the case. *Finite and Eternal Being* is no more a final version of *Potency and Act* than a replacement of it; nor is *Potency and Act* a mere first draft, but a point of departure. It holds an important place among Stein's writings first of all because by both its history and its content it ties her earlier treatment of the topic in the *Festschrift* article to her later great work, *Finite and Eternal Being*. Now if it is true that perspective, the angle from which we view the subject matter, is essential in philosophy, then each approach —the one discussing the references of potency and act in the structure of being, the other describing the ascent to the meaning of being, and both going back to the same thing, namely, the question of being— retains its essential relevance. Nor are the two works significant only as approaches, for each has a perspective essentially related to "the" thing that in either becomes a theme for discussion. To work out these essential perspectives of each work and compare them in their convergence is the task of future study.

[Phenomenology and Thomism]

We may see a third feature of *Potency and Act*, besides its particular perspective and its connection with the works of Thomas Aquinas, in its phenomenological procedure. The phenomenological interest is more in evidence here than in Stein's later work. This is clear not least because in *Potency and Act* her own understanding of phenomenology becomes sharper. Her excursus {xxxiii} on transcendental idealism in particular shows how she has made phenomenology her own and built upon it, and it illustrates in the context of her work as a whole how this phenomenological position gives her a base precisely from its bearing upon those matters that she is inquiring about. By shifting the thought of Thomas Aquinas beyond a methodological approach into the very objective context of phenomenology, she so frees phenomenology itself from its limitations that its fixation on a specific metaphysical position, transcendental idealism, is questioned and renounced.

We cannot but mention that her procedure will evoke a basic objection, *prima facie* less against the nature of her aim itself than its implementation. I mean that she may not have given enough thought to *how* a phenomenological analysis of the "things" that Thomas Aquinas was concerned with can and should proceed. In her forward she is content to point out that "the inquiry itself will give an account of the method she uses in this analysis" (p.3). However apt her remark and however much her procedure may have tallied with the thing-directed style of the Göttingen phenomenologists, for a reader outside this circle[77] and unfamiliar with its practices, it can be an obstacle to following her thought.

---

[77]   This already proved to be the case with Honecker, who lacked a background in phenomenology and did not see what Stein was aiming at in her work. Significantly, the first objection in his notes on *Potency and Act* is: "is all this supposed to be an explanation of Thomas?" (H. Ott, *Die Randnotizen Martin Honeckers*," op. cit., p. 141). Other terse remarks show that he also obviously misread Stein's implicitly methodological intention behind her approach to the *cogito sum* [I think, I am]. — Moreover, Stein did not learn of Honecker's criticisms, as a comparison of his notes with her later revision shows.

But there is another important point. For Stein herself there is obviously no problem that what she wishes to analyze in direct phenomenological access are at best "things" that have been thought previously and have their being first only in the form of received texts. She does not question whether the same phenomenological procedure is applicable here as in those cases wherein things are *not* mediated through texts, nor does she ask how far things can be separated at all from the form of their text.[78]

It is not really clear how a phenomenological study of things can proceed in this case. For if the {xxxiv} text is the occasion for turning to things, we may ask whether the things thus viewed are not previously determined by the text— say, when some philosophical position expressed in the text does not account therein for its own approach and thus manages the things it treats. But if the text is more than an occasion, we have a right to ask why it is not then a matter of text analysis that would inquire into the things of the text, hence into this and that text, as things.[79] Even if the text is but an occasion, we may insist that then especially we must begin by taking a better look at the text's foundations and making sure of them, in order to view the thing more clearly in the way it was conceived. Stein herself may have been conscious of an objection like this, and it may have led her to study the text far more thoroughly when she came to write *Finite and Eternal Being*.[80]

---

[78] For Edith Stein it is clearly a fact that "things" can {xxxiv} be detached from the terms in which a thinker has clothed them (see her forward to *Finite and Eternal Being*, ESWii p. xv).

[79] That *Potency and Act* is not responsive to such objections may also give the impression that in some passages she is merely oversimplifying Thomistic reasonings. Such a reading is supported by Honecker's comment on one passage that she does "not identify as necessary" a distinction from Thomas Aquinas but "assumes that it is found in Thomas and then goes ahead and discusses it" (*Randnotizen*, op. cit., p. 144).

Even, especially, a procedure wherein one ventures —of course not carelessly— upon untrodden ways, albeit conscious of being ill equipped for the venture, can be consistent with the commitment to be faithful to things. Edith Stein's risky effort brings a philosophical issue to light that goes beyond her own concerns and poses the question raised above: how are things related to texts and how can they be accessed *through* texts. The fact that although Edith Stein did not discuss this question, she did in fact pose it by taking the path she did in *Potency and Act* it —indeed actually exposing herself to its danger— is no small thing— particularly since the answer is still ours to find.

{xxxv}   **Transmission and formation of the Text**

The autograph of Edith Stein's *Potency and Act* has not come down to us. The text is extant today in two copies of a typewritten version.[81] One copy is found among Conrad-Martius's papers in the

---

[80]   Stein herself was aware that her attempt was inadequate. On Jan. 25, 1933 she writes to Ingarden: "Unfortunately I am still no connoisseur of scholasticism and St. Thomas" (Letter 156, ESWxiv, p. 233). And in the previous draft of her foreword to *Potency and Act* she stresses that she lacked "the essential basis of a comprehensive knowledge of medieval philosophy," consoling herself with the thought that: "perhaps it will help others to advance further" (see above, p.xxviii). She had made this last point in a letter of April 5, 1933 to Conrad-Martius (letter 139, ESWviii, p. 135) and, in modified fashion, in the foreword to *Finite and Eternal Being* (ESWii, p. xvf <CWESv, pp. 138f>).

[81]   Edith Stein probably had three copies made of the text (the typed original plus two carbon copies). At least she did this with *Finite and Eternal Being* (cf. her letter of 12, 9, 1935 to Ruth Kantorowicz, op. cit.). We know that in the fall of 1931 she gave copies to Husserl, Heidegger, and Honecker (cf. her letter of 9, 3, 1932 to Ingarden, op. cit.). She must have gotten Husserl's copy back during her stay in Freiburg in the winter of 1931-1932, for on April 29, 1932 she wrote to Ingarden: "I have only one copy here which I cannot very well part with. But Honecker and Heidegger still have

Bavarian State Library in Munich;[82] another is among the papers Stein left behind. When Stein went to live in the convent in Echt in 1938 she took her own copy with her along with other writings and personal documents. The writings that had been deposited in the Dutch convent of Herkenbosch after her arrest were heavily damaged in one of the last German air-raids at the end of 1944. This was also the fate of the Stein's manuscript of *Potency and Act.* Dr. Lucy Gelber, of the Archivum Carmelitanum Edith Stein, managed to reconstruct the manuscript, which is now complete except for pages 5, 8, and 12.

Stein had written her revisions in her copy in early 1935 and so the reconstruction represents her final version. If in fact there were two copies of the writing among Stein's papers —as the German editors of *Finite and Eternal Being* claimed[83]—, we would have to distinguish {xxxvi} four extant versions: A: the copy that was in Conrad-Martius's possession, B: Stein's own copy not completely preserved, C: a second copy found in her possession, also incomplete,[84] and D,

---

some..." (ESWxiv, letter 153, p. 229). In June of the same year she asks Honecker "may I ask you to send the ms. that I left with you to Breslau at the end of July...?" (letter in the Cologne Carmel). For during the summer vacation she spent with her family in Breslau she wanted to look the manuscript over in preparation for her course in Münster "The Structure of the Human Person." At the beginning of April, 1933, she sent one of the two copies now in her possession to Conrad-Martius (see above). But we cannot rule out that the third copy remained with Heidegger. The editors of the second volume of ESW mention, however, that Stein's copy was reconstructed from *two* carbon copies (ESWii, p. 490). If both copies were among the papers she left behind, it follows either that she got back Heidegger's copy or that there were originally more than three copies. See the following.

82   Call number F I 2 (cf. E. Avé-Lallemant, *Die Nachläße der Münchener Phänomenologen in der Bayerischen Staatsbibliothek <Catalogus codicum manu scriptorum Bibliothecae Monacensis*, t. 10, p. 1>, Wiesbaden, 1975, p. 250.

83   Cf. above, note 81.

84   This copy C should be critically examined to see whether it, too, shows

the manuscript reconstructed from B and C by Gelber. The text of the present volume is this D version.

The typewritten copy comprises 437 pages of text, a six-page index, and a coversheet with the title. In her letter of March 9, 1932 to Ingarden, Edith Stein speaks of "over 450 typed pages";[85] and in a letter of March 24, 1933 to Conrad-Martius she also mentions a bibliography which is no longer extant and, to judge from its length, contained more than the works that Stein cited (see p. 425).

Edith Stein wrote minor corrections, obvious typing errors, in the extant versions, probably right after the text was typed. On the other hand, Conrad-Martius's copy shows no later alterations. In our opinion, Stein must have made the later more extensive alterations in her copy from mid May to mid July of 1935, probably between the end of May and the beginning of June (cf. above p.xxvi). Stein obviously decided to make a completely fresh start on her topic after this interval. This dating is also supported by the fact that the alterations are not extensive in number or length, and also that they are made mainly in the first quarter of the work—[86] but, as we mentioned, Stein was especially dissatisfied with the last, the sixth, chapter containing her critical discussion of Conrad-Martius's *Metaphysische Gesprächen*. All this goes to show that quite soon after undertaking her revision Stein must have realized that she had to start all over again.

The present text represents Stein's final revision. All her alterations {xxxvii}have been taken into account as far as the reconstructed

---

traces of later revision. If so, we would have to speak of two copies. For the present edition I only had access to a copy of the reconstructed manuscript (the D version); hence I was unable to compare this D text with the B and C versions it was based upon.

[85]   ESWxiv, letter 152, p. 227.

[86]   However, it would be good to determine what pages in Gelber's reconstruction (see above) come from Stein's copy (B), and which do not. Cf. above, note 84.

manuscript (D) allowed. Since the collection of Stein's works was not intended to be a critical edition, her later changes are not included. Besides alterations (additions, deletions, replacements by new formulations), her own copy contains brief notes on revisions she wished to make and marks in the margin. The present edition does not take these additions into account; it remains a task for a future critical edition of her works.

We have left the text in the form that Edith Stein gave it. Only spelling and punctuation have been adapted to current usage. We did not think that a certain roughness of language —the text was not supposed to be ready for publication— reason enough to refine her style and diction or alter peculiarities like spelling variations (for example, "*anderen*"/ "*andern*") and the overuse of colons and semicolons. Wherever words or (as in the footnotes) references had to be supplied, they have been placed in angle brackets. Where clarity demanded, paragraph divisions have been added.

We had to depart from the manuscript in two cases involving later revision. We omitted two short footnotes that Stein inserted on pages 15 and 16 of her copy since the sheets were damaged and could only partially be read. Also, the reading of the typewritten foreword is unclear. Stein had actually signed it at the end of the long initial paragraph, and she placed square brackets around the next two shorter paragraphs in which she refers to Husserl and Heidegger. This could mean that she wished them to be considered deleted;[87] but since we cannot know this for certain, we have retained the two paragraphs.

Stein twice referred to extra sheets in her footnotes (cf. below pp. 34 and 39), but we could not fit the additions into these pages since there was {xxxviii} no indication of where they should be inserted; moreover, they did not fit into the main text without a break. Hence

---

[87] Cf. her remark in her letter of 12, 9, 1935 to R. Kantorowicz (op. cit.): "please omit what you find in square brackets."

we placed these texts in supplement I, marking the corresponding pages (cf. p. 54). These handwritten supplements with the original page numbers 56, 56a, 57a-c, and 58a-e are not found in Stein's copy of *Potenz and Akt*, but are contained in a bundle with the call number A I 4 ("loose sheets"). Reference is made on page 76 of the typed copy of *Potency and Act* (p. 73) to another additional text, also written by hand, found in the same bundle with the page numbers 76a-b; since this supplement cannot be matched with the main text, we include it as supplement II. The texts in both appendices has already been published in the third chapter of ESWxv in ignorance of their provenance.[88] Since these texts, because of their pagination and similar content, can clearly be assigned to *Potency and Act*, it seemed mandatory to print them again here in their rightful place.

[Acknowledgments]

We conclude these introductory remarks with a word of thanks. I am especially beholden to Dr. Peter Suchla, editor of Herder publishers, without whose support it would not have been possible to complete the edition in the allotted time. I also thank Sister Amata Neyer, O.C.D. of the Edith Stein Archiv in the Cologne Carmel for the confidence she placed in my work as well as for her valuable advice on many questions concerning Edith Stein's biography and on archival matters. In this regard I am also grateful for the research of Dr. Hugo Ott of Freiburg University, which has been helpful in my reconstruction of the genesis of the work. I thank Dr. Eberhard Avé-Lallemant of the University of Munich for making the literature available, and Mrs. Cornelia Billmeier, M.A., for her assistance in collating the text. I am

---

[88]   Pp. 57-62. Cf. the editor's introduction, p. 12f [*Knowledge and Faith*, pp. 75-80 and xxi-xxii].

also grateful to Dr. Walter Redmond (Austin) for his English translation of this introduction, undertaken with such great competence and care; and especially for his profound suggestions that have led to improvements in the original published text of *Potenz und Akt.*

Hans Rainer Sepp
Center for Theoretical Study
Prague

EDITH STEIN

Saint Theresa Benedicta of the Cross
Discalced Carmelite

Potency

And

Act

Studies
Toward A
Philosophy of Being

{3} Author's Foreword

[St. Thomas's method]

The following inquiries are the result of my efforts to gain access to an understanding of St. Thomas Aquinas's method. As I began to study his writings one question kept troubling me: what method is he actually following here? I was accustomed to the phenomenological way of thinking, which eschews all doctrinal lore, preferring to examine *ab ovo* whatever it needs to solve a problem, and I was puzzled by a procedure wherein conclusions are drawn from Scriptural passages, quotes from the Fathers, and principles of the ancient philosophers.

Yet we quite soon get the impression that St. Thomas's approach is not "unmethodical." We feel we are in the hands of a guide who is quite sure of his way. The abundant results of following his way vouch for its reliability; we reach solutions that bear the stamp of truth and prove their worth by illuminating entire areas of theory and practice that before lay dark.

We also quickly discover that Thomas cites "authorities" only after careful choice and assessment. He accepts a statement as valid not because this or that person made it but because it is sound and in this place gets him further on. However, he does not ordinarily tell us how he arrives at these positive assessments.

Principles he treats as items of knowledge generally accepted over a long time that we can go ahead work with. What criteria guarantee their truth? St. Thomas's way of handling opposing views gives us a clue. He dismisses them as soon as he shows them to be at odds with certain principles, and the views he does accept must agree with these principles. So in a negative way we are led to a basic stock of truths which serve as criteria for everything else.

On the positive side, a comparative consideration of how the Saint forms his arguments will also help us to trace the method he uses in practice, albeit we shall not get an explicit account of it from him. We see {4} that his arguments in the *Summa* of theology, when we look at them carefully, often have gaps. A conclusion may be plausible, but the reasoning as a whole is not really "conclusive." However, it will become conclusive as soon as we add a statement that he made elsewhere (for example, when he treats the same question in greater detail in the *Quaestiones disputatae* [Disputed Questions]).

The fact that the *Summa* is a textbook tells us why the saint could not nor would not always reason back to his ultimate grounds. If we went through all his works, filling in what we need to round out the logical structure, we should arrive at the organon of basic Thomistic concepts and principles. We would then have an insight into the method behind his work as a whole and into its systematic coherence. And we would have accomplished a huge task of interpretation (we need not discuss here how far the literature on Thomas has gotten in carrying out this task after well-nigh seven centuries.)

[Philosophical understanding]

But this accomplishment would still not tell us at all what the philosopher owes to St. Thomas. Indeed, I daresay all it would give us is the humanistic groundwork preliminary to the real work of philosophy. The humanities scholar may rest content when he has uncovered the inner connections of a self-contained thought world and can trace the links from cellar to gable. Such is the "understanding" we ask of him.

Philosophical understanding is different. The philosopher must not only be able to see and show the *fact* that someone else went about it in such and such a way; his insight must not only extend to the connections between the other's grounds [*Grund*] and consequences. The philosopher must also *grasp why* his predecessor went about it like this. He must get down into the grounds themselves and grasp *them*. And this means that the grounds must grip *him* and best him in the sense that he decides to accept them and retraces *within himself* the path the other followed from grounds to conclusions, perhaps even going beyond him. Or else he must best the *grounds*; I mean, he must decide to get free of them and take another path. To be bested by St. Thomas's "grounds" means to vanquish him philosophically for ourselves. To best his grounds means to "be done" with him philosophically.

[Husserl and Aquinas]

The author, whose philosophical thinking was formed by Edmund Husserl, has in recent years found a home in Aquinas's thought world. She now feels an inner need {5} to allow the two different ways of doing philosophy bearing their names to come to resolution within herself.[89] The way to do this, she believes, is an objective analysis of basic Thomistic concepts. In this analysis the inquiry itself will give an account of the method she will use.

Note [on Heidegger]

The way the author poses questions in this work and some of her attempts to solve them may suggest that it is a critical response to the

---

[89] A first attempt to do this was her short sketch "Husserls Phänomenologie und die Philosophie des Hl. Thomas von Aquino" in the supplementary issue in honor of Husserl's 70th birthday <of the *Jahrbuch für Philosophie und phänomenologische Forschung*, (Halle a. d. S, 1929, pp. 315-338), reprinted in *Husserl (Wege der Forschung*, vol. 40), ed. H. Hoack (Darmstadt, 1973, pp.1-86)> [English translation by W. Redmond together with original manuscript version, "Husserl and Aquinas: A Comparison," in *Knowledge and Faith*, CWESxiii, pp. 1-63)].

philosophy of Martin Heidegger. In fact, the personal circumstances of her life in recent years have yet to allow her such an —explicit— concern. She did, however, work through *Sein und Zeit* [*Being and Time*] soon after it was published [1927], and the strong impression the book made on her may linger in the present work.

Breslau; September, 1931

I
Issues of Act and Potency

§ 1
Introduction to the meaning of "act" and "potency"
according to the *De Potentia.*
Potency in God and creature.

[Organic whole]

It is a bold undertaking to pick out a single pair of concepts from a closed system in order to get to the bottom of them. For the "organon" of philosophy is *one*, and the individual concepts that we may isolate are so intertwined that each sheds light on the others and none can be treated exhaustively outside of its context.

Such is the dilemma of all human philosophizing: truth is but *one*, yet for us it falls into truth*s* (plural) that we must master step by step. At some point we must plunge in to discover a greater expanse; yet when this broader horizon does appear, a new depth will open up at our point of entry.

[Analogy]

We may take the idea of being and of the basic forms wherein being is determined as a core of the Thomistic organon. The contrast between potency and act relates to the ultimate questions of being. The discussion of these concepts leads us at once into the heart of Thomistic philosophy.[90] The first question that Thomas asks in his

---

[90] G. Manser, O.P. ("Das Wesen des Thomismus," in *Divus Thomas*, <38> <1924>, p. 10) calls the teaching on act and potency the "innermost essence of Thomism."

Quaestiones de potentia [questions on potency] is: *does God possess potency?*[91] And his answer distinguishes two meanings of potency and act. His entire system of basic concepts is bisected by a radical dividing line that splits each <basic concept>, starting with being, into two faces, one turned here below and the other pointing beyond: *nothing can be said in the same sense of God and creatures*. And we may use the same expressions for both only because they are *not univocal nor* simply *equivocal*, but *analogous [analog]* And {8} so we could call the dividing line itself the *"analogia entis* [analogy of being]," the term denoting the relationship between God and creature.

[Potency in God]

We may and ought to speak of potency in God, but His potency is not opposed to act. We must distinguish between active and passive potency; God's potency is active. God's act, of course, is not "act" in the same sense as the act of creatures. The creature's act is a working, effecting [*Wirken*], an activity [*Tätigkeit*], that starts and stops and presupposes a passive potency as its principle. God's working neither begins nor ends; it is from eternity unto eternity. And in Him there is nothing that is not act; He is *actus purus* [pure act]. This is why God's act does not presuppose any potency as its principle. Certainly there is no passive capability that needs to be set in motion, "activated [*aktivieren*]," from without.

Yet even the active potency we do attribute to Him does not subsist alongside of and outside of His act. For His "being able," His "power" [*Macht*], takes effect in His act. And although outside of Himself —in His creating, conserving, and managing the created world— He does not work, effect, everything He could effect and has the power to effect, and although being able and accomplishing seem

---

[91]   *Quaestiones disputatae. De potentia*, q. 1, a. 1.

to lie apart here, in fact, there is no more potency than act, there is no potency that is not brought to effect [*unausgewirkt*]. The reason is that the self-limitation of God's power in its external working is itself act and the effect of His power. God's potency is but *one* and His act is but *one*, and His potency is brought to effect completely in this act.

[Categories]

How many questions arise at this point! The modern thinker will be tempted to ask "well, how do we *know* everything you are saying about God?" And then he will delve into all the problems on how we know about God. The logician may feel uneasy about this system of categories where no category when applied to God retains its meaning, and this means that properly not a single category *is* applicable to Him.

The Aristotelian categories that Thomas adopts are divided into substance and nine genera of accidents. God is not a substance in the sense in which created things are substances. A thing's substance is *what* it is and its substance is different from its being; God is "Who is," and this —according to Augustine[92]— is the best way to say what He is. And there is no question at all of accidents in God, for He is eternally unchangeable nor can anything "happen" to Him or befall Him. Nevertheless category names are applicable to God, not in a proper but in an analogical sense, as long as we free them from the bounds [*entschränken*] set by the creatureliness that mark them. {9}

[Being, act and potency]

The analogy of all the names of God and creature harks back to the analogy of the *being* of God and creature. Everything that is,

---

[92]   *De trinitate*, 1:1.

insofar as it is, is something after the manner of divine being. But all being, save divine being, is tinged with nonbeing [*Nichtsein*]. And this has consequences for *what* it is, for all that it is. God is *actus purus*. Unbounded being is actual being. The greater a creature's "share in being [*Seinsanteil*]," the starker its actuality. As long as it is, something of what it is, but never everything that it is, is actual. It can be actually more or less of what it is, and what is actual can be more or less actual.

Hence in actuality there are differences of extent and degree. What is, without being actual, is potential, and potentiality shows parallel differences of extent and degree. Such is the *potentiality* of creatures. Actuality and potentiality, as we are taking them here, are *modes of being* [*Seinsmodus*]. Pure actuality is the divine mode of being. The modes of being of creatures are variously layered blends of actuality and potentiality (this means that they are equivalent to, but not identical with, blends of being and nonbeing). Pure potentiality is the mode of being of bare matter [*Materie*]; hence, like matter, it does not occur in fact.

In God there is no potentiality in this sense. *In potentia esse — in actu esse* [being in potency — being in act] are the modes of being of finite substances. God cannot but *esse in actu* [be in act]. Thus His potency is at the same time *in actu*. Substance, potency, and act coincide in Him. In the creature they are separate and stand in a real relation.

§ 2
The immanent starting point of philosophy.
Act and potency in the immanent sphere.
From the immanent to the transcendent sphere.

[Ontology]

Our preparative study, which we now concluding, has led us into a number of intertwined issues. In order to set out on a path that is methodically secure, it is essential to trace the order of these issues. This much should now be clear from all we have said: as long as we do not understand *being* we understand nothing. Hence we should call what we are going to do here "*ontology*."

The moment we mention being we must distinguish between the being of God and creature. How should we understand this? Are we bringing in ideas from theology or from a simple pretheoretical faith? Or do the words mean something that we may take in a purely ontological sense; that is, do they indicate formal distinctions in being for which we are but borrowing the names of the realities that correspond {10} to them and fill them materially [*material*]? This is the first question that we must answer.

[The starting point: my being]

The first and simplest fact of which we are immediately certain is the fact of our own being. This is the core of the reflections on doubt we find in Augustine, Descartes, and Husserl. My being is not a conclusion —*Cogito ergo sum* [I think, *therefore* I am]"— but a simple certainty: *cogito, sum* [I think, I am]— when thinking, feeling, willing or however I bestir myself spiritually, I *am* and am aware [*innesein*] of this being. This certainty of being comes before all knowledge. It does not mean that everything else is to be logically deduced from it —as from a principle—, nor that it is the criterion upon which all else is to be measured. It is rather a starting point behind which we cannot get further back. The certainty of being is an unreflective certainty, and it precedes all our rational knowledge.

When the intellect does concentrate on this simple fact in reflection, it sees it split into three aspects that pose questions. What is the being that I am aware of? What is the I that is aware of its being? And what is the act or the spiritual stirring wherein I am and wherein I am conscious of myself and of the stirring? When I turn to being, as it is in itself, it reveals two faces: being and nonbeing.[93] The "I am" does not withstand the look. The "wherein I am," the act, is different in each case, and since my being and my act are not separate, since I am "therein," my being, too, is different in each case. The being of the "just now" has passed away and made room for the being of the "now."

[Being and time]

We ought not to separate from temporality the being that I am aware of as of my own being. As actual being it involves discrete points: a "now" between a "no longer" and a "not yet." But since its flowing character is split into being and nonbeing, the *idea of pure being* unveils itself to us, a being which in itself has nothing of nonbeing, in which there is no "no longer," no "not yet," and which is not temporal but *eternal.* Thus eternal and temporal being, changeless and changeable being, as well as nonbeing, are ideas that the intellect comes upon within itself, for they are not borrowed from elsewhere.

---

[93]   H. Conrad-Martius vividly analyzed the frailty of temporal being and its relation to eternal being in her essay on "Die Zeit [time]" (*Philosophischer Anzeiger*, 2 <1927-1928, pp. 143-182, 354-390>1 <reprinted in H. Conrad-Martius, *Schriften zur Philosophie* [writings on philosophy], vol. 1, ed. E. Avé-Lallement, Munich, 1963, pp. 101-184>).

Here a philosophy built of natural knowledge has its legitimate starting point. The *analogia entis* also, understood as the relationship of temporal to eternal being, already comes to light at this starting point. Momentary being, at the {11} moment when it is, is something after the manner of being absolutely [*schlechthin*], of full being knowing no changes in tense. Yet because it is but a moment, neither is it at that moment full being; its frailty [*Hinfälligkeit*] already lies in its momentary being. This momentary being itself is but an analogue of eternal being that at every moment is full being.

[Tense, possibility, and actuality]

We need not ask here whether from the fact that temporal and eternal being are analogous we should infer a relation of origin [*Ursprungsrelation*] between them suggested by the words "Creator" and "creature." It is important first to make the most of the fact that is our starting point. Along with the idea of being and nonbeing we have met the idea of *actuality*, the being that is *esse in actu* [being in act]. But we have yet to finish our description of the fact.

What was but is no more and what will be but is not yet, is not simply nothing. Past being and future being are not simply nonbeing. This implies more than that past and future have cognitive being in remembrance and expectation, that they have an *esse in intellectu (sive in memoria)* [being in the intellect (or in the memory)]. From a purely ontic [*ontisch*] viewpoint, we cannot think of momentary actual being as existing all by itself— just as we cannot think of a point outside the line nor of the moment itself without duration in time. And from a phenomenal viewpoint this momentary actual being is given as something that issues from darkness and crosses a light beam only to sink again into darkness, or as the crest of a wave that itself forms part of a current.

These are all metaphors of a being that, though enduring, is not actual in its duration. In what I am now there lies something that I am now not actually, but will become actually at some time in the future. And what I now am actually, I already was previously, but not actually. My present being contains the *possibility* for future actual being and supposes a possibility in my earlier being. My present being is at once actual and potential being; and insofar as it is actual, it is the actualization of a potency that already existed earlier. As modes of being, actuality and potentiality are contained in the sheer fact of being [*schlichte Seinstatsache*] and from it they are to be inferred.

The potentiality that can pass into actuality —for its very meaning is to pass over into actuality— is not nonbeing. It is something between being and nonbeing, or it is being and nonbeing at once. What is in the present but is not actually is like this. What was once actually but is so no longer is like this, insofar as it can pass over into actuality from its present mode of being. What will be actually in the future is like this, insofar as it has that preparatory mode of being in its previous temporal duration.

So much for what the first and simplest fact of which we are certain says about being and the modes of being. Now, do we also know what act and potency are? {12}

[Actuality and activity]

We called "act" that wherein I come upon myself as be-ing [*seiend*]; we are tempted to say: my actual life. But this is still not exact. What is now actual at this moment stretches backwards and forwards. The momentary has existence only in what endures. What endures is not actual over its entire stretch, yet we were warranted in calling it "act" (taking "act" in the sense of actual), because the actual momentary phase lends a certain mark of actuality to the whole that it belongs to, as well as because each phase of the whole was once or will be actual.

If so, we would have to take "act" as being for a certain duration, wherein one phase after another momentarily becomes actual and then passes into inactuality. Being will be determined in a particular way in each case not only in its mode of being (actuality — inactuality) but in its content, for through their content acts are internally grouped and distinguished from other acts.

But we would jeopardize the formal character of the concept of act if we were to define act and its content materially [*materiell*]. The area of immanence wherein our study has thus far been confined suggests that we call act "conscious life" of a specific kind or, as we did just now, "spiritual stirring [*Regung*]."

But this would be to forestall the possibility of also speaking of "act" outside the immanent sphere, whereas the expression traditionally is understood as the *activity* [*Betätigung*] *of a be-ing* and as its *actuality, reality* [*Wirklichkeit*] in contrast to mere possibility, since only the real can be effective [*wirksam*] and active [*tätig*]. And ultimately "act" is traditionally what gives being and effectiveness [*Wirksamkeit*] to a be-ing and makes it what it is.

Accordingly, the kind of be-ing that it is is irrelevant, and there are physical as well as psychic acts. Without lifting for now the boundary of immanence, let us confine the definition of our concepts to a formal generality [*Allgemeinheit*], and not allow ourselves to be swayed by the particular nature of the immanent material.

We mentioned that in our traditional way of speaking "act" means not only "actuality [*Aktualität*]" but also "activity [*Aktivität*]." We have not yet discussed activity at all nor even given sufficient attention to actuality. Just as we got the idea of full, unbounded being from the fact of defective [*mangelhaft*], transitory being, so from the fact of defective act, rightfully called "act" only in its momentary phase, we get the idea of *pure act, actus purus*. Pure act is actual throughout; it does not go through phases, nor does it *become* instant by instant only to founder; rather, it is actually all that it is from eternity and hence at each moment. It is no accident that we must say again what we have said before: *pure being and pure act coincide* {13}. Our acts, which in a certain way represent our greatest "share in being,"[94] our closest approach to full being, themselves lie between being and nonbeing. We should not say, however, that insofar as they are potential they are *not*, for even potential being retains something of being in itself. We must ask another question about this potential being: can we also find in it the second meaning of "potency" (capacity [*Vermögen*] for activity)?

[Acts of a potency]

Act, we have learned, is that wherein we find ourselves be-ing. Is "*in potentia esse* [being in potency]" as immediately certain for me as "*in actu esse* [being in act]," and am I as certain of myself therein? Obviously not. What is "no longer" and "not yet," but is somehow "still" and "already" therein, is upheld [*halten*] from the actuality phase. Husserl called these phenomenal features of being "retentional" and "protentional."[95] We are justified in claiming these modes to be potential being because of the possibility —not only objectively but also phenomenally— of passing into actuality. *In potentia esse* means *in potentia alicujus actus esse* [being in potency *of some act*]: herein

---

94   Cf. the last part of this work, VI, § 23e.

95   For his entire account of the inner sphere see his "Vorlesungen zur Phänomenologie des inneren Zeitbewußtseins [lectures on the phenomenology of the inner consciousness of time]" (*Jahrbuch für Philosophie und phänomenologische Forschung*, vol. 9, 1928 <critical edition: E. Husserl, *Zur Phänomenologie des inneren Zeitbewußtseins* <*1893-1917, Husserliana*, vol. 10>, ed. R. Boehm, The Hague, 1966>); in 1917-1918 the [present] author worked up sketches in preparation for its publication.

lies the phenomenal tie of potentiality to actuality.

On the other hand the traditional dictum that every act is "an act of a potency" has another sense. We mean that the act, as what is real [*wirklich*] and effective, proceeds from a real [*real*] possibility preceding it in time— from a "predisposition for being [*Seinsanlage*]." But we are not thinking here of immediately conscious transitions from potential to actual being, such as we have in our daily experience.

Is there a phenomenal approach to all this? That we speak of act as "operation, activity [*Betätigung*]" suggests that there is. Activity implies that something activates itself [*sich betätigen*]. Something "has" the potency, and because it does, it can perform the relevant acts. However, our immanent analysis has taught us nothing about the "something," or about the "has," or, in this sense, about "potency and act." The difference between the immanent and transcendent considerations (in Husserl's sense) stands out quite clearly here. We surely see that in order to reach Aristotelian and scholastic categories we must cross over into the realm of transcendent objects. But we ought not to get there by leaping across. We are engaged {14} in a genuine consideration of origins and if we wish to understand what is ontically further by starting with what is closer, we must move ahead step by step.

[The I]

We have not concluded our analysis of the situation that is our starting point, namely the fact that *I* am in an act and therein find *myself*. We have considered being and act, but not yet the I. What does the I —me— imply, and what does the finding imply? I am thinking about some problem; this is now my actual being. And this being of thinking [*Denkend-Sein*] is accompanied by the consciousness of the being both of this thinking and of what is thinking therein.

In its original form this consciousness is not a new act turned toward the thinking and toward the thinking I. The more actual the thinking the more undivided it is and the more undivided I am therein; still, the thinking is conscious and self-conscious [*selbst-bewußt*].

The split may also come between an act that I do not reflect upon and a reflection that I direct toward it. Is then the I also "split"? Not in the strict sense. I —what is reflecting— do find myself —the thinking I— but it is the *same* I. It is no belated realization let alone a conclusion, since the former I and the latter I are the same. By reflecting I am immediately conscious of myself as of what is thinking. Even where there is a number of simultaneous acts, in consciousness it is the same I that thinks, perceives, wills, etc.; there is no special I in each act. And the very same I that holds on to what has passed away and goes forth to meet what is to come is just as much the same I that from the past lives its way into the future. Thus phenomenally the I is something that has duration, something that not only is now but was and will be, even though the content of its actual being is constantly new and different.

What am I conscious of it as? Husserl described it as a "pure I," as the bare subject of some act and of the subject's life as a whole connected in consciousness with the actual act. It is discrete in points of time, it lacks substance and properties, and it is distinct from other I's not in qualities but only because of the uniqueness [*Einzigkeit*] of the being of its I [*Ich-Sein*].

Of course my name and position, my accomplishments, and even the properties that I see in myself, in short everything I know about myself from my own experience and from the reports and judgments of others, lie outside the simple consciousness of my own being. And yet the being that I am conscious of and the I that is conscious of itself, do not lack for qualities. At this moment I am other than I was at a previous moment and other than I shall be at a later moment— I am different as my particular acts vary in kind. And yet throughout these variations I somehow also remain the same *in my qualities.*[96] And although the consciousness of my actual being includes no comparison with my previous being, nor am {15} I conscious of my being different without a comparison —I *can* be conscious of it—, nevertheless the I is conscious of itself as being of such a sort, and this, its *"quale* [what (it is) like]," is the basis it needs to compare and learn of its being thus and of its being different in comparison to its previous being, perhaps too, in comparison to the being of something else.

[Substance, *something*, I]

Am I not coming upon a depth here that is disclosed in our actual living? Does this not evince something lying behind it that cannot itself be grasped nor grasped directly? Is not this the first direction whither immanence points beyond itself and whence it obliges us to set out? Something exists [*dasein*] that "lies at the bottom" of the flow of our life, something that bears our living; I mean, a *substance.* I cannot catch sight of this something directly. *That* it is, as well as what it is like and *what* it is, makes itself known to me in what I am immediately certain of and in what, at the moment this something appears behind it, stands there evincing, effecting, activating this something.

Here we have access to act as attesting to a substance; we have access to the categories of *something, act,* and *substance.* These are not all on the same level. We had already to speak of *something* in the immanent sphere. *"Something"* is anything we say something about; it is the highest and most general logical category. Accordingly, *"something"* is anything that is, anything that is like this or like that, anything that is the case, etc. It is the highest and most general ontic category, as general as being itself. Nor is it restricted to any sphere of being, for

---

[96]   Cf. my remarks below on personal distinctiveness, especially VI, § 23 h.

the immanent and the transcendent enter this form equally.

"I" and "substance," unlike "something," are already limitations. We come upon the I in immanence, albeit in our usual way of speaking, and analogously [*sinngemäß*], we transfer the word to the transcendent that stands behind the pure, self-conscious [*selbst bewußt*] I. "Substance" points into the transcendent sphere, and in the immanent sphere it has no place.

[Substance, potency, and act]

We set out to seek the meaning of "potency" and came across substance. But this may be the place to find potency— as a predisposition for being. We were able to point to the phenomenal meaning of "*in potentia esse* [being in potency]." The being of the I, tending toward something that it still is not but is ready for, showed us the duration of the I, and its changing qualities brought us to something lying behind it. Thus "possibility," harking back to the past and heralding the future, points outside and beyond itself to an enduring determinedness of this something, that is, of the substance wherein the possibility of its acts is anchored as well as the diverse qualities of such "potencies" of the substance.

Hence substance, potency, and act go together. What is activates itself, what operates, in all its acts is the *one* substance, but the qualitative diversity of the acts is based on the fact that the substance "has" a number of potencies. We can understand the categories in formal generality without restricting them to a definite {16} area of transcendent objects, namely to the area of the soul, as our departure from the immanent sphere could suggest. On the basis of our analysis heretofore we are taking substance as a something whose being stretches over a duration and which activates [*betätigen*] what it is in certain effects. We are taking acts as these activations, operations

[*Betätigung*], and we are taking potencies as the substance's enduring determination to certain operations. We need not include in the concept of act the notion that such activity must be conscious life, for when wood thrown into the fire begins to burn, the burning is an act whose "possibility" it bore within itself.

[Substance and God]

Does having determined potencies belong necessarily to the idea of substance? The question arises when we recall what we learned about pure being. Pure being is pure act wherein nothing is merely potential; it does not start and stop, but *is* immutably from age to age.

In the first place, is the category of substance applicable at all to God? We said before[97] that God is not substance if we take "substance" as "essence" in contrast to "being," or as the "bearer" of "properties" that do not coincide with God Himself. But if we take "substance" only as we defined it just now, "a something whose being stretches over a duration and which activates what it is in certain effects," I daresay we may answer yes. True, God's duration is not a length of time but the duration of eternity fulfilling each temporal duration. No more is the effect of substance, said of God, an effect in these or those particular acts that begin and end and differ in kind. Accordingly, what takes effect in God's acts is from all that His substance is, not sometimes this and sometimes that. His being is *actus purus*— implying that all that this something is, is constantly coming to effect actually.

Hence in God's being there is no possibility that has not taken effect, no possibility determined to something that has yet to be. "Potency" here is but possibility brought to effect, *potentia in actu* [potency in act]. Nor is there any room for a plurality of potencies in

---

97   P. 7.

a substance that takes effect in *one* act. So substance, potency, and act in God, we must say, coincide *realiter* [really], even though in our idea we should keep them apart— precisely out of regard for what the categories, concerned as they are with what is finite, have in common with the issue at hand.

[Three spheres of being]

Starting from the simple, immediately certain fact of being, we have come to distinguish three spheres of being: [1] the immanent sphere, which is immediately and inseparably close to us and of which we are conscious, [2] a transcendent {17} sphere, which heralds itself in immanence, and [3] a third sphere radically different in its being from the immanent sphere as well as from this transcendent sphere. Of this pure being we have said so far that it discloses itself in immanent being only "in our idea," whereas we should take the evincing of finite substances in immanence as evidence of their existence [*Existenzbekundung*]. But what we have said does not rule out that the existence of this pure being may also be evinced in immanence. Let us now pursue this question.

I am conscious of myself in my actual being, and I am conscious of this being. My being is momentary, but it cannot be as purely momentary. Actual being emerges from a potential being and passes into a potential being, but all potentiality is phenomenally upheld [*halten*] by actuality and it cannot uphold [*Halt geben*] actuality. What upholds me in my temporally discrete existence between being and nonbeing? When I have pressed ahead into the transcendent sphere, I may conceive of the substance evinced in my flowing actual being as the bearer of this being.

But we have just seen that the being of finite substances is such that it has not come to full effect. It is destined to unfold in successive activities and ever retains in itself some unfulfilledness and frailty— a "not yet" and a "no longer." Its potentiality points ahead to the actuality wherein it is to fulfill itself, but it also points back beyond itself to a being that no longer unfolds in an alternating flow of actuality and potentiality but in the eternal unchangeableness of actual being.

Can anything uphold [*Halt geben*] my frail [*hinfällig*] being, which touches upon genuine existence [*Existenz*] only from one instant to another, save true being wherein nothing of nonbeing is found and which stands changeless by itself alone, unable to have, nor needing, any other upholding [*Halt*]? And does not the very frailty of my own being lend certainty— not only to the idea but to the reality [*Realität*] of this pure, true, "absolute [*absolut*]" being?

[Three paths to God]

I wish to claim that we must come to this conclusion *by thinking* and that the basis for an argument for God's existence is given in the sheer fact of being.[98] This does not mean, however, that the certainty of the existence of absolute being lies immediately in the sheer fact of being. I *do have* this certainty the moment I *believe*;[99] then I am reaching for the absolute hold [*Halt*] and by it I feel myself upheld. But the certainty of faith is blind certainty; believing is {18} not seeing. Indeed, it is doubtless possible to be conscious of God's actual being without making an act of faith in it or even to have faith in but a nonactual way.

There is also a certainty of being upheld absolutely, a certainty of the presence of God, that goes beyond the certainty of faith and is

---

98   This is *not* the ontological argument that deduces the reality of absolute being from its idea.

99   "Believe" in the religious sense of "*fides* [faith]," not as "*belief*." [St. Teresa Benedicta uses the English word here; the German word "*Glaube*" may mean religious faith or natural belief.]

no longer blind; any mystic can tell of it. But mystical awareness of God is not inseparably connected with the sheer fact of being. Were it so, there would no longer be any place for faith. Thus we shall have to posit the sphere of absolute being as a second transcendent sphere. Three paths lead to it from the immanent sphere: the path of mystical contemplation [*Schauen*], the path of faith, and the path of logical reasoning. The first way is compelling but not universal. The second is open to anyone but the will must help it reach the goal. The third is the way of natural knowledge which any reasonable person could take. Why this does not happen, why not only dull or indifferent people but even those having a theoretical interest do not take this path or stop along the way, and why so much energy has been spent to prove that this path cannot be traveled— is as unfathomable as the very mystery of the being itself that lies outside the divine or is opposed to the divine.

The world within, the world without, and the world above have disclosed themselves to us according to their form. Fullness of being [*Seinsfülle*] rather than frailty, eternity rather than temporality, mark the world above from the others. The fact that existing by itself [*Für-sich-Dasein*] cannot be separated from being marks off the immanent sphere from the transcendent. There are most general forms (like *something* and *being*) that run through all the spheres of being and in principle are accessible from any one of them. Other forms can find fulfillment only in one or perhaps two spheres of being, but as possible modifications they may be accessed in their empty formality even from the spheres where they find no fulfillment. The transcendent spheres of being, as materially [*material*] fulfilled and real [*real*], herald themselves to us in "our," the immanent, sphere.

Access to the world above is also possible in principle from the world without, since an analogous relationship is to be found between them, just as between the world within and the world above. (This is the way of Thomistic arguments for God's existence in contrast to the way from within that is paramount in Augustine.)

{19}   § 3
                A Methodological look back and ahead.

                        [The first steps]

We now have the beginnings of a methodological reflection on the way we have traveled so far. We were seeking a secure starting point to get to the bottom of the concepts of "potency" and "act"— as essential elements of the Thomistic organon as well as those of any philosophy of being. As their connection with the ultimate questions of being came to light, we needed to go back to the initial point of departure of all philosophizing.

That the "sheer fact of being," as I called it, is an initial point of departure hardly seems to me to need further warrant. If we were to bolster it by authority, besides Augustine, Descartes, and Husserl, we could call upon Thomas himself.[100] I think, however, that the very course our inquiry has taken is justification enough.

We could argue over whether we could also construct a philosophy from a quite different starting point. I believe we can manage to show this possibility, indeed from *this* starting point. But there is no getting away from it: what we did go back to is an ultimate and indemonstrable fact.

Our second methodological step was to put this fact to as much use as we could, I mean, to bring out from it whatever might be important for our question. A whole series of paths have now led off

---

[100]   For example, *De veritate*, q. 10, a. 8 (in my translation, *Des Hl. Thomas von Aquino Untersuchungen über die Wahrheit*, <vol. 1>, Breslau, 1931, p. 282 <new edition: Edith Steins Werke, vol. 3, Freiburg and Louvain, 1952, p.257>).

from this point of departure. But before venturing forward, we had to decide which path it would be best to follow.

[Approaches]

When using this fact as our starting point, we were obliged —just to be understood — to use terms repeatedly whose meaning we had not yet clarified sufficiently, and so a belated justification is called for. Prime examples are "form" and "matter [*Materie*]," the "forms of being" and those of "be-ings."

To seek the meaning of form and matter, to show how we can speak of forms detached from matter, to decide if we should understand act and potency in a formal sense— these are the tasks of a *formally ontological* treatment of our problem. So far our inquiry has found a meaning for "act" and "potency" both in the immanent and in the transcendent {20} spheres. To be able to make a legitimate shift from the immanent to the transcendent sphere, we must discuss the relation between the two in greater detail. This would be the task of transcendental philosophy, an inquiry that would be relevant both to the theory of knowledge and to *metaphysics*.

Once we find ourselves in the world of finite transcendent things, a series of materially [*material*] diverse regions of being opens up to us. Hence we should ask whether act and potency have a place in all of them as well as how they might differ in different regions. This would amount to a *materially ontological* inquiry.

Finally, we saw that by virtue of the *analogia entis* [analogy of being], act and potency are also relevant to the world above, and if we followed out this thread we would be led into theology.

[Transcendental philosophy]

In principle, it is just as possible and just as urgent to begin with a transcendental approach as with a formally ontological approach. By "transcendental philosophy" we mean what Husserl calls "transcendental phenomenology," that is, a description of the structures of consciousness in and through which a transcendent world is constructed from immanence. (The metaphysical aspect of the problem answers the question whether this world is a world relative to the constituting consciousness as well as conditioned and upheld by its constituting acts, or whether the shift from the immanent to the transcendent sphere is a transition into a world that is autonomous and independent of consciousness.) This transcendental perspective recommends itself as an initial approach, because it is a consideration of origins and because it starts from what is closest to us and leads us therefrom, advancing step by step, to what lies further afield.

"Closest" and "further" are obviously not to be taken here in a spatial sense, if for no other reason than because the immanent and the transcendent do not at all fit into a *single* spatial order, and so they cannot be compared spatially. The only thing spatial about the "closeness" of the immanent is that it is "here" in a unique sense.

Nor should we take the priority of the immanent in a temporal sense. If we watch how our knowledge develops over time, we see that the first domain of the objects that we know is certainly not the world within but the world without. "Closeness" means that this domain of objects cannot be severed or deleted. This is what we mean when we say that the immanent is what is first for us, and that by passing through it we must come to everything else.

[Formal ontology and constitution]

Now, as soon as we have gained access to the other spheres —our brief reflection on the departure point has already shown this —, the immanent sphere, without losing its central place {21} for us, descends to a specific area. Then formal ontology stands alone embracing all being, for its forms are the basic forms of being and of every be-ing, and for this reason it is itself πρώτη φιλοσοφία [first philosophy]. True, we must also ask how this formal ontology is constituted, and so as long as we ignore constitution problems, formal ontology remains unexplained in one direction.[101] On the other hand it is impossible to get clarity —even on terminology— as long as the basic ontological concepts have not been made clear. We can describe nothing, say nothing, in any area, without using ontological expressions, without presupposing ontological forms. Moreover, since our topic includes a discussion of such ontological forms, our most pressing task is obviously to begin with an ontological inquiry.

---

[101]   Cf. Husserl's remark on the relation of ontology and transcendental philosophy in *Méditations Cartésiennes*, Paris, 1931, pp. 115ff <critical edition of the original text in E. Husserl, *Cartesianische Meditationen und Pariser Vorträge* (*Husserliana*, vol. 1), ed. St. Strasser, The Hague, 1951; cf. § 29> as well as his *Formale und transzendentale Logik*, Halle, 1929 <critical edition in *Husserliana*, vol. 17, ed. P. Janssen, The Hague, 1974>.

II
Act and Potency
from the Perspective of
Formal Ontology

§ 1
"Form" in the sense of formal ontology.
The most general basic forms.
Formalization, generalization,
specification, individuation.

[Meanings of "form"]

Our first question, if we take formal ontology as the theory of the forms of being and of be-ings, must concern the meaning of "form" as such. Now, we speak of form in the most diverse ways. In visible things, the word refers first to geometrical shape opposed to the *matter* [*Stoff*] that is shaped. But it is also used —of *living* bodies— for the inner *power, force* [*Kraft*] that shapes the matter into a formed object and gives it its outer form. Moreover, in all *material* [*materiell*] things, the word is used of what their sensible nature as a whole goes back to: that is, to their *idea*. Form contrasts with what is wholly formless; such is *matter* [*Materie*] in the Aristotelian and scholastic sense of *prima materia* [prime matter]. Besides these forms of material things, there are *pure forms*: the *formae separatae* [separated forms] that do not confer qualities on any matter but exist [*existieren*] by themselves as pure be-ings of spirit [*Geistwesen*].

But in all these meanings (hardly all the possible or common meanings), form is something "having qualities [*qualifiziert*]" in the sense of something fulfilled in content or something material [*material*].

No geometrical shape (as purely geometrical) is like any other shape, no idea is like other ideas. But once we empty *these* forms of their content, we reach the forms in the sense they have in formal ontology.

[Individual, something, object, being]

What befalls us in experience are objects [*Gegenstand*] of a definite kind, material [*materiell*] or spiritual. They are in *such* wise definite that each is different from all the others, be it only by their location in space or time. The uniqueness and unrepeatability of an object setting it apart from all else, we call its "*individuality*," and the qualitative and quantitative fullness to which its individual existence is bound we call its *concreteness* [*Konkretion*].

In this fullness there is much that we can also find elsewhere and that we can lift out of its concreteness and consider *in abstracto* [in the abstract]. {23} But if we empty it entirely of its fullness, remove everything that sets it apart from all else, something still remains, namely, *something* that *is*. Every be-ing confronts us in this form. Here we have those completely empty forms of being that formal ontology is concerned with, namely "*something*" or "object [*Gegenstand*]" on the one hand and being [*Sein*] on the other.

The "*something*" has two other aspects: *what is* and *what it is*, the object, its fullness, and its being. Without fullness there is no being. That is why fullness, too, is an ontological form. *Aliquid* [something], *quod quid est* [what it is], *esse* [being]: these are the basic ontological forms. Their concrete unity is the *be-ing*: *ens*.

[Concept and abstraction]

We said much about being in our first section. does the word now have exactly the same meaning that it had then? The being that we spoke of, the being of God and creature, potential and actual being, are different fillings of the empty form of being. We may be tempted to call this form the "*concept*" of being, but this would be to confuse the issue. We can just as well speak of the "concept of actual being" or of the "concept of potential being" as of the "concept of being as such." Therefore passing from what has content to what is formal is not the same thing as passing to what is conceptual. Abstraction [*Abstraction*] is not simply concept formation. "*Abstrahere*" [to draw off, abstract] means —in this context— (1) negatively: disregarding the fullness and (2) positively: isolating the form. Both take place at what is, for fullness and form are located in the be-ing itself. But everything that is can be grasped conceptually; logical forms correspond to ontological forms. We are explaining this now only to define the area wherein we are moving.

[Empty forms and levels of generality]

Husserl called ontological forms "formal categories," and we spoke earlier in this sense of logical and formally ontological categories. We would like to avoid this expression for now, since it recalls the traditional table of categories, and we have yet to ask whether these categories —all or at least some of them— are really forms in the sense explained. So let us speak of "empty forms." We may not be able to point to more forms of the same generality as the three basic forms that we just mentioned.

By this we do not mean that empty forms represent the entire area of formal ontology. There may be forms of greater and lesser generality and, parallel to them, material content of greater and lesser generality; formalness does not coincide with generality, nor does materialness [*Materialität*] coincide with individuality or singularity. "Object [*Gegenstand*] as such" and "individual" are the highest and lowest degrees on a scale ranging from the general to the particular. But "individual" is itself {24} an empty form. Implied here is that this empty form denotes a singular *together with* all that fills it, and conversely, that it can *only* be filled immediately by a singular. We can imagine indefinitely many singulars that can fill the form. In this sense the form also possesses generality. On the other hand it can *only* be filled by what is singular.

And this qualifies "object [*Gegenstand*]" as a most general basic form. The form of object can be filled by something general. An example of such filling would be "triangle" or "material [*materiell*] thing." Something can be stated of either of them in this generality ("a triangle has angles totaling two right angles," "a material thing has physical properties"). They may, but need not, be filled further, that is, by individuals on the one hand ("this triangle is a section of this prism," "this piece of iron weighs three pounds") and on the other by something that is less general but not an individual ("the equilateral triangle is equiangular," "metals come in different mineral compounds").

A concrete individual may immediately fill the most general empty form or one of the lower forms. But whereas any individual can enter a most general form, the other forms can be filled only by a smaller set of individuals. Filling is linked to how these "forms" are related to one other. The pair "triangle" and "equilateral triangle" is not just a form plus something filling it. Each has a content and these contents are intrinsically connected. The two contents coincide in part, yet each also has its own special stock of meaning [*Sonderbestand*]; "triangle" indicates something fixed and definite as well as a series of possibilities definitely prescribed for it beforehand. The definite aspect reappears in "equilateral triangle," and "equilateral" specifies triangle in one of its possibilities that excludes the rest. The general content is contained in the more specific content, and conversely —in another sense, in that of being marked out beforehand— the more specific in the more general. This relationship we call "*differentiation*" or "*specification.*" Differentiation proceeds downwards to a fully determined content that cannot be further differentiated since it can only be filled by an individual. Then when we ascend toward greater generality on the scale of "material [*material*] forms" or "species," we finally come to something that is no longer a differentiation of something general. We may {25}use the traditional term "genus" ["*Genus*" — "*Gattung*"] of it.[102] Are the genera empty forms? And how are they related to empty forms?

[The Bohemian garnet]

Anticipating later inquiries, we may take "material thing" and "spiritual person" as genera [*Genera...Gattungen*]. To each belongs a domain of individuals. These belong to their genus because of *what* they are, and we should understand this "*what*," their species, as specifying the genus. This particular garnet is an individual of the species "Bohemian garnet" ("Bohemian" here does not refer to the place where it is found but to a definite quality, assuming that the Bohemian garnet is the lowest species, lacking further differentiation). Species may be found at different levels of generality between the lowest species and the genus; at all levels we have something determined materially, and between any two levels we have a difference in content.

But the relation of genus and species may be of another kind. In the case of genuine, proper specification the genus *must* be distributed into a number (possibly a definite, finite number) of species, and it cannot occur in individuals except as specified in one way or another.

---

[102]   We shall again seek to distinguish the ideas of "genus - species - individual" in several contexts in our material study, especially in VI, § 19.

In a broader sense (as in the our example) "specification" only implies the fact of a relation wherein a series of stocks of content exhibit, besides their own, a common stock that we call "generic [*generell*]." Later, in our material and genetic study, we shall endeavor to clarify the difference between these two kinds of specification.

[Kind, *individual*, and empty form]

The relation between the lowest species and the individual is not the same as that between genus and species. The species of a pair of Bohemian garnets, assuming they are quite identical, would be the same in this garnet over here and that one over there. The individuals could be distinguished only by being "here" and "there." So individuation [*Individuation*] is not specification. The species is "embodied," "realized [*realisiert*]" in its individuals. Yet nothing of the individuals enters the species. And since they do not lend the species any fullness of content, we cannot properly say that individuals "fill" the species. It seems much more appropriate to say that the species enters the individual. The species is what gives content to the individual. And this tells us once again that "individual" denotes a form.

We have something analogous at the other end of the scale. The genus "material [*materiell*] thing" is not a species of the empty form "*something*" or {26} "object." The genus "material thing" enters the form of "*something*" and can fill it, but it does not get its content from this form. Nor is it a differentiation of "object," since the empty form "object" lacks a content that could be differentiated.

We thus see that there are in fact levels of generality within the formal as well as within the material. We also see that the distinction of form and matter [*Materie*] in *this* sense is not relative, as if something could be related to a lower form and at the same time be for a higher matter. This shows that a distinction between a formal and material ontologies is warranted and required, yet at the same time it shows how closely they are connected.

Empty forms nowhere confront us in our experience as empty forms, for they are always fulfilled by a content. On the other hand every content occurs in a form. Finally, not just any content can enter any form; rather they are ordered to one another. Every genus and every species is something material in such wise that *this* species can belong only to *this* genus and *that* species only to *that* genus. But as such, genus and species are empty forms, the empty forms that stand in their generality between object as such and individual.

§ 2
Genus, Species, and Individual
in relation to the basic forms: object,
what, and being.
Primary and secondary objects.
Ideal objects.

[Object, *what*, being]

Let us return to our three basic forms: object, *what* [*Was*], and being, in order to see how they relate to genus, species, and individual. The object is what *is* and *what* it is, its content. If this is to become a valid material proposition [*Aussage*], then all the forms must be filled with content, and more precisely in such wise that the contents that enter the various empty place-holders be intrinsically connected. Being, when the object is an individual, conveys first "*esse in se* [being in itself]," selfsufficient being, grounded in itself, and then "concrete being." (I do not wish to discuss now whether it also means "real [*real*] being," since we lack the assumptions we need to treat the problem of reality.) The "what" in this case is a lowest species that cannot be further differentiated. Here the individual is not an empty form, but a concrete individual; *species in individuo* [the species in an individual] *is concretum* [something concrete, "grown together"] and a *concrete* individual *is* in more than a formal sense.

Being, when the object is a species, is an *"inesse* [being in]," an inhering in or a befitting [*Innewohnen*], and in the case of the lowest species it is an *"esse in individuo,"* being in an individual, and either real [*wirklich*] or {27} possible being. Later we shall discuss whether it is also possible for the species to exist [*Existenz*] outside of the individual.[103] The species is at the same time the *what* to which being in this form is attributed. The being of higher species and of the genus is just as much *esse in individuo*, but this *inesse* is mediated through the lowest species and so implies at the same time being in the lower species.

[Genus and species as objects]

We may wonder whether genus and species then admits of treatment as "objects [*Gegenstand*]." We can perhaps settle the question by examining the relevant logical relations. A logical-grammatical form corresponds to every ontological form. "Object" here means a "subject" of which something can be stated. Indeed, we can in principle state of any individual, of any species and of any genus *that* they are and *what* they are.

But here again misgivings arise about whether "object" in the ontological sense really means something other than logical subject. When I say "the genus is more general than the species," "the genus" is the subject of the sentence [*Satz*]. But it does not *only* have existence [*Bestand*] in the sentence, for its logical existence [*Existenz*] presupposes a prelogical existence. But we could say further that the genus as such may have being previous to and independent of its being

---

[103]   Cf. <supplement I, p. 417> [and 106ff].

a subject. But when it is not the subject of a sentence, what is the sense of continuing to call it an "object"? To be able to say something about it I must "make it into an object," meaning that I must direct my mental look at it, turn my "intention," to it. As I do this, it becomes an "intentional object," an "object for me."

This is not the same as "logical subject." But is it the same as what we earlier called the most general ontological form? And if it is *not* the same, does this most general form have yet another meaning? We should first ask whether "intentional object" is an ontological form at all. Then we should ask if it is the most general form.

In regard to the first question, being an intentional object means "existing [*dasein*] for a knowing subject." "Knowing subject" is no longer an empty form; it has a material meaning. Still, it permits formalization: "an object standing in a certain relation to an object of a certain kind." This empty form, however, is qualified [*Einschränkung*] to a large extent, and so it is not the most general ontological form. If we drop the qualification, we again have the most general form that can be filled by anything and everything. We should not be misled by the fact that we {28} are putting now one thing and now another into the empty place-holder for the object, for it is actually a necessary feature of empty forms to appear now with one filling, now with another.

[What it is and what it is like]

It could be however, that the form admits a more or less "proper [*eigentlich*]" fulfillment. For example, in the sentence "the body is heavy" a form appears that we have yet to discuss. "Heavy" does not answer the question "what is it?" but "what is it like [*wie*]"? It does not mean a "*quod quid est* [what it is]" but a "*quale* [what (it is) like]."

Is this form just as general as the form of object and the form of *what*? The object is what is; a *what* always belongs to it. Hence we can say with equal generality that every object is "something or other." Can we say with the same generality that every object is "like this or like that"? If the *quale* is located alongside the *quid*, it must differ from it, it must contrast with it at least by abstraction, even though it cannot be separated from it *realiter* [really].

This can be based ontologically on the fact that the *quid* is not altogether simple. If it is entirely simple, then at this simple *what* we can still focus on its own *quale* and hence we can also attribute it to the object. If the *quid* is composed, we may say that what is in the *quid*, insofar as it can only be *in* a *quid* but is not itself a *quid*, belongs to the *quid* itself and hence to the object (an "accident [*Akzidens*]"). And we can call it a quality insofar as it gives qualities to the *what* and the object.

[Language about God]

We can explain formal relations by means of the material content through which they find fulfillment. It is improper, we say, to call God wise, good, just, etc., since this way of speaking is merely transferred from the way we speak of creatures. And we think that it is more correct to say that He is wisdom, goodness, justice, etc., and still more correct to say that He is not this and that singly but all at once; He is His fully simple undivided essence. This means that we cannot attribute any accidents and qualities to Him, but this still does not say whether any *quale* can be proper to Him (as belonging inseparably to His *quid*). (Saying that God alone is *good*, God alone is *holy*, may be an attempt to state the *quale* that cannot be stated.)

Our material investigation will acquaint us with still other fillings of the simple *quid* and *quale*. We should distinguish, as distinct forms, the sole *quale* that is inherent in a simple *quid* and the *quale* that belongs to a *quid* as an accident (hence it is also better to keep them apart terminologically as "*quale*" and "quality").

Thus we have encountered forms here that are linked to a restricted domain of objects. The restriction applies to the species, too, and all the more so to the individual (to the individual as such and to the concrete individual's particular form{29} that has but a single possible filling) which reply to the question *quid*?

[Primary and secondary objects]

Moreover, *quale* and quality also turn out to be secondary in comparison to the *quid*. *Quale* and *quid* are not independent of each another nor are they at all arrayed *alongside* one another; they are rather in one another. *What* is simple has its *what it is like* [*Wie*], and what is composed is resolved in the *what it is like* (and in its other accidents) and is thereby determined.

We can say from the other side, that "qualities" make up the *quid*, insofar as we could regard them as "prior," presupposed, to the whole that it makes up. (We do not wish to go into the question of priority now.) But the *quale* belongs to the object throughout the *quid*. does this relate to how the two are themselves objects? The *quale* as well as any other form may be a logical subject. But its being is differentiated —indeed already *formally* differentiated— from the being of other forms, the "more primary" forms. What fills this form is not first-hand being. The *quale* in each case is in a *quod quid est* [what it is] and this in turn is in an "object" whose *what* it is.

An ambiguity in regard to "object" shows up at this point *within* formal ontology and corresponds to an ambiguity in regard to being. *What is in itself* is the *primary object*. What is in another, either immediately in a primary object or mediated by another, we may call a secondary object, parallel to the secondary being that it possesses. The word "primary" qualifies the most general form of object as such. Not just anything at all can enter this form. But whatever we do claim to be an object in the general sense of the word harks back to the primary object. A definite manner of filling pertains to this form; namely that it must be a be-ing that no longer harks back to another be-ing;[104] the individual obviously satisfies this requirement.

[Individuality and golden balls]

It is now essential to understand the individual exactly, to distinguish what is formal from what is material in it, and to explain its relation to the other ontological forms. The individual is singular, unique. This may be based upon <u>what</u> the individual is; that is, in the case where its *what* admits of no repetition. Thus the divine essence, encompassing all fullness, cannot exist in more than one instance. This is why God should be considered a genuine individual. {30}

If each angel represents a single species, as the Thomistic theory claims, we have another case of a *quid* that can exist *in individuo* [in an individual] but once. And if it is also true that no human individual is completely like another, we would have another example of singularity based on the object's *what*. (We are not asking here whether the essence of God, angel, and man is *in fact* like this; the corresponding ideas serve only as examples of a possible filling of the form that we are endeavoring to clarify.)

The further possibility is that the lowest species is instantiated [*vereinzeln*] in a number of individuals, limited or unlimited. We would have an example of a number limited in fact if we were to fashion an amount of matter into bodies completely alike; say, if we took all the gold in the world and made it into balls ten centimeters in diameter.

---

104   I mean it does not refer back to something else *in which* it would have to be. Referring back to another be-ing separate from it (for example, in the sense of a causal relation) should not be excluded.

These balls would then represent all the individuals of the species "gold balls with a diameter of ten centimeters" that are possible in fact. When we go from instances possible in fact to any possible instances whatever, we have unlimited instances. All material things are individuals of this type. Although all the blocks of granite in the world happen to be unalike, this fact is "accidental" to the essence of granite. A series of individuals that are alike is not inconsistent with granite as such.

The *principium individuationis* [individuation principle] here must lie outside the species. The principle has been widely held to be a spatial determination; for Thomas it is matter. We shall soon have to take up this question again.[105] For our present purposes we need only speak of two forms of individuality. In the one, "*haecceitas* [thisness]" (the "this being [*dieses Sein*]") is based on the "*quidditas* [whatness]"; in the other its base lies outside the *quid*. "Outside" here means that the *quid* within the individual must be adjoined to something which in itself is not fixed and for which it is as it were accidental to be fixed to this *quid*, that is, fixed to a formal sense of *matter* [*Materie*] still to be discussed. In either case the general form of individual is retained. The difference of forms indicates that it is fulfilled in different domains of objects.

[The existence of ideas; the artist]

Are we now warranted to take the individual as the "primary object" to which whatever can be called "object" harks back? Every individual is a "*species in individuo* [species in the individual]" or a "*quidditas* [whatness]" in "*haecceitate* [thisness]." Does the species or any other "*what*" have being outside the individual? We shall ask this first {31} of the lowest species, using our example of the gold balls ten centimeters in diameter.

---

[105]   Cf. <Supplement I, p. 417>

The lowest species is what each of its individuals is and what is in each of them. May I really say "is"? Rather, *are* there not just as many species as individuals? It cannot be denied that every individual has its *own* species. If it did not, it would be *nothing* and it would *not* be. But is the *same* species in all of them? This is the old dispute over the existence [*Existenz*] of "ideas" or "universals [*Universalien*]." Their special existence [*Sonderdasein*] in individuals is obvious; obvious, too, that this "being in" and the individual species itself depend upon the individual and its being. But does not our very example *make* it quite clear that something else precedes the existence [*Existenz*] of the individual species and of the individuals themselves? After all, they have been *formed* [*formen*] into instances of this species. "Of this species" refers to the general species that can be formed into many "instances." Hence the species *was* before the individuals were.

How was the species beforehand? Somebody, let us say, "had the idea," either the one who implemented it or somebody else who first ordered its implementation. For simplicity's sake let us assume that the "author" of the "idea" was the same as the one who carried it out. The idea, we say, existed [*existieren*] "in the mind" of the artist before its "realization [*Realisierung*]." What does it mean "to be in the mind"? To this we can give no complete answer, since we could do so only within an ontology of the spirit. Yet this much is clear. "To be in the mind" on the one hand signifies a link to a spiritual person, and so to an individual. On the other hand, the generality is not eliminated. After all, the "idea" does not cross over into the instances; it stays in the artist even after he has realized it. And, assuming a perfect [*vollkommen*] realization, it is the *same* idea "in his mind" and in all its instances. "Realization" would have no meaning at all were the generality not assumed to be "the same here and there."

[Finding and producing ideas]

When we say someone has gotten "a new idea," is his mind coming upon, finding [*vorfinden*] something general? Or do we mean that he is producing the idea from himself? And if the latter, how are we to understand that he, an individual, can bring something general out of himself? These questions arise here and invite us to explore their related constitution problems. In order to stay within our onto-logical discussion, we should not pursue this course for now. Were it in fact a question of "producing" or "bringing out" the general, this would imply that the general depends upon an individual. This then would also be true of God's creative mind (this is indeed the way the Augustinian-Thomistic tradition interprets the Platonic theory of the ideas: {32} as the archetypes of things in the divine mind).

On the other hand, were we to understand "getting" ideas as finding them outside the mind, we should ask what it means to find ideas and *what* we are finding them *as*. Finding refers us to epistemol-ogy, but we should be able to answer the "what as" question within our present discussion. The idea or species "gold ball ten centimeters in diameter" "pops up before me." It makes no difference whether I am picturing the ball in my imagination [*Phantasiebild*], having an abstract concept of it, or "intuiting" a general idea of it as something existing [*bestehen*] objectively [*objektiv*] and by itself (however we may think of this intuition); in all these cases there is a relation to what is individual. The picture itself in the imagination would be something individual; moreover, it would be joined to a general intention toward the many instances of the idea that would "represent [*vertreten*]" it. And the same intention toward a domain of individual instances would also lie in the concept and in the general idea. Now, this was just what we were looking for: an indication that the individual and individual being have the priority.

[Color, cubes, and the individual]

The higher species and the genus are like the lowest species in that they, too, have an *esse in individuo* [being in an individual] as well as another being outside the concreteness —"*in abstracto*"—, where the "abstract idea" in turn contains a reference to possible individual instances. In this case, the relation to the individuals passes through the lowest species. The relation of genus and species is joined to the relation of species and individual.

Let us compare color, red, and some definite shade of red as it is or can be concretely present here and there. Color can occur only as a species of color and red only in a definite shade of red. This means that color cannot be realized without its content being more closely determined at the same time. The possible ways in which it is determined are prescribed beforehand in color itself: color can become specific only within the color spectrum, not, say, in different spatial shapes, although it can occur concretely in different shapes.

The difference among specification, concreteness, and individuation stands out clearly here. Color receives individuality by entering the makeup of a concrete individual, in this case in the makeup of a spatial object. Concreteness is the "growing together" with the other elements [*Moment*] belonging to the individual's makeup. However, the lowest species able to occur in many instances (say, dark red cubes with sides of a certain length) —considered as an "idea"— is still not concrete; it is not concrete until the parts making it up have truly "grown together" as they become real [*Verwirklichung*] in the individual. Spatial determination {33) is unessential to color as such (although it is essential that it can only "occur" accompanied by spatial extension), but it is essential to color to be determined down to the last shade.

The relation between color as such and the colors of the spectrum is analogous to the relation between sound as such and the scale of tones; it is the formal relation of genus and species of which we spoke. But these forms with their fulfillment, as color in its species or sound in its species, have a distinctive kind of being. There is something objective [*sachlich*] here, something having its own laws [*Gesetzlichkeit*]. This objectivity [*Sachlichkeit*] exists [*Bestand*] independently of the individuals wherein it can be concretely realized; independent, too, of all knowing minds that may grasp it.[106]

[Three types of being]

Three types of being are apparent here: the being of concrete individuals with the elements making them up (insofar as they are "composed"), the being of empty forms, and the being of "material [*material*] ideas." The being of the individual we sought to characterize as being "in itself [*in sich*]." This may have to do with the fact that the concrete individual is completely "fulfilled," having in itself everything that belongs to it (notwithstanding the fact that much of what it is is not actual but only potential, nor that a bond to things other than itself may belong to its being.)

On the other hand the emptiness of the empty forms requires that they be filled in, and this need [*Bedürftigkeit*] also affects their being. The need, it seemed to us, is not satisfied until the forms are individually filled by concrete individuals or their elements. Conversely, once this takes place the empty forms enter the individuals; they partake of [*teilhaben*] their individual being, that is, they have their "being in" the individuals.

This relationship, however, becomes questionable because of the third type of being, that of material ideas. Of the lowest concrete species we can say first that they —like forms— have a "being" in their

---

106   What "dependence" on knowing spirits and "independence" from them may mean will be discussed elsewhere.

individuals; I mean, within the individual they are what fills the forms, they are their "fullness." But detached from the individuals, they have —again like forms— a "needful [*bedürftig*]" being. Form and full- ness in their special being [*Sondersein*] refer to each other and to the individual wherein they have their place and merge. But the forms that correspond to the concrete fullness are both the form of "individual" itself and the elements that make it up.

Material ideas on a higher level of generality make up the lower species and through them the individuals. These ideas (as well as {34} the lower species related on the one hand to the more general forms and to the individual on the other) are already a formed fullness. This fullness, however, can still enter further forms. As possible construc- tive elements they also have a "needful being." But their autonomous objective content lying behind this possibility as its basis, is something "in itself." Color, sound, geometrical shape —as well as the species wherein they are differentiated— are indifferent to the individuals whose makeup they can enter. We might be tempted to call them too "individuals." This is ruled out by their twofold character; that is, by the fact that they can have, besides their selfsufficient being, the being of a constructive element. But they are also "objects [*Gegenstand*]" in a special sense setting them apart from the general form of object [*Gegenstandsform*]. Let us agree to call them "ideal objects [*idealer Gegenstand*]."

[The search for order]

We have thus uncovered another basic ontological form. At first our sole aim was to display the area of formal ontology by identify- ing the forms of "act" and "potency" about which we were inquiring. But now we must seek an order among the various kinds of forms we have met.

§ 3
Classification of ontological forms according to their degrees of generality. Selfsufficiency / unselfsufficiency, whole / part, composition / simplicity.

[Generality]

Our first principle of order we found in generality. We saw that generality and formalness are not the same, for the empty forms themselves are more or less general. Everything and anything can enter the most general ontological form of "*something*" or of "object as such," which parallels the logical form of subject. Only genera can enter the form of genus, only species the form of species, only individuals the form of individual. Once we admit into the form of individual the "this" that fixes the individual in a definite way, the "this" can only be fulfilled by a *single* individual. (The "this" has a general range of meaning [*Sinnesbestand*], hence it is itself still a general form; but part of this meaning is that each "this" fixes one singular and we can think of it as individualizing the form itself.)

[Modes of being]

Besides "*something*," we said, *being* and *what* the object is are equally general basic forms. We should qualify "equally general" somewhat, it seems, since being and the *what* themselves can {35} enter the form of object. On the other hand every object is a *what* and a be-ing in the most general, formal sense of the word. Being is a general form that admits of several material fillings by different *modes of being*, but at the same time it admits of a formal variation that corresponds to these modes. All empty forms have their own characteristic mode of being— their "needful being" as we called it. This mode is a material fulfillment of the *general* form of being. But at the same time it is a special *form* of being [*Seinsform*] that corresponds to this mode, namely, being that stands in a relation R to another being (the material fulfillment of R is the reference to the being of the *concretum* [concrete thing] wherein the form finds its corresponding fullness and the "proper" being is what first fits into the place of the form's mode of being). Hence the forms of being are arrayed parallel to the forms of object according to their degrees of generality.

[Selfsufficiency]

Now, we have another division in our classification of the forms of being besides the classification according to generality, namely, the distinction between the *selfsufficient* [*selbständig*] and the *unselfsufficient* [*unselbständig*]. If we first speak only of being, the sole selfsufficient being would be being to which no relation pertained and which would exist completely in itself. Accordingly, the being of all empty forms is unselfsufficient. Hence generality and unselfsufficiency are not parallel. But neither does the converse hold. For the most general forms are not the least selfsufficient; indeed, we have seen that the being of genus and of its specific differences is more selfsufficient than that of the lowest species, which can no longer be differentiated. But just as the generality of objects parallels the generality of being, so also the selfsufficiency of objects parallels the selfsufficiency of being. We may say that all forms as such are unselfsufficient because emptiness signifies reference to fullness. The most general basic forms already show their unselfsufficiency by their mutual demand for one another. Every object *is*, and what is is an object; but the object is also *what* is.

Thus the distinctions of greater and lesser generality and self-sufficiency must also be found in the *what*. The *what* is the form of fullness required by the form of object. Moreover, a specific fullness corresponds to every form of object distinguished in generality and selfsufficiency. The *what* as such corresponds to *something* as such. The lowest species, which cannot be further differentiated corresponds to the individual. Genus and species as formed fullness are both differentiations of the form of object and of the form of *what* [*Was-Form*]. Only concrete objects can be selfsufficient, wherein all that is formal is filled and every fullness is formed. But their forms prefigure [*vorbilden*] selfsufficiency, as we saw in the case of the individual and, in a certain way too, in the case of the ideal object.

[Composition]

Two {36} other contrasts are connected with the distinction between selfsufficiency and unselfsufficiency, namely, the *whole* and the *part* and *composition* [*Zusammengesetztheit*] and *simplicity*. Only a whole can be selfsufficient; a part is always "needful." A whole may be simple or composed. A simple whole would be one wherein form and fullness as well as being and what it is coincide, and hence wherein all three basic forms are inseparably one. Such a whole would obviously be completely "unneedful" and hence selfsufficient. But a composed whole may also be selfsufficient; that is, when all forms are fulfilled in it. A part itself can in turn be simple or composed. Composed parts hark back to ultimate simple parts; both are unselfsufficient.

From these perspectives that we have gained, we shall bring together the forms that have so far emerged in a provisional overview, without claiming it to be complete or definitive <see diagram>.

{37}

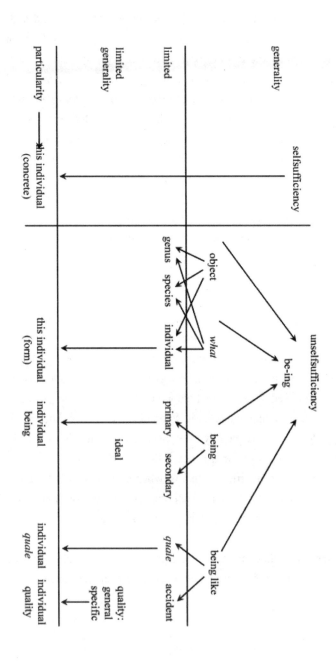

All forms are unselfsufficient, all are parts of a possible whole. General forms are simple. Insofar as the more general forms reappear in the more specific ones and are distinguishable from the specific stock, we may see them as parts of the specific forms, and these we may take to be composed, although the composition is not of course real. All concrete individuals are selfsufficient wholes, whether simple (applicable perfectly only to God) or composed.

Genus and species, taken as fulfilled forms, are of limited generality; they are possible parts of individuals and as such unselfsufficient. They may be composed, and as such they determine *what* the individual is. Or they may be simple, in which case they determine *what* the individual is *like*, and they may possibly make up *what* it is.

[Color and colors]

We have already given examples of both types of genus and species. "Color" and "blue" are determinations of the *what it is like* in the makeup of the individual, in this case a visible thing. At the same time they make up a part of *what* it is: a blue cube with sides of a certain length, etc. The lowest species making up its *what* is sure to be something composed. The "*qualities*" that make up the lowest species are, in relation to this species, parts of the whole and they are relatively simple. Ought we to see them as absolutely simple? Color and blue fit into a place in the thing's makeup and they are relative to each other. The thing is blue. It has a color. This color is blue. Blue is the quality of the concrete thing. Color is not the quality of the concrete thing. To the thing as a thing it is only proper to have *some* color, since color belongs to the makeup of the thing as such only as some definite color. Color can only occur in the concrete thing as this or that species of color.

Is color then a {38} "part" of this species, and is the species composed of "color" and the specific kind of color? Then again is color, and likewise the specific kind of color, some ultimate, simple thing? Color is not connected to the specific kind of color, as if color and blue were arranged alongside each other. When a thing has color, it means that it is red or blue or green, etc. If I say "the color is blue," I am not referring to a property of color; I am rather designating the color itself before me. Wherever there is color, there is always *a* color. There is a place in the thing's makeup where color —meaning *some* color— belongs.

Color is not an empty form that is filled with blue. There is a form that they both fill together, namely quality. That there can be no color without being red or blue or green is what is distinctive of genuine specification. Although they coincide in being, we may none-theless speak of composition. We can take color as something simple when we contrast its distinctiveness with that of sound. We can also take blue as something simple when comparing what is characteristic of it with what is characteristic of green. But when we consider blue in relation to color, there is at once coincidence and difference. Color is not only blue but blue or red or green, etc. Blue is color but a *definite* color. We may speak of composition in both cases insofar as we consider genus and species relative to one another.

These last observations show that *whole* and *part* themselves are empty forms able to be formally differentiated and fulfilled materially in many ways. The other principles of classification —generality, selfsufficiency, simplicity, as well as their opposites— are also empty forms. Common to all of them is that they presuppose the basic forms and express their relation to one other, not only the relation but its basis as well.

[Forms, act and potency]

We do not wish to pursue this general inquiry further. It has opened up the area of formal ontology and shown it to be a vast field for investigation. We must now examine the forms that we have already encountered to see what they can tell us about act and potency and perhaps to identify other forms relevant to our problem. {39}

§ 4
Potentiality and actuality
from the perspective of formal ontology.
Forms and the origin of becoming.
The aporia of ideas and creation.

[Senses of "act" and "potency"]

It became clear in our first section that act and potency have several traditional meanings. In the first place, the words are used for actuality and potentiality; I mean, for actual and potential being. This pair we should in turn take in two ways: (1) as real and as possible being, and (2) as the pitch of being [*Seinshöhe*] where being unfolds through time, and as the modes of being that precede and follow the pitch of being in the "now." In the second place, the words are used for the activity of a be-ing and for its capacity [*Fähigkeit*] for this activity— in this sense potency is a principle of act. Finally, "act" is also used for what gives being to what is not actual in its full stock or for what leads potential to actual being— in this sense act is presupposed to potency.

In actu esse [being in act] and *in potentia esse* [being in potency] are modes of being, material fulfillments of the form of being, hence as such they need to be elucidated in a material ontology. But at the same time they designate formal differences of being; namely, *"in potentia esse"* designates a being that refers to another (actual) being. These modes of being are to be elucidated formally as well as materially only in connection with the be-ing they correspond to. We have in fact seen that distinctions of being run parallel to distinctions of objects and of what these objects are. We must suppose from the start that not just any object can be actual or potential.

[God, absolute actuality]

If actual [*aktuell*] being, in the full sense of being that is real [*wirklich*] and unfolded to the utmost, is "unneedful being" —meaning being that has in itself no sort of reference [*Hinweis*] to another—, then only a selfsufficient be-ing, meaning only an individual, can be absolutely actual; yet only an individual wherein whatever it contains partakes of its actuality can be actual *absolutely* [*schlechthin*].

In contrast, only potential being can pertain to anything that by itself is unselfsufficient; that is, to all forms, to all that is general, to all parts. Our —purely formal— conclusion, then, is that only a perfectly simple whole can be absolutely actual. This can only be an individual whose being is no longer separate from what it is, an individual wherein all basic forms coincide, the be-ing absolutely. There cannot be more than *one* individual that satisfies this formal definition, since otherwise the *"what"* and the "instances" that the *what* occurs in would be separate.

Here again we encounter the idea of God in what is purely formal, the equation of *actus purus* and being absolutely. If all being that is not absolutely actual should be called "potential," then potential being, corresponding to {40} the various forms and modes of being that we have met, must differ in the various degrees in which they approach pure being.

[Actual and potential in whole and parts]

Does it make sense from a purely formal standpoint to talk about a being that is not "absolutely actual" yet not absolutely potential either, but partly actual and partly potential? We could be thinking here of individuals and perhaps of ideal objects whose modes of being set them apart from the modes of the empty forms and of the lowest species. We had called the being of individuals "selfsufficient," but doubts arise about the actuality of this selfsufficient being, since composed individuals contain parts in themselves and the being of their parts is unselfsufficient. If unselfsufficient being is potential being and the whole is made up of nothing but unselfsufficient, hence potential, parts, how can the whole be an actual whole? Or should we say that the being of the parts *in* the concrete individual is not potential? The parts are potential only when we consider them by themselves. But in the makeup of the individual the parts have no proper being at all; they partake of [*Anteil*] the being of the whole. And if the whole, because it is selfsufficient, should also be called "actual," should we not also attribute the actuality to its parts?

We shall in fact have to say that the "being in" of the parts of a whole is determined by the being of the whole, and on the other hand that the being of the whole is co-determined: we can say that the being of the parts must be potential when the being of the whole is potential. (When the architect has the plan of the house he wishes to build ready in his mind, a potential being accrues to the color of the house just as much as to the house as a whole.)

We cannot say in general that every part must be actual when the being of the whole is actual— for example, when <we> are no longer thinking of the yellow of this house as the color of the house but apart from it. Of course a real house also has a real color and shape. Only when we focus on the being of the part by itself must we call it potential— independently of the potentiality or actuality of the whole. (If we wish another material [*material*] explanation, we should think of a multiple potentiality of the parts as such; examples are a possible intentional being, say, of certain segments that the eye can pick out from the continuum of a line, or the possible being in other concrete individuals that is proper to genera and species.)[107]

[Principles of individuation]

But can a composed whole then be absolutely actual? To be able to answer this question we shall once again {41} have to keep the meaning of "absolutely actual" very clearly in mind. It means to be in *such* wise that nothing of nonbeing is included in the being— no being-not-yet, no being-no-longer, no possible nonbeing. Among the concrete individuals whose actual being we are now to examine, we distinguished between those that bear their *principium individuationis* [principle of individuation] in themselves and those for which it is external. We shall have to treat each case separately.

In the case of external individuation [*Individuation*], where a concrete species *in individuo* [in an individual] could also occur in other individuals, how are the parts related to the whole, and what is the being of either like? Besides its partaking of the being of the whole, a possible being "elsewhere" is proper to the species. Does this potentiality impair the being of the whole? Apparently not, for the existence of this red cube is indifferent to whether things like it exist or how many exist. But this species does not *demand* that it be realized in an individual here or elsewhere or anywhere at all. And this implies that it is possible for the species not to be *here*, and hence that it is possible for the whole, the concrete individual, not to be, which of course cannot be without this part, its species, and which is nothing at

---

[107]   <Cf. supplement I, p. 285zzz for the following.>

all besides this species here and now. This already settles the question: the individual whose individuation principle does not lie in the species is not absolutely actual.

So what sense is there to ascribe actuality to it at all? For one thing, we can describe it negatively; I mean, in contrast to the species that is not individuated [*individuieren*]. The being of the species *in individuo* [in the individual] is different from the being of the unindividuated species, and the potential being of the species is the possibility of having being *in individuo* wherein it is fulfilled. If we had to call the being of the species *in individuo* "potential" for including the possibility of nonbeing, this potentiality would in any case be different from the potentiality of the unindividuated species.

We ought also to ask how these two potentialities differ. One difference is that the relation between them is asymmetrical. One being, viewed from the other, appears as the real [*eigentlich*] being at which the other aims. Furthermore, it appears as the real being because it has something of a "fullness of being" in itself, that is, of actuality. It is not being through and through lacking nonbeing, but it does contain something of being in itself. This is why the mode of being of concrete individuals that are not individuated by the species is neither pure potentiality nor pure actuality, but at once potentiality and actuality.

Judging from what to we have learned so far, potentiality has seemed to accrue to the individual from the species. May we say that it owes its actuality to the form of individual? Obviously not, for the empty form is unselfsufficient {42} and as such potential. Hence actual being is proper neither to the form without fullness nor to the fullness without form. How does the whole acquire actual being from the two? The question seems pointless if this fullness and this form were never apart but have been one all along.

[The statue]

But the case is different when the fullness *enters* the form or the form is fulfilled. The examples that have always come to mind are artificial forms and organic becoming. If we wish to illustrate the formal relations in these material ones, we must of course, because of the two meanings of "form," be careful that the concept of "material [*material*] form," usual and required in real ontology and also called "idea" or "species," does not crowd out our formally ontological concept.

In our terminology, the individual was the form and the concrete species, the fullness corresponding to the form. This fullness, though, is already a formed fullness, since "species" itself is an empty form. When an artist carves the figure of a boy in marble, the finished statue is the concrete individual. "This here" is the form of the concrete individual. What "hovered before the mind" of the artist and now stands realized before him (in the ideal case where his idea is fully expressed) is the concrete species. It is composed of many kinds of simpler species: the shape down to the final touches, the marble color and all other visible qualities of the marble that enter the whole, etc.

How did it come it about that this "idea" was realized, or, in formal terms, that the species entered the form of the concrete individual? Obviously forces were joined without which we could not conceive of the realization, namely, the *matter* [*Stoff*] fashioned into this statue and the *work of shaping*. If either were lacking, "this thing here" would not exist nor would it be this one. The individual apparently owes the actuality of its being to these two factors, but does it owe it to both in the same sense? Before it was made into the statue the matter was already a concrete individual —"this block of marble"— and as such it had actual being. It brought this being over into its new form. At the same time it was possible for it to take on this or that new shape, and one of these possibilities, by entering the new form, passed from potential to actual being.

But by itself the matter could not effect this transition. What the artist's did brought about the transition from potentiality to actuality by taking the matter and reworking it according to his idea. The statue also had a potential being "in his idea"; *without* the matter he would not have been able to bring it from potential to actual being, and had he taken {43} other matter [*Stoff*], it would have become another individual. But that the matter could become a new individual or pass into this new form— the proximate or last cause of this is the artist's doing, which for its part is something actual— the work of a concrete individual. And since the artist's doing consists in forming his "idea" into the matter, the new individual owes *what* it is, and with it at the same time its being as this one, to the "idea" formed into the matter, which is also called its "form of essence [*Wesensform*]" or its "act." Form, matter, and idea are presupposed to the working, effecting, that causes the transition from potential to actual being.

[Emergence]

Let us see what we can gather in formal fashion from these material relations. Where form and content come together, further factors effect their union and the individual's actual being that emerges precisely as they come together. What is the formal counterpart of these factors? And must there always be a plurality of factors? Matter is what the concrete individual emerges *from*, and it is itself already a concrete individual.

Does a new concrete individual's emergence generally presuppose another individual that is transformed into it? "Emergence [*Entstehung*]" or "becoming" imply a new form, a mode of being that is oriented to actual being in a way different from the way potential being is related to it; that is, a transition from nonbeing to being. An object emerges that was not present before the creative activity. We can also say, though, that in our example a transition from potential to actual being does take place, since what becomes, i.e., the new object, had potential being previously in the matter and in the idea. But this transition from potential to actual being <is not the same as the one> we found in the duration in being of finite things wherein first one aspect of what they are becomes actual and then another. A thing still does not count as be-ing as long as it is potential in its entire stock. Besides this potentiality, the thing's becoming presupposes a twofold actual being: the act causing the transition and the being of the matter which was before it entered the new form. This second actual being does not cease, and the object whose being it is "does not pass away" by the new object coming to be. The old object perdures in the new form and has its being *as* the new object, albeit its *what* has changed.

[Emerging out of nothing]

Still, this is not *the* form of becoming in the absolute sense. Besides the becoming of one concrete individual out of another, there exists the formal possibility of a becoming "out of nothing [*aus nichts*]." "Out of" here means something different from becoming out of an actual be-ing. "Nothing" is not matter that is transformed. "Out of nothing" means that what is becoming was nothing beforehand, {44} nor was it "in another form."

Does not the becoming of a new individual also presuppose a potential being? We have already seen that a twofold potentiality exists previously in a work of art as the basis of its becoming: the potentiality of the "matter" and the potentiality "in the idea." The first does not apply to becoming out of nothing. Does the second also fail to apply? To answer this question we must explain the role of the "idea" more clearly.

[Idea as goal]

Matter is that out of which the new individual is made; the idea is the goal at which it aims and the type or original [*Urbild*] according to which it is formed. The goal, by the way, does not refer to any external purpose but to *what* the new individual is after becoming. What it is now actually it was potentially before. But even this potentiality was already bound to an actuality. The artist's idea as such had actuality, for the "being in his mind" was actual (no matter how we interpret "in the mind"). It is *the same species* that was in the artist's mind beforehand as an idea and now is embodied in the statue *as well*. "As well" because the idea in the artist's mind did not cross over into the matter nor is it now the individual's *what* in the way that the previously existing matter continues to exist in the new form. This is just why we cannot say that the statue has emerged *out of* the idea as it emerges out of matter The matter has been shaped *according to* the idea, or the individual itself has been shaped into an instance of the "ideal" species.

[Creation of matter]

We must now consider *both* of the following possibilities: becoming out of matter without any idea being involved and being formed according to an idea into an instance of the idea without any matter being involved. We can imagine several cases that illustrate this second possibility: (1) the original creation of material things, (2) the creation of pure spirits, (3) artistic conception, that is, the formation of the very idea in the artist's mind.

According to the view of the emergence of the world in Christian philosophy, which follows the creation account but differs from other theories of natural philosophy, the Creator did not first form a preexisting [*vorausexistieren*] matter [*Materie*] but created matter and the many different shapes wherein it occurs at the same time. That is, He shaped the matter itself, *by* creating it, into concrete individuals according to a fullness of ideas of all kinds. So matter [*Stoff*] would exist in this case but not pre-existing matter. The concrete individual would owe its actuality to the creating "*fiat* [let there be]" alone. This is a calling into existence [*Ins-Dasein-Rufen*] by the absolutely Actual from something nonbe-ing beforehand, an imparting of being.

[Pure spirits and individuation from within]

We also have this imparting of being in pure spirits. In their case it is clearer still that nothing is present "out of which" they emerge, since the phrase "pure spirits" obviously means that even after coming {45} into existence they have nothing of matter in themselves but are pure species individuated in themselves. To be sure, we have yet to see if this "matterlessness" actually holds true in every sense.

Does not only "out of which" (the individual is formed) fail to apply here but also "according to which"? Or may we speak of an idea that this individual species imitates or is copied from [*nachbilden*]? It surely belongs to the idea of creation that the Creator, Who calls the creature into existence, knows beforehand what He wishes to create and so has an idea of angel. Here there is but a single instance of the species; the created spirit corresponds to the idea in the divine mind feature by feature as a perfect "likeness, image, or copy [*Abbild*]" of the "archetype or original [*Urbild*]."

Although the idea and its likeness tally completely in content, we should not see them as "the same," since when God calls something into existence, this of course means that He gives it being apart from His divine being, that something comes about that did not exist before. The created pure spirits are concrete individuals, substances of no less selfsufficiency and fullness in being than material things. This kind of becoming is actually our first example of genuine emergence whereas the first kind, "becoming out of," meant rather being transformed or re-formed [*umformen*].

[Artistic creation]

A certain analogue of the "act" of creation also lay in the artist's "creating," without which the matter and the species of the work of art of course do not "come together." However, creatures "creating" does not mean that they bestow actual being but that they *use* actual being as it were, that is, the being of the matter, in order to "bring out" the idea.

But how about the artistic idea itself? Is it not actually a "creature" in the artist's mind, I mean, something that he calls into existence "in itself" unaided by anything existing previously? We can hardly find a more mysterious spiritual process than how the artist "conceives" his ideas, nor is this the place to examine the process or the various ways he executes it. This much we can say without further analysis. Voluntary [*willensmäßig*] intervention plays a greater or lesser role in artistic conception, but it proceeds from material present "on the inside," and at the same time this material is organized involuntarily [*unwillkürlich*] and in a manner that is largely hidden from us.

There can be no question here of a divine *fiat* bestowing being absolutely. The only analogy is that a voluntary doing is involved when a new individual emerges. And we have always found this to be the case in the several kinds of becoming we have considered. May we claim in formal generality that all becoming requires creative doing (either primary = genuine creating or secondary = transforming)? Or can we imagine {46} that an idea enters into existence of itself? Or lastly —the question we have asked before but not yet answered— can we conceive that a thing of matter was formed anew without any forming action and without any idea according to which it would be formed?

[The kaffir lily]

Organic becoming seems to be the best example here. I have a kaffir lily [*Clivia*] before me. Yesterday a leaf was tightly wrapped around the flower stem which I could hardly see. Today the stem has gotten loose from the leaf, turned upwards, and risen quite a ways. The buds, still pressed closely around the stem, will soon spread and push apart on all sides. One by one they will redden slightly at the tip and open into a red calyx of flowers. By then the whole plant will be standing there, fully self-contained, elegantly proportioned, an object that is now what it was to become.

The kaffir lily developed like this from the inside out; nothing else had to be done. "It is now what it was to become"— we said this only to describe the phenomenon, not to suppose that some goal was set objectively [*objectiv*]. The shape before us has in itself something of an inner necessity, and the becoming that we watched as it developed seemed to aim at this result and to find its fulfillment therein.

Here, too, an individual has emerged that *realizes* an "idea." The idea is not brought to the matter from outside and formed into it; there is no "unorganized" —implying "unformed"— matter at all. The growth of the matter here is at the same time a growth into the shape that is its goal. We actually "watch" the shaping from inside out, and so we are inclined to speak of an "inner form" or "entelechy [*Entelechie*]" (insofar as the shaping from within is directed to a goal).

The matter, the guiding idea, and the shaping work that in artistic creation are really separate we find here together: the inner form at work in the matter and progressively shaping it outwards. For each actual being we have always been assuming another actual being in such wise that the same individual is constantly both actual and potential, and that the actuality is constantly passing over into potentiality and potentiality into actuality, analogously to the way we found it taking place in immanence. But this process, just as artistic creation, is timebound; for its becoming fulfills a duration, and we watch it begin and end.

[Causes of art]

In a work of art, becoming commences the moment the artist begins his creative doing. His action need not coincide with his conception of the idea, but it *may* coincide with it, as when the initial idea is accompanied by an intention to implement it. As long as the conception is but a "plan" in the artist's mind and lacks a practical intention, the artwork {47} is only potential, still not underway, still not "becoming." Becoming begins when the artist decides to carry out his plan, and it ends when he finishes the work (I mean, when he stops working on it even if it remains unfinished in itself).

All the factors that contribute to the artwork coming about we may call "*causes*" in some sense, but what initiates the becoming, the "*proximate cause*," the setting about the work, especially deserves the name "cause."

[Germination and inner form]

Where do we find something analogous in organic becoming? Obviously when a seed begins to sprout. The seed itself, or its inner form, cannot "decide" to sprout, as the artist decides to execute his work, nor can it "set about it." External conditions, material forces acting on the matter of the seed, give it the "disposition" it needs to germinate, but the onset of the becoming lies within. It is not essential here to understand the inner form as such; we need only focus on the particular form of becoming that we are considering. Here no spiritual act seems to give the impulse to being as do the divine and artistic *fiat*.

When we examine the external conditions affecting the seed that is about to sprout, we find causal connections similar to those found in inanimate nature. But why is it that when acted upon by purely material, mechanical forces or by any physical forces, certain things show certain like external changes and behaviors [*Verhaltensweise*], while in others life begins to stir— *life*, meaning actual, but not spiritual, being (in the usual sense of the word "spiritual"). We shall eventually answer these questions from the perspective of material ontology, but we can eventually approach them formally as well.[108] For now let us be content to point out the different forms of becoming.

[Causes]

We have found a radical distinction between what we may call *absolute becoming*, where something quite new comes into existence without previously having had any actual being in some other form, and *becoming out of something*, where something having actual being is transformed into something else. In absolute becoming, something comes into existence as actual being, and at the same time *what* it is is bestowed upon it. The proximate, last, *cause* is the *act that bestows being*, and for this such an act —that is, however, something being actually— is presupposed. Another cause, no less original and inseparable from the act, is the *idea* according to which what becomes is shaped. (To be sure, {48} this "inseparability" holds in one way only, for we can think of the idea without the act that bestows being,

---

[108]   VI, § 18.

but not the act without the idea.) We should think of becoming as momentary: the "creature's" actual being begins at the moment set by the creating *fiat*.

But this being may itself be a becoming in the second sense. I mean, the moment it comes into existence there commences an enduring forming process of the new individual according to an idea. A succession of such transformations [*Umformung*], each according to a different idea, may also take place within the duration of its being. We found that several different causes were required in each of these transformations. [1] That *which* is transformed; in other words that *out of which* the new individual becomes, namely, the matter. [2] That *according to which* it is formed; that is, the idea. [3] That *by which* it is formed: the forming activity that here is the last cause.

We may go on —with Aristotle— to distinguish [4] that "*into which*" the thing is formed from that *according to which* it is formed; that is, the idea and *what* the thing is becoming and later will be. "That into which" the thing is made, if we take it to mean the concrete thing that it is to be, is not included among the causes of its becoming, for it is but its result. If we take it as the species, whose instance the individual will become, it does not differ from the *according to which* aspect, the ideal species. The work of art owes to the species the fact that it becomes *that* into which it is made, and in this sense the species is a cause. However, the species owes the *fact* of its becoming an effective factor to its being "taken up" into the artist's mind. In the ideal species, the two aspects, *according to which* and *into which*, are the same; but in each case the "*in individuo* [in the individual]" aspect is different, and since it shares in the becoming in the *according to which* aspect, we may speak of four causes. But this applies only to the case where matter and idea are distributed among different individuals (artistic shapes).

[Organic becoming]

A second possible case of becoming in the "improper" sense is where matter and idea are united in one individual and the working comes not from the outside but from within (organic becoming). Here the four causes collapse into two: the matter and the "form" working from within. There is, however, something new: an outside (material [*materiell*]) action affecting the matter. Both the purely spiritual shaping and the organic becoming take place within an individual. Moreover, matter [*Stoff*] (albeit immaterial [*immateriell*]) is also present here, as well as a kind of forming process that, like organic formation, works from the inside out— I mean, in this matter. But we also see that a free shaping of the matter affects it from without, albeit within the individual. Lastly, the matter and through it the becoming depend upon external (material) conditions.

[Material becoming]

Finally {49}, in "material [*materiell*]" becoming, I mean, in the becoming of "lifeless [*tot*]" material things, outside (material) forces transform the matter, as when the weather carves stones into objects resembling human works of art. Here there is matter *out of* which the object is made or becomes and something *into which* it is made, but there is no goal, merely an end-product. It lacks an idea *according to which* it is fashioned even though it accords with some such idea, and that *by which* it becomes is the material effect from without. In all these cases the second, improper, kind of becoming presupposes a be-ing as its matter. Does this imply that an initial becoming of this be-ing, a becoming in the proper and absolute sense, is presupposed? And can there be any kind of first becoming besides that of being brought forth by an act that bestows being?

[The absolutely actual that does not become]

Were *no* becoming presupposed, matter [*Stoff*] would have to be from eternity. (Materially [*material*] this would mean that matter [*Materie*] is eternal or —in the case of immanent spiritual forming— that immanent being is eternal.) Here we need only ask, in purely formal fashion, if it is conceivable that something that is now in the becoming mode of being —where that actuality is constantly passing into potentiality and potentiality into actuality so that it is undergoing constant alteration in its *what*— has possessed actual being from eternity.

This something either must have been absolutely actual being, an actuality that contained in itself nothing of potentiality, or else it must have been in just this mode containing actuality and potentiality. It is inconceivable that absolute actual being pass immediately into the becoming mode, for in what is actually all it can be, in what contains in itself nothing of potentiality, no transition from potentiality to actuality is possible. Hence it would first have had to relinquish its being, that is, this be-ing must have given up something of what it was actually, and in so doing it would have had to downgrade its very being to a partially potential being. But this would entail that within the absolutely actual, being could be separated from <u>what</u> it is, and for this *what*, at least for a part of it, this would entail the possibility of nonbeing. But if so it would not be absolutely actual. So we are left with the other possibility: an eternal becoming.

[Eternal becoming]

Is it conceivable that something has been constantly passing from actuality into potentiality and from potentiality into actuality from all eternity? We again have two possibilities: that it has thus existed either from itself or owing to something else. Becoming is a continual transition not only from potentiality into actuality and vice versa but at the same time a transition to a *what* that is ever new. Something that is becoming is not what it is to become until it stops {50} becoming. Throughout the duration of its becoming it is always headed toward this goal as it passes through this *what*, that *what*, and yet another *what* that lie on the way to the goal. This passing through, which takes place in a moment, may be a material fulfillment of the general form of being, but it is a mode of being that harks back to another (an enduring) mode, since a moment is possible only in a duration, and so occurring momentarily is possible only in the context of a being and of an occurring that endure.[109]

[Substance, upholding, the absolutely actual]

Hence all becoming and everything that becomes needs enduring being to "uphold" it. For one thing it must have something enduring within itself that allows us to say that "it" is becoming and "passing though" first this and then that stage. This enduring something that underpins what is changing we called "substance." We can think of several further aspects here. First, we may refer to what the individual, <as> enduring, preserves throughout all its changes and what enables us already to say that it *is* during its becoming (the Aristotelian "first substance"). Another aspect is *what* the thing is becoming, or the various whatnesses [*washeiten*] it passes through in its becoming ("second substances"). All this, taken *in specie* [in the species], not *in individuo*

---

[109]   On momentary processes and duration cf. "Über das Wesen der Bewegung [on the essence of motion]" in Adolf Reinach's *Gesammelte Schriften*, Halle, 1921 <critical re-edition in A. Reinach's *Sämtliche Werke*, edited by K. Schuhmann and B. Smith, Munich, Hamden, and Vienna, 1989, pp. 551-588>; Thomas Aquinas, *De veritate*, q. 28, a. 2 ad 10 (in my translation *Des Hl. Thomas von Aquino Untersuchungen über die Wahrheit*, Vol. 2, Breslau, 1932, P. 457 <re-edition: *Edith Steins Werke*, vol. 4, Freiburg/Louvain, 1955, p. 397>).

[in the individual], is what endures, remains untouched in its enduring being by the individual's passing through and becoming. Do these kinds of substance —the "first" or the "second" or both together— uphold the becoming and do they suffice to uphold becoming?

Genera and species determine *what* concrete things are, but they cannot of themselves lend them their *what*, they cannot call them into existence. Their mode of being, as we have seen, is a combination of actuality and potentiality that differs from the combination found in concrete individuals. Genera and species are what they are constantly and changelessly, but their being allows for the possibility of another kind of being that is correlated to them, namely the being of their corresponding individuals. But this possibility is passive; the transition from "ideality" to "reality [*Realität*]" (if we may anticipate this expression which we have yet to clarify fully) is inconceivable from the ideality side. So second substances do uphold the individuals' becoming, but they do not suffice to uphold it; I mean, such upholding must be *given* to the individual.

Now, "the first substances" are what the individuals {51} themselves are throughout all their changes. We should distinguish from first substance the empty form "this individual" that abides but is unable, in the emptiness and needfulness of its being, to fulfill itself with a content and thereby to attain actual being. Nor should we consider the empty form as "substance" before it is fulfilled, for this is first accomplished by the form with a certain fulfillment. This fulfillment is not the lowest species in its full stock, since it contains changing constituent parts; I mean those that replace one another in the course of becoming.

What changes, however, is the filling of what abides. Genera and species prescribe beforehand a framework that abides throughout the individual's entire duration in being and is concretely fulfilled successively by variable [*veränderlich*] accidents. We should then take substance here (in the sense of "second substance") as an instantiated general species. It becomes a concrete individual by being successively filled, and for the first time actual being accrues to the concrete individual— with its abiding stock *as well as* its changing stock. Actuality cannot be due either to the abiding stock, or to the changing stock, or to the form of the individual; for each of these "abstract parts" of the concrete individual requires the others, nor can the individual being bring them about or draw them into itself. Thus all mutable being, all becoming, points to an upholding outside of itself, to something immutable, to absolutely actual being. What *becomes* must take its origin [*Ursprung*] from what *is* immutably and thereby it must be upheld.

[Matter with and without beginning]

Purely ontological considerations do not rule out the possibility that this upholding has gone on from eternity. It is quite conceivable that eternal, immutable, absolutely actual being constantly releases what becomes, what is mutable and alternates between actuality and potentiality.[110]

If we assume a beginning in time, it is clearer that what becomes cannot come into existence by itself, than if we assume an eternal duration of becoming. We have seen that all becoming of the second kind, that is, all transformation, presupposes some matter that the forming can affect. All becoming is conceivable only on the basis of absolute [*absolut*] being, that is, absolutely [*schlechthin*] actual being.

We ought also to ask if we can think of matter that has had actual being from eternity and began in time to be subject to transformation,

---

110   Such is Thomas's view that the eternity of the world can neither be proven nor disproven philosophically, but should be rejected in view of the creation account (cf. *De potentia*, question 3, article 14).

either of its own accord or through another actual being. If we can, we would have to assume a twofold eternal actual being, hence {52} two principles: matter and a forming principle. But we have already seen that something that is absolutely actual, meaning that it is all it can be, allows of no variation. Consequently matter, even were it from eternity, would always have been mutable, that is, not absolutely actual but at least partially potential. But then it is conditioned and upheld in its being by absolutely actual being.

[God and creature]

We have thus arrived at a radical split between absolutely actual being and being that lies between actual and potential being. Parallel to this distinction is that between the be-ing that is immutably from eternity and is from itself, and the mutable be-ing, perhaps beginning and ending in time, which "becomes" from the immutable be-ing and is transformed under the action of diverse secondary "causes."

[Ideal being]

We have yet to inquire about the act that bestows being, the act by which actual being calls something else into existence. We learned first, in purely ontological fashion, that the one being depends upon the other. Merely borrowing the terms from theology, we may call this purely formal relation "creating" or "being created (as act or state) [*Geschaffenwerden und -sein*]," and we may call eternal being "Creator" and the created be-ing "creature." We found the realm of creatures or of becoming to be the area of alternation between "*in actu esse*" and "*in potentia esse.*" We saw a certain formal makeup of these creatures, wherein ontological forms, already partially famil- iar, play a role. But quite new forms also have come to light here.

Before we go into them, however, we should consider the third item we distinguished from the absolutely actual and from becoming: the "ideal being [*ideales Sein*]"of the genera and species and these "ideal objects" themselves.

We saw that these objects play a role in becoming yet do not themselves become. This red, the pencil's color, has become as *its* color and can pass away again. But color as such, red as such, as well as the definite shade as such, do not come about and pass away. What they are in themselves, apart from their possible entry into concrete individuals, contains nothing of potentiality in the sense of pure possibility that has not taken effect. Being color admits of no heightening [*Steigerung*] or diminishing [*Minderung*] (it contains an empty placeholder only in the sense that it can and must be this or that species which are mutually exclusive). Nor can we imagine anything out of which, as out of matter, color could become.

[Ideas and creation]

Can we think of anything *according to which* color would be formed, an idea separated from it? Color is related a priori to everything confronting {53} us as colors in the sensible world, as well as in contrast to all the "ideas of colors" of finite spirits. Does it makes sense to say that the Creator created color and all genera and species according to "archetypes" in His mind; I mean, as an objective [*objektiv*] world of ideas separate from Himself?

Obviously not. I daresay a created world of ideas could be created from eternity, but if so it would be possible for it not to be and for it to be different. For if we claimed that the creation of the world of ideas is *necessary*, that is, if the Creator cannot but set forth a world of ideas from Himself, indeed this particular world of ideas, we could account for this necessity only if absolutely actual being had need of completion— but this is ruled out by the very meaning of absolutely actual being. If ideal being is such that it rules out ideal objects not being and being other than they are, it can be included only in absolutely actual being. Ideal objects cannot be created; that is, set forth from absolutely actual being; they should rather be thought to belong to this absolute being itself from eternity and inseparably.[111]

[St. Thomas's account]

But is it not wrong to speak here of an ideal being as a third item between absolutely actual being and becoming, or even to speak of ideal objects at all? How is a plurality of ideal objects compatible with a perfectly simple and undivided actual being? Thomas sees them as compatible in his teaching on God because he identifies the one simple divine essence with the many ideas and explains their plurality as a relation of the divine essence to the many creatures, actual and possible, all resembling the one essence in different ways.[112] We must ask if this account allows of a tenable formal interpretation. We have

---

[111]   <Cf. supplement II, below p. 423> [and 106].

[112]   Cf. for example, *De veritate*, q. 3, a. 2 (<in St. Theresa Benedicta's translation vol. 1> op. cit., p. 97ff <new edition p. 94f>): "...the intellect of God, Who works [*wirken*; Thomas: *operare*] everything, brings forth [*hervorbringen*; *producere*] everything according to the likeness [*Bild*; *similitudo*] of His essence; hence His essence is the idea of things.... Created things, however, do not portray [*abbilden*; *imitari*] the divine essence perfectly; hence His essence is not taken by the divine intellect as the idea of things absolutely, but relative [*im verhältnis*; *cum proportione*] to the thing to be created in accordance with the divine essence itself, according as it falls short of it or resembles [*nachbilden*; *imitari*] it. Now, different things resemble the divine essence in different ways, and each in its own way, since it is proper to each to be distinct from the other. And so the divine essence itself, when the different relations of things to His essence are also taken into account [*hinzugedacht*; *cointellectis diversis proportionibus rerum ad eam*], is the idea of each thing. Therefore, since the proportions of things are different, there must be a plurality [*Vielheit*; *plures*] of ideas.

not after all taken the idea of absolutely actual being from any material theology; we have rather gotten it through purely formal ontology, and from {54} that quarter we must endeavor to solve the difficulty.

In the case of absolutely actual being we denied that it can be separated from *what* it is, since it would be possible for it not to be. We also denied that its *what* can be divided, since it would be possible for certain parts in the whole to be different and hence not to be. The manifold of the ideas, supposing them to be inseparable from absolutely actual being, seems to indicate a division in its *what*.

Can we do without this plurality? The formal structure of the absolutely actual being we saw as necessary not only in itself but also, as the upholding they need, for the being of creatures, that is, of individuals whose being is a becoming. The plurality of ideas was a consequence not of absolutely actual being but of the diversity of creatures. And, if we supposed the ideas to be an "upholding" of individuals, the only possible place for them was the absolutely actual.

But is there really a need for a manifold between the one and the many, between the absolutely actual and what lies between actuality and potentiality? I daresay we shall not be able to answer this question without considering the nature of the act that "bestows being" and the way we should view the origin of creatures from absolutely actual being. We did say earlier, in order to show the need for ideas as the archetypes of creatures, that the Creator must know what He wishes to create, but we did so as a material [*material*] illustration of formal relations and not for the sake of the ideas. This already implies that absolutely actual being is spiritual, that its activity is knowledge - will - deed [*Tat*]. But these are all material ideas. They would be warranted methodologically in a formally ontological study only if we could show in formal fashion that absolutely actual being can be nothing but spirit. But whether such a proof can succeed remains questionable.

III
Transition from a
Formal to a
Material Inquiry

Our conclusion at this point is that we cannot avoid discussing the relation between formal and material ontology. On the formal side we must close for now with an aporia [*Aporie*]: the distinction between an absolutely actual being and a being incorporating actuality and potentiality, more precisely a being passing from actuality to potentiality (perhaps also conversely), was only to be taken formally, as was also the dependence of becoming on absolute being. The third kind of being that seemed to emerge, that of "ideal objects," that is, of genera and species, or (if we wish to use Plato's word) ideas, has become questionable within a formal approach, and on this formal ground, it seems, the issue cannot be definitely settled.

§ 1
"Matter" and "material" in material ontology.
Prime matter.
"Form" and "matter" as empty forms.

[Senses of "matter" and "form"]

It can help us to understand what a materially ontological inquiry involves to take another look at the "forms" that we met again in our analysis of becoming. But first we must settle what we mean by "matter [*Materie*]" and "material [*Material*]." Our foregoing study has already suggested two meanings of "matter [*Materie*]" parallel to the two meanings of "form." The forms we were discussing within formal ontology contrasted with the *fullness* that enters those empty forms. And in the case of fulfilled forms we spoke of something material [*material*]. Thus color, sound, and shape are material ideas that contrast with the empty form "quality."

Then when examining becoming we encountered *matter* [*Stoff*], formed either from without or from within. "Form" was either an "entelechy" working from within (in living things) or an "idea" working from without (in a work of art), where both form and matter are something material [*material*]. Here a scale of possible formings came to light ultimately harking back to an ultimate, completely unformed matter, *prima materia* [prime matter].

Is prime matter a formal or a material idea? And how is this sense of "matter [*Materie*]" related to that of "fullness"? We come upon the idea of matter in natural philosophy, where it appears as that out of which all things of nature are made, and hence are called "material [*materiell*]" things. Thomas calls matter "pure potency" because it is receptive of all "forms," that is, of all the species of sensible things, and because it acquires no actual being at all until it receives some species or other.

[Form and matter in the soul]

Thus we can form a *concept of the form* of *matter* [*Materie*] as what is purely potential. But the question is whether something else satisfies this form besides the matter of material things. Thomas is wont to say with Aristotle that the soul is *in potentia* [in potency] toward all forms of knowledge just as matter is in potency toward all forms of nature. But the soul's actual being does not tally with its knowing; hence it is possible for the soul to be {56} knowing in potency and yet to have actual being, albeit not absolutely actual being.

A material study of the soul will show us that we must distinguish therein an inner principle of form and something that corresponds to the empty, formal concept of matter.[113] In the immanent sphere, too, we encounter a "matter [*Stoff*]" that has potential being with respect to the diverse forms it can enter, and indeed in several senses. We may see sense data as matter formed through mental conceptions into acts of perception, memory, or imagination [*Phantasie*]. But we can also understand the "matter" of our inner living as the life of the I welling up and formed by its shifting contents into different "living experiences." The one harks back to the other. We can grasp sense material [*material*] only through the spiritual activity that processes it, yet it becomes graspable as something that can be actual without this intellectual forming, that is, as "bare sensation."

Now, this "bare sensation" is not completely unformed matter, for the sense *datum* [*Sinnesdatum*] as such —I mean, as it has entered into the actuality of a life— is "formed matter," and it is so in two senses. [1] Sensible material contains a forming and actual being by being received into the life stream of a living thing open to receiving it. [2] On the other hand, the inner life, too, not just the sensitive life but the higher, spiritual life as well, is formed and actualized by receiving contents, in such wise that in this kind of living too, we should acknowledge the presence of form and matter. Working out more exactly what this means must also await our material inquiry.[114]

[Formal and material]

We thus are finding "formed matter [*Materie*]" in the most diverse material [*material*] areas. In each, "form" and "matter" have a different material meaning; that is, we should see them as empty forms allowing of different material fillings. At the same time formal differences run parallel to different material fulfillments. We

---

[113]   Vi., § 22.

[114]   Vi., § 22.

should admit a specific empty form for each "formed fullness" (where "fullness" in general means "formed matter [*Materie*]" and includes unformed matter only as the limiting case).

On the other hand, we must derive specific empty forms in a purely formal way. Nor are they to be filled materially in any way we please, for they place certain restrictions on the matter which can enter them. But we cannot reach this matter itself through a purely formal procedure. (Our method has already shown this in practice, for we needed {57} material descriptions to help us bring out the formal relations.) Thus our formal inquiries show a need for a material procedure to supplement them.

§ 2
The method of material ontology:
intuition and thought.
Formal and material intuition.
Abstraction: sensible, ideating, and generalizing.
Variation.
The *mathesis universalis*—
the possibility of systematizing
ontological disciplines.

[Formal and material approaches]

Our task now is to find a method that can take us further into this new area. We may begin by considering the examples that have often helped us to identify formal relations in the second chapter. These analyses showed that we are dealing here with a number of different areas. We must ask if this diversity is manageable and ordered. If it is, we may hope to find the subareas wherein "act" and "potency" have their place as the "activity" and "capacity [*Vermögen*]" of a substance as well as act as the underlying inner principle of form. We can see the difference between formal and material approaches when in mathematics, say analytical geometry, after intuiting the shapes we go on to formulate the equations about them and calculate the results, and when —as so often in our preceding study— we illustrate an idea (like becoming) with a concrete example and then decide what we should say about it formally.

[Intuition and thinking]

This difference is by no means the same as that between sense intuition and thinking. Our examples have already shown this. We do use sense intuition to help us understand what a parabola or a hyperbola is, but we cannot find pure geometrical shapes in any sense experience. This is clearer still in becoming, which indeed we cannot grasp at all with our senses. A spiritual act is no doubt involved here; to be precise, an act of the understanding. If we were to take "thinking" as a general term for the acts of the understanding, we should say that the distinction between formal and material approaches is found within thinking (or better, we should say that the distinction bisects the distinction between sense intuition and thinking, for we may well be able to show that {58} an analogous distinction is to be made *within* sense intuition).

It is more usual to restrict the word "thinking" to a certain kind of acts of the understanding, to those we commonly consider specifically logical or rational processes such as drawing conclusions from premises, judging, inferring, defining—everything Thomas calls "*ratio* [reason]."[115] Here we certainly have a formal procedure; I mean, one wherein we reach results without regard for the "fullness"

---

[115]   In one of the many meanings of the word; cf. the glossary in my translation of the *Quaestiones de veritate* <Breslau, 1935> under "*ratio*," pp., 45f.

of the objects we are dealing with. In contrast, "spiritual intuition" [*"Anschauung" oder "Intuition"*] will denote an act of the understanding whereby we grasp something that has content; for example, when I fix my "mind's eye" on something like color or sound or shape. (It is hardly possible to describe this without borrowing expressions from physical sight.)

But this is not the final distinction we must make. Before the understanding can proceed logically, judge, or infer, it must "grasp" something, in order to operate on it and by virtue of it. This "grasping" may first be registering it sensibly. But as the starting point of logical activity this does not suffice, because what the senses register must be brought into logical form, or the form that it *has* must be brought into focus.

On the other hand two further things are possible when I "direct my mind" to something, for I can direct it either at the form or at the fullness. Hence we may go ahead and speak of *formal* and *material intuition*. Describing these acts in detail and evaluating them critically is a task for epistemology. Here we wish only to point out briefly that there are specifically distinct means of knowledge that belong to different disciplines.

[From above and from below]

The object of our material ontology is now the *what* that fulfills the empty forms, and we acquire this knowledge by means of material, mental intuition. does this mean that our proper procedure is to take any things whatsoever and display their whatness [*Washeit*] by looking at them mentally? And what is this whatness? does the "*what*" of things mean the concrete fullness proper to them?

In this way we cannot tell how we are supposed to attain a science. At best we could get a description, such as we have, say, in the biological sciences. But of course such descriptions cannot comprise the full concrete fullness. Linguistic expressions are always general (so instead of describing things, we would have to call them by their proper names; but names —given what our human names are like— could never completely express the thing they denote). Consequently any {59} description is already an abstraction and a classification. Is it possible to reach a systematic understanding [*Systematik*] within this classification? And it is possible to reach it "from below," that is, starting from any things whatsoever given in experience? Or can and should we come to it "from above"; I mean, is there some specification of the basic idea of "fullness"?

We must also distinguish several senses of "from below" and "from above." We could take them first as induction and deduction; that is, acquiring general ideas and items of knowledge from the particular experiences we bring together, or deducing more specific ideas from more general ideas and deducing truths about individual objects from general truths.

Or again we could understand them as the contrast between *a posteriori* and *a priori*, which is not the same as that between particular and general. What we know *from* experience is *a posteriori*, whether it concerns a definite particular thing or is a general truth about particular things gotten from experiences. Whatever is not to be gotten from experience is *a priori*, even if it is gotten on the occasion of experience, whether or not it concerns the particular or the general. This raises far-reaching epistemological and ontological questions. We shall again put aside these epistemological problems here. The ontological discussion directly affects only the object now engaging us.

[Fullness and abstraction]

Can we say anything *a priori* and in general about fullness? We had also to consider fullness in its most general sense as an empty form; I mean, as what corresponds to the empty form of *something* as completing it. Either a *single* thing which contains in itself all material fullness whatever corresponds to the empty form as its material fullness, or else a differentiation of the *what* must come into play. This holds for fullness *a priori* and generally. Is it a *material* truth? Not yet, obviously.

Fullness implies first what is possible from the perspective of the form. Material knowing [*Wissen*] can only be derived from an *intuition* of the one or the many. The idea of the divine essence corresponds to the one, to be viewed from the formal perspective, and since only one thing can correspond to the divine essence, any other filling is out of the question. How we get this idea, from what sources we are to acquire it, does not pertain to our present discussion. The difference between the particular and the general would not apply here; we may leave undecided for now whether the distinction between the *a priori* and the *a posteriori*, too, would fail to apply.

The other possibility implied is fullness as plurality and so as a plurality of different contents. And from this we learned, from our formal perspective, that differences can come "from without" or "from within": they come from without when the same *what* enters different compounds and from within when the whatnesses {60} themselves are different. External differences hark back to inner differences, I mean, to a last simple *quale* [what (it is) like], or more exactly, to many such *qualia*. On the other hand, from inner differences we should gather what external differences are possible. The simple *quale* is accessible to material intuition and only to material intuition. So a first possible task of material ontology would be to identify these simple *qualia*. The search for them would be neither induction nor deduction, but something that could perhaps supply both with material.

Is this procedure empirical? In experience we never meet anything absolutely simple. All the objects of our experience have complex structure. We get to the simple from experience through *analysis*, that is, by breaking down the complex, and through *abstraction*, by disregarding what the simple is combined with, perhaps fused with, in the complex, and by viewing it in isolation. The question is how we are to conceive this abstraction and whether we can inspect the simple merely by analyzing experience or whether there is another way.

[Kinds of abstraction]

We can perform abstraction in virtue of a sense intuition, for example, when we focus only on the top of the tree, not the trunk. We are then abstracting *from* a concrete piece of a sensible thing and picking out another concrete piece by abstraction. This abstracting intuition remains a sensible, concrete intuition, but the abstracting itself *can* at least be an actively spiritual function.

A deeper detachment is involved when instead of a concrete piece I pick out an element that makes the thing up, an "abstract part," say, its color. The concrete piece might exist by itself but not the abstract part; not, that is, in the same mode of being. And this is just where the deeper detachment lies, for a transition to another mode of being takes place therein, or rather may take place. I can concentrate on the thing's concrete color, say, a fully determined shade of red, in a "purely intentional" way; I mean, I "pay attention" only to the thing's color, not its shape or the other qualities it may have.

But the abstraction may also be "*ideating* [*ideierend*]," as when I no longer take red as the color of the thing, but *in specie* [in its species], perhaps along with the insight that the "same" red could also "occur" elsewhere. In *generalizing* [*verallgemeinernd*] abstraction we can ascend from the definite shade to red in general and to color in general. In both ideating and generalizing abstraction something beyond sense intuition is involved. When I intuit a definite color it does not matter if I disregard the individuating elements of the case at hand or pick out the identical red in a series of different shades, nor does it matter whether I ascend from red directly to color or grasp {61} the general element common to red and green. There is always something identical that I get hold of and there is always a specific act that conceives it, namely, a material intuition *a priori* that makes the abstracting possible in the positive as well as in the negative sense.

By virtue of this sort of intuition we can make *a priori* and general judgments and statements [*aussagen*] about these material ideas and their interrelations. Hence the material intuition and the abstraction it allows for can lead from concrete individuals to the simple *qualia* that enter their structure, and can examine these *qualia* in themselves. Through ideating and generalizing abstraction we arrive at ultimate ideas that cannot be reduced to simpler material (the genera of qualities, such as color, sound, shape, etc.), and we can make them the objects of the sciences, which include all truths relevant to the particular genus and the species under the genus; I mean a pure color theory, a pure sound theory, a theory of spatial shapes (= geometry; "pure" here means "*a priori*"). These are branches of material ontology.

But it is also possible, to concentrate not on the elements but on the "structure" of the individuals into which the elements fit *in concreto* [in the concrete]. We then get to the *essentiae rerum* [essences of the things]. (*Essentia* and *quidditas*, essence [*Wesen*] and whatness [*Washeit*], are often used interchangeably. We could so distinguish them that "*quidditas*" would mean the full concrete *what* and "*essentia*" the fixed "framework" of the thing that abides throughout all its changes in appearance.) Here, too, we can, by ascending, come to ultimate ideas no longer reducible materially, to the genera of individuals (material thing, living thing, spiritual person, etc.) and to the corresponding sciences.

[Universal science?]

We saw that each genus and each species admits of formalization. Is a *"mathesis universalis* [univeral mathematics]"[116] conceivable that would deduce all possible specific forms from the ontological basic forms, thus setting up a closed system of forms, in such wise that material ontology would have only to fit in the relevant fullness throughout? Were there such a formal system, it would still not tell us whether a filling existed for a particular form or which form it would belong to. This we can only learn through material intuition. We can no more come to a closed systematic theory of fulfilled forms, of material ideas, in this way than by ascending from below, as we did above.

I daresay it is conceivable in principle in both ways, but practically it cannot be carried out in either. The first way would assume that we have a finished formal ontology (or *mathesis universalis*) and that all material involved in filling the forms, —that is, anything that we can experience at all, including anything that is intuitively possible — {62} would be readily accessible. The other way would also have to meet this second requirement— I mean that we must be assured of having an complete overview of the domain of possible experience and of really [*real*] possible being.

Both ways go against the fact that human experience and science are unfinished in principle. We would already have gained much if, from the formal side, we knew the possible genera [*Gattung*] of a being and, through material intuition, the fullness of these genera, and thus had a closed overview of the branches of the material ontology they require. The case is analogous in particular disciplines. Once we have, according to the form, the genus [*Genus*] that marks off an area, we can then determine its species in formal procedures and seek to fill them in a material intuition.

---

116   [Leibniz's *mathématique universelle*, general theory of relations.]

[Learning about color]

We saw that we can also get to the species and genus by ascending from individuals; the only question is how we can be sure we are including *all* the species of the genus— and so in a sense all the individuals belonging to it. As we do this we should remember that within what is material [*material*] we can pass from one item to another connected with it: from species to genus in generalizing abstraction (as we have already seen), from genus to species in specification, but also from one species to another in the same genus.

Let us illustrate this again with our color example. We see that we can grasp color intuitively, indeed as such, only in a species. This intuition differs from grasping the species itself, say red, in that red is taken as "a color," or color itself is taken in *this* specification whose place could be taken by any other color. Does this presuppose that a color is given in experience, or is it possible in principle to get from the genus "color" to its species, to the whole spectrum of colors? Certainly, in the normal course of human knowledge, we first know particular colors and learn their names but only much later grasp the general idea of "color." However, our ability to grasp the general as such by itself implies that we have already grasped it all along in the particular, long before we become conceptually aware of it by itself. Even the blind associate a meaning with the words "color" and "red," surely more than the purely empty, formal sense "the quality that I cannot imagine." It is quite conceivable that a person who was born blind and then gains his sight and learns how to see (I mean, accustoms his organs to seeing), rediscovers in the visible world what he previously "thought." (This "thinking," though, should not be interpreted as imaginative intuiting).

Nor are the colors and shades that we meet for the first time completely new and startling for us {63}. We may be conscious of not having seen any color like this before, but it fits at once into the species that we are familiar with at its place in the spectrum. Moreover, we can "picture" colors between the ones we know and blends of colors that we never experienced. All this goes to show that there are connections which have *a priori* existence [*Bestand*] and in which our knowledge makes headway without the aid of experience and without any logical procedure. This is why we can start anywhere we wish in order to come by a particular insight.

[God's sight]

We have yet to consider whether *access* is also possible without the aid of experience and whether we can reach a systematic understanding from such an unsystematic starting point. Let us imagine the idea of perfect knowledge, such as Thomas, for example, describes it in his account of divine knowledge.[117] This is the knowledge of a mind that surveys everything knowable as such *uno intuitu*, in a single look. Here there is no ascent from individuals to species and genus nor descent from a genus to its specifications, but a surveying of all of it in its connections, the whole field of the pure theory of colors in a perfectly complete systematic view.

[Structuring of material ontology]

If there are connections between the genus and its species and among the species, we can also think of knowledge leading from one to the other— since this knowledge is not complete from the outset but gained gradually. If the connections among them are grounded in the forms, headway will be logical; if they are grounded in the contents, in the fullness, headway will be made in material intuition.

---

[117]   He probably does so in greatest detail in the *Quaestiones disputatae de veritate*, q. 2.

In ideating and generalizing abstraction we saw such an intuitive procedure leading from individuals to species and genera. We also mentioned the possibility of the reverse procedure: specification— an intuition that would "see" how the genus is "broken down" into its species. When the nature of a particular genus requires that the number of its species be limited and that a definite order exist among them, it must be possible even for a finite mind to identify each and every species by starting from the genus, and to know that these are all the species there are.

But it would also have to be possible to get from one species to the others within the genus and eventually to conclude that there are no more species to be found. The procedure would then not be generalization or specification, but *variation*, meaning locating the various {64} species given in intuition as far as possible; that is, within the limits set by the genus. "Possibility" is shown to be the case practically when the intuition can be performed, "impossibility" when it cannot, and the "limit" is marked by where it cannot. Therefore for minds that depend on the intuition of concrete individuals as the starting point of their knowledge, these are the progressive stages: individual, concrete intuition, ideation, and from ideation variation and generalization (either or both). We may also formalize at any stage, and starting from the empty form, we may reach the forms connected with it in a formal procedure.

Euclidian geometry is a prime example of a fully constructed material ontology. From its methods we can get a clear idea of the difference between formal and material approaches. The limited number of its elements and principles as well as the law-governed connections in form and content among all its objects have allowed it to be constructed as an axiomatic system, as a self-contained discipline, albeit for us it is unfinished. Nothing like this has yet been done for colors and sounds. We could seek the first steps in several places (for example, in Goethe's color theory) and assess them, but above all we must ask the basic question: will the nature of the other areas permit a construction analogous to geometry?

One question we have already asked is especially relevant to our present discussion: can we define the area covered by material ontology? I mean, can we find a limited number of genera that will assure us of covering all its subareas?

§ 3
The terms "category" and "transcendentals."

[The ambiguity of "category"]

We need first to get our bearings on terminology. In our ontological approach so far, we have tried to avoid speaking of *categories* (we did so several times in the first chapter), since the word comes to us burdened with a history in several ways and even in an individual philosopher it is ambiguous. Based of our foregoing reflections, in particular our distinction of disciplines that differ in principle, we can perhaps settle on one usage and make any, perhaps unavoidable, ambiguity harmless.

"Category" is already ambiguous in Aristotle. The word refers on the one hand to possible forms of propositions [*Aussage*], and so to logical forms, but at the same time it denotes forms of being, more precisely, forms of be-ings and {65} what befits them, hence ontological forms.[118] These two senses are analogous and necessary because the ontic and the logical are parallel and mutually related and hence there must be corresponding forms on either side. The Aristotelian table has ten categories, substance and nine kinds of accidents. (We are concerned here only with the ontological aspect.)

---

[118] We shall shortly ask whether they include everything be-ing or are limited to a particular area.

[Substance]

We have remarked several times that "substance" itself is ambiguous. In one sense, substance is what abides and perdures throughout the change in the accidents and the appearances of the particular thing (the concrete individual); it is the bearer of the accidents and its being underlies their being. In a second sense, substance is *what* the individual is, taken *in specie* [in its species] as invariable [*unveränderlich*].[119] Apart from these historical definitions we suggested another meaning of "substance" from the immanent perspective: "something whose being stretches over a duration and which activates all that it is in certain effects."[120]

The contrast of substance and accidents shows that in the table of categories first substance is obviously meant and that second substance is clearly out of place among the categories of being. Substance as something enduring that activates what it is in certain effects is wider, since the something is not limited to what has accidents. Here, too, a limitation of the *something* as such is already present.

Even less should we see the Aristotelian category as a form of highest generality. In both versions something material [*material*] is included. Thomas understands his distinction between substance and accident in a purely formal way as what is not in another and what is in another, and he sees it at the same time as a determination of a being by its mode of being.[121] But even taken in this way the table of categories does not include absolutely every be-ing. There are forms of greater generality that it does not contain.

---

119 P. 68-9.

120 P. 15ff.

121 Cf. *De veritate*, q. 1, a. 1, corpus; *De spiritualibus creaturis*, a. 11.

[Transcendentals, the be-ing, categories and substance]

Thomistic philosophy distinguishes the *transcendentals* from the categories, into which the transcendentals do not fit; they are: *aliquid* [something], *ens*, [be-ing], *unum* [one], *verum* [true], and *bonum* [good]. We can understand the *be-ing* in such a way that it does not enter the table of categories, but is presupposed by it; that is, in the general sense wherein both the selfsufficient and the unselfsufficient "are." The be-ing thus comes *before* the division of substance and accident.

In our section on formal ontology we stressed {66} the three basic forms: the form of object, or *something*, the form of *what* the object is, and the form of being. Speaking now of how these forms and the be-ing that embodies them can possibly be filled, we find that a be-ing may be absolutely simple, wherein the three forms are indistinguishable, or it may be something wherein they can be distinguished and perhaps separated. The formal concept of substance, what is not in another, would apply to both, but it would be further determined in a way proper to each. The concept of the simple be-ing (which at the same time is *absolutely* selfsufficient) is further determined as that wherein nothing is separable, and the concept of the composed being as that wherein another is.

In the first sense "substance" would exclude accidents and in the second sense it would include them. In the table of categories substance and accidents are contrasted, obviously not in the sense that they exclude one another but that they are correlated. In this second sense they could encompass not *every* be-ing but perhaps every composed be-ing (for certain reasons we also called it created). Substance would then be the same as the form of the individual (that is, of the created individual), and the other categories would be variations of the correlative form of accident, that is, the possible elements making up the individual.

Does this category list, we should ask, contain *all* possible forms of accidents? If the list proves to be complete and the categories all turn out to be formal, we would have a closed formal framework for the material ontology of the created world. We would then arrive at the <u>genera</u> [*Gattungen*] of a be-ing if, in a material intuition, we sought how the forms may possibly be filled. (For this we may well have to start from the category of substance itself and from the *ti* <*something*>.)

[Formal and material categories]

But need we define the term "category" in this way? If we recall the parallelism between logical and ontological categories, the most general ontological form of object or *something* corresponds to the logical basic category of subject, and so a version of the ontological concept of category that would include *every* be-ing within its scope seems to make more sense.[122] We shall then be distinguishing between *formal categories* (and among them we may include all empty forms coming from formal ontology) and *material categories*, I mean, those material ideas that do not admit {67} of generalizing but only further formalizing. In them we shall have the *genera* [*Gattungen* (*genera*)] of the be-ing that define for us the branch disciplines about the be-ing. If every be-ing has its own measure of being (mode), as our material study will show, the distinctions of the categories must at the same time be *distinctions of being*. The term "*genera* [*genera*]," however, will receive its own warrant when we uncover its several ontic *Geneses*.[123]

---

[122]   Husserl does this, for example in the first section of *Ideas* <*zu einer reinen Phänomenologie und phänomenologischen Philosophie*, bk. 1, Halle a.d.S., 1913; new critical edition: *Husserliana*, vol. 3, 1, edited by K. Schuhmann, The Hague, 1976*>.

[123]   VI, § 19 and the final part.

[Transcendentals: one and true; logic]

Let us take a brief look at the other transcendentals: *unum*, *verum*, and *bonum* to see how they are related to the categories. They denote nothing save a be-ing, but a be-ing grasped solely from some aspect other than its being. The *unum* grasps what we called "*something*" in the be-ing, that is, what enables it to be grasped by itself and apart from others (Thomas's note on the etymology of the word illustrates this: "*aliquid* [something] is "*aliud quid* [another what]").[124] Thus it is an ontological form of the same generality as be-ing in the wider sense of the word; I mean that it is a formal category, not a category in the narrower sense.

Verum and *bonum* are distinguished from *ens* and *unum* in that the be-ing is grasped not in itself but in relation to a be-ing of a particular kind. The *verum* is the be-ing insofar as it is known or knowable, hence in its relation to a knowing mind, indeed in a specific relation: that of correspondence [*Übereinstimmung*]. *Verum* does not restrict the be-ing to a particular set of objects, since the be-ing is knowable as such (even if not *every* be-ing is knowable for *every* knowing mind); *ens* and *verum* are therefore equivalent.

On the other hand, since there is something material [*material*] in the relation to the knowing mind, we may hesitate to call *verum* an empty form. "Mind [*Geist*]" has a material sense and so do "knowledge" and "being knowable"; consequently "truth," too, has a material sense, albeit it is usually seen as formal in relation to individual "truths." A curious twofold position is in fact proper to truth. In its full sense "truth" denotes a special area of be-ing, namely the area presupposed by the encounter of a be-ing with possible knowledge. We cannot claim that truth is a genus because it does not fall into species, nor does it define a domain of individuals of a definite sort.

---

[124]   *De veritate*, q. 1, a. 1, corpus.

Logic is the discipline that analyzes what truth is and sets forth all the "truths" pertaining to it. Insofar as logic has to do with a particular area of being, we could think of it as a branch of material ontology. But {68} insofar as truth is related to *every* be-ing and comprises the *forms* in which a be-ing as such of whatever area can be known and which correspond to the forms of the be-ing itself, logic should be seen as a *formal* discipline, one having the same scope as formal ontology.

Finally, it is possible to formalize the *verum* itself. I mean, we can first strip mind and knowledge of its material sense and reduce them to their form; then we can define the *verum* by the relation of the be-ing as such to this specific form. In this case the science of the *verum* becomes a branch of formal ontology. Thus we can speak of *verum* as a formal as well as a material category (in the broad sense of the word). It has no place in the table of categories of substance and accidents, for it is neither substance nor accident. But we would still have to examine its particular relation to the table of categories.

[The transcendental good]

Bonum is the be-ing insofar as it is the goal of an intention of the will and fulfills the intention. Here, too, something material gets into the meaning because of its relation to the will, which is something materially determined. If we understand "*bonum*" (= value [*Wert*])[125] in this way, we can take it as the title of a specific area of the be-ing and assign to this area a value theory as a discipline that corresponds to it. But in this case neither would "*bonum*" denote a genus of individuals, but something that presupposes a relation of every be-ing to a definite be-ing: I mean just this dependence through the encounter of a be-ing with a will.

---

125   In modern terminology the *bonum* corresponds (1) to the *good* [*das Gut*] that is, a thing of value [*wertvoll*], and (2) to the *value*, that is, what gives the thing value.

Unlike truth, "value" is specified into values, and so we may speak of it as a genus. We may also say that the be-ing and the good are equivalent. But in what sense are we taking "be-ing" here: in its formal generality or in some specific sense? Our answer will tell us if the same universality that applies to formal logic applies to the discipline that is to explain what value is as such —without regard to particular values—; that is, to the formal theory of value or axiology.[126] A formal value theory would in any case require a supplementary material theory to determine how the idea of value is differentiated as well as how the genus {69} "value" is specified to a scale of values and what these species of value entail.[127] On the other hand we can again formalize "will" and "value," thereby reducing formal axiology to a branch of formal ontology. Hence we can also grasp the *bonum* as a formal as well as a material category. Moreover, I daresay we may bring it under a category of accident. We cannot see how this can be done before taking a closer look at these categories.

---

[126] Husserl outlined such a parallel discipline for formal logic in the lectures on "formal axiology and practice," which he gave decades before in Göttingen; unfortunately they have not been published. <Available now in: E. Husserl, *Vorlesungen über Ethik und Wertlehre 1908-1914* [lectures on ethics and axiology] (*Husserliana*, vol. 28), edited by U. Melle, Dordrecht, Boston, and London, 1988.>

[127] The most valuable beginnings of a material value theory are found in Max Scheler's works.

§ 4
The task of material ontology.
Method: formal or material?
Attempt to classify material ontology according to
immanence / transcendence or
spirit / sensibility / nonspiritual.

[Act and Potency in the formal]

We are assuming the distinction we made in our preliminary study between two uses of the term "category": "formal category" refers to the empty forms of formal ontology, and "material category" to material ideas marking off particular areas of being together with their disciplines. The be-ing, as something that is, is the defining category for formal ontology, the be-ing as an object of knowledge is the defining category for formal logic, and the be-ing as an object of striving [*streben*] is the defining category for formal axiology.

Do act and potency have a place in these formal disciplines? We have sought to show what formal ontology says about act and potency. We found, first, that they are different interrelated modes of being (actuality and potentiality). Then —as activity and capability— they are accidents of a substance that are interrelated in a certain way. Finally, act designates what in a be-ing makes it into a be-ing, that is, gives it actuality and determines *what* it is.

[Method: material and formal]

In all these meanings the formal categories admit of various material fillings. Accidents are differentiated according to the substance whose accidents they are, and we must discover their differences by considering the be-ing materially. But we need also to supplement actual and potential being with a material study, since being in its full sense, that is, not reduced to its formal sense, implies a fullness accessible only to material intuition.

Accordingly, material ontology signifies at once a theory of being in its fullness and a theory of the be-ing in its different genera. It will hardly {70} be necessary and may well not even be possible to treat them separately, since different modes of being correspond to the different genera of the be-ing and cannot be understood in their fullness apart from *what is* in this way or that. Now is the time, then, to seek the genera of the be-ing.

We seem to be limited here to *that* sort of be-ing which is split into genera; that is, we are limited to creatures. For the present we shall not regard the one, simple, be-ing wherein there is no such split, wherein being and what is are no longer distinct. But we shall have to come back to it again, since everything else points to it again and again, and our introductory study has already shown us that act and potency have their place therein.

Now, are we using a formal or a material method as we do this? Actually, the preceding paragraphs have already settled the matter practically: if we had a finished formal ontology, it would contain the system of all the possible genera of objects. But all we have are the beginnings of a formal ontology, and where we managed to make discoveries in this area, we usually did so with the aid of the material method that allowed us to spot certain connections and enabled us to highlight their formal relations. Thus we find ourselves sent down the path of the material method. We may start from some points we have made previously, in order to organize them into a whole and supplement them.

[The three realms]

We have envisioned three realms from the immanent point of

view: the world within (the immanent world), the world without (the transcendent world), and the world above. We may say that all possible be-ing is contained therein, insofar as we cannot conceive of anything except as something that belongs to the subject itself, something that the subject runs up against outside itself, and something that becomes evident [*sich dokumentieren*] both within and without as beyond. But as we do this, we are grasping everything from one particular point of view, namely, the relationship to the subject. And what the three realms signify in themselves remains open.

[Self-conscious being]

We can define the sphere of the immanent through the basic category of *consciousness* in its full meaning: being that is conscious of itself [*seiner selbst bewußtes Sein*], of the be-ing and the being which exists for itself [*für sich selbst dasein*] in the manner that it exists for itself. We must add this qualification since not all self-conscious being is immanent being. The subject, after all, encounters other subjects "out there" which are no less self-conscious in the way it, the subject, itself is self-conscious, but which for the subject belong to the transcendent world, the world without. And the world above should also be called self-conscious being.

["Spirit"]

If we take being that is conscious of itself, or the be-ing that is {71} conscious of itself, without the qualifying phrase binding it into itself, we come to another material category that ranges throughout all three realms: *spirit* or *mind* [*Geist*].[128] Spirit is within us, outside us,

---

[128]   We shall explain below that self-conscious being does not entirely mark off the sphere of spirit; rather it denotes only the primary objectiveness and the highest mode of being of the spiritual sphere (cf. V, § 2).

above us. So does this not invalidate the division we just suggested? Must we brush it aside as something arbitrary [*willkürlich*], dragged in from outside?

The division certainly has epistemological import. A somewhat closer consideration of the self-conscious be-ing should tell us whether it is also warranted in material ontology. We have seen that it was objectively necessary to distinguish the uncreated spirit from created spirits, because there is an analogy between them yet their essences are not alike [*Wesensgleichheit*]. It is characteristic for the created spirit to be closed in itself yet at the same time open to the outside. This is the objective [*sachlich*] basis for the division between immanence and transcendence.

There is another ontological reason for distinguishing between spirit and the immanent. We have defined "immanent" as the be-ing that is conscious of itself or as what exists for itself. But this does not mean that it is *totally* conscious of itself; that is, it does not mean that *everything* that it itself is exists for itself. It is the nature of spirit to be completely transparent [*durchsichtig*] (intelligible): more precisely, it is the nature of the *subjective* spirit in the highest mode of its being.

[Immanent, immanently transcendent, transcendent]

The immanent is spiritual insofar as it is conscious of itself. But it may not be transparent as a whole and it may not be a subject of self-consciousness as a whole, for there may be a distinction between subject and object in the immanent itself. And this is indeed true of the human spirit, where spiritualness is based upon the sensibility. Thomas says that sense data are something immaterial in relation to the things of the outside world, but in relation to the intellect they are things, as it were.[129] This sheds light on our present concern. The

---

[129]   *De veritate*, q. 1, a. 11, corpus.

sensibility is the border area. We could call it a first transcendence in immanence: immanent because the subject is conscious of the sensibility as something that belongs to it, to the subject itself, and transcendent because it is not transparent to itself nor to the spirit.

We can thus arrive at this classification: the purely immanent, the immanently transcendent [*immanent transzendent*], and the absolutely transcendent. The absolutely transcendent we could take as denoting what is transcendent not only for *one* subject but as something that does not enter the inwardness of any subject. The classification would then be quite objective [*objektiv*] {72} and it would seem to coincide with that other division of pure spirit, sensibility, and the nonspiritual [*ungeistig*]. We can see the sensibility as a border area insofar as it shows a lower degree of the consciousness that is the trademark of spiritual activity and moreover can enter into that characteristic union with the spiritual that allows us to claim that the sensibility is immanent.

But these are still not categories that can serve to define areas of objects [*Gegenstand*]. Sensibility denotes not a genus of individuals (individual substances), but a genus of something that has its place in the context of a be-ing of a particular genus. It is still not clear enough what "pure spirit" means. It is even less clear how we should understand the nonspiritual, which of course is but a negative depiction— the answer we are inclined to give is "material [*materiell*]." But then we must take another look at the material, consider how the sensible is related to it and to the spiritual, and then ask whether these three genera cover every conceivable be-ing whatever.

IV
Attempt to Define Matter Materially

§ 1
Problems concerning matter.
The fourfold potentiality of matter.

[Pure potency]

In our formal approach, we defined "*materia prima*" as what is absolutely potential and unformed, and it was already clear that this empty form can be filled in many ways. In our ordinary way of speaking, both inside and outside of science and in philosophy as well, "matter [*Materie*]" has a material [*material*] meaning, for we speak of "material nature" and of "material things," and from time immemorial we have associated matter in this sense with space. Plato (in the *Timaeus*) wished to equate matter with empty space. The Aristotelian-Thomistic view understands the word as the unformed matter [*Stoff*] that confronts us as formed in the things of nature.

We defined the mode of being of matter as pure potentiality, but we have not spoken about its *what*. After thinking away all "form" —that is, all the species making up the thing's *what*— what do we have left? Matter has no color, makes no sound, is neither hard nor heavy. But it is what takes on all these qualities and fills space with them (hence it is not empty space). Matter acquires actual being only by taking on qualities [*Qualität*]. On the other hand matter enables species to exist [*Dasein*] concretely in space, for it is what individuates them. Because of the potentiality of its being we characterized matter as unselfsufficient, as what cannot have its being from itself but must be created. Matter is untransparent in the sense that what is material cannot take in something else material— it can only make way for it.

[Matter and spirit]

We have yet to ask if the material [*materiell*] can take in the spiritual. The spiritual cannot take the material into its "interior" [*Inneres*]"; the material is what spirit comes up against as against something foreign to itself that it cannot penetrate. Spirit on the other hand is transparent; it is transparent both for itself [*für sich*] —in the form of self-consciousness— and for something else which it takes in by knowing it. Spirit, by knowing, penetrates the other and the other penetrates spirit, for one spirit can displace itself into another spirit. Everything that happens to matter is done to it from {74} outside; it is *passive*. But what happens to spirit comes from inside; it is *activity* [*Tätigkeit*], *spirit is active* [*aktiv*].

Here we meet the *second sense* of "*potency*" and "*act*": act as activity and potency as capacity for activity. The relation between first and second act also comes in here. What is actual takes effect from the inside out; it is active [*tätig*]. What is potential needs something actual to place it in activity. The possibility of being placed in such activity is a *passive potency*; the possibility of being active from itself is an *active potency*.

How can something material be known if it does not enter the spirit? Obviously, because it is not pure matter but formed by species. How can matter be formed by species, how can it receive qualities? And how should we regard these qualities or species: as material, spiritual, or something else? Furthermore, the rigidity, the passivity, of matter, prompts us to call it *lifeless* [*tot*], but to say that spirit is *alive*. Yet we do speak of *living*, animated matter and distinguish it from nonliving matter, usually without going so far as to mean *spiri-*

tual life. How is life related to spirit and matter? How can matter take life into itself?

[Knowing matter]

To the first question, about how matter is knowable, Thomas gives three replies that correspond to the three types of knowledge that he treats: the knowledge of God, of angels, and of men. God bears within Himself the archetypes of all things, their ideas, and Thomas assumes there is also an archetype for matter. Angels bear in their minds the "forms" that God bestows upon them as a natural endowment enabling them to know things. Men must acquire these forms for themselves. First they receive a sense "image [*Bild*]" from things, and from the image their understanding works out the species of the understanding— the *intellectus agens* makes the things *actu intelligibiles* [intelligible in act] that before were intelligible potentially. "*Intelligibilis*" here has two senses: "knowable" (= "graspable by the mind") and "spiritual." The two are thought to be inseparable, for the mind can only take in what is of its own nature, and what is spiritual in its nature can enter the knowing mind.

Our comments here should be taken as ontology, not as a theory of knowledge. How are we to take the "idea of matter" and the emergence of matter from its idea? How should we regard "species"— in the mind of angels, in the human mind, in the senses, in things? We shall soon {75} broach the problem of the being of ideas —hence also the being of the idea of matter— "in the divine mind."[130] Our formal treatment has already taught us that the being of matter is conceivable only on the basis of a creative act.[131] To understand this origin lies beyond our power.

---

[130]   Pp. 105ff.

[131]   II, § 4.

[Creation, kinds of potentiality and actuality]

Philosophy based on natural reason brings us to the act of creation which alone is able to bridge the gulf between being and nonbeing, to leap from spirit to matter. But here philosophy halts before a locked gate: creation, as taught by faith, remains a mystery for our knowledge. What is absolutely spiritual and actual calls into being its direct opposite: what is nonspiritual and potential.

Matter represents the utmost in potentiality. This potentiality is fourfold: (1) the potentiality of being as the possibility of passing into actual being, (2), the potentiality of being formed as the readiness to receive certain species, (3) the potentiality of functioning, working [*Wirken*] as the possibility of being affected and of being shifted to active working, and (4) the potentiality of becoming known as the possibility of passing into intelligible being. They are all intrinsically connected.

Potentiality can be understood only from the viewpoint of actuality. The most original meaning of "actuality" is being, and it parallels initial potentiality, the possibility of passing into being. Since matter is brought to actual being by taking in form, the potentiality of being necessarily requires the potentiality of being formed. Activity belongs to actuality, hence the potentiality of working belongs to the potentiality of being and forming. Since pure actuality is spiritual being, and anything, insofar as it is spiritual, can enter knowledge, the potentiality of becoming known also belongs to the potentiality of being.

§ 2
The potentiality of being.

We said earlier that potential being lies between being (that is, pure, absolutely actual being) and nonbeing, or that it is at once being and nonbeing. We were not thinking of some third thing between being and nonbeing, nor a mixture of both. We meant rather that there are degrees of being and corresponding levels or degrees of potentiality; I mean degrees of nearness to pure being.

Materia prima is on the lowest rung on this scale of be-ings. Here it is {76} pure potentiality, not actual being present *beside* potential being—as in the case of formed matter. This lowest mode of being differs from nonbeing in that it is ordered to actual being. Matter differs from the nonbe-ing by being *determinable*. This determinability, in contrast to the nonbe-ing, implies something positive, although in comparison to definite being it implies something negative as well; I mean that it is *undetermined*.

§ 3
The potentiality of forms or species
The problem of "ideas."
Idea and spirit.

[Ideal objects]

Determinability is the readiness to receive forms or species. Receiving means passing from the absolutely potential being of *materia prima* to the higher mode of being of formed matter that includes something of actuality; it means that a particular be-ing, a material thing, emerges. To understand this transition and this mode of being, it is now important to answer our previous questions about how we should conceive species, what their being is like, and how they enter into matter.

When examining concrete things, we met their "forms," their genera and species, describing them as what makes things what they are. Their forms, we saw, can be abstracted and have their own proper being, their own existence [*Bestand*] in themselves, in their connectedness, which is the relationship of their genera and species. These "material [*material*] forms" or "ideas," which cannot be further reduced and are interrelated in a fixed order, we called "ideal objects," and from them we distinguished the concrete *what*, the lowest species that is individuated in particular things. And we regarded matter as their principle of individuation, for according to Thomas matter, a principle of individuation, is not the wholly unformed *materia prima* but *materia signata* [marked matter], the "piece of matter [*Stück Materie*]" determined in size. Unsolved problems remain in all this.

[Divine ideas]

Genera and species, it seemed, possess in their law-governed connectedness a mode of being setting them apart. For this reason we called them "ideal objects." We could not as yet really understand this mode of being. On the one hand it is ordered to the being of individuals wherein the genera and species are instantiated but without getting dissolved into the "being in" the individuals. On the other hand this mode of being is akin to and even belongs to the divine being.

We could not but recall the Augustinian interpretation of the ideas as the archetypes of things in the divine mind, yet we could not explain what it means {77} to "be in the divine mind" nor how this is compatible with the simplicity of the divine being. We should also bear in mind that "ideas in the divine mind" would include not only ideal objects but also the lowest concrete species, since after all the whole concrete thing must be foreseen in the Creator's mind. This would in turn jeopardize the privileged position of the ideal objects, or else we would have to assume different modes of being for different divine ideas. (Plato had already concerned himself with the difficulty of how we should understand the word "idea.")[132]

[Eternal states of affairs]

The feature of ideal objects that allows us to connect them to the divine being, is their timelessness, the eternalness of their being. It makes no sense to say that numbers, colors, sounds, geometrical shapes, emerge in time or are created, as heaven and earth, plants and animals and people emerge in time. Certainly, before the creation of the world "there could be" no colors and sounds "in the world." But color as such and in its varieties in the spectrum, sound as such as well as the qualities of its various species, have a being that does not coincide with their "occurrence [*Vorkommen*] in the world." It was the case —indeed not in a purely formal, but in a material sense— that red was different from green and the pitch C was different from D before any note sounded and before any color shone in the world. And not only was it a valid statement [*Satz*], but the corresponding state of affairs [*Sachverhalt*] had existence [*Bestand*] from eternity. Now, since it belongs to the idea of divine being as of the absolutely actual that there can be no other being independent from it, we are led to regard the "eternal ideas" as belonging to the divine mind, as something upon which God rests His gaze from all eternity.

[A plurality of ideas]

We have already spoken of Thomas's view of how God, ideas, and things are related. In his account[133] God beholds Himself, His own being, from eternity. His knowledge of the divine essence in its unity

---

132   In the *Theaetetus* (186A) and the *Philebus* (16C).

133   *De veritate*, questions 2-4.

expresses itself —inwardly, in God— in the divine Word, the second Person of the Trinity, and His knowledge of the divine essence in its relation to the plurality of things expresses itself in the ideas.

When discussing this we paused before the puzzling nature of this combination of unity and plurality.[134] We must now take up the question again. Is it enough to set the absolutely simple divine essence on the one side and on the other the plurality of created things {78} called into existence by the act of creation (or of such things that could be created but in fact are not)? (On the other hand we should not think of this act as something particular and separate within the Godhead, for it is included in the unity of the divine essence, which is actuality and activity.) What obliges us to suppose "ideas" as a second plurality in addition to the plurality of concrete individual things?

[The intention to create]

We have seen how the ideas, in virtue of our intuition of things, stand out as something realized here and there and as having its own laws. It is precisely the connections between genera and species, which stand on their own [*eigenständig*], that make it impossible to reduce this entire region of ideal being to that of the "real [*real*]," that is, to the region of concrete individual things.

It seems to me, however, that we must explain further how the ideas are marked off from the simple divine essence —or better, sorted out from it— by the intention toward a plurality of things created or to be created. We may be able to imagine God's being without creation: the one simple divine essence resting in itself, without outside effect. If we also think away any intention toward a creation, we may well have to say that the ontic basic framework of a world of individual

---

[134]   II, § 4 toward the end.

things, that is, the world of ideas, would collapse. Even if the being of the ideal world cannot be reduced to the intention toward individual things, the intention is still indissolubly connected to its being.

On the other hand, as soon as we posit in God the intention toward a creation, even if only a possible creation, we must see this intention as eternal, and the whole image of the creation and the order ruling it, the "basic framework," must have stood before the mind of God from eternity. "Before the mind of God"— the creation thus belongs to Him without suppressing His unity and simplicity.

[Possible worlds, necessity and choice]

We must also ask whether the eternal order, the realm of ideas, is called into existence through God's intention as an eternal creation before the creation in time. His bond to this intention seems to indicate this. On the other hand, can we then seriously imagine God's mind without this intention? The *need* to create the world would place a limitation on the divine will; still, necessity is not given with this intention. Removing the intention toward a *possible* creation would obviously put a limitation on the divine intellect, since the idea of a possible creation must be included in His perfect, all-embracing knowledge.

What stands before God from eternity is the eternal truth; it is not created by His choice [*Willkür*] nor is it to be altered by His choice. Here belongs the order of the realm of ideas, the connections among genera and species that reveal {79} themselves to us as "*a-priori* truths" with the mark of necessity. In these immutable connections the possible combinations of ideas, the "possible worlds" and, in the particular, the possible concrete species, are prescribed beforehand. They are involved as the archetypes for things to be created and they leave room for choice [*Willkür*] and selection [*Wahl*].

[Potency and possibility]

The mode of being of ideal objects which has already concerned us in our formal approach has now been clarified. Standing before God is immutable, actual being. The potentiality connected with it implies both God's potency —active potency, not opposed to act— to call the relevant things into existence, as well as a passive potency of the things, that is, the possibility of passing from nonbeing to being. Thus the mode of being of ideal beings is higher than that of created things. Also confirmed is the fact that the being of ideal objects, of genera and their specifications, is distinct from the being of the lowest concrete species, of their possible combinations. Their "possibility" is an *ideal* possibility and as such it is in turn actual being before God, connected with potentiality in the two senses just mentioned.

But this being is not purely actual being, for possibility connotes a secondary being, being owing to another —namely, being based on the ideal objects— and it connotes a certain nothingness [*Nichtigkeit*] in itself, a contingency [*Zufälligkeit*]. Possibility as such surely cannot be eliminated; however, a world is conceivable wherein many of these possibilities would not be realized, whereas a world that would contradict the eternal order is inconceivable. Thus in the end the nothingness [*Nichtigkeit*] of the concrete species, too, has its place not in the region of ideal being, but in the region of "real" being.

[Spirit and idea]

Concrete species confront us individualized [*individuieren*] in material things. Here for the first time, in the area of becoming, the area of the transition from nonbeing to being, we meet the puzzling connection between idea and matter. We have endeavored to clarify what the ideas are in order to understand this connection, and I believe we have come a little closer to understanding it. We are seeing that material things presuppose ideas and, on the other side, matter. The encounter of the two and their unification requires a third thing: a creative *spirit*. The contrast of spirit and matter is already clear; now we must ask if spirit or mind and idea must be distinguished.

The original manner in which spirit exists [*Existenz*] is actuality and it is life. Functioning, working, pertains to life, and so actuality and activity belong together, for actuality takes effect in activity and activity presupposes actuality. At first glance an idea appears to be something lifeless, dead, and ineffective. By {80} itself the idea of man cannot bring forth a man.[135] This seems to gainsay what we said earlier, that things are called into existence by ideas, even matter by the idea of matter. We made this claim in the context of Thomas and it should be understood in reference to his explanation of the Augustinian conception of the ideas "in the divine mind."

[Thomas and St. John's Gospel]

This conception is closely connected with the Neoplatonic-Augustinian view of the *Logos* that finds its characteristic expression in an interpretation of a well-known Scriptural passage that differs from the current reading. Today we read the opening of St. John's Gospel in this way:

In the beginning was the Word and the Word was with God and the Word was God.... Through it everything was made, and without it nothing was made *that was made. In it was life....*

---

[135] The κίνησις [movement] of the εἴδη [ideas] was already a problem for Plato. The central place that he assigns to the idea of the good (in the *Republic*) seems to preview the Augustinian conception.

The older reading, which we also find in Thomas's works, is:

... without it nothing was made. *What was made is life in Him*....[136]

Thomas, in accord with this reading, speaks of a being of things in the Word which precedes their being in themselves and which is a higher mode of being than their being in themselves.

It is indeed to be gathered from this Biblical passage so interpreted that the being of things in themselves —their real being, as we were saying— should be referred back to the being of their corresponding ideas in God. So this is an answer to our present question: how are we to understand the transition of things from nonbeing to being and the entry of ideas into matter? Ideas are —on this view— archetypes of things and the things are their likenesses or copies. But the ideas owe the fact that they have the power to call their likenesses into existence and to form the matter into copies of themselves to their being in the *Logos*, who makes them alive [*lebendig*], hence effective as well.

[Ideas and the divine mind]

This view of course needs further analysis. First, it casts fresh light of how the ideas belong to the divine mind. So far we have taken the being of the ideas only as a standing before the divine mind. And seen from this angle, they do seem rigid and lifeless, like our own human "ideas" or "concepts," the sort of rigid, dead things that we operate with. But we know that these items which we say are "in our mind" can show a quite lively effectiveness. The artist's "idea" gives

---

[136]   [The German Bible (*Die Bibel/ Einheitsübersetzung*, 1980) gives the "older" reading, seeing the other as "less probable." There is actually a parallel to this "older" reading among the Dead Sea Scrolls: *Manual of Discipline* (composed 100-75 B.C.), 1QS 11:11 (*The New Jerome Biblical Commentary*, 1990, 61:22 and 67:83).]

him no rest as it drives him to creative activity— an activity {81} through which a new object comes into existence in the visible world, but in the course of which the idea itself, too, may change.

This description of human mental processes, a mere suggestion, is intended here only to help us get a bit closer to the analogous processes in the divine mind and to the connections between mind and idea. What is in God cannot be lifeless, since His being is actuality, life, and because it is a being that is one, simple, undivided. God's being is a spiritual being, and spiritual being is being illumined for itself [*Für-sich-durchleuchtet-Sein*]; that is, it is a knowing and a being-known. God as He Who is known by Himself [*von sich selbst erkannt*]— this is the *Logos*, this is the divine Word, the Word that is God and is life. Through the Word everything has been made, because the creative intention is included in the unity of the divine life.

[Intentionality]

Now then, is what has been made life in Him? Our difficulty, of course, was that the ideas, which are many, are *in* God, Who is one and simple. This is why we understood their being as being *before* God. We can and must, however, assume a living, creative intention that is itself *one* but takes effect in the midst of the manifold of the ideas —not in what happens in time, but from eternity— and "sets them in motion," makes them alive and effective. The eternalness of the effective intention to create [*Schöpfungsintention*] is not inconsistent with the fact that this becoming effective is something temporal, if, as we should, we think of the temporal order itself as posited by the intention to create. It pertains to mind or spirit in its original form that something stands before it.[137] It also pertains to spirit to be living and, what is more, to be able to put life into what stands before it. Just as

---

137   Husserl calls this property "intentionality."

indissolubly it pertains to what stands before the mind to stand before the mind, for such is its mode of being. (Mind here is the eternal mind or spirit, the divine mind; we have yet to ask whether there is an analogous relation in created minds.) It further pertains to what stands before the mind that of itself it has no life, yet it can take life into itself from the mind.

We have called what stands before the mind "ideal [*ideal*]"; it is also commonly called "spiritual." Thomas uses the term "*intelligibilis* [intelligible]" for both —for mind as well as for what stands before it—; but in many places he distinguishes between *intellectualis* [intellectual] and *intelligibilis*. In previous works I distinguished between the "subjective" and "objective spirit."[138] These expressions seem apt to me because they bring out {82} both what is common and what is different. But we ought not to worry here about the history attached to the phrase "objective spirit." The world of ideas represents a first realm of objective spirit. We shall meet others.

---

138   Cf. "Beiträge zu philosophischen Begründung der Psychologie und der Geisteswissenschaften" <"I. Physische Kausalität," "II. Individuum und Gemeinschaft"> (*Jahrbuch für Philosophie und phänomenologische Forschung*, vol. 5 <1922, pp. 1-282; reedition, Tübingen, 1970>), especially pp. 267ff. However, there it is primarily a question of distinguishing between the human mind and the works it creates.

§ 4
The formation of matter.
The nature (substance, form, species) of the thing;
its mode of being.
Need for supplementation by the
ontology of the spirit.

[Informing]

We now have some appreciation for ideal being as well as for the way the ideas can be set in motion and the way they can work. Let us return now to the material [*materiell*]. The existence of matter [*Materie*], we said, we are to understand as posited solely by the creative act, and its *what* as that which is absolutely potential and nonspritual. For this *what* to be able to enter into existence, something must be added to it so that it can have actual being, for matter can only come into existence as formed by concrete species. The creative act, we said, we are taking as the last cause of the existence of matter as well of its forming.

But how should we think of this forming itself? As the species crossing over into materialness? Definitely not, according to Plato and the Augustinian and Thomistic interpretation of the theory of ideas. They rather suppose a relation between archetype [*Urbild*] and likeness or copy [*Abbild*] and attribute to each its own mode of being. They speak of "*imprimere*," "pressing into," and "*indere*," "putting into." The first word recalls how matter [*Stoff*] is shaped into a work of art from without and the second how a living thing is provided with an "inner form" that shapes it from within.

[Matter: nonliving and living]

These are analogies [*Analoga*] that we can bring in from our experience to help us understand what we cannot experience; admittedly these relations themselves are still quite puzzling and unclear. We ought not to conceive of matter [*Materie*] as an item of matter [*Stoff*] present to us and formed into an object by outside mechanical agency; any item of matter that we know by experience, of course, is already formed. Nor is matter a living thing that something happens to from the inside. Pure, "lifeless" matter differs from living matter in that whatever is done to it, all additional formings that it can undergo, come from outside. Nonliving matter does share with living matter the fact that they both come into existence with a "determination" prescribing beforehand what can happen to it from without; that is, they come into existence as a thing with a determined "*nature*." {83}

[Nature, substance, form, species]

The "nature" of a thing is distinguished from the ideal species that corresponds to it by being bound to "a piece of matter." A series of like natures, each individuated [*individuieren*] by the spatial-temporal determination of a "piece of matter," may correspond to one and the same ideal species. Every piece of matter is completely controlled by its nature. This is the "*inesse* [being in]" of the "form" in the matter. It implies that the thing's being, the formed matter, is not completely undetermined potentiality, but *a potentiality in determined directions*. It can become actually this or that, or like this or like that, and at any one time it *is* actually something of that which it can become, or something the likes of which it can become.

The nature then contains within itself a series of potencies, more precisely *passive potencies*, which are nonetheless partially actualized, and as they are actualized they are shifted into active potencies. We say that the transition from passivity into activity and from potentiality to actuality "happens" to it, and since in the case of matter everything happens to it from the outside, this transition is tantamount to being thus shifted. What is actualized can work, have an effect, in the sense that it can lead something else in turn from potency to act. We may call the nature "*substance*" as it "underlies as its basis [*zugrunde liegen*]" the alteration of potency and act and persists throughout this alteration, and we may call the nature "*form*" as it determines the entire process of becoming as well as its outer appearance; we may even call the nature "species" as it is a likeness of the ideal species.

[Nature of the material thing]

Is the nature of the material thing itself something material? It certainly is not matter [*Materie*]; for a nature is not undetermined but determined and determining. Nor is the nature pure potentiality; it is rather a potentiality which can be actualized in a definite way and which is partially actualized. But the *in actu esse* [being in act] of a nature and its *agere* [acting] does not come from itself but is effected in it, and through it it is effected in the matter. The nature is bound to matter with its being; the paradoxical phrase "material form" reflects this. The form's *inesse* [being in] in the matter implies that the idea is as it were materialized [*Materialisierung*] and the matter spiritualized [*Vergeistigung*]. The idea does not become matter nor does the matter become idea or spirit. The unit of both, the *material thing*, is the existent [*Existierendes*] in the proper sense; it is that wherein matter and form when united receive actuality in the sense of *real* [*real*] *being*. Real being, according to what we have learned so far, means being that is detached in a particular sense from the creating spirit to which it owes its existence [*Dasein*] and contrasts with the ideal being that coexists [*Koexistent*] with the creative spirit and belongs to it.

[Matter and spirit]

We set out to identify —completely if we could— the realms of material [*material*] being and to examine the role act and potency play in each of them. A first area we isolated is the region of material things. This region, as we saw, contrasts with other regions which because of this very contrast are {84} already somewhat clear but need to be studied on their own. These other regions are that of the spirit and that of ideal objects; in other words the regions of the subjective and objective spirit. The material [*material*] idea or *basic category* governing this area and marking the scope of the corresponding material ontology is *the idea of the material* [*materiell*] *thing*. The individuals of this genus are the be-ings of this area, and reality [*Realität*] is their specific mode of being. Our essential task is to investigate this basic category, in regard to its inner makeup, as well as the mode of being of reality. Another is to identify the species into which the guiding idea of this genus may be differentiated.

Our inquiry so far can only be preliminary, especially since it has shown that the "material [*materiell*]" thing is not purely material and should properly be understood in its makeup first from the viewpoint of spirit. This is why we have not revisited all the questions that arose when we were discussing the material thing, such as how the material can be known, how it "enters" the knowing mind. Our analysis of the material thing that took us as far as its spiritual origin and portrayed its "nature" as something which itself is not material suggests that we can also understand how it is received into the mind in knowledge.

But this understanding cannot come *merely* from an analysis of the material; it also requires that we first analyze spirit and then explain it in a study of knowledge. A further area appeared in connection with these questions: the area of living matter. It seems to hold an ontic position between spirit and matter. But we found we had to bring in the spiritual to shed light on the material, while we could leave what is "just living" unexplained. Hence our most pressing task is to undertake the ontology of the spirit, since from that quarter we may expect to get pointers for all of ontology.[139]

---

[139]   The study of material nature will be taken up again in VI, § 12ff.

V
Attempt to Define Spirit

§ 1
Provisional description of spiritual being.

[Spiritual life]

We have already made several claims about the essence of spirit as such when distinguishing it from matter, and within spirit we have distinguished between *subjective* and *objective* spirit, between God's *infinite* spirit and *created* spirits and between *pure* spirit and its connections with what is not spiritual.

We may begin by using the polarity of subject and object that we are calling *"intentionality"* to describe *what being that is spiritual in the subjective sense is. Spiritual life* or *living*, the highest form of spiritual being, means being stretched between these two poles and aiming at an object.[140] "Life" we would define as movement from itself and "the living" as what moves from itself. This is also a strict definition since it applies to life and to nothing else, but it does not cover the fullness of the meaning of "life," nor can any definition encompass life since it is something ultimate.

[Act]

We may take *"Intentionality," "intelligibility,"* and *"personhood"* as special distinctive marks of *spiritual* living. In modern philosophy the intentional life of the spirit is called *act* [*Akt*],[141] but the word here

---

[140] We shall presently show that this is not the only form of spiritual being.

[141] I have done this myself in all my earlier works, following Husserl's terminology.

envisages something much more limited than what we take it to mean in our present work following scholastic usage. We have found three meanings for the scholastic term "act": [1] an inner principle of form, [2] the "act of *being*," and [3] the "act of *activity* [*Tätigkeit*]" or as we usually say, [2] "actuality [*Aktualität*]" and [3] "activity [*Aktivität*]." The idea of activity prevails in the modern concept of act, but it does include actuality (activity, after all, presupposes actuality).

Taken in a wider sense, "activity" scarcely implies more than intentionality; I mean, the specific effect of the being of spirit, which can {86} be further divided into activity and passivity (as "*actus*" in the Thomistic sense, too, is subdivided into "*actio* [action]" and "*passio* [undergoing]").[142] But this already limits the concept of act to the spiritual area, which lies far from the scholastic concept of act. (However, there is a certain ontological basis for this limitation which can be gathered from our previous remarks and will shortly be taken up again.)[143]

[Eternal and temporal spirit]

The preference of modern philosophy for *finite* spirits brings in another restriction, for it sees act as something timebound, something having a beginning and an end, or even something momentary. *This* restriction at any rate we must lift if we wish to get to the essence of spirit as such. If the highest form of spiritual being is an actuality that takes effect in intentional activity, then an infinite spirit must be actual and active from eternity and for all eternity, its "act" must lack beginning and end. In contrast, a temporal act appears as a limitation of actuality and so as a lower form of spiritual being.

---

[142]   In my German translation of the *Quaestiones de veritate*: vol. 1, loc. cit., note, p. 329 <reedition, p. 296>.

[143]   P. 127.

[Actuality, intentionality, intelligibility]

We are claiming that actuality, as the highest form of being, pertains to spirit; an actuality which takes effect in that special activity we call intentionality. Acts can be classified according to their different objects as well as according to their directions toward these objects. We shall deal with this possibility later when we consider the differences between the infinite spirit and finite spirits.

Now, what we called "being illumined [*Durchleuchtetsein*]," *intelligibilitas* [intelligibility], also pertains necessarily to any kind of spiritualness. It does not belong to every form of spiritual being *actually* but to the highest form it can attain. For the subjective spirit this means existing for itself and for what is objectively spiritual it means existing for a spiritual subject.

§ 2
Subjective and objective spirit.
The I, person, spiritual substance.

[Subject, substance, person]

In order to describe briefly what spirit is as such and its mode of being, we must say something more about the kinds or *forms of spiritual objects* [*Gegenstandsform des Geistigen*]. If before we could not get along without bringing in its different forms, now we can do so even less. *Subject* and *object* [*Objekt*] are the two possible forms of objects [*Gegenstand*]. The distinction is not logical (since both may be a logical subject) but ontological. Subjectivity is the original form {87} of spiritual object. In contrast, being a spiritual object in the sense of existing for a subject, is derived.

The "*subjectum*" = "ὑποκείμενον [*hypokeimenon*]," literally, is what lies under, the bearer [*Träger*] of spiritual life. There are, by the way, differences in the use of the Latin and Greek terms. "Ὑποκείμενον" is usually used for a *logical* subject and secondarily for matter [*Materie*], as what underlies the forming, but not so much for what we are getting at here. For *this* sense we use the word "ὑπόστασις" = hypostasis, which is the *linguistic* counterpart to "substance." "Substance" and "subject," however, have different meanings. The subject is what the spiritual life proceeds from and what is primary for it. The spiritual subject is inconceivable without spiritual life, for such is its being. Still, the spiritual subject does not "presuppose" spiritual life; it is rather the other way around, for in spiritual life the subject "finds fulfillment." This implies that the subject "underlies it as its basis." It is a beginning of being.

This does not imply that the spiritual subject must be "from itself." Finite spirits are not from themselves; that is, they do not come into existence through their own power. But they are "by themselves [*für sich*]"; that is, by entering into existence they are on their own. "Hypostasis" is the specific term for this self-constancy [*Selbst-Ständigkeit*]. We shall even go ahead and restrict the word to this purely formal sense that does not include spiritualness, and we shall call what is selfsufficient, insofar as it is something spiritual, a "*person.*" We would therefore have to identify "spiritual subject" and "*person.*" The person is what *is* spiritual originally. Does "person" mean only the be-ing's original form as an object in the region of the spirit? To answer this question, it may help to ask another: is the person a substance?

[Individuation of the I]

"Substance," if we take the word in the Thomistic sense as what is not in another, means the same as "hypostasis" and is included in "person." If we take "substance" for what activates its being in certain effects and —where it is something variable— persists throughout its variations, we intend something more than what selfsufficiency implies, even though without this something selfsufficiency is not possible *realiter*. We intend, namely, the fact that something objective [*sachlich*], something material [*material*], must exist [*vorhanden sein*] that can persist and activate itself in a definite way. In the spiritual area, this means that there must be something that is more than a pure subject of spiritual living devoid of qualities (which I called the "pure I" in the first chapter, using Husserl's term). A spiritual substance is a spiritual subject having a *what* of definite content.

Because every I is something singular, the spiritual subject is an individual. We have seen that there are {88} several principles of individuation. The species itself realized in a concrete individual may be something unique, one of a kind in its qualities; or a species admitting of multiple realizations may be individuated by an external principle. In the case of lifeless things, we found the individuation principle to be the "piece of matter" informed by some species.

Now, how are spiritual individuals individuated? Here it may be precisely the species that is doing the individuating (according to Thomas such is the case with the angels). It is also conceivable that the species is individuated by the fact that the being of the spiritual subject is bound to a piece of matter, its *material* body (according to Thomas such is the case with human individuals; on this theory we have yet to take a stand).

[A third individuation theory]

Now, there is a third theory to be considered, namely, that the I as such *is* an individual, even apart from its bond to a material body and apart from the species that distinguishes it from other individuals in its qualities. Being separate from everything else lies in the being of the I, and the I can grasp it in its consciousness of itself. This self-consciousness is something that cannot be mistaken for any consciousness of something else; an I can only call itself "I" and can "have" itself in such wise that it can say "I."

But it is possible to distinguish among subjects other than my own only on the basis of one of the two above-mentioned individuation principles that differentiate individuals through their qualities. But even though the I as such is not individuated by its qualities, this does not mean that it could *be* without qualities. The being of the I is conscious life ("consciousness" here may still include differences; I mean, various kinds and degrees of consciousness), and in the continuity of such living a "stream of consciousness," as it is called, is built up. Although we can conceive of the I without qualities, we cannot conceive of the stream of consciousness without qualities, for it must be qualitatively fulfilled.

[I and person]

Where does this fullness come from, and where does the I get its qualities? The life of the I is stimulated at [*an*] something outside, at "objects [*Gegenstand*]" that "come to consciousness." But the I is not an empty form that life is put into from without; its life rather comes from itself. Hence something exists that takes effect in living, and this something must have its own qualities and it must bestow qualities, although the objects whereat conscious life is stimulated *also* give qualities to the stream of consciousness. So we cannot imagine any being of the I where the I lacked substance; spiritual being requires a spiritual substance. Consequently, we may answer our question in this way: being a spiritual substance pertains to the person. Person denotes not just the form of object in the spiritual region, but at the same time the need for an individual substance to fill this form.

§ 3
Infinite and finite persons.

[Two senses of selfsufficiency and duration]

Living is spiritual being in its highest form. Life springs from a living thing. This living thing is the person. The person has self-sufficient and enduring being. Both "selfsufficiency" and "duration" have two senses. "Selfsufficiency" can mean being by itself, *in se, non in alio esse* [being in itself, not in another]. This is true of any finite person. Or "selfsufficiency" may mean to be through itself or from itself— *a se, non ab alio esse* [from itself, not from another]. This applies only to an uncreated person, not to any created person.

"Duration" can mean to be in time, fulfill a length of time. Or it can mean to be from eternity and hence to be throughout all time. The former sense applies to finite persons, the second to an infinite person. What is in time can only be *ab alio* and ultimately can stem only from the One, which is not *ab alio* but *a se*. From the One all finite persons and all spiritual life —all creation for that matter— must come forth. Here alone is the original —in the strict sense— be-ing of the spiritual region as well as of any other. What begins to be can only be brought about by an activity that goes forth from something actual. All actuality harks back to the pure actuality proper only to the infinite, pure spirit. A pure act in the full sense that includes actuality and activity is God's being, the being of the infinite, pure spirit. (The ontological basis for restricting the word "act" to spiritual activity we should see in the fact that all activity ultimately harks back to spiritual activity.)[144]

---

[144] Cf. p. 122 above.

[Persons divine and finite]

Wherein lies the common ground between God and finite persons that allows us to speak of "person" in either case? It lies in the analogy of being [*Analogie des Seins*], in the analogy of being a person and of spiritual living. God alone possesses personhood as selfsufficiency in the unrestricted sense of *aseitas* [being from oneself] But there is a genuine analogy between the infinite person and created spiritual subjects that justifies our speaking of them, too, as persons. Every spiritual subject is a *beginning* wherefrom two things come forth: the subject's own spiritual living and something that this spiritual living brings about but after coming into existence has its own being, or in other words, something that continually depends on the spirit that produces it and something that becomes independent of it. The latter are "spiritual objects [*geistiges Objekt*]" or items that are spiritual in the objective sense [*objektiv-geistiges Gebilde*].

God's being is from eternity and is immutable, for He *has* no beginning and *in Him* nothing begins. His whole being is *one* act; that is, He is eternal actuality and activity. But He *is the* beginning, the {90} *principium* [beginning, principle]. *From Him* whatever has a beginning sets forth. Created things have a beginning and in them something constantly has its beginning, and this is their *major dissimilitudo* [greater unlikeness] to the divine being.

[Analogies]

But what begins in created things, their acts that come to be and pass away, are finite analogues of God's infinite actuality and activity. The continuity of life maintaining itself throughout constant change is an analogue of the unchanging divine life. New being springing from spiritual acts is analogous to the divine creating power. Those acts that are called "act" in the specific sense of being "free" or "deliberate"[145] are an analogue of divine freedom. That acts are *conscious*, that is, existing for themselves in a certain way, is analogous to divine self-knowledge. Acts that conceive something else, grasping it in its order and connectedness and treating it in accordance with this order, are analogous to divine wisdom and reason.

All this is but a title for more extensive analyses that would everywhere follow out the *similitudo* [likeness] and *maior dissimilitudo* [greater unlikeness] of God and created subjects. All we wanted to do here was sketch briefly what "personhood" has in common to God and creature; namely, that a person is something whose being is enduring spiritual living and in this living is free, conscious, rational, creative activity.[146]

§ 4

Spiritual life as intellectual life.

Living means being in motion from within. Living *spiritually* also means being aware of this motion, being illumined for oneself, being conscious of oneself and possibly of something else— *intelligere* [understanding]—, setting oneself and something else in motion from oneself. In God all of this is one and simple; in us it is a manifold of different acts. God beholds Himself from eternity; from eternity He holds the creation and its order before His eyes as well as all possible worlds that He has not made real [*verwirklichen*]. From eternity He has destined the real [*wirklich*] world for its reality [*Wirklichkeit*] and called it into existence for a determined time. What stands before the divine spirit from eternity, the world of ideas, we have called a first

---

145   Cf. my analysis in "Beiträge zur philosophischen Begründung der Psychologie und der Geisteswissenschaften," <loc. cit.>, pp. 46ff.

146   More on the *analogia entis* [analogy of being] of the person is found below, pp. 218ff and 406ff.

realm of *objective spirit.* We used this expression first because <the ideas> {91} belong to the spirit but also because the divine life takes effect in their midst and makes them effective in His creation.

All this has analogies in created spirits. Their living falls into several dimensions. [1] Acts follow one after another in temporal sequence [*Nacheinander*], [2] acts occur beside one another at the same time [*Nebeneinander*], and [3] acts are from one another in their qualities [*Auseinander*] (and this in two senses: an act is separate from others and stems from others in a network). But whatever is separate springs from *one* living impulse and merges with it again into a unity of being that is not a composition. The separating and splitting take place when "contents" are taken in and processed. A world of objects is built up therein for the subject.

§ 5
Created pure spirits
(knowledge of God, self, material things, others).

[Thomistic angelology]

We must, however, distinguish between spirits that come into existence already having an actual spiritual possession and those that acquire their entire actual spiritual possession during their lifetime. The Thomistic theory of angels describes the former case.[147] Thomas says we should think of angels as pure, yet created, spirits. They have once begun to be; their being has been bestowed upon them along with a particular endowment. He explains the knowledge of angels as an intuition of things through species with which they are naturally endowed. They know themselves through their essence, which is always present

---

[147]   For St. Thomas's theory of angels see *De veritate*, questions 8 and 9, and *De spiritualibus creaturis* (*Quaestiones disputatis*, III).

to them. They know God through the divine essence, which unites itself <to> them as an inner form or species. And they communicate with one another through a spiritual turning of attention which is their "speech."

[Act and potency in angels]

This account raises a number of questions which should not be ignored here. If the being of pure spirits is not absolutely actual, is there an opposition of act and (unactualized) potency in them? Yes, of course, on this theory.[148] The pure spirit's "pureness" means that it lacks any connection with what is spatially material.

However, we see a division in these spirits that is not found in God. First, what they are is distinct from their being. They are not always actually everything that they are. This, as {92} we learned in the formal part of this work, has to do with the fact that they are creatures. In anything that is not *a se* [from itself] and has received its being, what it is is related to the being that it receives as potency to act, and the possibility of nonbeing remains ever open, the possibility that the actuality and what is actual ceases in whole or in part.[149] What such a created spirit itself is and what it is in itself [*an sich*] —its essence [*seine Essenz, sein Wesen*]— we should consider as actual throughout the entire duration of its being.

[Self-awareness]

Now, there are several forms and degrees of the actual being of angels. The highest degree is that of conscious being, where "consciousness" has two senses, for angels are aware both of their own

---

148   Thomas argues that act and potency are found in spiritual substances explicitly in *De spiritualibus creaturis*, a. 1.

149   We shall show later (pp. 349z and 382ff) that *what* a finite spirit is, is also an act (− form) of something absolutely potential.

being and of their own essence [*Essenz*] (which in their case, according to Thomas, is an individual species). Thomas does not regard their awareness of their own essence as enduring actual knowledge. The enduring actuality of their essence involves only a potentiality for self-knowledge. We should surely not see the transition from potential to actual self-knowledge as a heightening of their being [*Seinssteigerung*]; I mean, it is not a transition from some lower degree of spiritual being (unconscious, unillumined) to a higher one (conscious, illumined). Clearly, we should take the self-knowledge of the pure spirit as an actual turning of its attention toward its self [*Selbst*] (to its being or to its essence).

Self-consciousness, however, need not entail turning toward oneself. It is precisely in the deepest concentration of our mental life that we are turned mainly not towards ourselves but to the object that we are concerned with and are giving our undivided attention to. In regard to what the pure spirit is in itself, its essence (or as we shall say later, its personal core [*personaler Kern*]), we should see this highest form of the being of its concentrated spiritual life, but not its turning toward itself, as enduring.[150] The case is different with what the created spirit is not of itself but with what it has or what applies to it accidentally. The knowledge it has of God is not its own in virtue of its own essence nor does it belong to its own being; God rather gives it this knowledge by uniting His divine essence to the essence of this creature.

[Prophets and the knowledge of God]

Unlike matter, spirit is not impenetrable. One spirit can be where another is. Since spirits are nonspatial, this does not mean that they are in the same place; it means either that they are mentally grasping the same object (whenever the object is spatial it is also meaningful to say

---

150   Cf. pp. 200f.

that they are at the same place) or that one is in the other.

The prophet is "grasped [*ergreifen*] {93} by God." "God speaks from him"— things that he cannot know of his natural knowledge, perhaps in a language that in his natural mental state he does not know at all. His spirit, when grasped by God, is not suppressed or displaced by the divine spirit grasping it; rather, it is actually "grasped," pervaded. The prophet is also said to be enlightened by the divine light, because to him it is given to see things inaccessible to the "natural light" of his own understanding. "And in thy light we behold the light."[151]

Spiritual being in the actuality of living [*Lebensaktualität*] is transparent (intelligible) being. It is first of all transparent for itself [*für sich selbst durchsichtig*]. God is conscious of Himself; but the one He grasps can also become conscious of the divine being grasping him. Where the measure of grasping and being grasped is different, there is also a difference in the measure of knowing God; there are degrees of being enlightened. Higher angels differ from lower angels, says Thomas, by having more enlightenment, but he is thinking here of their "natural light," that is, of the knowing power they are endowed with, the hallmark of their own spiritual essence.

[Supernatural enlightenment]

We should see this light as something that the angels possess enduringly, yet not as something immutably fixed. This is so in the first place because angels are open to "supernatural [*übernatürlich*]" enlightenment from the divine light. This openness [*Zugänglichkeit*] itself is a *potency*, more precisely a *passive* potency, proper to the created spirit. It is shifted into actuality when the created spirit is grasped

---

[151]   <Psalm 35 [36]:10.>

by God. This new act is therefore a higher mode of being than the natural act. At the same time, it is an "act" in the sense of activity, of a new activation of the enlightened spirit's living [*Lebensbetätigung*]; it is an "act of knowing God."

We may consider this supernatural knowledge of God as something that is freely given to pure spirits from the very beginning and for the duration of their being, but it might also be bestowed upon them only temporarily. In neither case should we think that it is a gift that God leaves with the recipient as a possession without further troubling about it. Rather, the gift is actually in effect throughout the entire duration of its being by God's presence in the angel's spirit.

[Communication among angels]

Just as God works in the created spirits by bringing about a transition from potentiality to actuality, that is, to a higher mode of being and, as its result, to a new spiritual activity, the created spirits also affect one another and thereby cause change in their actual living, in their being. No angel is like another; the essence of each is its own individual {94} species, and each has its own mode of being as well. A different "natural light," that is, a particular measure of knowledge, corresponds to each mode of being. Thomas assumes that the lower angels can be "enlightened" by the higher, hence that their being and knowledge can be heightened. Indeed, he even assumes that the lower angels are enlightened *only* through the mediation of higher angels and not directly by God since God has assigned this work to the angels as their highest likeness to God.

He is, however, taking "enlightenment" here in a sense that differs somewhat from its previous use, for he means in particular strengthening the knowing power to know external things. He does not seem to be thinking of mediating the knowledge of God, in the sense of that "supernatural" knowledge that only the divine essence can give. The *natural* knowledge of God, which Thomas also attributes to angels, could also be heightened by a higher angel raising the natural knowing power of the lower.

We may find a better way to understand this heightening and the connections among the angels that it supposes by asking what kinds of knowledge they have besides their knowledge of God and of themselves. I mean that we should ask how angels know one other's essences, how they know what is taking place in the other angels, and how they know external things.

[Angelic and human knowledge of material things]

According to Thomas the knowledge of material things is knowledge through forms that the human understanding works out for itself, whereas the angels are provided with them by nature. This is his reason. All knowledge rests on a similarity of the knower and the known. The resemblance can rest on one being the cause of the other. In this way God's essence is the cause of things, and this is why things are likenesses of His essence and why He can know them through their archetype.

In human knowledge the resemblance rests on the fact that the things known are the primal cause [*Ur-sache*] and the primal type [*Ur-bild*] of the forms that our understanding receives. Upon receiving them the understanding functions both actively and passively. Two transitions from potentiality to actuality take place here at the same time. [1] The forms of the things become *actu intelligibiles* [understandable in act], more precisely through the activity of the understanding, through the *intellectus agens* [agent intellect], and [2] our *intellectus possibilis* [possible intellect] passes over to actual knowledge.

We cannot as yet enter upon a closer study and interpretation of the "active" and "possible" (= ready for knowledge) intellect. The process should obviously be so interpreted that the result, the actual knowledge, is simple. Indeed, it is even quite often claimed that the knower and object of his knowledge "become one" or "coincide" in knowledge. There are {95} two starting points, and on both sides there is an actual and a potential aspect. [1] The "form" or "species" of material things is actual as their *own* form, but it is *"potentiā intelligibilis* [intelligible in potency]"; it is a possible object [*Gegenstand*] of knowledge. [2] The understanding is potential insofar as it is not yet *in actu illius formae* [in the act of that form]; I mean that it still does not possess actual knowledge of the thing in question, but it does have the possibility and even the positive readiness to pass over into this actual knowledge. And the understanding is actual insofar as it is a living spirit and as such it is in motion; that is, the *intellectus agens* that sets out for knowledge.

The work of the agent intellect regarding this particular actuality of knowledge is conditioned by an activity coming from the other side: the effect of the thing's form. The thing's species and the intellect shift mutually from potency to act. This shifting would not be possible if something absolutely material stood on the one side and something absolutely spiritual stood on the other since potency and act must belong to the same genus. According to Thomas, the shifting is made possible by the mediating position of the sensibility. We have still not gotten far enough to be able to understand this; here we needed an account of the Thomistic theory of the human knowledge of material things —as much as we have included— only to contrast it with angelic knowledge.

[Angelic knowledge of things]

Since pure spirits have nothing in common with matter, they cannot be affected by material things. If they are to have knowledge corresponding to material things, they cannot receive it from without but must possess the species corresponding to them by nature. They need not, however, be always intuiting actually everything that is naturally accessible to them. The will, not only the understanding, plays a role in knowledge. In ourselves, the will shares in bringing about actual knowledge by moving the *intellectus agens*. In angels, the will contributes by actualizing some of the knowledge they possess naturally; the will determines what is actualized and how much of it is actualized.

Unlike us, angels do not gradually acquire additional knowledge; in them there is no "discursive" knowing. The number of forms "in the mind" of the angel does not correspond to the number of individual things that their knowledge covers. They see individual things through general forms and with a single look they take in all the things that correspond to the actualized form. The more general, hence the fewer, the forms and the more that can be encompassed by one form, the higher the knowledge (God encompasses all real and possible individual things with his simple essence). Thus the difference in the knowledge of the higher and lower angels consists in the number of their forms and in their power {96} to grasp them, but "enlightenment" takes place when the higher angel shares its knowledge with the lower and the lower intuits it in the "higher."

[Communication among angels]

How does this contact between one angel and another come about? On the one hand it occurs when one "opens, discloses, itself" to the other. A lower angel may also open itself to a higher one. No angel by itself can see inside another since this cannot occur unless the angel that is to be known wills it. Only God can penetrate the will and move it from within.

On the other hand, what lies in one angel becomes accessible to another if the latter freely turns its attention to it, thus allowing something to become actual in itself. This is angelic "speech." However, they have need of this speech —so it seems— only to share what is taking place in them actually. Their knowledge of each other's essence, insofar as it is common to them, takes place through the essence proper to each. But to know the species belonging to each, they need forms impressed upon them, similarly to their knowledge of things.

[Knowledge in God and in the higher angels]

The knowledge that angels have in God, their intuition of creatures in the Word (called "morning knowledge" after St. Augustine), differs from the knowledge they have by nature through their essence and their impressed forms. There seems to be an essential difference between their intuition in God and their intuition in a higher angel (and so between their being enlightened by God and by a higher angel). We described enlightenment by God as a union of essence [*Wesenseinigung*]; since God's knowledge pertains to His essence, one must, insofar as one is grasped by Him, also become privy to His knowledge (it is impossible for any creature to do this perfectly).

[Essence and knowledge]

Can there also be a union of essence among created spirits? A generic commonness of essence [*Wesensgemeinsamkeit*] enables one angel to know the generic essence through its own essence without actual union. It may be the knowledge that the knowing angel itself has of its own (generic) essence joined to the knowledge that this generic essence is also proper to the other angels without this knowledge being "in them." Analogously, the knowledge of another angel's specific essence can be knowledge (that is, a becoming actual) of the corresponding form in the knowing angel together with an intention toward the other angel without being knowledge of the species *in* the other's specific essence known through the form.

In such knowledge, provided it is not essential, one angel does not enter into the knowledge possessed by another. One created spirit does not enter the other unless the latter wills it. But where admission is sought and granted, and insofar as this is the case, there does seem to be a union. Here both the generic and the specific knowledge of the other angel's essence may be {97} knowledge in the "other," and here for the first time there is full actual knowledge in the sense of the "coinciding" of knower and known. In virtue of such voluntary union, knowledge of what the other angel knows is also possible "in it."

§ 6
Problems of *species intelligibiles*
and objective spirit.

[Forms in angels, God, and human beings]

We have found the actual and the potential in pure spirits. What these spirits are essentially, namely the person and its substance, which is an individual species, is enduringly actual. Spiritual living is actuality; it includes knowing and willing and represents a movement wherein changing forms are shifted from potency to act. I daresay that these forms continue to be what is most troublesome. They do not belong to the essence but are "*inditae*" —"put into" it—, "*innatae*" —"inborn [*eingeboren*]" in it—, "*impressae*" — "pressed" into it.

These expressions are all metaphors. What is the meaning behind them? Our analogues here are the ideas of the divine spirit that we sought to characterize as a realm of "objective spirit" which does not inhere in God's personal essence but "stands before Him" as well as the "concepts" and "ideas" of the human mind. An analysis of what lies closest to us can best help us clarify all these items and thus settle the meaning of "objective spirit" as such.

a. Human "ideas."

[Idea and concept]

"Concept," "idea"— these words are by no means unambiguous even for us today. They have something in common —and precisely what is germane to our discussion—; namely, they are the middle ground between the knowing mind (the subjective, personal spirit) and its objects [*Gegenstand*]. We say of a man or even of an essay that they are "full of ideas" but lack precise concepts. We could also use "thought [*Gedanke*]" instead of "idea" in this sense. The present Chancellor[152] has come in with a whole series of "new ideas [*Idee*]" to conduct the affairs of the Republic; for example, he has the idea of lowering salaries and prices. Here we could not replace "idea" with "concept." Idea in this last sense is very complicated, and it includes the intention to shape actual living conditions; it is a *practical* idea. "Idea" as such does not necessarily include the two senses, theoretical and practical, but it does allow {98} them, whereas "concept" excludes *this* sort of "combination" as well as the practical sense. A concept is a purely theoretical item; I mean, its task is to grasp objects [*Gegenstand*] with the understanding.

There are ideas that are simpler than the one mentioned above and such as are purely theoretical. We can speak of the "idea of price" and of the "concept of price." The two here are quite close, and they

---

[152]   [Heinrich Brüning was *Reichskanzler* of the Weimar Republic when Edith was writing.]

allow us to form a sharper definition. Anyone reading or hearing the above sentence *understands* the word "price" and associates a definite *sense* or *meaning* with it. But by no means will everybody be able to spell out what he "means by the word" or narrow it down ("define" it) so that it is unambiguous and cannot be confused with anything else. Only someone having the "concept of price" can do this.

The sense of a word or phrase, perhaps apart from its link to a definite sound, is a possible meaning of "idea."[153] It is a meaningful whole [*Sinnganzes*] that does not require analysis. On the other hand, a concept "consists" of elements that should be sharply distinguished ("notes [*Merkmal*]"), that can enable us to define its "range" unambiguously. Either may serve to examine the middle ground between the knowing spirit and its objects.

[The chestnut tree]

"The leaf-buds on our chestnut tree opened yesterday." I intend a quite definite individual thing here: the chestnut tree in our garden. But I mean it "under a general [*allgemein*] idea." When I looked out into the garden, I knew it was a chestnut by its thick, shiny buds, and yesterday I deliberately looked to see if it had leaves.

What role does the general idea play in the intuition of the individual thing? We may see trees without knowing what kind they are, but we know at least that we have a tree before us. In any clear, distinct intuition (in perceiving [*Wahrnehmung*] or in picturing [*Vergegenwärtigung*]), the individual thing is "conceived as something" or "considered under a general idea." And we are missing something in the intuition if it is so vague and blurred that we cannot conceive the object as something definite; an intention toward some-

---

153   We have earlier seen another meaning of "idea"; we need not explain here how the two are connected.

thing definite does exist, but it is unfulfilled, empty.

Intuiting differs from the mere fact that the "senses are affected [*Affektion*]" in that an intuition is {99} "filled with spirit" and "an idea (usually a whole series of ideas) lives in the intuition." The expressions "filled with spirit" and "the idea living in the intuition" show exactly what we have just now been after. It is not the quite the same thing when I "look for the chestnut tree" and when I "know it as a chestnut tree." When I am looking for the tree, I focus on some definite thing whose shape is familiar to me in several ways (I name it after these familiar features). I need no "image, picture [*Bild*]" of what "chestnut tree" conveys *besides* the tree that I see before me, nor need I make any comparison.

Only the "intention," the direction toward the tree as the tree with this shape, is "in me"; it is an intention fulfilled in a definite way when I direct my look at *the* tree with this shape that I was looking for. As long as my look had not found the tree that I was "looking for," the intention was different, and the two stand in a particular relationship that we call "fulfillment."[154]

Instead of saying "the intention is in me," I could more aptly say "I am in the intention." Being directed to something in this way or that way is indeed my spiritual living; and "this way or that" are features that I can discern in my various "acts." An "image" in the strict sense of the word is not present at all in such an intention. It is neither inside myself (in the most proper sense no image at all can be in a spiritual subject) nor outside myself; the thing I mean stands before me in my intuition, but it fails to portray anything for me. (In our present con-

---

[154]   The term comes from Husserl's *Logische Untersuchungen* <new critical edition in *Husserliana*, vol. 19, 1, edited by U. Panzer, The Hague, Boston, Lancaster, 1948> [English translation *Logical Investigations*, by J. N. Findlay, 2 vols., New York, Humanities Press, 1970], where the relationship between intention and fulfillment is treated in detail (cf. especially the sixth investigation published in a separate volume <II, 2> in the reedition of 1921).

cern, the analysis of the intuition itself, it does not matter if it portrays anything objectively [*objektiv*].) In the thing itself, I see the species "chestnut tree" that corresponds to my intention.

[Recognizing a chestnut tree]

The process is somewhat different when I know the tree as a chestnut. I saw the tree the other day with its thick, shiny buds, and I suddenly realized: why, that's a chestnut tree. There is a duality here: the tree I see before me and what I know it as. An image *may* play a part here when I picture a chestnut tree that I have seen elsewhere. But it *need* not play a part.

It may also happen that the tree I see before me "snaps into" the type that I know, or that the type confronts me when I had {100} not been expecting it (as in the case just mentioned). However, to come upon something I know (= knowing it as something) is a definite sort of intention "wherein I am." There will be two specifically different intentions when encountering something is foreseen and when it is unexpected. But if recalling also plays a part, the species I perceive in the tree must be the same as the species in the tree that I am imagining if picturing is to help us to "know it as."

[Idea vs. perception and imagination of the chestnut]

Is the species that confronts me as an intuitive type the species of the thing? The question is still not unambiguous. From the concrete species, from the entire *what* of the thing as it is now, we have distinguished the more general species and the genus (chestnut tree, tree, plant) that are also realized in the thing. We can do with the inclusive term "*idea*" for the whole "general" aspect realized in the particular thing (following the Platonic use of the word). Our question now is whether we must distinguish *this* idea as an *objective* [*objektiv*] idea from what we called an idea in our previous analysis or whether the two are the same.

What the word "chestnut tree" means for me may be an intuitive type.[155] It does not mean everything I have before me in a sense perception of a particular tree (which contains much that is "contingent," what is proper to this tree alone, perhaps only at the present time, wherein the meaning of the name is not fulfilled for me). On the other hand, much that belongs to my idea may be missing in what I have before me; for example, when I see the tree before it blossoms, while its distinctive flowers are what primarily determines the meaning of the word for me.

"My idea," therefore, is clearly distinct from the concrete appearance of the individuals in question as they confront me when I perceive or imagine them. I can find my idea again and focus on it only in each of such intuitions, even though I may find only a part of its stock of content [*Bestand*]. Unlike the individual appearances or the real things that appear in them like this or like that, the idea is characterized as a unity rather than a plurality.

[Our ideas and objective ideas]

Now, is this idea *of mine* as a unit the same as the ideas others associate with the word "chestnut tree"? By no means can we say this. There are people who have less accurate knowledge than my own and so their idea is "poorer"; on the other hand botanists have a much "richer" idea than mine. The total content of our ideas is different in each of us; the idea of some people may contain something that does not jibe with reality at all. Hence the idea is bound to the individual {101} mind.

---

[155]   The question of the intuitability of the idea will be taken up again below, p. 145.

On the other hand we ascribe an objective meaning to our words and through them we make ourselves understood; but then there must be meaningful content [*Bedeutungsgehalt*] common to our words. Just by speaking we claim to be understood and are convinced that our meaning is objective. When I read or hear a word that I do not understand, I automatically assume that it "means something" although "I do not associate any definite meaning with it." In many cases I know that the idea I associate with a word is quite meager and does not come anywhere near its objective meaning.

[Objective meaning]

Now, what is this "objective meaning"? Is it something in the things themselves? We do say that our ideas find complete or partial fulfillment in our intuition of things. When I say that the chestnut tree in the cemetery is further along than the one in the garden, by my words I mean a definite individual thing here and another definite thing there, as well as something identical in both, and anyone who hears these words will understand it in this way. We are thus directed to the things outside in the world and to the same things as well as to the same "universal [*Allgemeines*]" in them— "through" our several ideas.

Is this universal the "objective meaning" of the term? The universal is the species "chestnut tree" which is effective in the tree as its inner form and makes it an object of such a sort and also makes it appear to us like this and like that. Supposing that a botanist knew everything about chestnut tree as such; would his idea then be the objective idea, would it coincide with the species in the thing?

[Approach to the objective]

We spoke just now of the "subjective idea" as an intuitive type that can be brought into greater or lesser focus at the appearance of the thing. The species in the thing is not intuitive in this sense; it *determines* the appearance but does not enter it. But even the subjective idea need not be intuitive or in any case not in every respect. No doubt a good deal of what the scientist knows, but what cannot become intuitive at all, enters his idea. "Our" ideas may be intuitive, and they may be abstract; the average idea is a mixture of both.

When we go from the idea to the concept —obviously the case in scientific thought— the entire stock of content is "abstract." Although the concept may correspond in content to the species in the thing more fully than the intuitive idea, it is an object of the understanding freely acting, and it is acquired and formed by thinking. This is why in the concept the bond to the thinking spirit stands out in particularly stark relief, nor can there be any question of equating it with the species in the thing. Hence we must say that all "subjective" ideas can {102} but tally more or less with the objective species; they coincide completely in the ideal case, but they are never identical. Human knowledge can never reach the ideal of complete agreement; yet such is the aim of all our labors to acquire knowledge.

[Noesis and Noema]

We must then distinguish another, a third, thing from the objective species and from the many subjective ideas that corresponds to it, namely, the subjective idea that is *idealiter* [ideally] brought to completion [*vollenden*], and because of its completeness [*Vollendung*] attains the character of a relative objectivity [*Objektivität*]. When we speak, we mean the things themselves (in our usual, unreflective attitude). But our ideas of things "bear" this intention and at the same time point beyond themselves to the "ideal idea" that would tally perfectly with the species of the thing. This, the place where all subjective ideas meet and if brought to completion would coincide, is the objective meaning of the term.

This analysis of our ideas has led us to espy something that clearly lies between the subjective (personal) spirit and its objects. They constitute a realm that belongs to a particular personal spirit. Actual spiritual life is lived in intentions. Husserl introduced the word "noesis" for this subjective aspect of the spiritual life in all its forms (of which we have only seen one) and "noema" for its objective (that is, relatively objective) correlate.

There is a thorough correlation between noesis and noema; they are two sides of the same thing. In our present case this implies that I cannot mean anything without meaning it "under an idea." In the limiting case, where the material content of the thing is completely undetermined, the empty, formal "this here" remains, and we take it that it has a content. The middle position of the ideas shows two links. [1] They would tally with what the thing is (in our analysis we have taken the general species as the *what*; we could also have taken the concrete whatness or the genus). [2] Also, they "bear" the intention of the intuiting or thinking spirit; they are "animated" by it; the intention "goes through them." What do all these metaphorical expressions mean?

[The mountain]

What an intellectually mature man can discern in himself (that is, immanently) when he reflects on the acts through which he experiences something from the world outside will always be a spiritual movement wherein already existing ideas play a part. Our present concern does not allow us to go into the genesis of this spiritual possession or discuss how we might make immanent statements about the first beginnings of spiritual living. A systematic phenomenology of knowledge would not ignore these questions. For our {103} purpose we shall content ourselves with the simplest case possible, one that occurs often in the spiritual life of an adult.

I am traveling in a mountainous region unfamiliar to me. Some time before I arrive at my destination something appears on the horizon. At first I cannot tell what it is, whether it is a cloud or a mountain peak. Soon sharply defined contours take shape; it is the mountain, and my journey's end lies at its foot. During my stay I learn more and more about the mountain. On my walks I come to see it from all sides; its form and color reveal themselves in all their different aspects. I learn what sorts of rock it is made of, what kind of forest covers it, what flowers grow on its slopes. From the summit I look out in all directions and from other places. When the time comes to leave, the mountain has become familiar and dear to me, and later whenever I hear its name it is as if I am reminded of an old friend.

My initial contact was quite simple: I notice a change in my field of vision. There is something over there! What is it? There is an interplay of the outer and the inner. Something outside —the change or something new appearing— stirs me inwardly and sets me in motion.

[The single mental process]

"There is something over there— what is it?" These phrases indicate two kinds of intention. They do not lie unconnected side by side; rather one proceeds from the other. My noticing evokes my asking the question, and it does so precisely because what strikes me in the object that suddenly becomes visible is its vagueness. The noticing may be called "motivating" and the asking "motivated." One stems from the other— I pass from one intention to the other, but the first does not cease, for it is taken up by the second and survives in it. My spiritual living is both together until "I realize" that the object is a mountain. My question is answered and ceases. My noticing has become more definite; the *something* has been fulfilled. New questions are prompted and will eventually be answered, and in this process the *something* which at first was empty is increasingly fulfilled.

From the moment I noticed the object for the first time until my "acquaintance" with it ceases —when I am no longer concerned about it actually— a *single* ongoing intention is living in me during all these changing intentions, and a unified whole thereby takes shape throughout this duration. (Husserl introduced the term "living experience [*Erlebnis*]" for this unity; but the word has been used in so many different, often obscure, senses that we almost fear to use it.) {104}

[The mountain and my spiritual world]

Although intentions, both changing and enduring, arise from one another and may merge into one another, and my mental life consists in them, nevertheless, strictly speaking, they do not set each other in motion (they do not motivate each other). They are motivated by what enters my spiritual world and builds it up over time. The real [*real*] thing is not what enters my world. All the time I have something undetermined before me, the real thing has been totally determined all along, and nothing in its stock of content is modified by the fact that my knowledge stems from it.

The undetermined something that refers to the determined real object is now in my spiritual world. It has been taken up into a world that already exists and belongs to me, and it has been taken up *through* what already exists therein. I already had the idea of "something definite" as well as the ideas of "mountain" and "cloud" that came up as possible fillings of the *something*. The partial definiteness —the indefiniteness and definiteness— of what I newly take in prompts me to perform various acts wherein I learn more and more about it and "fit it into my image of the thing."

"My idea" thus continues to grow as my spiritual activity progresses. It remains when I no longer have the real mountain before me, for I have taken my idea along with me, and I bear it even when I am no longer thinking of the mountain at all. My idea is not "actual," but it may become actual again. When I hear its name, everything it means to me "comes back" and "I relive it." I can also learn something new about it (for example, when I hear of a change that has taken place in the mountain). The idea "coming back" may involve an intuitive memory that conjures up the mountain before me, perhaps a whole series of "memories." The intentions concerning the mountain "revive"— seldom all of them, but what is no longer actual now is still somehow connoted in what is actual.

The intentions are also connected with what they have taken up and with what they were motivated through. The inseparability and interdependence of noesis and noema allow us and even oblige us to call the noematic, too, "spiritual," "a world of spirit" or "objective spirit" (despite its dependence on the subject). And it even makes sense to speak of a "life" of these spiritual objects, since they come about and grow in connection with the life of the subject. On the other hand, we cannot conceive of any life of a subject without spiritual objects, for the subject cannot have life unless surrounded by a spiritual world, a world borne by and dependent upon the spirit.

We have by no means finished describing this material; very many problems remain. We treated {105} it here only to help us to understand the "forms" in the mind of the angels of which Thomas speaks.

b. The principles of knowledge and of the understanding.

[The original possessions of angels and human beings]

Pure spirits must also have a world of ideas, a world of objects which they bear and which belong to them, objects that represent to them the real [*real*] world independent from them. The great difference is that their world of ideas, unlike our own, does not develop gradually throughout their spiritual living; rather —in its principal stock— they possess it as their own from the very beginning of their existence.

Is there an analogy to this in ourselves? And how can we imagine a life of the subject where no new ideas arise? Thomas himself gives the analogue, namely, the principles [*Prinzip*] of knowledge that he takes to be the original endowment of our mind. He is thinking here of the logical principles presupposed to all thinking and knowing. Still, some of his remarks suggest that even on his own view there must be many more principles than the traditional principles [*Grundsatz*] of logic.

[Contradiction]

Our main question is how we should understand this original possession. *What* should we take these principles to be, and what *mode of being* should we attribute to them? They are certainly not the principles formulated in traditional logic. After all, logicians today disagree on the "identity principle" and the "principle of contradiction," and people who have not studied logic know nothing about them.

However, anyone who hears the words "this rose is red and not red" feels that they are stating an impossibility. He senses the *contradiction* [*Widerspruch*] in the statement [*Behauptung*] —its logical aspect— as well as the clash, the *contraposition* [*Widerstreit*] in what it states —its ontological aspect—.[156] All is clear sailing until he gets to the second predicate, which at once, since it cancels out the first, calls for an inner protest: "this doesn't work." To sense this he does not even have to know what the sentence is about.

---

[156]　The distinction between "contradiction" and "contraposition" is Husserl's.

[Logical categories]

What is it in us that causes this protest? Obviously even without accounting for it we have an "idea" of subject and predicate and their interrelation. I am referring to logical categories: the basic forms into which we gather whatever we think, hence also whatever we say and understand. What does not fit into them is, as it were, dashed to pieces against them; we dismiss it as a "logical impossibility." Anyone who has language, anyone who can {106} use his mind and understand speech (uttering sounds is not essential), possesses these forms. They are not things he normally thinks about (they may become so), but they do affect his thinking.

Before children are old enough to speak, we can see no sign of these categories, but while they are learning to talk, we get the clear impression that the categories are beginning to have an effect—not all at once but little by little. What warrants our claim that children already "had" these forms before they could think and speak? If it makes sense to say that they already had understanding, then we must admit in the same sense that the forms were previously present. What does "understanding" and "having understanding" mean in the first place?

[Understanding]

This question brings us right back to the central problem behind our whole discussion, for Thomas holds that the "understanding [*Verstand*]" (*intellectus* [intellect]) is a *potency* of the human soul.[157] However, he uses "*intellectus*" in several ways. The word also denotes the *insight* [*Verstandeseinsicht*] of the understanding, that is, an individual act of a knowing mind. He also speaks of the "intellect"

---

[157]   Cf. *De veritate*, q. 15, a. 1; for his theory of the intellect see also especially qq. 1, 2, 10, and 22, a. 10-1.

of pure spirits, both of the angels and of God, in Whom there is no contrast of act and potency and in Whom, as Thomas himself says, *intellectus, intelligere* [to understand] and *intellectum* (the knowing mind, actual knowing and what is known) are one.

God's understanding may be our best approach to the original meaning of "intellect." The many uses of the term, after all, are not purely equivocal, but imply that all of its meanings belong together objectively [*sachlich*]. In God "*intelligere*" means actual insight. (For "*intelligere*" we could also use "actually knowing, recognizing," but if we do, we should not associate any beginning with the *re*-cognizing [*Er-kennen*], as the word suggests, since God's knowing is not a gain of new insight.) "Having understanding" implies for Thomas only "*intelligentem esse* [to be understanding]" or "*in actu intellectus esse* [for the understanding to be in an act]"; the *intellectus* is always actual insight.

Our *intelligere* is an analogue of the divine *intelligere*; it is a temporal, passing act of knowing (momentary, in a "flash" of insight but lasting a limited time if the insight lingers). For us, "having understanding" does not mean "*intelligentes esse* [to be understanding]" absolutely but "*intelligere posse* [to be able to understand]"; it denotes the *possibility* of {107} passing into actual knowledge. Our understanding is not enduring, complete actuality.

[Non-materialness of understanding]

If we wish to appreciate what finite understanding is, we must free ourselves from ideas coming from our dealings with the material world that would constantly intrude themselves through our language, formed as it is largely on the material world. The spirit or soul is not an extended thing, nor is the understanding a spatial part of such a thing. The understanding is not a kind of drawer we can shove things into. It is not a material body than can be molded and impressed with forms like visible, tangible shapes.

[Being illumined and open]

We have yet to ask whether and how far the human soul is altered in its mode of being through its bond to a material body. If we consider the pure spirit and the soul only insofar as it is spirit, the understanding or intellect denotes an essential property of spirit: *being illumined* [*durchleuchtet*] (that is, being visible to oneself [*für sich selbst sichtbar*]) and *being open* [*geöffnet*] (turning the attention to something else by grasping it). In God both are infinite. This is why His understanding is eternally actual and perfect knowledge of Himself and of all else knowable. Finite spirits are not everything they are in enduringly changeless actuality. Their being is parceled out to them, confined to a limited measure. Their being illumined and open is also limited. The *mode* of their being [*Seinsmodus*] denotes first the *degree* of the actuality of their being as well as of the being of their knowing [*Erkennendsein*] and second the *range* of what they can *in general* turn to by knowing and of what they can turn to in the highest measure of their actuality.

[Actuality of knowing]

We have seen again and again that potentiality implies not only possibility but a lower level of being (or a whole series of levels) between nonbeing and the highest actuality, pure act. Ascribing potency to a be-ing means attributing to it a being that admits of heightening to higher actuality. Ascribing "understanding" as a potency to a be-ing means assigning to it a spiritual being that has yet to include actual knowing but makes the transition to actual knowing possible.

Should we take "has yet to include actual knowing" to mean that there is no minimal measure of actuality? Can we conceive of any spiritual being at all that lacks a minimum of actual knowledge? Were being enlightened and open attributes of the being of spirit in all its forms and modes, then being conscious of oneself and having something before oneself would have to belong to spiritual being, even though both would involve a quite low level of actual knowledge.

[A materialistic view of consciousness]

There are states of sleep that do not interrupt {108} the continuity of spiritual being. We know how we pass from a lucid mental life when awake to confusion and half-consciousness when dreaming and conversely, and we pass through these stages without "getting lost." One inclined to give a materialistic interpretation to mental life and what occurs therein will say the following. Even while the conscious life of the spirit is suspended for certain time, the material body continues to exist and its functions do not cease— at least not all of them. The corporeal dispositions, too, which are preconditions for the life of the spirit and may also be acquired in a certain sense in past spiritual living (or through the corresponding physical processes), continue to exist and provide continuity when mental life is resumed after the interruption.

A critique of the background of this interpretation must await an adequate study of the interrelations of body and soul. We would have misgivings about the interpretation itself, for though it may explain how mental life resumes, it does not account for the continuity of consciousness over the "empty stretch." After all, what is this "empty stretch" under closer inspection? Looking back on it, can we say that there was really nothing in between the two periods of conscious, materially fulfilled living? I do not think so.

An inner consciousness belonging to my "stream of consciousness" that develops along with it and takes part in its development —a
consciousness of duration continuously filled with my living— crosses
the "empty" stretch. Not only do I realize that time must have passed
objectively between the two fulfilled periods, but also the living duration goes through them, although without any fulfillment that I can
detect. Indeed, looking back on my stream of consciousness, I see
that even segments in my waking life have gaps; I am frequently conscious only "that something was there," but my memory does not tell
me *what* it was. It obviously depends on the level of actuality of our
spiritual life how faithfully we retain its material content in memory.

[The onset of mental life]

And we should add that there is a form of spiritual being which,
though not conscious life of the spirit, has the potency to be raised
into conscious life, and we learn of this heightening *afterwards* when
we look back on it from its vantage. Should we conceive the onset
of spiritual living in a child as such an awakening from unconscious
being to a conscious spiritual life? We may do so, but such awakening does not explain it entirely, for not only is the mode of spiritual
being heightened, but its range expands, too. I mean, it is more than
what was occurring on the inside yet could neither be known from the
inside nor noticed on the outside and now can be detected {109} both
inwardly and outwardly. For something new is increasingly happening that presumably was not happening before. So spiritual existence,
we should say, does not necessarily begin when it first becomes verifi-
able for us. The onset of verifiability points to a change in the be-ing
itself, a transition to a higher type of spiritualness, to intellectuality; it
marks a heightening of the actuality of life and consciousness and at
the same time an expansion in the range of openness.

[Differences of mind]

Not every spiritual subject has access to everything that can be known. God's essence is completely knowable to God alone. Created spirits know more or less of His essence in proportion to their power to grasp it. Even among spirits of the *same* species, hence among men, the range to which they have natural access varies. Relatively few men possesses knowledge of higher mathematics. This is partially because such knowledge can only be acquired in definite ways, and few have the opportunity to find out about them and to learn to follow them. But even of those who do, not all reach the goal, for some have the "necessary gift" while others do not.

What is this necessary gift? A certain kind of understanding is needed to learn mathematics: a "feeling" for mathematical objects, for the peculiar nature of numbers, for spatial forms and for quantities, as well as a more general ability to think abstractly, to draw conclusions from premises, etc.— what mathematicians and logicians have in common. If "having understanding" means "*intelligere posse* [being able to understand]," this potency does not extend to everything for everybody nor even to the same things for everybody. The "born" mathematician is from the outset of his being *in potentia illorum intelligibilium* [in potency toward those intelligibles], that is, he is ready for these kinds of knowledge (it does not matter if his potency is ever put into act during his lifetime or not).

Certain directions are naturally proper to every understanding. If the knowing spirit comes upon *intelligibilia*, objects of knowledge, when taking one of these directions, it will pass easily from potency into act and will be encouraged to move further into the intricacies of the area. We hear that in principle any normal person may be taught mathematical truths (so that the failure to learn mathematics will be due to the ineptitude of the teacher). There may be some truth in this, for *some* potentiality for mathematics belongs to the human mind as such. Still, individuals have more or less facility for passing from potency into act, and these differences make them {110} more or less dependent upon particular learning strategies.

[Principles of mind]

These specific directions in potentiality may well be what we mean by "*inborn* [*angeboren*] *forms of the understanding.*" As long as the spirit, meaning the spiritual subject itself, is merely "in potency" in regard to these forms, the forms do not lie before the subject, they are not yet a spiritual object [*Objekt*]. As soon as the spirit passes into actuality in this direction, it has something before it by knowing it actually. In our example, it thus has mathematical objects and —as understanding advances — the truths founded upon them. We should also think of the "*principles*" proper to the human mind as such as forms in this sense. They determine the type of mind. We can say metaphorically that the principles "tense [*spannen*]" the mind toward a certain goal (the material principles), toward a certain means or a series of possible means to the goal (the formal principles), and toward a certain kind of intellectual movement (which we may call its "natural light"[158] or "mental power").

c. Potency, act, habit.

[Recalling the tetrahedron]

This last point needs more clarification in several respects. We are taking potency and act as degrees of being but in such a way that

---

[158]   "Natural light" usually has the wider sense of the entire endowment of the natural understanding.

each term denotes a whole series of ranks with a dividing line running through them marking the transition from potency to act. But there is a third thing here. When I acquire an item of knowledge, for example when I see a tetrahedron for the first time and learn what it is, there is a transition from potency to act, from "possible" to "real [*wirklich*]" knowledge. The knowledge I gain does not remain enduringly actual [*aktuell*]; I move on to other things and no longer think of tetrahedrons. But the transition to potentiality that takes place here is not a return to the *same* potency that existed before in regard to this item of knowledge. I have gotten the idea of tetrahedron, and it remains in my possession. I know what the word means when I hear it; it stands before me at once (made present intuitively or *in abstracto* [in the abstract]), or I know that I know what people are talking about, and I could "bring it back up" whenever I wished.

[Habit]

We are speaking here of a *habitus* [habit], more precisely of an *acquired* habit, since the knowledge {111} was gained through actual knowing.[159] Thomas also speaks of the "*habitus principiorum* [habit of principles]," but this is a *natural* or inborn habit, not acquired. When I say that a sentence [*Satz*] stating a contradiction is false and thereby realize in general that contradictory things cannot stand together, I am not gaining a new insight; I am bringing up something I already know; I am stating something "self-evident," something that I "have always known."

A habit (whether inborn, acquired, or infused— a third kind of which Thomas speaks) is called a *completion of the potency* wherein the potency acquires an ease and readiness to pass over into act. From

---

[159]　For the concept of habit see *De veritate* q. 12, a. 1, q. 14, a. 7, q. 16, a. 1, q. 17, a. 1.

the subject's viewpoint ("noetically") we can again understand habit, relative to potency, as but a higher degree of spiritual being, as a closer approach to the boundary of actuality. Noematically, we can point out another characteristic. In any actual knowledge a mental object is constituted that now remains in my mental world. This continued existence that allows me to bring the object back up, this spiritual "possession," is the noematic side of habit.

[Natural habit]

Natural habit poses other, special, problems. Before a habit is actualized, its spiritual objects are not in my possession. And as long as no spiritual life can be verified at all, neither can any habit be perceived. We may say that a natural habit is present and that there is a preference in the knowledge potency for what must be newly acquired, only insofar as the subject is ready for actualization *as soon as* he awakens to mental actuality. We may even say in a sense that a certain actualization is already taking place here, for the principles regulate the actuality of knowledge and take effect in knowledge without themselves as yet being constituted as mental objects in actual knowing and without having become a habit, a mental "possession" in the noematic sense. An acquired habit, too, is "implicitly" actualized in the same way (if we may so describe it) in the mental acts that it determines. All that I am habitually affects my actual living, but it need not come to the fore in an actuality of its own nor constitute an objectivity [*Gegenständlichkeit*] of its own; nevertheless, this *can* come about at any time. {112}

d. Alternation of actuality and habituality.

Participation of the will.

[Actuality and habituality]

Now, what determines the transition from habituality to actuality and from actuality to habituality? My understanding, as my potency for knowledge, as my "*intellectus possibilis* [possible intellect],"[160] determines what is accessible to my knowledge in principle. But I cannot know everything actually all at once; I cannot encompass it all in one spiritual look. One reason for this is that our human mind is set to acquire its knowledge step by step. Another is that every spiritual individual has a certain range of its own beyond which its actuality cannot extend. This is why we need to step back from actuality into habituality.

The transition from habituality to actuality is conditioned to a large extent from without. What I hear and see and what my mind actually grasps as present therein touches a number of things in my mental world and makes them come before me; at the same time it brings their noetic counterpart back to life. (The phenomena of the memory, remembrance, association and recall are relevant here and need further clarification.)

[Free will]

Besides this involuntary reappearance and revival of things, we can, within certain limits, *freely will* to bring things back and reawaken them. I have some —but not unlimited— control over my spiritual realm. Here we meet the second potency of the spirit, the *will* (we

---

160   For the distinction between the "*intellectus agens* [agent intellect]" and the "*possible* [possible intellect]" see p. 168f.

shall consider now only how it shares in the life of the understanding). Spiritual being is not only being illumined for itself [*für sich selbst durchleuchtet*], that is, it is not only intellectual being conscious of itself, it is at the same time being that the spiritual subject can determine, being that is free and deliberate.

When something affects me inwardly I *may* follow the bid, but I do not *have* to do so necessarily and unavoidably. When I hear a word that sounds familiar and highlights an entire area in my spiritual world in such a way that I feel a pull toward it, I can recall all the things the word reminds me of one after another and deal with them both in actuality renewed and in new actuality. But I can also withstand the pull and remain with my actuality in my external surroundings or in the objects I am thinking of.

[The activeness of knowledge and the will]

Let us try to imagine the opposite case— mental processes running in a purely mechanical fashion. We find something quite like this in those suffering from a serious mental disorder known as the "flight of ideas." They {113} seize upon some word they hear, usually outside of its context; this "idea" then triggers others and they cannot stop the process. They construe no world, no fixed, meaningful frame of reference; they have neither external surroundings (at least not as a whole, only fragments) nor a spiritual world of their own. Had no spiritual life of their own been present, they could not construct any mental world at all.

Is such "mechanical" knowing conceivable at all? If we mean that something could "impress" itself upon a mind while it remains passive, certainly not. The actuality of spiritual living, after all, is at the same time activity, and its activity is intentionality. But intentionality, that is, the subject's direction toward an object, already has some activity in the heightened sense of something spontaneous [*spontan*] to be carried out by the subject. All knowing entails that the knowing mind grasps and embraces what is known, and if the knowing takes place step by step as it does in human knowing, it entails that the mind adds the new to the old and holds on to what it has gotten and so some doing is always involved. Even when it is "affected" in a way that it could not choose, this "contact" bids the "free" I to set out on its own down the path that the contact has opened up. And if "all it can do" is follow the bidding since other motives are missing and its acting (even its failure to act) is a motivated doing, it would still be its *own* doing, not something done to it without it doing its part.

So we can understand the part the will plays in determining what becomes actual for a spiritual subject in the following way. The subject can decide, say, to continue an actual train of thought that is disclosing something new to it. In this case it must let go of the past insofar as it does not need it to conceive what is present now; I mean it must send it back into the mode of habituality or allow it to remain there. Or else the subject can decide to heed a stimulation to sink into the past and so break off its present train of thought.

§ 7
Habit and act in pure spirits.

[Angelic knowledge and the limitation of creatures]

Let us return to the kind of spirit whose knowledge and spiritual world do not grow gradually, that is, to pure spirits. We have now gained some appreciation for the "forms" that are proper to them by nature and mark the domain of the objects of their natural knowledge. We should think of these forms in a way analogous to principles, and since the spiritual life of angels is awake [*wach*] from the beginning of their existence, their forms are more {114} than pure potency; they are a potency that is affected and effecting, and hence they are at least habit if not act.

We can see why created spirits do not actually know all at once everything accessible to them in principle even though they have no need to acquire it for the first time. The reason is that at any one time they are not actually all that they are. This in turn is so, Thomas explains, because their essence [*Wesen*] (substance or essence [*Essenz*]) is not the same as their being (*esse*). The identity of essence and being, he repeatedly stresses, is found only in the first principle, the one uncreated be-ing, but for any creature it is impossible. Every created thing has received its being as something added on to what it is. *What* it is must be limited, since otherwise it would be a duplicate of the divine essence. This is why something else, something accidental, can be added on to what it is in its nature— essentially. The measure of being that it can receive is determined by its limited *what*. However, the "measure of being," the mode of its being, is not something extended (at least primarily). The *what* is not a vessel that would be spatially filled with being.

Neither is temporal duration the measure of being, although being does have duration. God's infinite being is infinite at every instant. It is the highest actuality, pure actuality. The reception of being is the contact with this actuality. Should this contact cease, the creature would at once cease to exist. Should the creature, with everything that it is, contact the divine being, it would be raised at once to divine being, without, of course, being able to embrace it in its entirety. The natural being of the creature moves between these two extremes. Now with this part of its *what*, now with that part, it enters the highest actuality it can reach, and for this reason its being must extend over a duration. How much of its essence —at one moment and over the full duration of its being— becomes actual is determined by the measure of its being, and to this the rank of the be-ing corresponds.

[Angelic species and knowledge potential]

We said that for Thomas the essence of angels is enduringly actual and only what accrues to them over and above their essence is subject to change.[161] We should take what "accrues" to their essence to be in particular the forms through which they know. We also saw that there is an alternation of habituality and actuality in them. If we disregard the "forms," what content is left to their "essence"? The answer is: the species proper to each angel, determined it seems to me, by the measure of the being they are able to grasp.

This measure takes effect {115} in the actuality of their living, which is concerned either with creatures or with God (the either-or is not exclusive.) Since the forms provide access to creatures, the only other actuality in the life of a pure essence is its relationship with God, and so the measure of their being is identical to what they grasp of God. They cannot, however, grasp the divine being by themselves (without any mediation by creatures); they must be raised to it. Their enduring actuality is therefore their union with God, that is, their supernatural being wrought by God, to which their only natural contribution is a potency.

[Angelic knowledge]

Knowing is something proper to spiritual being itself. If no creature can *be* everything that it is at one moment, then neither can it at one moment know everything that it can know in principle. The contrast of potency (or habit) and act is involved here. An angel habitually encompasses from the outset and as long as its being endures what is accessible to its natural knowledge. And by turning its attention to it, it has the power to make anything it wishes become

---

[161]   P. 130.

actual from its spiritual world.

Here too, of course, we should think of the attention as motivated. While we should also take "outside" influences into account, we ought not to think of them as an outside world in the spatial sense. To be sure, angels can also let changing parts of the spatial world become actual to them. But the reason they can do so is not because they have access only to the changing parts— as in our own case, where access depends upon the spatial location of our body. They "know" the whole spatial world, and for them each part is equally near or far. The bid to turn toward this or that part can only be spiritual, for example a command [*Befehl*] from God directing them to some place or a human cry for help. The act wherein they live enduringly is their intuition of God to which they are raised by God working beyond their nature, as well as the intuition of things in God ("morning knowledge"). The natural life of their spirit is a changing actualization of their habitual knowledge due to the bidding from other spirits.

[Difference in knowledge in angels and men]

Thomas stresses that the knowledge of higher angels differs from that of the lower in that the former know through a smaller number of forms. God knows everything through one single thing: His essence. The closer a knowing spirit is to God the fewer forms it needs. These relations, too, we can clarify by analogy to human knowledge. Say three people hear the name of a person who is absent. The first knows him well and is deeply attached to him. The second knows the name but has not met {116} him personally and knows nothing else about him. The third does not even know who they are talking about.

So the name will mean something different to each one. Each will associate a certain meaning with the name, and there is a stock of meaning [*Sinnesbestand*] common to what they all are thinking.

However, the third conceives only something empty and formal. The form that the second has is filled to some extent but is quite poor, vague, sketchy. But the word conjures up a rich fullness before the soul of the first man (even though at the moment he cannot bring up everything it includes), and at the same time it touches him deeply and awakens this depth to actual life.

Something similar occurs when a science is mentioned. One does not understand the word at all, a second knows roughly what it is about, while a third is an expert in the field. Here again we see that the word means much to one and little to the others.

[Mental power in angels and men]

The ability to grasp a fullness through a *single* form also implies a higher degree of spiritual being. This fluctuates in the life of a particular spiritual subject, for its mental activity shows a greater and lesser intensity, more or less of what it is is awakened to actual life. But for each subject there are limits within which these fluctuations occur. There is a lower limit below which we cannot speak of wakeful [*wach*] spiritual living at all and an upper limit above which the tension and range cannot be increased naturally. We called this feature of the mode of being "mental power" or "natural light." A spirit so endowed cannot go beyond these limits by itself. But it can, as we have seen, be raised out of its natural limits under the action of another.

We have analogues for this, too, in human life. There are people who have the necessary intellectual talent for quite good scientific achievement, but who left to themselves lack the needed energy and so make no headway. But contact with an especially lively, agile spirit will give them the stimulus they need; they will become "infected" with its power, swept along by it, and now they can rise to surprising heights.

Others there are who, though lively and ever pushing ahead, would not get far by themselves. But if they join forces with other "more productive" spirits, by taking their cue from them, they will come to insights, to a spiritual possession, that they could not attain through their own gifts.

In either case, one spirit, by joining with another, comes to share in the other's mode of being. We need not discuss here how this union is achieved. The case {117} of pure spirits will be different from that of spirits structured as body and soul. For the present we have done enough if we have gotten some appreciation of how a lower angel is "enlightened" by a higher one; namely that the higher angel heightens the other's mode of being and the intensity of its knowledge while the lower angel can know things through the forms of the higher.

§ 8
Attempt to define the human spirit.

Our comparison of the infinite, uncreated spirit with created pure spirits has already given us a some notion of the human spirit [*Menschengeist*]. But we must fill it in in several directions. Our treatment of the three types of subjective spirit is still biased toward the intellectual side. Our explanation of the objective spirit is still inadequate. And to understand the human spirit we must ask how it is shaped as a soul in human love.

a. Intellect and will.
Intellectus agens and *intellectus possibilis.*

[Spirit as mind and will]

It has now become clear that "spirit, mind [*Geist*]" and "intellect

[*Intellect*]" do not mean the same thing; that is, spirit cannot be merely understanding [*Verstand*] and nothing else. The life of the spirit is movement (nonspatial, of course). Spiritual movement proceeds from the I. It involves the will, albeit in a more general, elementary sense, I mean, not always in the specific form of proper will acts. Understanding and will are essential attributes [*Wesensattribut*] of the subjective spirit. No spiritual life is conceivable wherein one or the other would not come to the fore at typical moments.

We saw two features of the intellectual side of spirit. The first is being illumined, that is, being conscious of self— and it may be the "consciousness" which accompanies mental life without becoming a proper act of reflection but which can pass into such an act. The second feature is being open to objects other than the spiritual subject itself— and in the case of finite spirits this also implies that they are endowed with forms of knowledge, that is, that they are naturally set for a definite domain of objects. But even the intellectual life, the specific activity of the understanding, is not possible without the participation of the will.

[Possible and active intellect]

In regard to the lowest, step-by-step, type of acquiring knowledge, we characterized understanding in two ways: as an "*intellectus possibilis* [possible intellect]" and as an "*intellectus agens* [agent intellect]." We cannot define {118} their relationship as potency and act since we find potency and act in both. The most exact literal translation of "*Intellectus possibilis*" would be "possible insight [*Einsicht*]." If we stress "possible" in the phrase, we highlight the "potency," that is, the openness of the understanding and its direction to the objects that it is open to (perhaps *especially* open to). And we can say, using a spatial metaphor that is now unlikely to lead us astray, that this potency is the "place" for the forms of the understanding, for the *species intelligibiles* [intelligible species].

We can also stress the "insight" of possible insight, and then the phrase will signify the actualized potency, the actual insight, that has the character of taking in [*Aufnehmen*] or receiving [*Empfangen*] and hence does not involve the *intellectus agens* [*acting* intellect]. Finally, we should ascribe insight to the "*intellectus possibilis*" because it signifies that a *possession* of knowledge is acquired which the *intellectus possibilis* "stores" after it passes into habituality.

We can take "*intellectus agens*" as *agere* [doing, acting], hence as an *actus* of the understanding. This act, then, I mean this working toward an actual instance of knowledge, differs from insight. This is the reason why the *intellectus agens* is found only in spirits that know discursively but not in other kinds of spirits.

We can take the "active intellect" in turn as the potency for such "doing," for this movement that aims at knowledge. But all "doing," even the doing that aims at knowledge, involves the will. Hence we should say that the active intellect is just as much a potency of the will as it is of the understanding.

[Role of the will]

Furthermore, all doing, all movement, is motivated, and the motive is "received"; all doing, all movement, is directed toward a goal and comes to rest at the goal. The "receiving" and the "resting at the goal" are an *actu intelligere* [understanding in act] on different levels, both involve the *intellectus possibilis*. An "*intellectus*" that would be *agens* [acting]" but not "*possibilis*" is quite inconceivable. On the other hand, a minimum of activity lies even in "receiving" the "motive," and a higher degree of activity lies in "resting in the insight gained." For the intellect is not completely helpless before either, since it can "turn toward" and "turn away," it can "open" and "close."

Hence we cannot imagine the *intellectus possibilis* without any activity or without any participation of the will, even though we can imagine it without an action preparing for the *actu intelligere* [understanding in act] but separate from it in content and in time. So we shall have to say that the "*agere intellectus* [the acting of the intellect]" and the "*actu intelligere* [understanding in act]" are different modes of actuality of the spiritual subject that is at once knowing and willing and actualizes the two potencies, *intellectus* and *voluntas* [will] in each of its acts but in different measure.

[Knowledge and will in angels and God]

While we do not attribute {119} an *intellectus agens* to pure spirits, which do not know discursively, as a proper activity of acquiring knowledge, nor its corresponding potency, their *actu intelligere* is nevertheless marked by an immanent determination by the will, a free turning away and turning toward, that also enables them to actualize successively their habitual possessions of knowledge and to be enriched by being enlightened by higher spirits.

In God there is no alternation of actual and habitual knowledge, no increase or decrease in His possessions of knowledge, no contrast of potency, habit, and act; He is eternal, immutable *actus purus*. Is this *actus purus intellectus purus* [pure understanding]? By no means. God's *intelligere* is not only active knowing but "creative knowing," and hence it is at once the highest work of His understanding and His will. God's knowing —as we have seen— differs from human knowing. It signifies that everything that was or is or will be, even everything that will never come into existence, stands before the mind of God from eternity.

At the same time, however, God measures being out to each

thing that He marks for being, He "places it in existence" with its own mode of being and for a certain duration, and He withholds being from what is not to be. But He affirms Himself in His being Who is from eternity and has never first been placed in existence. His is not only a being conscious of itself but a being approving itself [*zustimmen*] in the highest form of approval [*Zustimmung*]: love; His being is blessed self-love. All this is comprised in the simple act that is God Himself. Thus far we have considered but a tiny part of this simple fullness that in created spirits is found split into diversity and diminished to an analogue, the *similitudo et maior dissimilitudo* [likeness but greater unlikeness].

b. Creative activity. Objective spirit.

[Creation in knowledge and action]

Human acts, as we have seen, include knowing and doing. To illustrate the universal participation of the will, we chose knowledge activity as the paramount example. What the *intellectus agens* does aims at knowledge, which is its goal and possibly its outcome. Is this doing analogous to divine creative doing?

The action of the agent intellect brings about nothing in the external world, changes nothing. Yet we do have some warrant for saying that something is created. With every new insight something is "incorporated" into the knower's mental world. His world is the richer by one idea, and this may alter much throughout the entire stock of his knowledge, and place what was already there in a new light. The spiritual subject, too, "grows" thereby, at least in its knowing power, in its ability to take in new things. Knowledge activity, then, does create and {120} re-create [*umschaffen*] in the area of the subjective and objective spirit. Here "objective spirit" continues to signify a world of objects [*Objektwelt*] dependent on, upheld by, and borne by the subjective spirit.

Now, there is also a doing of created spirits that reaches beyond them, beyond the world of their spirit and affects the world outside. We usually think of it only when speaking of a man's creative activity, and we have discussed artistic creation several times. But we should not only be thinking of artistic creation but of any transformation [*Umwandlung*] in the outside world due to a man's planned intervention.

Human creating differs essentially from divine creating in that it never brings about something from nothing but shapes or reshapes [*Umgestalten*] material [*Material*] already given. Both knowledge and will play a part as they do in all that man does. The subject must grasp the material and also what the material could become as well as the ways and means apt to bring it about. This is the role of the understanding (we are speaking of *practical* knowledge here since knowing serves doing). The subject must set what the material is to become as a goal and decide what must be done to reach it. Such is the role of the will, which imitates the doing and continues to live therein.

[The purse]

A piece of leather is cut out, folded into shape, and sewn into a purse. With relatively few deft actions a new object has been created. The piece of leather is the same, but it has been made into another object. What allows us to speak like this? The "piece of matter" has gotten a new "form," a new external shape. But along with the shape it has gotten a new "meaning"; it embodies another idea, indeed, a "practical" idea, for by virtue of its shape and its other qualities it can serve definite purposes. As the material is worked according to a plan, a meaning is given to it, an idea is shaped in it. There is always purpose here (but not always a "practical" purpose in the sense of "useful"), for the thing becomes something meaningful for a man and something that he may deal with accordingly.

The meaning which he puts into things, and in accordance with which he uses them and perhaps shapes them, is spiritual. This means first that the meaning has come from his mind. The leatherworker saw the piece of leather and thought he could make a purse out of it. Or he was asked to make a purse and looked around his workshop until he found a suitable piece of leather. The purse existed as "his idea" before it existed "in reality"; through his idea and through his deliberate action it became reality. And now {121} the idea "lives" in the material thing and from it "speaks" to men.

[External things]

"Living" and "speaking" are metaphors. The thing is not moved from within by the idea. Whatever can happen to the thing in accordance with this idea must be done to it by something other than the thing itself. Nor has the idea shaped the matter by itself, for the matter had to be "formed into it" by a living subject. To illustrate the creative process we would have to bring in the mediator role that the body [*Leib*] plays in human creating and shaping in the external world— the body as at once belonging to the outside world yet closely bound up with the spiritual soul into a unity. This we can do later; here we can but offer a preliminary analysis.

Dealing with things outside ourselves is an essential part of human living. We are closely bound up with the things we know and are familiar with. We know what they are for and how they should be handled; we count on them and use them practically as members of our own body. Each thing has potencies, possibilities for being effective that we can actualize, and we have the potency (possibly the habit) to make them effective. When we meet something for the first time, we look at it to see what we could do with it, how it could fit into the context of our life.

"It speaks to us" means that the qualities we see in the thing motivate intentions in us to use it in accordance with this or that practical meaning, to reshape it if necessary to make it serve this or that purpose. "A meaning lives in" the thing signifies that it is apt to evoke certain acts in a spiritual subject that encounters it. "Putting meaning into" a thing means that the subject grasps it as it is meaningful for its life, perhaps shaping it so that its outer appearance will suggest to others that they should view it with this same meaning.

[Objectivity of meanings]

Hence all "objective spirit" or all "spiritual objects" are "spiritual" because they are actually, or may be, included in the life of spiritual subjects. When we say that external things that bear spiritual meaning, unlike ideas, are independent of subjects, we mean first that mere material things (apart from the spiritual meaning they may bear) are not bound to this or that subject as are its ideas.

But we also mean that their spiritual meaning, as a potency grounded in the things themselves, is also "objective [*objektiv*]," that is, their meaning is not enduringly upheld by a subject but only referred to spiritual subjects (perhaps to particular subjects) so that they may actualize it, and a meaning may be imparted to the thing by a spiritual subject shaping it for this purpose.

[Self-shaping]

The shaping power of created spirits extends not {122} only to the material world; it is more than a potency for a doing that brings external things into the spiritual context of their lives. This power includes the ability of spirits to shape themselves and other spiritual subjects by virtue of their own doing. We had already spoken of self-shaping in one sense. I mean that with every intellectual activity the spiritual subject widens its world of objects (now to be taken in two ways: the subject's ideas and the domain of external objects that it knows how to deal with) and grows in its habitual being as well. What we have shown here in regard to the understanding applies no less to that other aspect of spiritual life, the will, as well as to something closely connected with the will but which needs further treatment both in its own right and because of its connection with the will: I mean emotion, the sense appetite [*Gemüt*].

c. Emotion

[Understanding, will, and emotion]

Actus purus, as we saw, is being, it is knowledge that encompasses everything perfectly, and it is creative will and approval of itself (and of everything created as well) in the highest form of approval, love. All that in pure act is the oneness of a single act, in created spirits falls into a series of objectively [*sachlich*] and temporally separate acts and potencies which, however, are interrelated in a definite way. Under the heading "understanding" we are grouping all real and possible acts which aim at knowing some be-ing and in which this knowledge is acquired. Under "will" we include all acts through which something that is grasped as possible but not yet actual is marked for being and possibly placed in existence (by means of a doing initiated by the willing).

Between the person's taking in the world through his understanding and shaping the world through his willing lies an inner give-and-take with the world in his emotions or sense appetite [*Gemüt*]. As a rule, the spiritual subject does not merely encounter an object in the understanding; it does more than receive it in knowledge. The subject is inwardly affected by the object and challenged to take a stance on it.

This contact is marked by an opposition between liking [*Lust*] and disliking, [*Unlust*].[162] The analogous attitudes are approval [*Zustimmung*] and disapproval [*Ablehnung*], which in their extreme form are *love* and *hate*. This polarity is found {123} not only when a person encounters something else, but also when he encounters himself within his own being (this "encounter" with himself does not apply to the ordinary case but only to quite special forms of the objectification of the I).

[What and how I am]

We have described the intellectual aspect of spiritual being as being open and being illumined. Being illumined, meaning being conscious of oneself [*Seiner-selbst-bewußt-Sein*], is not merely consciousness of one's own being but also of *what* the be-ing, the person, is and *how* he is [*wie*] at any one time. Consciousness of what I am and how I am is not rational knowledge. This "what" is still ambiguous. It may mean what the spiritual person is as such, hence something general, or it may mean what I am "quite personally"— something individual, something absolutely unique.[163]

After laboring long to understand what I am, I can gain a certain rational knowledge of what I am in my general essence [*Wesen*]. I mean that I can acquire knowledge that I can frame in general concepts and words. However, my immediate self-consciousness is not

---

162 It is debated whether there is a mean, some "*adiaphoron* [indifferent]" thing, between these extremes, that is, an encounter wherein the subject is not inwardly affected. It doubtless appears so. We could perhaps settle the matter to the effect that although any encounter may be apt to affect the subject inwardly, the subject is not always so disposed.

163 The question of the individuality of the person in principle will be taken up on pp. 394ff.

knowledge like this; it is but one of the starting points I use to arrive at it. What I am as a spiritual individual is not accessible to rational knowledge at all (in the sense just defined). As something absolutely unique, it cannot be brought under general concepts; at most it can be denoted by a proper name. Yet for this reason it is not completely unknowable or unknown. <I> am what I am —or I am with what I am— for myself (and also for others) in a certain way.

[Mood]

Now, the *what* lies in a *how*. I am at every moment in some particular actuality; in this actuality my attention is turned toward this or that object [*Gegenständliches*], but at the same time I "feel [*fühlen*]" that I am in this or that "mood [*gestimmt*]." The "mood [*Stimmung*]" is my present inner state of mind [*Verfassung*]: this is *how* I am at present— because of what I am and because of what is just now affecting me inwardly. My "feeling [*Fühlen*]" is my consciousness of this mood. The *what* is enduringly present throughout the variation of the *how* (the *what* also determines the *how* and gives it its individual coloring) and throughout the variation of all that befalls me from outside. I am determined enduringly (albeit not immutably) by what I am and successively by what befalls me. To feel in a mood inwardly means to be affected by myself. If it is to my liking, I am in harmony, at rest and at peace, with myself; the attitude that it motivates is approval, self-love. If it is not to my liking, it prompts me to disapprove of myself, to fly from myself, to hate myself. {124}

[Attitude and behavior toward objects]

Like and dislike in one's own being (in the *what* it is and in the *that* it is) point to something positive or negative in the be-ing itself, to a *bonum* [good] or a *malum* [bad]. (This does not mean that the evidence is unmistakable; but connections come to light here between the be-ing (*ens*), the value [*Wert*] or the worthy be-ing (*bonum*), and the evincing [*Bekundung*] of what is of value in the emotions.)

The mood I am in comes first of all from within myself and tells me something about what I am and how I am inwardly. But it also commonly comes from outside myself, and I am usually conscious of being inwardly affected in one way or another by this or that thing. The immediate marks of this contact are "like" and "dislike" (which differ greatly in amount and kind). In this contact I see that the objects affecting me have corresponding qualities —values—, and as I turn my attention to them I take certain stances toward them. I mean that I affirm their being or deny it, I am pleased with them and feel drawn to them, or I am disgusted and repelled by them.

From these stances spring different ways of voluntary behaving and deliberate doing. I seek after objects, or I shun them; I let them alone, leave them as they are, or I try to alter or even destroy [*vernichten*] them. These are all kinds of the person's "give-and-take" with what befalls him and, depending on his like or dislike of the contact, not only grazes him on the surface but seizes him inwardly at greater or lesser depth by furthering and heightening his being or by diminishing and threatening it.

We are most strongly seized inwardly, and so the give-and-take is most intense, when the be-ing that we encounter is another person. Here approval and disapproval take the form of love and hate.

d. Shaping oneself — Character formation.

[Self-shaping, virtue and vice]

The forces prompting the decisions of the will and the shaping action of persons are in the emotions. Depending on the "impressions [*Eindruck*]" they receive from themselves, from things, and from other persons, they feel impelled to behave toward these threefold world in one way or another and to intervene in it, perhaps by shaping it. Here again we meet the question of shaping oneself. What does "shaping oneself" mean?

The person is shaped by all of his living. His mental world grows through his intellectual *doing*, and his knowing potency is formed in habits [*habituell*]. Through his willing and doing, a region that he affects outside himself accrues to him, and an expanded bodiliness [*Leiblichkeit*], as it were, is bound up with his interior. This means that his willing potency, too, is formed in habits. As the person feels {125} inwardly affected by himself and by others in some way or another, his emotions awaken to actuality, and are thereby shaped in habits (in his "sentiments [*Gesinnung*]," "inclinations [*Neigung*]," etc.).

On the interplay of potency, act, and habit (set in motion by a "motive [*Motif*]" that actualizes the potency) rests the possibility of *freely* shaping both oneself and others. We saw that actuality, insofar as it is activity, must be brought about freely. Within certain limits I am master of it. Motives stimulate my doing, but I am not helpless before them, for I am not forced to follow them. Just as it lies in my power to go through a rational process in order to gain insight and sharpen my understanding or to refuse to do this thus foregoing the possible gain, I can let rising anger or a grudge take root and give in to it, even let myself be carried away by it to do certain things, or I can stop it, impede it, suppress it. All this depends upon how these or those habitual attitudes of the sense appetite and the will (called "virtues" or "vices" when evaluated ethically) have developed.

[Forming character]

The "shape" the person assumes when his potencies are formed in habits we could call his "*character*."[164] Planned "character formation" (in the sense of shaping oneself freely) presupposes that we know the general essence of the person and have a definite goal in mind (an "ideal character"). We should look for the motives behind such self-improvement —disregarding for the moment the influences of personal environment, tradition, education, etc.— in the way the person "feels about himself." A person who is "at peace" with himself will have no incentive to change. But someone who feels an inner "unease" — coming from within, not connected with anything outside— will be motivated to do something to escape it.

This incentive may urge him in different directions. It may prompt him to flee from his own I, which is causing his unease, into the world outside or to things in the world likely to impress him and put him in another "mood." Or it may prompt him to think about what is "wrong" with him, to try to understand his own interior. So he may ask himself if "there is something I should change" and look for ways to put to practical use what he has learned from his voluntary self-shaping.

Is it what the person is that is reshaped here? The person's actual life springs from what he is and from what befalls {126} him, and in this actuality what we are calling his "character" takes shape. In our ordinary way of speaking, we cannot say that the person *is* his character but that he *has* a character. Therefore what he *has*, not what he

---

164   If we distinguish "innate" and "acquired" character, we should see them as potency and habit respectively.

himself *is*, seems to lend itself to shaping. But what does this "having" mean for the person? Is this not the point of all we have said about all "having" coming down to "being"?

[Habit and character]

Let us think about the meaning of *"habitus"* as it has emerged for us. Literally of course it means "having." We identified two related aspects of having. First, what the subject actually "has," his "belongings, holdings [*Habe*]," the mental possession or property [*Besitz*] that accrues to him through his actual doing— this is something noematic. But we have also seen that something noetic parallels the noematic, that is, a "behaving [*Gehaben*]," enduring directions in the person's spiritual being, attitudes of understanding, will, and emotion that are effective in the actual life of his spirit. This is no longer a "possession" that can be contrasted with the person. He does not *have* a habit in the noetic sense any more than he has an act or he has potencies, if we take "potency," "habit," and "act" as degrees of actuality and so as modes of being.

Then character, too, can be seen as the person's overall habitual shape (to be taken noetically), not as something that he has. Only when we transfer the word "habit" to *what* is habitual at any one time, does character tell us something about what the person is. In the first sense character does not say *what* he is but *how* he is at a certain time. The *what* never lacks a *how*, in the twofold sense of a mode of being and of the *quale* (as we saw, we can grasp the *what* only in the *how*), for the person's being is being in changing modes and qualities. Insofar as character formation is a shift from the potential to the habitual, we may have some justification for saying that the person shapes himself by "forming his character."

e. The core of the person.

1. Can the core be changed?

When we say that the person's core[165] is what he is in himself and what perdures as the *how* varies, and ask whether the core persists entirely unaltered throughout all the changes, we must again take care not to be misled {127} by the spatial image. The only being we can imagine for the core is one that is actualized in spiritual living and hence, insofar as actual living is actualization of potencies, one that shapes character and reshapes it over time. Hence we must say that the person himself is constantly changing, although the core that determines the whole shaping process from within is not shaped or changed in this way.

Is the core then completely immutable? When we say that a man has changed radically, should we not see this as a change in his core? What is *shaped* before the transformation appears to be at odds with what is shaped after the transformation, and they are opposed in such a way that we cannot understand the later stage on the basis of the former, as we can in the case of unbroken development. The transformation comes from the depths, from something assailing him in his innermost heart; we shall see later whether the innermost depth itself allows of transformation.[166]

---

[165] For the character and the core of the person see my dissertation *Zum Problem der Einfühlung* (Halle, 1917 <new edition, Munich, 1980>), p. 109 [English translation, *On the Problem of Empathy* by Waltraut Stein, CWESiii, 1964, third edition 1989], and the treatise on "Individuum und Gemeinschaft [individual and community]" <"Beiträge zur philosophischen Begründung der Psychologie und der Geisteswissenschaften," II ibid>, pp. 204ff; below, pp. 397ff.

[166] Cf. pp. 401ff.

2. Actuality of the core.
Relation to the actuality of life.
External dependence of the actuality of life.

[Stratification]

There is a further question here. Is this core of the person what he is in himself, perhaps independently of any outside determination, throughout the entire duration of his being *in actu*? What the person is in himself lives in all his acts but not in all in the same measure. Changing acts are more or less "personal," more or less determined from within. Hence more or less of the person's core will enter into his actual living. Apparently even in the core there is an opposition of act and potency, a change in its mode of being. Several strata in the person's being become apparent here and hence several strata wherein act and potency have a place.

[Being behind conscious life]

Conscious spiritual life is what is most apparent, the succession of acts that come from a potentiality and after running their course (indeed progressing during their course) fall back into inactuality (potentiality or perhaps habituality). "Coming from a potentiality" may mean that something which before had one mode of being now has another. This happens when something "pops up from memory," and the same is true analogously of "falling back into inactuality."

But this may also mean that an act (in the sense of a timebound spiritual {128} event) is constituted for the first time in virtue of a previous potency. The act, as the living experience of this particular content, may have been "possible" before, but it did not as yet exist *realiter* [really], except in the lower mode of potentiality. The potency, which preexisted [*bestehen voraus*] *realiter*, is the subject's potency to pass into this act, but this is never all that the content of the act and its coming about presuppose; rather something objective [*gegenständlich*] is always presupposed at the same time. We thus arrive at a being of the person that stands behind his conscious life but becomes actual in it and is its basis.

We see on the other hand that spiritual living is not nourished and borne by its subject, the person, alone. We must now ask whether and how far what the person is in himself must enter each of his acts and how far the person's spiritual life has the capacity to be borne by external factors.

[Personal involvement]

Spiritual living borne only from without would be an "impersonal [*unpersönlich*]" life. Can there be anything like this at all? We notice that one person's spiritual life is more strongly determined from without and less from within than another's, and also that at different times the same individual person lives more or less from without or from within. Then we see that a person's involvement differs according to the particular content of his acts, for in every act the subject aims at something objective by accepting it or opposing it.

External perceptions may take place with very little "personal involvement." When I am at work, what I see and hear around me may practically slip by me. They are not just sense impressions but real perceptions wherein I grasp the meaning of what I am sensing. For example, I hear the noise as the beating of a carpet, and I see the picture as a Madonna. But what I hear and see makes no inner impression on me. I am wrapped up in my own problems. However, the same noises could also assail me inwardly. When a noise disturbs me when I am at work, I may find it annoying, and it may even arouse violent anger. The *fact* that it disturbs me is already a sign that it is affecting me inwardly. The noise itself may be what is disturbing me (apart from what it conveys), say, when it is discordant. I can still understand the *dis*cord objectively as something attached to the object. But the other aspect may be present: it hurts me and causes suffering. Then it is something wherein I "feel myself"; I sense my being determined in a characteristic way.

All that we call "feelings," from the {129} lowest sensible feelings to the highest spiritual feelings, are contents in the experience of which the person lives, I mean, wherein something of him is actual. I have called these contents "proper to the I [*ichlich*]" to distinguish them from contents (such as external sense data) that set something objective [*gegenständlich*] before our eyes, something foreign to the I [*ichfremd*].[167] *What* of the person becomes actual here is not always the same.

3. Depth levels and the simplicity of the core.

[Metaphors]

We speak of various "depths of the I [*Ichtiefe*]"[168] that apply to contents as such. However, it is hard to see what "depth" means here. Contents have the feature of seizing the person at some depth or other, and it seems odd when they do not affect him at the right depth. But the person's core, what he is in himself, is not spatial; it is not even composed of parts, as if we could easily translate the spatial relation of surface and depth into a nonspatial analogy.

We have used intentionality to describe spiritual living; it means that a person turns his attention toward objects [*gegenständlich*], his

---

[167]   Cf. my treatises on "psychic causality" and "individual and community" <*Beiträge zur philosophischen Begründung der Psychologie und der Geisteswissenschaften*, ibid.>, especially pp. 136ff.

[168]   Ibid. pp. 204ff.

act aims at them. This does seem to suggest the possibility of a spatial analogy. The intentional act seems to have two poles: the I and the object, and we seem justified in speaking of a "surface" where the contact with the object takes place. When external impressions "slip by us," we may perceive the things but they make no dent —as we say—; there is something here that reminds us of two bodies touching on a surface. But something making contact from outside may also strike at depth immediately.

[Reaction to environment]

The same harsh noise that at one time I simply allow to slip by me but that at another time annoys me by its discord and so gets to a certain depth, may also upset me at my deepest level. Let us say that it is all important for me to concentrate on what I am working on. I think I am on the point of solving a key problem and definitely hope to do so if only I stay with it. Then comes the jarring noise and it tears me away from everything. I am angry over the disturbance and distressed over the loss, and I despair because I let {130} myself get distracted so easily.

In all three cases it is the same sound, even the discord is the same. But its significance for me is different, and the reason is that each time I am in a different frame of mind. If the noise slips by me, it may be because I am insensitive to discord. But it may also be because I am concentrating so deeply that what touches me on the surface cannot reach me at depth. Again, I may hear the sound as discordant and it distresses me but not so much as to distract me from what I am doing. The distress does not get down into the depth where I am working on my problem. There seems to be one path from surface to depth for someone concentrating and a different path for someone else who allows himself to become easily distracted. And then the one who falls into despair over the distraction *is* in his depth in a different way than someone who calmly gets back to work after getting distracted.

[Surface and depth]

There are different ways the depth can be reached from the outside world, different ways impressions are engaged at the various levels, different ways one level affects the others. The differences also point up individual differences, since all the contrasts that we mentioned are more pronounced in different individuals than in the same individual at different times. Some live mainly at depth, but others seem so entirely given over to changing surface impressions that we are tempted to say they have no depth at all or at least they do not live at depth actually.

All these are but particular suggestions and need to be worked out systematically in a theory of the structure of the person and of personal types. All they show is that it is meaningful to speak of "surface" and "depth" and may help us to understand what it means somewhat better. What touches the surface may penetrate to the depths gradually or at the moment of contact. This shows how inept these spatial images are, for the depth may lie on the surface so to speak, I mean when the depth is struck immediately upon contact. When we say that a subject's mind is "concentrating" or "distracted" or "dispersed," we mean that he may be at one point of his interior region *completely*, he may be as it were drawing itself together there, or he <may be> at several points at once, perhaps spread out over its entire surface.

[Two dimensions]

How does this relate to what is distinctive of personal being and how does it tell us *what* the person is? For one thing, as we have seen, not {131} everything that the person is, is actual at the same time in his conscious spiritual living. So must not this "*what*" have parts and be extended even though the extension be quite nonspatial? If the extension is not spatial, can it then be temporal? For a person's spiritual living and his acts, as we know, occur one after another, and one "part" after another passes over into actuality only to fall back into inactuality. The person behind the succession, too, is formed over time. For we have seen that "character" develops gradually and that the development also shows an alternation of potency, habit, and act.

But a temporal succession of one act after another will not quite do here. There already is a simultaneity in the acts for different acts occur beside one another, and a *single* subject lives at the same time in several acts of different content. The diversity of potencies and habits corresponds to the diversity of (the species) of the acts. So here, too, besides the succession in time, we have discrete contents separate from one another — a second dimension if you will.

But this still does not give us what we are after. Acts and potencies come not only in different kinds but also in different values or degrees of importance in the overall makeup of the person.

[A third dimension]

Recalling for the moment our generic distinction of acts and potencies in the understanding, sense appetite, and will, we see that in our understanding we have an external engagement with the world, in our sense appetite a give-and-take with the world, and an outreach into the world in our will. These three are intrinsically connected, for the inner give-and-take presupposes some engagement with the outside, and the deliberate intervention in the world presupposes a certain inner give-and-take.

This gives us a starting point for understanding the "surface." It makes sense to call a mere external contact "living on the surface," I mean, merely engaging objects externally without being inwardly affected by them. (Penetrating things with the understanding goes further, since, as active, it is the work of the will [*Willensleistung*] and as such must come from the depths.) "The sense appetite" will appear as an "inner space," and feelings, appetitive stances, and emotions [*Affect*] (these are but expressions for actual living in this area; their specific meanings should be analyzed) will have their specific "place" within this "space."

The corresponding potencies and habits (temperaments and character traits, sentiments, etc.) are also organized according to surface and depth. Not everything that can be truly said of a person is equally characteristic of him nor equally relevant for judging his character. If, as we have just said, objects {132} penetrate to a depth proper to them, the surrounding world [*Umwelt*] of objects appears to be decisive for this "third dimension" of acts and potencies. On the other hand "penetrating to a depth" implies that the depth exists independently of what does or does not penetrate it. Thus the person himself, in what he is in himself, in his core, seems to be what has a dimension in depth and is the deciding factor in determining the depth of acts, habits, and potencies.

[Qualities, time, and God]

Do the other two "dimensions," extension in time and diversity in qualities, also apply to the person? The difference in qualities, I would say, comes purely from the objective [*gegenständlich*] side and is not founded in the person. To be sure, the person does not lack qualities; he has qualities in himself, and he has a say in the qualities of his acts and potencies; still, his *quale* [what he is like] is simple.

Now, as far as extension in time is concerned, the person doubt-less *is* throughout the entire duration of his actual life and of the development that takes place therein. Still, I am inclined to think that the person himself is not in the *same* temporality wherein his development takes place; he rather takes effect into the midst of this time in such a way that what he shapes has duration in time.

We would then have here an analogy with God's being which is throughout all time and yet is not in time. Of course God's being is eternal, and we are speaking now of finite persons having a beginning in time. This means that their actual life, which is lived into time, begins. The questions of whether their own being is temporal and what kind of being they have are connected with the other question that we asked earlier and postponed: is the core subject to change?

4. The three questions interrelated.

[Engaging and affecting the world]

What is the person, if we disregard all the things that play out one after another in the course of his life? He is something put into the world as a center to engage the world —in the form of the intellect— in such wise that he is either beset by the world or penetrates into it by overcoming it. This either-or is not exclusive. The two forms of the intellect lie beside one another within the individual and mesh with one another, as we have seen. But the relation between them is not the same in all individuals. As the world has an order, indeed not only an order of one thing separate from another and stemming from another [*Auseinander*] but an order of rank, the spirit must have a makeup able to engage the world in such a way that it can do justice to these differences in rank. I mean that the mind must have a depth that corresponds to these differences.

The spirit grasps the rank of things as it is affected by them. This is why knowing {133} adequately is an act wherein understanding and emotion pervade one another. (They no more pervade each other completely in us than our knowledge is adequate.) When our being is affected by things, the inner effect reaches the point where we are pressed to behave practically in a relevant way toward what we know. For the person is at the same time a center wherefrom his working reaches out into the world. Neither engaging the world nor working in it and on it are altogether colorless; they do have characteristic qualities due to the center from which they proceed. The human person has neither the *breadth* to engage the entire world, nor the *depth* to grasp all the ranks of a be-ing, nor the capacity to be moved, the *power* to be inwardly affected by all of them in a living way nor to be prompted to effect bring them about practically. Depth, breadth, and power —different in each individual— describe the measure of being that is proper to particular persons as well as the possibilities a person has to effect what he is in himself in his actual living.

[Actuality and potentiality of the core]

If by the person's core, that is, what the person is in himself, we understand this distinctive something having qualities and certain dimensions, we must now ask again what act his being is and how it relates to his actual living. We have seen again and again that not all that the person is, is continually converted into actual living. Does this mean that it is not itself actual? We can and perhaps must say that the person's core is potential relative to his actual life, that is, to his conscious spiritual living and also to the process of development that accompanies it; the core is the possibility of this actual life. This possibility is not merely logical but real; the person's core is the basis for his actual living, it *is really* [*wirklich*]."

And insofar as we interpret actuality as reality in contrast to mere possibility and act as the act of being, the person's core has actual being. On the other hand, it is potential in the sense that it is a lower level of real being, so that the same thing that at one time is potential at another becomes actual, or rather may become actual. Conscious spiritual living is the highest level of actuality and so the highest mode of being of the person's core. The core as a whole is potential relative to this higher mode of being of actuality, but the core enters the mode with one "part" of itself after another, now with this part and now with that. We must now discuss what these "parts" are.

["Parts" of the core]

We had, however, decided that we should see the core as simple. Surely there are no real pieces that can be separated as parts of a material body. What becomes actual does not get detached from what remains potential. A whole always lies behind anything that is actual at any one time. More precisely, {134} something belonging to the whole enters the mode of actuality without withdrawing from the wholeness, as something relatively selfsufficient yet connected with the wholeness. If we wish to use a spatial metaphor again, we can say that a ray of light strikes a small spot on a surface; the bright spot stands out from the surrounding dark area, but it is not cut off from the rest of the surface.

In a spatial continuum we can break off any part we wish (if we are referring not to purely mathematical objects but to empirical bodies or their surfaces and edges). We cannot do this to the "parts" of the personal core. It is not a spatial sort of continuum. We have already seen curious differences between "dimensions" of the core and spatial dimensions. The "distance" between surface and depth varies in different individuals and in the same individual at different times, and the center may even lie on the surface. For this reason we cannot, it seems to me, separate what is actual in the person's core from what is potential. At the same time we should consider the possibility of a kind of separateness [*Abtrennung*] wherein an actual life would exist that did not come from the person's core.

["Impersonal" life]

We have yet to answer the question we asked about the possibility of such an "impersonal" life. We took the "most impersonal" living to be external perception that "slips by" us without making an inner impression. Does a purely surface contact between subject and object really take place here? And if so, could we still speak of an "act"? Who would be its "bearer"? I mean, what be-ing would activate itself in the act? Perceptions that arise involuntarily and are not pursued for the sake of some interest nor awaken interest as they occur do seem to leave the person untouched with what he is in himself.

We do find very little here to ponder on the side of the subject. The subject merely engages what falls upon the senses in its objective significance; the "meaning [*meinen*]" or the "knowing [*Wissen*]" that lives therein is the minimum activity the understanding contributes here. I daresay it is a fiction that the subject is in *no way* affected. Even when something leaves us indifferent, the indifference is a "mood" or an element in the overall mood of the moment.

If we do grant this fiction, we arrive at a purely intellectual subject (we should eliminate from it only whatever is "inner," but not the sensibility, which gives the content). The subject itself would no more be affected by what it perceives than its {135} personal distinctiveness would color the perception. Assuming the same sense data, we could imagine that a series of subjects would have exactly the same perception of a thing from the same standpoint. A subject that lived like this would be a person that lacks what he is in himself, it would merely engage what it takes in without any given-and-take with it. The potency actualized here would be the *intellectus possibilis* with minimum involvement of the *intellectus agens*. The subject appears, as it were, at the mercy of the world outside, a stage of shifting impressions. If true we would have to distinguish in what the person is between what he is in himself and his potency to take things in.

[Closing the window]

It is questionable whether we can imagine a practical intervention in the world set in motion only by impressions from outside and not issuing from the center, from the core. There is indeed a mechanical action where the person seems to have no more inner involvement than when perceptions slip by him. When I shut the window so that the breeze does not blow my papers away, I can do it without thinking about it beforehand, even without knowing what I am doing. A few minutes later I may be surprised that the window is closed. My action was an instinctual [*triebartig*] reaction to what the air was doing, not a free act in the sense of deliberately doing something that I choose in full awareness. Yet my action is not completely "unconscious." My degree of consciousness is only much lower in comparison to my "central" concern at the time. My consciousness is so low that I may not retain it later; I shall not remember that it happened.

Neither may we say that such a reaction occurs without the emotions taking part. For my reaction consists in warding something off that I perceived as unpleasant; still, for this reason something has gotten into me, even if the unease does not affect me at my center any more than what causes the unease.

[Center and periphery]

(The contrast of "center" and "periphery" may need brief clarification. We have seen that several spiritual stirrings of different content may be actual at the same time. Usually there is one that I prefer
to live in —whose object is what "really" concerns me—, while other
things are only going on incidentally <on the periphery>.
This contrast is obviously different from that of surface and
depth. Something may be occupying me centrally without reaching
into my depths, and something may be in my depths that only makes
itself felt peripherally. Depth and surface have to do primarily with
the content of the acts, center and periphery with the ways the acts are
performed, the degrees of actuality, still within actual life.)
    A good sign {136} that such involuntary actions come from
within is the fact that the way they are performed, the movements, etc.,
are characteristic of the person. This, to be sure, can be clarified only
by studying bodiliness.

[Mechanical delivery]

    Doing something mechanically is somewhat different from
reacting involuntarily. Mechanically repeating something from memory is an example. When a child recites a poem without thinking about
what it means or without understanding it, his words do not appear to
come from within. He may of course be proud that he can recite the
poem or annoyed because he is forced to recite it, but such things are
not essential. And all this may take place outside of a social setting, as
when the child simply spouts whatever comes into his head.
    The want of inner involvement usually shows itself in inappro-
priate emphasis. But lack of meaningful emphasis does not imply that
there is no inner involvement. On the other hand there may be appro-

priate emphasis with no inner involvement; we may detect an inner void— it impresses us as hollow pathos. This is often the case when a person begins to read or recite from memory with inner involvement and regard for the meaning, but then his articulation gradually becomes mechanical. In the change of delivery, now stiff, a lifeless reproduction, we notice what his inner involvement is like and learn of the character that it reveals.

How recitation can become mechanical is of course another problem. We must not, I think, call an entirely mechanical process "spiritual." It is a psychological process formed from the spiritual, but the spirit no longer lives therein. Again, we must study bodiliness in order to understand this whole question. A mechanical process is no longer a personal, actual living of the spirit. Such processes are no longer borne by the person; they are but a semblance of actual spiritual living, an appearance that when taken for genuine spiritual life is deceptive.

[Fake art appreciation]

We have another example of a deceitful semblance of living when a person associates with others while in his core he has no sufficient reason to do so. He belongs, say, to a milieu of art lovers and acts as if he, too, were interested in artworks and enjoyed them, whereas in truth he has no "artistic sense." He need not fake or consciously feign enjoyment and interest. In conscious deception, {137} one deliberately expresses on the outside what is missing on the inside, for there is no spontaneous movement that he could display.

In the first case the person may actually believe that he is interested in art and enjoys it, but his interest and enjoyment are quite "lifeless," nor would he bother about such things were it not for the group pressure. Of course when he has something he is *really* interested in and *really* enjoys, he must realize the difference himself. Then too, he may feel real enjoyment in these things, but left to himself he would not bother about them— he is "swept along" by the others. All this needs further clarification.

[Artistic sense]

What is "artistic sense" in the first place? It is the potency to appreciate something in its beauty and to derive enjoyment from it. A person's intellectual and affective attitude toward art lies in his natural predispositions, that is, in what he is potentially from the beginning of his existence. When he encounters art objects, his potency passes into an actual mode and, after the aesthetic acts cease, is retained as habit. I hardly think any spiritual person lacks this potency altogether, but it does show quite considerable variation. Where the potency is minimal, it will not prompt the person to seek out objects of art (as it does in those who possess a great deal of it). And when he does come across such objects, his emotion [*Affect*] (without pressure from others) will show scant vitality and warmth. The warmer and more vital his affective reaction, the more the person is moved by the artworks ("the warmer and the more vital... the more" means that the warmth and vitality show how much the person is affected) and the more his core is actualized therein.

When someone with little yen for esthetic experience goes out of his way to create the conditions for it, and, though little affected himself, acts and talks as though he were deeply moved, —whether he is aware of it or not, and whether or not he wills it— there is a discrepancy between his inside and his outside. His outward behavior pretends that something exists that actually does not (perhaps even for the person himself), or his behavior seems hollow and phony.

The discrepancy may come out when the person outwardly acts as art-lovers do but cannot "keep up" with them on the inside. He may be able to keep up intellectually but not affectively. It is odder still if he "joins in" affectively as well. In these cases the person lacks any great natural sensitivity to art, but inclines easily to strong emotion. He is actually affected inwardly, not by the art {138} but by how others are reacting affectively. More precisely, he does not enjoy the others' enjoyment as they enjoy the works of art; rather, the others' joy affects him and he experiences it as enjoyment of the work of art without any inner bond to it. Here his inner behavior itself is not semblance, nor is his expression of it hollow and lifeless. His external and internal behavior only become deceptive when it leads someone else to attribute to him the artistic sense found only in his associates.

We can understand such association only with the help of a philosophy of community living.[169] In the work and passage just cited I wish only to show that persons have a life that to a large extent is borne by others— to a large extent, but not completely. For "associating with others [*Mitleben*]" presupposes that the person's being has the potency to be affected by the life of others, and it presupposes some familiarity with the special area, even if this familiarity does not correspond to the life he shares with them.

[Conclusion]

In regard to how what the person is in himself is related to his actual living, we may conclude that his living is borne not only from within but also from without, and from the things he encounters as well as from the persons he associates with. Living that at first is spiritual may become mechanical, when it is no longer spiritual living and the person does not continue to live therein. Such mechanized

---

169   Cf. my work on "Individuum und Gemeinschaft [individual and community]" <"*Beiträge zur philosophischen Begründung der Psychologie und der Geisteswissenschaften*," II, op. cit.> and in the present work, pp. 386ff.

processes nonetheless presuppose a genuine personal life.

A person's living may to a large extent be borne by that of others. When this happens, his living is not the pure, unmistakable effect of what he is in himself; still, his living too is grounded in what he is. Hence we may not gather what a person is in himself merely from his actual living. Yet even if his entire actual living were a pure, unmistakable consequence of what he is in himself, we would not *identify* [*ganz haben*] him with it, since he does not enter into his actual living with all that he is; for more or less of what he is enters into his particular acts, but not everything that he is, not even throughout his entire life. {139}

5. Can the core be completely actualized?
Can it be annihilated fully or partially?

[The dark core]

What the person is, therefore, remains ever mysterious for him and for others, it is never completely disclosed nor disclosable. Never— that is, insofar as and as long as his being alternates between potentiality and actuality over time. "Insofar as," since his being is more than this alternation. What lies behind this flow of life without becoming actual and hence transparent (*intelligibilis*) therein should not simply be defined after its mode of being. Insofar as all that it is allows in principle for actualization in the flow of spiritual living, the person's entire core is in potency to this actualization, and spiritual actuality, conscious of itself, is its highest mode of being.

But insofar as the core, even when it is not actualized in the flow of life or when it is not transparent but lies behind it "darkly [*dunkel*]," has not only a "possible" but an actual and effective being, this being, too, should be called actual. It is an actuality analogous to that of material things. Just as their nature unfolds and becomes understandable in their working in a causal context, so "spiritual natures" unfold in the flow of their life. The difference in being is that spiritual working is transparent whereas material working is not. Hence what "lies behind" can become transparent in the one case but not in the other.

[Time and eternity]

We said that the core of a person cannot be completely disclosed, insofar and *as long as* its being is an alternation of potentiality and actuality. This is the reason why the being of a person need not in principle be such an alternation nor need it be so always. We have stressed again and again that in God there is no contrast of potentiality and actuality, of what has and has not taken effect, of what is and is not transparent. But finite spirits cannot be *actus purus* like God. They are not immutably, in highest actuality, everything that they are and can be. To the limitation of their being belongs the possibility that this being be diminished and heightened by the action of other spirits (as we have seen in the angels). But we may imagine that what they are in themselves is enduringly actualized and intelligible in the greatest measure of spiritual living that they can attain. This is obviously the way we should understand St. Thomas's view described earlier, that the angels' essence is enduringly actual and present to them.

And I daresay we should also understand the *status termini* [state "of the end," i.e., in the afterlife] of human persons in an analogous way. I mean, as the enduring, highest attainable actuality of what they are in themselves, in such wise that nothing dark and unknown any longer lies behind their actual spiritual living, and in the person's core the alternation of potentiality and {140} actuality is superseded, the core itself being released from temporality and placed into eternity. We should not regard this release from temporality as complete, since in the blessed and in the angels there is still a flow of life wherein actuality and potentiality alternate in their intellectual and practical behavior toward things and through their contact with other spirits. On the other hand, we should not understand this being placed into eternity as if it began absolutely at the end of earthly life. The end of earthly life and the entry into eternal life would mean that "darkness" fades away and the entire personal core becomes actual and transparent. However, it is clear at the same time that the core has already been in eternity throughout the entire duration of its earthly life. Time is in eternity and never ceases therein. And what is in time is for this very reason in eternity, but it is in eternity in a way other that it is in time. The person's earthly life is temporal; it has a beginning and an end in time and fulfills the duration between them. This temporal life includes several other things, as we have seen, such as the flow of spiritual living and the "stream of consciousness" that unfolds therein, as well as the development of the human person occurring in tandem with this conscious life, the unfolding of predispositions, and the forming of character.

In Catholic teaching development ceases when earthly life ends. But the person does not cease to be; he continues to be what he is —this is clear from the phrase "*status termini*"—, and he enters eternity with what he has acquired, as what he has become. In what he has become, however, lies what he has been from the start: it is kept or lost. The core of the person that he brings with him into his earthly life prescribes beforehand how his life can and should be lived and what he can and should become. What the person is in himself is to be actualized and retained as habitual —as far as it is at all possible—; when this happens, it is gained for eternity. What could have been actualized but was not is lost for eternity (though not under all circumstances, as we shall presently show). How much further can we clarify these facts? In the first place, how are we to understand that something that can and should become does not become and is lost?

[The buried talent]

We are thinking of the parable of the buried talent.[170] Someone has a great gift for poetry, say, and feels obliged to develop it as well as he can, to write the poem he has in mind as perfectly as possible. All sorts of obstacles stand in his way. He needs {141} all sorts of background studies, but they are hard to come by and some he cannot obtain at all. Health problems interrupt and hamper his work. If he is to finish his poem, he must summon all his powers, forego most of life's pleasures and even some activities that in themselves are good and beneficial. He has misgivings about whether it makes sense to stake everything on the one card, to sacrifice so much, perhaps only to achieve nothing. And besides all this, the deep concentration involved in spiritual creation demands painful exertion and is an enormous venture from which he repeatedly shrinks. Given all this, is it not quite unlikely that such a man will reach his goal?

If despite all his exertion he is overcome by the external obstacles, his failure is a loss for the objective [*objektiv*] world of spirit, which now is missing something which would have made it the richer. But in his inner world the inevitable happened, for in his extreme exertion he actualized the ultimate depth, brought it up to the highest degree of being it could reach. On the other hand, the loss is not only external but internal as well if the person, granted that he could have overcome the external impediments, did not execute the work or left it unfinished because of inner obstacles such as the dread of sacrifice or intense exertion required. For he did not grow in creative power as <he> could have if he had created the poem; his depth has not entered

---

[170]   [Mt. 25:14-30.]

his actual living. He lives his life on the surface, perhaps to a large extent mechanically, lifelessly. What is left unused may remain hidden to others and to himself. He does retain the possibility of actualizing it until the final moment of his earthly existence. Then the talent he buried will be taken from him.

This language suggests that something that was passes into nonbeing and that it does so not by itself but through one's own act. Just as the actualization of what a man is is to a large extent left up to his free deed, so we should interpret it as a free deed when the divine judge raises what he "has made of himself" to a higher mode of being or annihilates [*vernichten*] what he has failed to use. Ought we to view these alternatives only as a complete raising or annihilating of the person as a whole, or may they be partial? This question is related to another: is the personal core simple or divisible?

[Purgatory]

The teaching on a place of purification apparently points to the possibility of partial annihilation [*Vernichtung*] and partial retention [*Bewahrung*]. The soul's union with God in the *visio beatifica* [beatific vision] presupposes the absence of stain. But not only do souls without stain [*Makellosigkeit*] enter eternity. Rather, after {142} earthly life ceases and before the *visio beatifica* begins there is an intermediate state wherein stains are purified. How are we to interpret these stains ontically? Theology calls them "*peccatum veniale*," venial sin. Sin is defined theologically as a violation of a divine commandment [*Gebot*]. It is serious when the matter is grave and the violation fully voluntary, and venial when the matter is not grave or the violation is not willed in full freedom.

[Violation of a commandment]

Breaking a command [*Gebot*] is the deed of a man. The command exists independently of the man to whom it is given. It has a content or matter wherein a specific doing is enjoined or forbidden, and it has a form whereby it addresses the man's will and requires him to submit to the command, comply with its matter. The understanding must grasp the command in content and form in order for the will to be able to comply.

What a man does may be at odds with the matter of a command while he is ignorant of it. In this case the infringement is not voluntary nor culpable (provided that his ignorance itself is not culpable). The offense is not voluntary unless the person understands the command in matter and form and then acts otherwise. The violation is sin when the command comes from God. When the discrepancy between the command and the man's action is only objective [*objektiv*] and the infringement is not voluntary, the action may either be free or instinctive [*triebhaft*] and more or less deeply anchored in the person. His action is freely willed when it is a fully conscious violation of the command. Here there are several possibilities. The violation may come from a strong desire to do what conflicts with the command *despite* the conflict, or it may occur in rebellion against the command as such and against the one who has given it. In either case the person is affected in his depth. In the second case there is a confrontation in the ultimate depth.

[Decision making]

Every time a person makes a completely free decision —I mean, does not allow himself to be more or less instinctively swayed by some motive, but weighs several practical possibilities, in the limiting case just to act or not to act, and then of his own accord chooses one of the possibilities—, he performs an act from the center and depth of his being. He as it were gathers his whole being together at one point and lets it become active in his free decision. This is why decisions are highpoints in a person's life.

But the person's being is always involved here. Weighing practical {143} possibilities always entails a value judgment, for we try to find what is "better." "Better" may mean better for the choosing person himself, that is, enhancing his being or at least not threatening it. Or it may mean better absolutely, that is, apart from its significance for the person, something higher in rank of being for which by his decision he may be ready to sacrifice something of his own being. (But in the objective and absolute sense he will always gain if he decides for what is objectively better for the sake of its objective worth, since such a decision in itself represents a heightening in his being.) In the dread of making decisions, which is found in most people and in many is pathological, may lie the dim knowledge that by deciding we are "forging our destiny." This attitude, though, fails to appreciate that we can in no way escape decision, since by failing to act and by evading decision we also determine our being. Hence every decision entails a heightening or lessening of being.

[Sin]

Now if my decision involves a confrontation with God —and it does when I am fully conscious of a divine commandment [*Gebot*] and decide for or against it—, being or nonbeing are at stake. Deciding against God is called sinning. Deciding against Him means deciding against the absolute being that bears all created being; hence it means deciding for nonbeing and for annihilation [*Vernichtung*]. The worst case is where the commandment as such is rejected (not merely because of its matter). The response is a displacement into nonbeing [*Nichtsein*], which is the mode of being of the demons and of the damned. Is it not absurd to call nonbeing a mode of being? We shall put off this discussion a moment and attempt first to explain the less radical cases.

[The murderer]

The murderer knows that it is God's commandment not to kill. He is not out to revolt against God; he just wants the money a lone hiker on a country road has in his pocket, and he kills him because he cannot get it in any other way. We say that he is stained [*beflecken*] with a grave sin; he turned away from God and God from him. What does this stain consist in? A murder, moreover a murder committed during a robbery, a murder out of greed, is disgusting and outrages our natural feelings.

But what does our disgust mean ontically, and what knowledge lies behind our outrage? Someone who murders in order to rob places material goods above life. And this reverses the hierarchy of being. The murderer wills to annihilate life and hence to annihilate being, and this is evil absolutely. It means (in the Catholic view of the "last things")[171] exposing {144} the person to the annihilation [*Vernichtung*] of his being for all eternity, and this is Satan's work. It means breaking the bond that joined all men from the beginning and made all human life dear to each man, and this is a breach in the order of nature. All told, these are disorders, disturbances in the cosmos. But they cause disorders in the being of the murderer himself and in his relationship to God.

---

[171] [Death, judgment, heaven, hell.]

[Natural moral knowledge]

The "normal" man has a natural "sense" for what is right, for the lawful and moral order of the world. According to Thomas, this sense is a natural habit which, quite as much as the principles of theoretical knowledge, is an original possession of spirit. The traditional name for this habit is "*synteresis*"[172] By virtue of this habit we perceive a disturbance in the moral order as such, and from this habit comes the desire to reestablish the balance, to readjust the dislocation. A disturbance of the order of law and morality can be brought about only by free acts.

The restoration must begin at the point where the disturbance originated, I mean in the person who committed the wrong. What a person does is a consequence of what he is. If he does wrong, something must not be right with him. If in practice he puts material goods over human life, he has an intellectual lack or flaw [*Mangel*] that keeps him from recognizing the right order, or else he has a lack in his sense appetite and in his will that causes him to act against his better judgment. The restoration of the order outside himself for which he is responsible can result from an act that does not come from him, but happens to him, that is, it is a *punishment*. The order within himself cannot be reestablished without his doing something about it. How should we understand this disorder in the person? Is it a lack in his personal core?

[Expressing what one is]

We have taken the person's core to be what he is in himself and what prescribes how his life can or should be lived and what he himself can or should become. "Can" or "should" do not mean "must." It

---

172   [Or "*synderesis*" (*Summa theologica*, 1:79:12), the habit of universal practical principles of moral action.]

is possible that the core does not unfold [*Entfaltung*] fully [*rein*] in its development [*Entwicklung*]. The person himself has a sense of how he could and should be but in fact is not. And this discord confronts him in others as well. A man is kind and warmhearted "down deep," but he cannot show it in his relationship with others because he is reserved and distrustful and shuts himself off from them. If he could get rid of his inner inhibitions, he would start really to become and appear to be what he is down deep.

The word "inhibitions" conveys something negative. Mistrust and reserve are enduring tendencies that determine the person's actual behavior, but they are not "habits" in the sense of positive posses-sions. They are "*privations* [*Privation*]," lacks in his being that make {145} it impossible or at least difficult for him to perform certain acts. Accordingly, we should take all the bad habits, failings, weaknesses of men as privations — including the root from which they all spring, the corruption of human nature through original sin. But how should we understand privation? As something that is not?

[Privation]

Being distrustful is not the same as not being trustful. Not being trustful is purely negative; it means the person lacks a habit without saying what traits he actually does have. The nonbeing that lies in a privation is of another sort. To be trusting means possessing a habit by which we easily pass into actual trusting in our contact with other per-sons. Being distrustful means having traits that get in the way of this transition and cause the opposite behavior. For distrust is a behavior, an act of the person; the word implies more than the absence of trust-ing. Distrusting means believing someone capable of evil, fearing he is a threat to our own or another's being, in particular when we do not know that we have a sufficient basis for our belief and fear.

Expecting the worst from a man need not be distrust; it may have a rational basis and spring from something positive: the habit of judging human nature. The negative side of distrust is the lack [*Mangel*] of this rational basis. When we call the traits that such behavior springs from "privation," we are not referring to something nonbe-ing absolutely, but something missing, flawed [*mangelhaft*], something falling short of what nature or reason requires. The measure by which everything is measured is perfect being, perfect goodness, perfect knowledge, etc. Everything finite, limited, created, falls short of this absolute measure.

[The positive, the negative, and merits]

There are two aspects of any finite be-ing. One is what it is positively, I mean the measure of its being whereby it resembles [*nachbilden*] the absolute be-ing. The other is a limitation of its being, what keeps it back, hinders it from becoming fully and completely what is should and could be positively and from attaining the highest measure of being it can reach. The "predisposition" a man brings with him into the world, the totality of his potential being, includes both.

On the other hand, by the person's "core" we should obviously understand only the positive side. If during his earthly existence a person by virtue of his freedom has overcome the obstacles as far as he could, then in the *status termini* or in the purification after death everything that hindered him, all privation, fades away and the core enters eternity without dross.

In the purification, therefore, nothing positive is destroyed; rather the impediments {146} blocking the pure effect of the positive be-ing are removed, for purifying is not annihilating [*vernichten*] but bringing about [*Herstellung*]. We said[173] that upon entry into eternity

---

[173]   Pp. 201ff.

what was actualized in earthly life is retained and raised to a higher mode of being. But we need not stop here; we may assume that in this transition *everything* included in the core is actualized and raised. On the other hand, where there has been culpable neglect of something that should have been actualized, we ought not to think that this is all that is lost and that the rest of the core is retained. Either the guilt is forgiven, in which case *everything* is gained, or it is not forgiven, in which case all is lost.

When we hear that a man's merits determine his eternal destiny and that there are degrees of blessedness, this does not mean that more or less of his personal core enters eternity. If he is saved [*retten*], he is saved *completely*. We should rather interpret it to mean that the higher the heightening of being undergone in eternity, which carries with it an infinite number of degrees of nearness to absolute being, the more has been actualized in earthly life through free will [*freier Wille*]. Thus the teaching on purification and the *status termini* does not contradict the conception of the personal core as simple but rather supports it. However, the core is not simple in the way that the divine being is simple since its *what* and its being can be separated and its mode of being may vary. Nor does the whole have a single mode of being throughout its entire duration but only in the *status termini*.

[Doubts about the mutability of the core]

Consequently it is not true without qualification that the core is something immutable, something that during its earthly existence merely makes itself more or less felt in actual living, but is the same at the end as it was in the beginning. Certainly, what a man really is is hidden from others, who see him from outside, and even from himself insofar as he sees himself as others see him; it is hidden by what he becomes outwardly in the course of his life. The child matures into a man, the man grows old— those who have lived with him see the changes and hardly continue to notice anything of what he was before, while those who met him lately know him only as he is now and can hardly imagine how he was once different.

But the man himself, when he does not see himself from outside but falls back on his innermost feeling of being alive, in a way remains ever the same as he was and can hardly conceive that he is supposed to be what others see him as. The more he lives {147} from his depth, the more fully [*rein*] he will unfold [*entfalten*] his core, the less important will the external changes be, and all of us must enter the kingdom of heaven as "children." Does this mean they enter the kingdom exactly as they were originally? We spoke just now of "unfolding the core." But this indicates that the core, too, purely on the inside, may not remain completely fixed and unaltered. The aporia that comes up at this point will be resolved later.[174]

[Nonbeing and the naught]

At the transition into eternity, with guilt and forgiveness, being or nonbeing are at stake. How are we to understand forgiveness and bringing about [*Herstellung*] being? These we shall not understand as long as we do not understand nonbeing. We saw that the most drastic stand against absolute being is rebellion against the divine command as such. Deliberately breaking a commandment when the offender is tempted by what is at odds with it is not explicit rebellion, but it does imply a disregard for the divine will and for the divine being as well. It is called turning away [*Abkehr*] (*aversio*) from God by turning toward [*Hinwendung*] creatures.

Venial sin is not a deliberate turning away from God. We are most likely to learn about nonbeing from the most drastic rejection

---

[174]   Pp. 391ff.

of the divine being: "I shall not do what God commands *because* He commands it." What could a person who would say this be like? The overall activity of a be-ing is the effect of what it is. Hence taking a stand against absolute being must come from a "be-ing" which in itself is most opposed to absolute being. The greatest antithesis to absolute being is nonbeing (insofar as absolute being is at the same time the absolute good or Goodness in person, its opposite must be evil or the Evil One, and we can thus see why evil has been defined as the nonbe-ing [*das Nichtseiende*]).

We may *say* this, but can we *comprehend* it? *Agere sequitur esse* [doing follows *being*]: being, or the be-ing, as such is effective in activity— but how is nonbeing and the nonbe-ing supposed to work, be active? If this is to make sense, such nonbeing must differ from the nonbeing of what never was nor is nor ever shall be, or from the nonbeing of what once was but is no more or what once will be but is not yet. A negative existential judgment (and with a certain modification, any negative judgment) denotes *something that is not*.

The separability of *esse* [being] and es*sentia* [essence] in every finite be-ing also makes it possible {148} to contrast a *quid* [what], a something of determined content, with its nonbeing. This separability is the essential difference between a finite be-ing and the infinite, absolute be-ing. In what is most diametrically opposed to absolute being, the separation must be increased to the utmost. In a something that is not (but could be) this is not the case, but it would be, I daresay, in a *naught that is* [*Nichts, das ist*]. This seems to be an utter paradox, and, seen in itself indeed it would be. This being of a naught [*Sein eines Nichts*] cannot, of course, be borne by the naught nor can it be from the naught; it must rather be maintained by the be-ing. Nor is the naught to be grasped in itself but only from the vantage of a something that has once stood in its place and was annihilated [*vernichten*].

The original negation or denial [*Negation*] must be thought of as an act of a be-ing, not, of course, of absolute being that cannot negate [*negieren*] itself. Now this obviously contradicts what we have just said: negation is possible only as an act of a nonbe-ing. But this statement had already proved to be intrinsically impossible, or else it demands an interpretation that would make it possible and at the same time compatible with the claim we have just made.

[Deciding against being]

A be-ing of a particular kind must have decided against absolute being, and precisely by so doing it must have passed into naught [*Nichts*]. This passing is momentary, but it involves more than what becomes naught since this does not have the power to annihilate [*vernichten*]. It also involves absolute being, and we should also take it as an effect of absolute being that the naught and the negation [*Negation*] are maintained [*erhalten*] in being.

The decision against being is a spiritual act; hence the subject performing it is a person. Even after being annihilated [*Vernichtung*], the being still maintained by the subject must be spiritual and have the form of personal being. But it is completely emptied, for it can be nothing but pure negation directed against every be-ing. Yet of itself the person can annihilate nothing, for his "potency [*Potenz*]" is im-potence [*Ohn-Macht*]. Nothing can ever be annihilated except by absolute being, and in the case of persons this is conditioned by their free decision against being, and hence for nonbeing, as it first took place in the original negation.

Breaking a divine commandment for the sake of its matter, not its form, is not a direct negation, denial, of absolute being. The violation implies a negation in that the person decides in favor of something at odds with the commandment, and the violation becomes explicit since for the sake of the matter he also decides against its form. But he does not will the negation as such, and the negation of being is never total because the desire that leads him to break the commandment contains the affirmation of a be-ing, and every affirmation of a be-ing implies the affirmation of absolute being. A {149} basis is thereby given from which, after the turning away [*Abwendung*], a turning back [*Rückwendung*] is ever motivated (even though it does not becomes actual).

[Damnation, mortal sin, atheism]

In this whole discussion of sin and justification the person's being and nonbeing is at stake. The absolute negation of absolute being brings about [*bedingen*] the annihilation [*Vernichtung*] of what the person is, as what is annihilated is maintained in a "null being [*nichtiges Sein*]"; I mean damnation [*Verdammnis*]. We may well venture the claim that absolute negation is purely diabolical and that in men during their earthly existence some affirmation of some be-ing or other, and hence of being as such, will always remain present.

The state of the mortal sinner comes close to the state of damnation. His annihilation has not yet ensued, but he courts it, and it may occur at any moment. His being is not pure negation; it is still "something," and the core of the person whose being it is continues to be effective in its spiritual actuality. He goes on working at his calling, say, even working quite hard, perhaps out of a natural desire for the good. But negation, denial, is in his being.

If he believes in the God whose commandment he flouts, in the almighty and just One, he will live in dread of being annihilated. He will be conscious of his being as threatened, exposed to annihilation [*Nichtigkeit*], and he will perceive all he does as provisional and invalid [*hinfällig*] so that the hovering between being and nonbeing that belongs to all finite being holds a central place in his consciousness and dominates the entire actual life of his spirit.

At first there seems to be no negation when the person does not believe in the existence of God nor therefore in the binding nature of His commandments as such, nor did he act in marked opposition to them but was rather unconcerned about them. In this case the negation does not lie in a rejection of the commandments. It is however —implicitly or explicitly— a denial of God, a theoretical negation of absolute being. We do not wish to inquire now how far this negation itself is a sin. It objectively implies a negation of all being —insofar as all being is brought about by absolute being—, and thus the negation in turn enters the being of the person himself. He need not realize explicitly the consequences of his intellectual attitude toward absolute being, but the entire life of his spirit will be more or less subverted by skepticism and with it the consciousness of his own being, in turn the consciousness of a null being.

For fear of "falling into the hands of the living God," sinners take refuge in theoretical denial, but their flight only leads to another kind of dread [*Angst*]: dread of the naught [*Nichts*]. In all these cases the negation impairs an existing personal being to a greater or lesser extent; {150} it will always be possible for this being to be freed from the negation. (We have yet to discuss how far this liberation can go, since after all a certain negation lies in finite being as such.)

[Turning to God, grace and justification]

For this liberation a free turning toward absolute being is needed. This turning toward, we said, is ever motivated in a positive attitude that belongs to personal being toward some be-ing or other as long as the absolute denial [*Negation*] of absolute being has not occurred. In all of man's doing aimed at maintaining his being, even in the dread of annihilation, there lies an affirmation of his own being and with it —implicitly— of absolute being by which he himself is.

A theoretical explanation of the connections between absolute and finite being can lead to a reversal of the theoretical denial of absolute being (the way of the arguments for God's existence). Here instead of negation there is affirmation, that is, a theoretical turning toward [*Zuwendung*]. And if the intellectual attitude to absolute being is not impeded in its effect, from it will spring the affective [*affektiv*] affirmation of absolute being as well as the practical behavior that it demands. And just as on the part of absolute being annihilating may respond to the negation or turning away [*Abwendung*], so a heightening in being, a raising to a higher mode of being that we call "*grace*," may respond to the turning toward. The negation of the negation in freely turning toward and the heightening in being together yield *justification*.

The path to justification need not begin from theoretical explanations. This is the rule when the negation was primarily practical. In the sinner who breaks a commandment for the sake of its matter despite his belief in God and in the binding character of His commandments, there is an inner contradiction between his theoretical and practical behavior toward absolute being. He is conscious of this conflict in his own being. It makes itself felt in an inner unease that prompts him to suppress this state of mind either by trying to get rid of it by a theoretical negation that gives his practical behavior a legal basis or by negating the practical negation, by turning back to absolute being and submitting to the commandment that in turn makes the elevation possible.

Venial sin also connotes an inner conflict, not between intellectual behavior and affective or practical behavior toward absolute being since no turning away from Him has resulted, but between the behavior required by the turning toward and the de facto practical behavior. The conflict is eliminated by taking an inner stance against the disordered practical behavior and by correcting it or, when this cannot be done externally, standing ready to correct it. The response

{151} does not of course require that the sinner be welcomed anew by absolute being, as is the case of mortal sin, since no separation has occurred; however, a heightening in being (an increase in grace) is also possible here.

In the *status termini*, what remains fixed is the attitude toward absolute being: either turning away or turning toward, intellectually and affectively. On the other hand the *status termini* allows for any reparation that is still owed for practical transgressions as well as the elimination of any inner conflict that continues to hinder the full positive effect of personal being in its turning toward absolute being.

6. Summary of the provisional results on the core of the person.

[The four questions]

We did not make these last points out of theological concern but in order to understand better what we are calling the person's core about which we had already discovered much. Four questions kept reappearing in the most diverse contexts and seemed to demand one answer at one time and the opposite at another. (1) Is the person's core actual or potential? (2) Is it simple or divisible? (3) Is it mutable or immutable? (4) Is the person's actual life entirely or only partially anchored in his core, or can he live out his life without his core taking any part in it— that is, can he live "impersonally"? We can summarize all our analyses in the following way.

1) [The actual and potential]

The person's core is the be-ing which the person is in himself and through which he is a *similitudo* [likeness] of divine being. It is what positively lies behind the *analogia entis* [analogy of being] as its basis.[175] What makes the *analogia entis* a *maior dissimilitudo* [greater unlikeness] does not belong in the person's core. The core is an *actu ens*, a be-ing in act in contrast to sheer possibility; more precisely, it contrasts not only with logical possibility but also with sheer potency in the sense of undeveloped capability. However, the core is not *actus purus* but something actual that is capable of being heightened in being, indeed heightened to the form of being of the conscious life of spirit. The being of the core may be called potential in respect to this heightening in being.

2) [Simple and complex]

This be-ing approaches the simplicity of divine being in the following ways. (a) The core is not in time in the same way that the course of development that it underlies is in time. (b) The core is a simple *quale* [what (it is) like] without separate qualities and potencies which first appear {152} in what develops from the core. (c) Everything that it is can be gathered together in one act (in the sense of spiritual actuality) in the greatest heightening of its being: at particular moments during earthly life, and enduringly in eternal life.

This be-ing falls short of the simplicity of divine life in the following ways. (a) This concentration of all that it is, is not its constant mode of being but —*in statu viae* [in the state of earthly life]— the highest measure it can attain at certain moments. And even in eternity it is not absolutely constant because what it is itself is capable of being enriched and heightened and because what it has —its spiritual possessions— must be distinguished from what it is. Its possessions need not lie enduringly as a whole before its spiritual regard as it does in

---

175   For the person's *analogia entis* cf. p. 128 above and pp. 406f below.

the all-embracing divine knowing. (b) Therefore in the actuality of its living, what it is and what it has emerges in succession or in alternation— hence partially. (c) The extension of its being into a network of separate things [*Auseinander*] is not only a temporal continuum but stretches between surface and depth. (d) What emerges from its being in the actuality of its life has the form of being central or peripheral. (e) It also has various degrees of intensity.

3) [Changeless and changing]

The mutability of the core is the issue that we have least resolved. So far we have seen only that the core lies behind the person's process of development —his actual living and the ongoing formation of his potencies into habits— but it does not itself undergo this development. Still, there were several hints that the core itself does experience a change which we called "unfolding"[176] and which cannot be clarified before further investigation.

4) [The core and actual living]

The person's actual living is not founded on its core alone, but also: (a) on the world of objects with which he comes into contact, (b) on other persons with whom he lives, (c) on his dispositions that in the beginning are altogether potential, allow a series of potencies to be differentiated, and develop to a greater or lesser extent into habits (or also privations) in the course of living. Pure spirits lack any initial conditioning for their actual living outside of their core, and in lieu thereof they are provided with forms of the understanding that are more than purely potential dispositions. For this reason we should assume that both are *in ratione materiae* [by reason of the matter],

---

[176]   [Reading *Entfaltung* instead of ms. *Enthaltung*.]

that is, that they have their root in the material basis of human being a person [*menschliches Personsein*].

In pure spirits there is no actual living that is not an effect of their personal core or an actualization of the forms of their understanding, though it may also be caused by other persons. In human beings [*Mensch*] we found {153} three kinds of apparently "impersonal" living: [1] a life lived purely on the surface awakened by the world outside, [2] a life taken over by other persons and borne by them, and [3] a mechanical life. None are *totally* impersonal. External things touch the person even if only superficially. To be affected by the life of others the person must be in living contact [*Fühlung*] with them, and he may not be entirely closed to the objects that move them; the fact that a life has become mechanized presupposes that it was originally personal.

[Analyzing the human person]

To cast light upon what remains obscure about the being of the person, we must see how the person is integrated into the material and spiritual world. In particular we cannot analyze the *human person* adequately from the purely spiritual viewpoint before considering how he is shaped in body and soul.

However, after the many turns our analyses have taken in this last part, we must first summarize what we learned about the ontology of the spirit and apply it to our central problem: potency and act.

§ 9
Summary of previous results
for an ontology of the spirit.

The basic ontological forms, *object* [*Gegenstand*] (*something*), *what* (what the object is), and *being*, have appeared repeatedly in our material inquiry, although we could not always keep them apart nor avoid passing from one to the other. These forms can serve now as guiding lines for a summary.

[The object]

There are different forms of object [*Gegenstandsform*] in the realm of the spirit. The basic form to which the others hark back is the hypostasis. (1) The hypostasis is what is from itself and by itself [*aus sich und für sich sein*]. (*From* itself refers to something that is the principle of its being albeit not the ultimate principle. *By* itself means something that is in itself [*in sich*] and not in others, that is, it is a substance). This is subdivided into what exists not only from and by itself but also *through* itself [*durch sich selbst existieren*]—absolute being— and what receives its being from the absolute being. The further formal relation of existing-for-its-self [*für-sich-selbst-Dasein*] defines the hypostasis of the *person*: the *one* infinite person and the manifold of possible finite persons. These are the two forms of *subjective spirit* or of spiritual subjects.

(2) The second basic form of spiritual object is the *objective spirit*. Objective spirit is the spiritual that exists in dependence upon subjective spirits; it is the world of objective spirit surrounding each person and {154} borne by the person (his "ideas") or by the objects that are placed in existence by persons and go on existing apart from them; that is, ideas formed into matter (the person's "works").

(3) The third basic form is what is inherent in the subjective spirit and determines its being: its *forms* or *species*. There may be a transition, however, from the second to the third form and conversely.[177]

---

[177]   Cf. p. 227-8.

[The *what*]

The *what* that fills these forms is both common to them all, justifying the common name "spirit," yet different in each. The common *what* we may take negatively as immaterial [*immateriell*]; it does not fill space, is not bound to time in the same way as a material *what* is timebound, and lacks sensible qualities.

Positively, we may understand the *what* as being illumined, open, and active, or able to be illuminated, open and active. Illumination and openness in the subjective spirit mean becoming conscious of itself [*Seiner-selbst-Bewußtwerden*] and knowing [*Erkennen*], and in the objective spirit they mean becoming transparent [*Durchsichtigwerden*] and becoming-known [*Erkanntwerden*]. Activity in the subjective spirit is a free doing and in the objective spirit a working [*Wirken*] similar to the workings of nature.

The species, however, are the means that the subjective spirit uses to disclose the objective [*objektiv*]. We are aware of species in their effects analogously to the way we are aware of the doings of the subjective spirit without them being an object nor being known as an object, yet able to be objectified and to become known.

[The *what* proper to each form]

We have thus differentiated *what* is in the realm of spirit and so in a certain sense its being as well. We must now show the different contents that correspond to the several forms of the *what*. The person is what *is* as original in the realm of the spirit, it is what is conscious of (or knows) itself and of other being and of other be-ings, and it is what is active in willing freely.

The infinite person is absolute being. Absolute being has appeared again and again in all our formal and material inquiries as the principle and measure of all being and every be-ing: knowing, power, etc. It is being itself in Person; its diametrical opposite is the naught [*Nichts*] in person.

Between the two are positive finite persons, who are limited in what they are and in their being. What they are is in part something fixed which they bring with them into existence and retain according to their *what* throughout the duration of their being. We called it the person's core, and Thomas saw it as the essence or species of pure spirits. It is something individual, that is, numerically and qualitatively unique. It is also given a further stock of be-ings: the forms of the understanding that enables {155} it to know other being.[178] In a part of their stock of content the forms are general, but they are individuated by their being in persons. In pure spirits, the forms comprise a fixed stock in their totality.

In men, the forms they receive in addition are the principles, the "seeds," by using which they expand their stock of forms over time. Thus in men something is joined to what they *are* enduringly; something that becomes and grows and changes. What becomes is already something at the beginning of its becoming and throughout its entire duration, and we call this something, which materially [*material*] underlies the becoming, the person's "*predispositions*" or his stock of potencies. They are [1] the ability to use forms, to acquire new ones, and through them to know (intellect), [2] the ability to be set in motion inwardly through what the person knows and through his own being or what he is in himself (emotion), and [3] the ability to commit himself to something, to act and to shape (will, practical and creative powers). What each person has become, what his dispositions have developed into, are his habits and privations, and, taken as a whole, his *character*.

---

[178]   I should like to leave it open here whether there are analogous forms for the sense appetite and the will.

We have already found that what the person is includes the third basic form of spiritual objects mentioned above, that is, the forms or species that are in the spiritual subject and determine its being. The second basic form, the ideas and the works of persons, together with their *what*, comprises the meaningful content [*Sinngehalt*] of all real and possible things.

[Being]

Differences in spiritual being correspond to the differences of form and content of spiritual objects. The highest mode of being is actual conscious living that is a free doing as well. When immutable, it is absolute being; for finite persons it represents the limit which their being approaches in many different degrees. We call this highest degree of being pure "actuality" (*actus purus*). We also use "*actuality*" of the <degrees> of nearness to it (albeit they already contain something of potentiality). And we call "*habituality*" and "*potentiality*" the more distant degrees, each ordered to higher degrees and permitting access to them.

The being of finite persons is at once potential, habitual, and actual, but it is relative to different things and also has different meanings. In pure spirits, the core (their species) is enduringly actualized in conscious life. The forms of their understanding are partially actual and partially habitual as is also, analogously, the world of ideas they bear. The being of pure spirits is potential insofar as it allows {156} for elevation to a spiritual life higher than the life that corresponds to their essence and insofar as it is exposed to possible annihilation.

In human persons the core is not actualized as a whole in conscious spiritual life. What is not thus actualized is potential or habitual relative to the highest degree of actuality that the core can reach by itself. Nevertheless, when we claim that the core as a whole is enduring actual, the words "actuality" and "potentiality" mean something different from what they meant before. For we also speak of "potentiality" and "actuality" in the material world where actuality does not imply any conscious spiritual life nor does potentiality imply a degree of being that allows for a transition to the conscious life of the spirit. Actuality in matter means *effective* [*wirksam*] (but not conscious) being and potentiality means a lower degree of being that allows for a transition to that higher degree. This actuality is also found in what is spiritual in the subjective sense but with the difference that here it is joined to the potentiality of passing over into a conscious spiritual life, whereas the actual, in the sense of being effective in the material area, represents the highest actuality that material substance can attain without any possibility of passing into conscious spiritual life. It permits only a transition into the actuality of the spiritual being in the objective sense through its effects deriving from the spiritual.

[The being of spiritual objects]

Here we are broaching the question of the being of spiritual objects. Their being differs from the being of persons in that they are not from or by themselves, much less do they exist through themselves or by themselves. They are *through* persons, that is, they have received their being from persons either directly through God's creative act or through the creative activity of finite persons. (The former objects are the purely *natural* things [*Naturding*] which we call "material [*materiell*]" insofar as they are formed matter but which we should also call "spiritual" insofar as an idea of God is effective in them as their form. The latter objects are the works of men (or also of created pure spirits) that we group under the heading "*culture*" and represent a sort of second creation, analogous to the world created by God).

Spiritual objects are not by themselves; they are either maintained through the spiritual activity of persons or borne by matter. Nor are they from themselves, for they are not a principle of being and working as are, analogously to the first principle, finite persons by virtue of their freedom. They do not exist for themselves; their being is not conscious spiritual life. We may call their being "illumined" (intelligible) only insofar as it can be transparent for persons; we may call it "spiritual" as well, since it can unfold effects in spiritual persons. (We have not as yet discussed this kind of effectiveness adequately; it has to do with {157} how the person is integrated into the spiritual and material world.)

The contrast of actuality and potentiality is not found in God's ideas, which belong to divine being and are eternally actual. The forms found in natural things have actual being inasmuch as: (1) they inform matter, (2) they condition the external effectiveness of the material things in the causal network of material nature, and (3) they are known actually by persons and share in determining their spiritual being. These forms are potential inasmuch as: (1) they can be annihilated (not in themselves but in the concrete wholes whose form they are), (2) they do not take full effect in matter, rather the forming comes about successively in a temporal process, moreover it may not be complete for the entire duration of the thing, (3) their possibilities of being effective in the causal network of the material world are only partially and successively actualized, and (4) the possibility of their affecting the being of spiritual persons also becomes actual only successively and partially. An analogue is the relation of actuality and potentiality in the works [*Werk*] of finite persons.

[Ideas and species]

The ideas of finite persons are actual inasmuch as (1) they stand before the mind in conscious spiritual living and belong to it inseparably, and (2) by means of their shaping they are effective in actual spiritual living in the development of the person himself and in the world outside. They are potential inasmuch as (1) they have passed completely or partially into the mode of inactuality characteristic of the immanent sphere, and (2) not all their possibilities of being effective are realized.

The *species intelligibiles* have their being *in* persons; they have being actually insofar as they function as "means" in the actual life of the spirit, and potentially or habitually insofar as this possibility is not actualized. Their being can pass over into the being of ideas insofar as they are known and hence can lie before the mind. On the other hand, the ideas can pass from their objective status into a functioning status in such wise that they, too, must be regarded as forms of the spirit. Hence we should draw no sharp dividing line between them. (A more specific inquiry would define their mutual relationship.)

What we call "potencies" and "habits" are also forms of the spirit which are potential or habitual respectively and are actualized in the corresponding acts of the person. This explains the variation in the use of these words. On the one hand they denote modes of being yet something be-ing as well: properties, dispositions, states of substances, and even the substantial [*substantiell*] form itself. The person (and any other substance) is what he is in his various modes of being, and terms for these modes are transferred to what is in this way.

VI
Finite Things as
Hierarchy of "Formed Matter"
In Contrast to the
Metaphysische Gespräche
By H. Conrad-Martius

§ 1
The significance of human nature
for issues of act and potency.

Our study of matter [*Materie*] has led us to spirit, and our study of spirit has brought us back to material objects. The things we deal with in our experience are units of spirit and matter, matter formed by spirit. Material things bear something spiritual in the objective sense within themselves, in their "nature." In man we have a compenetration of personal spirit and matter (in the usual sense of the word). In the course of our investigation as we seek to be clear about inanimate things and human personalness, we shall also be learning how spirit and matter are connected in lower living things, which lie on a level between nonliving things and human persons. For all these objects of spirit and matter in their totality form a hierarchy wherein the higher in a certain way include the lower. Since for us spirit in its purest form represents pure actuality and unformed matter pure potentiality, and if we are right in viewing the relation of soul and body as one of form and matter or act and potency, then the study of human nature must also tell us more about act and potency.

§ 2
Possible approaches
to the relation of body and soul.
Matter and spirit.

[St. Thomas's theory]

Thomas conceives the soul as a spiritual substance, the lowest in the realm of spirit. As such it adjoins the highest material substance, the human body [*Körper*], and can unite with it as its form.[179] When {159} he defends his view of the soul as the form of the body against other views and rejects a purely external connection between them, his reason is that the body [*Leib*], once it is separated from the soul, no longer remains a body; that is, the eye is no longer an eye, etc. At this point we are referred to phenomenological analysis, which can tell us about the essence of body and soul and help us to understand its ultimate ontic structure.

[Two approaches]

We met with the distinction between spirit and sensibility in our immanent analysis. We claimed that the activity of the subject, which is self-conscious life in the most proper sense, is spiritual (spiritual in the subjective sense). From this we distinguished immanent data. These data appeared as belonging to the I, not as objects independent of it (not as transcendent objects); however, they also appeared as something foreign to the I, something immanently transcendent [*immanent transzendent*]. Our study in the preceding section was confined to the spiritual and only occasionally touched upon this area as a whole, for there our intention was to contrast the life of the human spirit with the

---

[179]   *Quaestiones disputatae de spiritualibus creaturis*, a. 11 and *De anima*.

life of pure spirits. We may perhaps begin here to understand how a living spirit penetrates what is not spiritual. This penetration also confronts us phenomenally in the body [*Leib*] (especially another's body) that stands before us as *animated*, *having soul*, and we perceive the body (especially our own body) from within as belonging to the spirit and animated by it. This would be a second approach. But we shall also have to ask whether the connection of the spirit to what is not spiritual suffices to distinguish the soul from pure spirits, or whether we might not see the soul in itself as an item of its own kind.

§ 3
Attempt to distinguish soul and spirit
by comparison with the divine spirit.

[Conrad-Martius's elemental spirits]

H. Conrad-Martius has taken this approach in her "Gespräch über die Seele [discourse on the soul]."[180] And in my *Individuum und Gemeinschaft* [Individual and Community] I, too, took this as my point of departure. We shall ask then to which spiritual beings [*Wesen*] we are and are not assigning a soul and seek the reason for this distinction in order to find out "what the soul truly is."[181]

So far {160}we have considered two chief kinds of "pure" spirits: God and angels. H. Conrad-Martius also considers elemental spirits [*Elementargeist*] of spiritual and bodily shape such as the elves, nymphs, etc., familiar from fairy tales and sagas. Were it necessary to collect and compare all possible types of spirits, we would have to

---

[180] *Metaphysische Gespräche*, Halle, 1921. Although at first she is careful to keep "soul" apart from "spirit," after her preliminary discussion of spirit she takes soul as a kind of *spiritual* object.

[181] Loc. cit., p. 26.

do a preliminary study listing them all. But a complete induction is unnecessary in principle since it is not a matter of induction but of an ideating abstraction based on sufficiently clear intuitive material. We shall begin with the kinds of spirit that we have already discussed.

[God and man, goodness and soul]

We speak of God's spirit but not of His soul. Is it His infinity that forbids us to attribute soul to Him? Or is it the originalness of His being (the fact that He is the *ens primum* [first be-ing] through Himself and the principle of all else)? Or is it His pure actuality or His simplicity?

To begin with His simplicity, we say that a man has a soul, but of God we could say only that He *is* soul, since He *is* all that can be said of Him. *May* we say that God is soul as we say that He is goodness [*Güte*], whereas man only has goodness or is good [*gütig*]? We may say neither. Man is not "animate [*seelisch*]" in the way that he is good. The soul is not a property [*Eigenschaft*]. If we may say that man "has soul [*Seele haben*]," we must ask what we mean by this. What does "having" mean? And do not "having soul" and "having *a* soul" mean different things?

We have previously attributed spiritual "belongings [*Habe*]" to the person ("habit" in the noematic sense); that is, his world of ideas which (in finite persons) is only partially actualized at any one time but from which everything can in principle be recalled (successively) and considered actually. But we distinguished this noematic habit from habit in the noetic sense, which is not what a person has as his own but what he himself *is* or what he himself *is* like [*wie*][182] habitually. Parallel thereto is what he is potentially and what he is actually. His potencies, habits,

---

[182]   "What he is *like* [*wie*]" understood not as a mode of being but as a quality of the be-ing.

acts —that is, what is potential, habitual, actual at any one time— are not "belongings," "possessions," like his world of ideas.

This is why we are already speaking improperly if we say that a man is goodness, for it is more appropriate to say that he is good. It is obvious why the soul is not a "belonging" in the sense given. When we say that a man has soul and body, we do not mean an external (material or spiritual) possession nor something accidental, nor what or how he may be at one time, but what he is essentially, that wherein his {161} being necessarily unfolds. Everything we can ascribe to him belongs to his body or to his soul (or to both at once).

Accordingly we could, in better keeping with the sense, render "man has soul" as "man *is* as an animate essence." This locates him within a particular genus of be-ing and ascribes to him a particular way of being [*Seinsweise*]. And so it already appears clear why we cannot say that God "has soul." For God cannot be fitted into any genus of be-ing, and no particular way of being can be attributed to Him since He is being itself, being without qualification.

[Belonging to God and having (a) soul]

A difficulty seems to arise at this point. Have we not constantly called God a spiritual being [*Wesen*] and assigned a special way of being to Him and Himself assigned to a particular region [*Region*]? On the other hand, we sought to use "spirit" to label a particular region of be-ings; so if we were to conceive God as a particular object in this region, we would be ignoring the fact that He transcends all regions. However if every be-ing bears an analogy to divine being and in divine being has its measure, this is preeminently true of spiritual being. God *is* spirit. Spirit in its purest form is pure act or pure being. This is why although God does not belong to any region of being, a region of being does belong to Him in a special way. Indeed, the region itself has been burst open so to speak by its belonging to him, since every be-ing as such has a share in the spirit. But not every be-ing has "a share in the soul." For a be-ing to share in the spirit means that something spiritual has entered into its makeup, that is, a spiritual subject or an idea. "Something of soul" can enter the structure of a be-ing only in the sense that "a soul dwells therein." And a soul does not dwell in every be-ing, nor does every be-ing "have a soul."

We just asked if "having soul" and "having a soul" mean different things. "Having soul" we interpreted as belonging to a definite genus of be-ings. (We leave it undecided for now whether "soul" itself is this genus.) "A soul" denotes an individual. "The man has a soul" implies that something individual dwells in him that we call "soul." Hence it implies at the same time that this man has *this* soul. We cannot say that he *is* this soul insofar as "is" would mean equating the object with all that he is. In this sense we could say the man is the whole consisting of this body and this soul. We may even say "he is in this soul" insofar as the soul's entire being is the man's being, and we may say "this soul is in him" insofar as he is a whole that includes more than the soul. If we ought not to say that God has soul, neither ought we, *eo ipso* [by this very fact], to say that He has {162} "a soul." This is incompatible with the simplicity and with the infinity of divine being.

§ 4

Comparison of the soul with
"soulless" finite spirits.

[Soul, spirit, and man]

It follows from what we have said that the soul is limited and that it forms part of a whole. It shares this first feature with other cre-ated spirits, and the second distinguishes it from "pure" created spirits.

Now, to make this clear, we must say more about being a part. There are wholes that are made up of selfsufficient parts (from parts that can exist outside of the whole) and are selfsufficient relative to these parts (individual parts can be lost without the whole ceasing to exist). In this sense the angels can be called "parts" of the heavenly court.

The soul on the other hand is an *essential* part of man; without the soul the whole wherein it is cannot exist. Is the soul also unselfsufficient relative to the whole? I mean, is it true to say that it cannot exist outside the whole, it cannot exist without being connected to a body? Popular belief both past and present has invested "departed souls" with a shadowy body and portrayed them as longing for their body of flesh and blood. This implies two things: the separation from the body is both possible and unnatural. It is not very promising to discuss this as long as we are not clear about what the soul and body are. If the connection of body and soul could not be broken and if it could be modified only to the extent that the soul could be separated in a certain way (to be further discussed) without completely ceasing to exist, obviously we should then assume that it is just this bond to a body that distinguishes the soul from pure spirits.

[Conrad-Martius: soulless spirits]

This view would be inconsistent with the possibility that there are spirits that have spirit and body but no soul. H. Conrad-Martius brought in elemental spirits that have such a nature, because a comparison of be-ings [*Wesen*] of body and spirit with those of body, soul, and spirit, she claims, would be most likely to tell us about what the soul is. (Opposing "spirit" and "soul" in this way already implies that they are incompatible, whereas in the Thomistic view the soul is spirit; to this we must return later.) It may be, of course, that the bodiliness of be-ings "with souls [*seelenhaft*]" must differ in principle from the bodiliness of spirits without souls [*seelenlos*]. If on the other hand the essence of the soul, and hence the soul itself, could {163} be conceived as "pure" spirit without defining it by its connection with a body, we might also be able to distinguish the soul from other pure spirits as another kind of be-ing.

[Conrad-Martius: elemental spirits, angels, men]

For H. Conrad-Martius what distinguishes be-ings that have souls from those that do not is a kind of weight [*Schwere*]. Elemental spirits are entirely confined to the natural sphere to which they belong; they embody the spirit of their sphere; they *are* this spirit in person and live it out in constant actuality. The angels, too, are confined to the heavenly sphere and live from it.

But man [*Mensch*] is set into a central self [*Selbst*] and with it he must engage the world. The world engulfs this center —namely, the soul—; the center is burdened with the world and must bear it. Man is shaped in three ways from the root that fashions him [*Bildungswurzel*]. He is raised to spirit and shaped by his body into the outside world, but in his soul he is truly at home. The soul is the midpoint of his being, yet from it he lives as from a ground that lies beyond. For the soul never enters completely into the actuality of living. With his life on the periphery man constantly distances himself from his central self, and there are "as it were, soulless" men whose central self is not quickened at all in a life that remains entirely on the surface.

[Two views on the core]

There is much in H. Conrad-Martius's descriptions that recalls what we said in the last section about the person's core. This therefore will be the best vantage from which we may contrast our two views.

Both views presuppose a basis for the being [*Seinsgrundlage*] of actual living that does not enter completely into the actuality of living yet could in principle become actual as a whole (she considers this possibility without deciding for or against it). Both also assume that we are dealing with what is "innermost" in man, what he is in himself and that with which he takes up all else into himself (insofar as he does take it into himself). In both views the emotional life [*Gemütsleben*] belongs more properly to this center than does intellectual living, which engages what lies without. Also there is a distinction, depending on the participation of the center, between living actually on the surface and at depth, and this is the mark of different kinds of persons.

We differ from Conrad-Martius when she distinguishes spirit and soul in man and rejects soul in the higher spirits. To proceed further here, we must inquire into the concept of spirit behind her claims.[183]

[Conrad-Martius: the spiritual]

Conrad-Martius stresses {164} (speaking of the meaning of the word "*spiritus*") that the essence of what is spiritual is that it breathes, spreads its essence about itself as an aura [*Hauch*]. This "breathing out, exhaling" or "spiriting [*Geisten*]" wherein the be-ing gives itself away by radiating, corresponds to "breathing in, inhaling" or a "bodying [*Leiben*]" wherein the be-ing takes possession of its very fullness and conserves itself.

She does not intend any sort of material [*materiell*] bodiliness here, and so we may say of God, Who is spirit in the most perfect sense but whose essence also takes effect most perfectly, that He "spirits" and "bodies" most perfectly, streams forth perfectly, yet at the same time conserves His total fullness. Breathing is not only proper to

---

183   She does not discuss spirit in her discourse on "*Die Seele* [the soul]" but does so in the following "*Um den Menschen* [on man]" (<H. Conrad-Martius, *Metaphysicische Gespräche*, loc. cit,> especially pp. 128ff).

personal spirits, for even things like a landscape and a melody radiate their own aura. She speaks of "objective spirit" in this sense. Her view obviously differs from our own, presented earlier in this work. Objective spirit is not attributed to every item shaped by an inner form nor even to every human work, but only to one that in a certain (but not completely specified) sense is alive.

[Conrad-Martius: God, souls, demons]

Material bodying differs from spiritual bodying. In the former, fixing one's own essence means weighting, burdening, stiffening. Moreover, "hungering spirits [*Hungergeist*]" are different from substantial spirits. The former cannot "body"; they can only "spirit," but they do so not in the sense of breathing out their own fullness, but by longing after, craving, the fullness they lack. Such are demons and departed souls.

The demon, "albeit a dreadful unbe-ing [*Unwesen*]," is nonetheless "shaped" as a "be-ing [*Wesen*]" of a certain kind —this contradiction is actually its distinctive feature— insofar as it lives and "issues [*west*]" from itself and must raise itself within itself to a certain kind of spirit. But insofar as the demon does not really raise itself to itself, since after all it cannot reach itself at all but is only driven and as it were possessed by the life that gives it its qualities yet without possessing its life nor resting in it by possessing it, neither can the spirit that it "breathes out" manage really to spread itself out or freely reach the substantiality that would offer it its essence and would be proper to it as such. Just as the whole be-ing hungers after itself, after true essentiality [*Wesenhaftigkeit*], so its "spirit" also hungers after itself, "after true spiritualness."[184]

---

[184]   Conrad-Martius, *Metaphysicische Gespräche*, op./ loc. cit., pp. 138ff.

This is diametrically opposed to God, Who rises [*erstehen*] from Himself from age to age, "free of nature" yet not "without nature." God,

> from His primeval, sheer, ungraspable stillness, has engendered and awakened in Himself a primal, quality-giving life of nature. Thus *even* in his very first "beginning" and ground, He is free of the life of nature and master of it.

This is the "first point of freedom," {165} the

> *punctum saliens* [crucial point] of any possibility of substantialization [*Substanzialisierung*], wherein the entity [*Entität*] no longer has any quality-giving life behind itself nor is "had" by it, but has its life before itself, *getting hold* [*habhaft*] of it. Its own essence and being becomes a personal "property [*Habe*]"— without which there is no body, no spirit. All of this, by the way, we may take as much as we like as impersonal and as happening only as passive fate.[185]

The "poor souls" are banned from the existence of bodily fullness into the abyss of their hungering, starving life, whereas in the demons

> their insatiable hungering spirit belongs to their nature essentially as shapings of their quality-giving primal life. Indeed, they *are* nothing except just this personified rush after effecting and shaping.[186]

[Conrad-Martius: soullessness in demons and elemental spirits]

---

185   Loc. cit., p. 141.

186   Loc. cit., p. 148.

Demons and elemental spirits differ as spirits "born of nature" and "born of spirit." Demons "come back [*urständen*]" in "primal nature" "as personified primal life in its many possible shapes." That spirit of nature or of things of nature, which is objective, essential, and exhaled, is personified and shaped in elemental spirits. They "revive" in a secondary life because "no objective spirit can exist, unless first led up from the primal life that gives them their qualities.[187]

Elemental spirits "are soulless" precisely "because they come back in the spirit but not in primal life since they develop not from down up but from up down."[188] Creatures born from spirit lack soul "because they do not reach down into the depths within themselves."[189] Nor can one quite properly use the word "soul" of the spirits of the depth "until the soul has been made the midpoint of a be-ing [*Wesen*] that is shaped truly and now itself bodies and spirits out of the soul into manifest existence."[190] On the one hand one may sooner speak of "soul" in the case of an animal than a demon, since the animal truly bodies. On the other hand, one could attribute soul in a more proper sense to a demon than to an animal because the demon, but not the animal, is a personal being. The demon is "naked life— having taken shape as such" hence a "be-ing of soul [*Seelenwesen*]" that has taken shape purely as "having a soul [*seelenhaft*]."[191]

The phenomenon is purer still in the "unsubstantialized [*entsub-stanzialisiert*]" dead called {166} the "poor souls,"

since here it is really the "leftover" soul, that is, the quality-giving midpoint of life in itself, raised to personal essentiality

---

[187]   Loc. cit., p.150.

[188]   Loc. cit, p.151.

[189]   Ibid.

[190]   Loc. cit., p. 152.

[191]   Loc. cit., p. 153.

and no longer able to be divested from this its own formation, yet now unsubstantialized— unbodied and unspirited.[192]

[Conrad-Martius: soul in higher animals and man]

The distinguishing feature of the soul according to H. Conrad-Martius is being the midpoint of life. Later on she also takes "soul" in a wider sense, no longer restricting it, as she did in the beginning, to higher animals and humans but applying it also to plants and lower animals as well as to higher spirits. "We can apply the word in the general and purely objective sense to what itself gives qualities."[193] This comes close to the Aristotelian-scholastic view, which also speaks of the "soul of plants." "But it is the plant itself that still lies completely outside its soul," but in the animal, a depth wherein the animal itself dwells breaks open, "and the higher animal, which begins to dwell in the depth that gives it qualities and from it to live and act personally, is the first to have a soul in the precise sense."[194]

When she speaks here of the animal's "personal life," she does not accord it any personhood or "personal soul." "The plant is... totally immersed in its bodied shape and for this very reason is not master of it."[195]

But the animal, drawn back out of this bodied shape and immersed in its quality-giving ground, is the personal master of its body. This means that here for the first time the bodied shape *becomes* a body in the precise sense.[196]

---

[192] Ibid.

[193] Loc. cit., p. 206.

[194] Ibid.

[195] Ibid.

[196] Loc. cit., pp.206f.

The plant is still not master of its body, which therefore is "impersonal."

The animal has a personal body but not a personal soul; for although it is master of this body because it has its base no longer in the body but in its soul, it is not master of its soul precisely *because* it has its base in the soul.[197]

On the other hand, the base of a man is shifted into his spirit, and so he can have his soul and master it. The shift of base into spirit, however, is not the same thing as sinking into the center of the soul, but

as such an unselving, becoming radically free and loose from fixedness {167} in the enclosing and binding self."[198]

Since "it is important for the be-ing of this base to unselve [*entselbsten*] and be free in it and with it," a man, by rising into the spirit, becomes "not only free toward and master of the center of his own soul but also free toward and master of his own spirit.'[199] It is just this "being raised, constitutive of being, into the unselved height of the spirit... that makes the person a person."[200] Man's being enthroned freely over himself seems less wonderful in the case of persons who issue properly speaking in the spiritual, that is, in the case of substantial pure spirits, than in man in whom "the self" is constituted "not from the fullness of the spiritual but from the fullness of the subterranean powers of nature."[201]

---

[197]   Loc. cit., p. 207.

[198]   Loc. cit., p. 218.

[199]   Loc. cit., p. 219.

[200]   Loc. cit., p. 220.

[201]   Loc. cit., p. 230.

[Conrad-Martius: man's spirit and soul]

In the broader meaning of "soul" as the "quality-giving ground of each living be-ing"

> spirits, too, would have a soul, specifically a "spiritual" soul, whereas soul in the exact and narrower sense applies to that ground and center of nature that takes its fullness and life from the deep and dark.[202]

Here Conrad-Martius distinguished between the impersonal and personal soul, and of the latter one can say

> that *only* man has a soul but not other be-ings of nature nor the pure spirits, not beings of nature because their soul is impersonal and not pure spirits because their soul is spiritual.[203]

But man, "rooted in the unfathomed depths and freely raised above himself," "growing" on "darkest soil and enthroned in the light," is twice born."[204]

> Begotten and formed from the quality-giving bottomless primal grounds of nature, yet at the same time is he born from the "spirit"— hence he issues [*wesend*] personally from below and from above.[205]

Man *qua* man is a be-ing born of nature, *not* born of spirit," he

---

202 Ibid.

203 Loc. cit., p. 321.

204 Ibid.

205 Loc. cit., p. 235.

takes himself totally up from below; but to be able to take himself from below as a person, he must take his freedom in the spirit from above. So not only his spirit but also his soul becomes his free personal property. Thus he is enabled to lead {168} all that lives and drives in the dark of his soul up into the light and into freedom."[206]

That place of absolute freedom, that place of the free birth of the I [*Ichgeburt*] or of the constitution of the I... must needs be the portal, metaphysically open, through which God's spirit can freely pass. Man has his own spirit stemming from the depth of his personal individual essence [*Einzelwesen*], but his spirit is to be transfigured and raised by God's spirit into the Absolute.[207]

When the triune Godhead is said to dwell most personally in man's soul, this cannot be true of his "soul of nature." "It is possible only where man's soul has emerged in the spirit and from the spirit —as from a second birthplace— or is strengthened in the spirit."[208]

[Conrad-Martius: personal spirit]

Within our present context we cannot do justice to the wealth of intuitions and ideas contained in H. Conrad-Martius's little book. We shall begin by describing the apparent differences between her discourse on "*Die Seele* [the Soul]" following the summary we have just given and our own analysis of spirit in the present work.

The author now acknowledges a narrower and a broader sense of "soul." She also attributes soul in the wider sense of "quality-giv-

---

[206]   Loc. cit., p. 237.

[207]   Loc. cit., pp. 237f.

[208]   Loc. cit., p. 239.

ing ground" to the pure spirits. However, we may, I think, understand this "quality-giving ground" of what the pure spirits are in themselves, their species or their personal core whose mode of being, in their case, is the subjective life of the spirit. To distinguish spirit and soul we should keep in mind not only this twofold sense of "spirit" but also the many different aspects under which spirit is understood.

Whereas at first she stressed that spirit is characterized by a living inhaling and exhaling, "spiriting" and "bodying," and supposed that this may take place quite unconsciously and involuntarily and that it is also possible as "objective spirit," she later distinguishes "spirit in the personal sense" from this sense of "spirit" and adds "it is not possible to be a spirit in the personal sense or to have a spirit in the personal sense without being *an I*'— and a radically new, free "beginning" as well:

> a self without selfhood [*Selbstigkeit*],... a being yet without being, and for the first time, with all this emptiness and detachment and freedom, the personal *par excellence*."[209]

She then {169} stresses

> that such a beginning cannot be created, set or formed out of nature and with nature, that only the primal begetter [*Urzeuger*] itself can raise itself from itself from age to age from the abysmal, primal grounds of its nature to radical freedom, can engender itself to a free primal beginning in itself, and then whatever in the same freedom, whatever as spirit, is to issue and live, can do so only by personally taking part in this one substantial primal spirit and primal beginning. For how could a finite thing, a creature, stand and stay as beginning by itself

---

[209]   Loc. cit., p. 234.

alone in radical freedom? No, coming forth immediately from the primal I [*Ur-ich*]—not as created but as lastingly begotten or born thereof or dwelling therein— it is itself an I.[210]

The "radical selfless form" of this self-unfolding and breathing out that is proper to spirit becomes in the personal spirit the "radically selfless way" to contact and embrace something, a way that is the "hallmark of intellectual having, of understanding and knowing."[211]

[Conrad-Martius: the unspiritual soul]

Conrad-Martius, gradually feeling her way forward in her *Discourses*, reaches a highpoint when she sees spiritualness in the most proper sense in God's personal spirit, free and intellectual. "Raised to spirit" means "raised to God" and raised to being similar to God. This is why the author attributes a "spiritual" soul to the pure spirits and also why she calls man's soul "spiritual" insofar as it has undergone this elevation.

But can there then be an "unspiritual" soul? Only what is spiritual can be raised to a personal kind of spiritual being. The main reason, it seems to me, why we cannot clearly distinguish between soul and spirit in the way Conrad-Martius describes them in the *Gespräche* is that, while she repeatedly attempts to discover the *way of being* of what has soul and what has spirit, as well as to identify what is essential to the form of the object, she fails to determine the *what*.

Identifying God and spirit, however, demands specifying the *what*. If God, pure being, is spirit, then all that is must be through spirit and bear something of spirit in itself. In this way we have arrived at a much broader version of "objective" spirit. All creatures are what

---

[210]   Loc. cit., pp. 234f.

[211]   Loc. cit., pp. 215f.

they are through the spiritual put into them, through their inner "form" or "nature." And only through it *are* they actually. This is why we cannot speak of a "nature" and a "soul of nature" as something unspiritual. The distinctions gained in the analyses of the *Gespräche* should not again be blurred in this way. It may well be correct to distinguish {170} between "soul of nature" and "soul of spirit" but in a sense that does not do away with the spiritualness of the soul as such.

[Procedure]

Let us first try to say what the soul is following the themes Conrad-Martius, cautiously feeling her way forward, has brought together in her *Gespräche* from the most varied sources. We shall comment on the senses of "soul" that she distinguishes: first the broadest sense, then the narrower, and finally the narrowest. Soul in the widest sense is the quality-giving ground of every living being. In the narrower sense, soul is the quality-giving depth wherein the animate be-ing [*Wesen*] dwells and from which it lives and acts personally[212] as a natural ground and center, taking its fullness and life from the deep and dark.[213] And in the narrowest sense, soul is this natural ground raised to personal being, to spirit. If a common term is warranted in all three cases here, something objectively common must lie behind them.

§ 5
The soul of plants.

["Soul" and spirit]

If we wished to call "soul" simply what gives qualities, we

---

[212]   Loc. cit., p. 206.

[213]   Loc. cit., p. 230.

would also identify it with the inner form that we find as the quality-giving ground in every be-ing [*Seiendes*]. What is the distinctive feature of soul that sets it off from the forms of "lifeless things" and is proper only to living be-ings [*Wesen*]? (In this way we would arrive at the same time at the essence [*Wesen*] that characterizes the "living" in contrast to the "nonliving.") Living things [*Lebewesen*] obviously receive their qualities progressively from within —they are shaped and reshaped— over the entire duration of their being *as* living things, whereas nonliving things are "finished" from the beginning of their existence and are not further shaped and reshaped unless "set in motion" by outside forces. Being moved and shaped from within is the peculiarity of living things, their mode of being; it is *life*. And the *living* inner form that gives life is the soul. The forming and shaping of the whole that the soul belongs to is the effect of bringing the potential to actuality, for the soul itself is actual and active.

According to the ontic definition of spirit that we attempted in the last section, we ought to call this actual life-giving soul "spirit." I mean that we should see it as an objectively spiritual item but not as a spiritual subject or person since its living works from the inside out; in itself it is nothing; its being is not an inner spiritual {171} living, self-conscious and receptive of and open to the outside. Does "spiriting," the free breathing out of one's own essence, that according to the *Gesprächen* is the first characteristic of spirit, also apply to the "plant soul"? And does another kind of spiritual being besides the "objectively spiritual [*objektiv-geistig*]" in the sense that we have maintained until now, also apply?

[Flowers and granite]

The essence or inner form of the flower addresses us from its visible shape— it also speaks to us, often with greater force and concentration, from its fragrance; here the plant soul comes to us, as it were, as its aura. But what speaks to us in its external shape is the *same thing* that speaks to us in its scent (it is disconcerting if the same be-ing [*Wesen*] seems not to speak from both). It is a *spiritual aura*, which we cannot see or perceive with any other sense, that affects us inwardly; it is an aura given off by an object that sensibly tenders itself.

And yet this is true not only of living things but also of lifeless "items of matter [*Stoff*]." Granite tells us things about itself that marble does not tell us about itself; Gold reveals things that iron does not. We are thus led to attribute "spirit" not only to living be-ings but to every be-ing— as indeed we have already claimed on other grounds. And we are led to attribute two kinds of being and working to this spirit: it forms itself into a clearly defined shape, and it radiates itself freely— hence there is a "bodying" and a "spiriting" for every be-ing.

This "freedom" of objective spirit and this "spiriting" is not personal; it is not freedom of the will, nor is this type of spiritual being self-conscious being. (It is, however, one that can penetrate into spiritual persons in a certain way, as we have seen.) But it is actual being; in it the be-ing [*Wesen*] is fully open. Here we can speak of potentiality only in the sense of a possible transition into nonbeing and in the sense of unactualized possibilities of working through contact with another be-ing.

§ 6
The soul of animals.

[The inside and two outsides]

The *animal soul* [*Tierseele*], the quality-giving depth wherein dwells the be-ing [*Wesen*] that has soul and wherefrom it lives and acts personally, was distinguished from the "soul of plants," the form of a living thing [*Lebewesen*] giving shape from the inside out in a living process of becoming. The animal soul is also a form that shapes from the inside out in a living process of becoming, but at the same time it is open to the inside, for the soul is aware of itself, of what it is, and of its being. Moreover, this being does not merely shape itself toward the outside or radiate itself; it is also an inner process [*Geschehen*].

What comes from outside is taken up {172} inwardly and sets the interior in motion; then from the inside the "reaction" breaks forth. "From outside" here means the world without, not *that* outside into which the soul has been shaped, its *body*. This "outside" of the soul is inseparably one with the "inside" of the animal [*Lebewesen*]. The soul is "enclosed" by the body, through the body the soul marks itself off and marks off the entire be-ing whose form it is from what lies further outside. Through the body the soul receives what comes to it from outside and through the body it reaches beyond itself into the world without.

[Conrad-Martius: sensation]

When the be-ing that has soul is aware of itself and thus "has" and "possesses" itself as nonliving things and plants do not, what it is aware of is the whole of soul and body, and at this level being aware [*Innesein*] is *sensation* [*Empfinden*]. H. Conrad-Martius described sensation as

> having and possessing itself personally in the body.... For what dwells personally in itself —not in an objective and distributed way as plants, but in an interiorized, personal, and subjective way as animals— must of course *also share* any fate that befalls this possession on the inside or outside, by sensing and feeling it....[214]

---

[214]   Loc. cit., p. 212.

Yet this sensation is not *understanding*, it is not an intellectual being conscious of itself. The animal does not *know* that it is, that it has a body and a soul, nor does it know what its body and soul are like and what is happening in either and to either. Sensation is a "selfish [*selbstisch*]" having. In it the self remains fixed on itself— and "the essence of its own life or of its bodiliness" entails "that here the self appears fixed on the fullness of its selfness [*Selbstheit*]." The animal senses its own body and has it in sensation, together with

> whatever comes within reach of its sensation— whatever, by affecting it directly, *also* comes into the field of what it selfishly masters and has.... Body and sensation are just as indissolubly connected in essence as spirit and understanding.

Body here is "not at all restricted to the material body," but includes anything "that in full measure enters into the be-ing posited as body."[215] Even in "psychic sensations," in feelings, "I 'have' and experience sensibly, insofar as I dwell as body... in my interiorized self.[216]

[Animal spirit]

Sensation is consciousness on a lower level. The soul that owns [*innehaben*] itself and its body in sensation is no longer just objective spirit; it is subjective, yet it is still not a spiritual person. It is not a person since the soul's spiritual being is not open to itself and to what is not itself; the soul cannot "contact {173} and embrace" in "that radically selfless way" which is the "hallmark of intellectual having, understanding and knowing."[217]

---

215   Loc. cit., p. 214.

216   Loc. cit., pp. 214f.

217   Loc. cit., p. 216.

Nor does the soul have the freedom to master itself and take charge of itself. The animal has a personal body but not a personal soul, for while it is master of this body since it no longer has its base in its body but in its soul, it is not master of the soul, precisely *because* it has its base in the soul. That radiation of its own essence, called spiritual being in the objective sense in the *Gesprächen*, is also proper to the animal soul. The tiger's spirit is different from the bear's, the goat's spirit from the lamb's. If of these be-ings we use "spirit" in this sense, when for the first time —according to H. Conrad-Martius— we may speak of a soul "in the precise sense," we may feel that it means something different from what she called their soul (as well as from what she called man's spirit).

We are certainly warranted to speak of the spirit of the tiger. But it does not inhere [*innewohnen*] in the individual living things as indissolubly, it seems, as their soul inheres in them (or as "his spirit" inheres in a man). The "tiger spirit" is proper to every animal of the species even though one tiger can strike us as "more tigerlike" than another. Spirit in this sense is obviously proper to the species, not the individual. But each has *its own* soul.

[Spirit and soul]

It is clear from the points we have considered thus far that by "spirit" we mean the specific essence [*Wesen*] of things. The "spirit" of granite or marble is proper to these kinds of matter, not to the individual piece. All the individual pieces may differ in fact and on the outside but not "from the inside out." And because their individual traits are not shaped from within, we cannot speak of a soul in their case. In the plant as well as in the animal, what we call "spirit" also attaches to the species [*Spezies*] (not only with the "species [*Art*]" in the biological sense, of course, but also to its "varieties," strains, etc.).

No individual rose and no dove has its own spirit; yet each living thing does have a soul of its own as its inner principle of form, even though outside forces share in shaping it.

So although the "spirit" and the "soul" of a living thing are not simply identical, we nevertheless should not think of them as really separate as, say, two forms, one general and the other singular, within the individual that they shape. It is not essential to spirit as such, nor even to the specific spirit that addresses us from a natural be-ing [*Naturwesen*] (the "idea" or "species"), to inhere in a piece of matter and to form it. But *insofar as* the spirit does inhere in {174} a determined piece of matter and shape it, it *is* soul and forms the matter according to the particular character of the species. But it does so at the same time in accordance with the "conditions of the matter [*Materie*]" (*its* matter) and with the forces at work on the whole individual, in such wise that the resulting "shape" is not *only*, nor always equally, a pure expression of the spirit, although the spirit will always speak from the shape. Hence the soul *is* spirit, yet not "pure idea" (this expression is perhaps more apt than the usual scholastic one, "pure *form*" since "form" connotes the relation to what is to be formed) insofar as the soul is bound to a piece of matter to which it gives life and shape.

This accords with the soul being the midpoint of life. Conrad-Martius distinguished the animal soul from the plant soul in their *what*, in that the former is not only a *quale* determined in itself and a form giving qualities to its matter, but a "world within" open in sensation for itself. Corresponding to this, as the form of object for the soul itself and at the same time for the whole be-ing having a soul that is the midpoint of its life, is the form of subject as of an object [*Gegenstand*] that exists by itself and "has" itself in this sense (not yet in the sense of an "outer" possession, either material or spiritual, relatively detached from itself). It also has itself in the sense that it can keep itself available, be its own master. In this sense, the "having" no longer embraces the *entire* self but only the body.

The soul's being is, first, an ongoing shaping into the body, a forming of the body. It is also (and this is not found in the plant soul) an inner appropriation of what is formed as it becomes conscious in sensation. It is movement of the body (movement in the narrower sense of local motion) and thus a working into the world outside. It is an *inner* movement (of the soul) that is sensibly conscious. And finally the soul's being is a "free" spiritual "breathing itself out" which, however, also has an "inside" here and hence a specific "feeling of being alive [*Lebensgefühl*]," a sensibly dull consciousness of its own kind.

§ 7
Man's spirit, body, soul
(individuality).

["Spirit" and "mind," freedom]

Conrad-Martius called the ascent from the animal soul to man's soul elevation to spirit. What can this mean if we must already grant an objective spirit to all things in the sense of an idea that forms them and a "subjective" spirit to all animals?

We are now taking "spirit" as personal spirit marked by intellectuality and freedom. We earlier defined intellectual being as being illumined and being open. Being illumined meant being conscious of oneself, not in the dullness {175} of the senses, however, but in freedom and clarity. "Freedom" here refers to the possibility as it were to detach oneself from oneself and to face oneself as foreign, as an object. And "clarity" means the possibility of "intuiting" oneself, knowing oneself. "Oneself" refers first to the subject that lives in its "acts" and also to this living. "Being open" means being able to engage what is other than oneself, stand over against it, turn toward it intentionally.

For us, spiritual living was synonymous with intentionality and "acts" with an actual turning toward an object. Since in our ordinary way of speaking we have come constantly to equate "spirit [*Geist*]" with "mind, intellect [*Intellekt*]," and we do this all the time even in philosophy, this use must have some objective [*sachlich*] basis. The basis, as we have seen, is the fact that being open for oneself and for what is other is the highest and hence also the most proper form of spirit whereto all other spiritual being harks back.

Then *personal freedom* means to be master of oneself and, in its highest form, *being* through oneself. — What is our warrant for saying now that man is raised to the highest form of spiritual being, to personal being in intellectuality and freedom? "Transparency" does not have as simple a meaning for man as it does for God since in man being and *what* are not the same nor is man's *what* simple. We may well say that man is conscious of himself, indeed not only in the dullness of his senses but in a higher way. Now, what this means will remain quite vague until we settle what "being" means; that is, what the "he" means when we say of man that "he is conscious of his being." Is "he" man? The body and soul as a whole? Again, is "he" man or *this* man?

[Soul, body, I]

To this last question we choose the second answer. We are thinking of the individual when we speak of consciousness of our own being. When we say that we are conscious of ourselves in an intellectual way, we cannot say this of our body. We do of course have intellectual knowledge of our body, but it is mediated in many ways and for most people it is quite meager. The enduring consciousness that belongs to the body as such is a given of sensation in both man and animal.[218] Of the soul as the form of the body giving it its qualities we

---

[218]   On "spiritualizing" the body and sensation in man compare p. 263f.

can say in turn that knowledge of the being of its form is possible only in a very complicated and indirect way; we {176} can hardly speak of an immediate consciousness of the being of form. To a large extent we are conscious in sensation of the body's movement from within, but we are conscious in a higher sense of being master of the body which plays a role therein.

Here in the whole of body and soul, in the human individual, something stands out which more properly than the whole can be called the "I" and calls itself "I." This is the freely active I that governs the body and is intellectually conscious of guiding it and of its being able to guide it. The I "is in the body," insofar as what senses in the body and at the body and what freely has charge of the body is the same in consciousness. The I "is in the soul" inasmuch as it senses and feels what is going on in itself and at the same time is its master in a certain way and conscious that it is its master. It is the I that can *know* in free doing; it can grasp objects other than itself, but it can also move its body and soul, wherein it is, away from itself, and take possession of them spiritually by knowing and willing. *As* intellectual the I is at the same time free and through both, personal.

[Spirit and soul]

Man, the whole individual of body and soul, is raised above the animal and so above himself insofar as he is animal, by something that is in him, namely, his personally shaped I with its actuality of understanding and will as well as with the potentiality belonging to understanding and will, his "spirit [*Geist*]" ("*mens*," distinguished from "*intellectus* [intellect]" and "*anima* [soul]"), meaning the highest form of spiritualness, yet in this sense still not "pure spirit" since it is immersed in and bound up with that whole of body and soul which is not transparent to itself or free. Nor is it unlimitedly transparent to the spirit, nor can it be unlimitedly mastered by spirit. —

How is man's spirit related to his soul? Or what characterizes the human soul as such? Man's soul as a quality-giving form coincides with the soul of plants and animals, and as the midpoint of a sensibly conscious life of body and soul it coincides with animals. However, the human soul is not merely aware of what goes on within itself in the dull manner of the senses. The human soul *feels* joy and sorrow, pain and anger, love and hate, in itself;[219] they fulfill its interior. But it is aware of them in an intellectual manner, for the I that enjoys and is conscious of this joy can turn to it in reflection and know it. Moreover, in joy the I is turned toward something objective [*gegenständlich*], for the joy is *intentional*; it is a joy for which the object enjoyed stands there. Thus the life of the soul is "illumined" and "open" and so spiritual in the specific sense of the word. The spiritual I lives therein, and it also lives therein as free, for it may either give in to the stirrings of the soul or withdraw from them, thus halting or at least modifying them.

Lastly, in this inner life the soul's very depth {177} opens up, and albeit (according to Conrad-Martius's discourse on "the soul") the soul remains a "ground beyond" which does not fully enter its actual life, nevertheless what the soul is in itself lights up in its inner life. And as we have seen, it is possible for the soul to pass into a form of being wherein it is entirely actual, hence entirely illumined. We also saw that the free activity of the I, what is specifically personal, proceeds from its "interior." From here, too, the real [*real*] unity of soul and body evinces itself.

Now let us also consider spiritual being in the objective sense, breathing knowledge [*Wissen*] out. If such being is proper to any earthly be-ing [*Wesen*], it is proper to the soul; at least nothing else touches us inwardly with so much force. But its way of being is not

---

[219]   [*sie in ihrer Seele*, where *sie* refers to *Seele*.]

exactly the same as in objects that are spiritual in the objective sense. We have already seen that there is something in the "spirit" of animals that corresponds to it inwardly: a specific feeling of being alive. So here the objective becomes "subjective." In man does it become something personal in a spiritual sense [*geistig-persönlich*]?

[Consciousness of children]

The child is surely unaware of the blissful aura issuing from its pure soul. But is its unawareness the unconsciousness of dull sensation, let alone of "lifeless" things? The child does not *know* what it is nor what it is like inwardly. It is given over wholly to its actual living, radiates itself therein without restraint, and this is precisely why the aura it gives off is so strong.[220]

The adult may reflect and say: "I am still just as I was as a child." He can do this only by remembering, that is, because of the continuity of consciousness retaining what was once actual. If consciousness did not exist originally, it cannot come later; all that can come later is a heightening in the degree of consciousness and in the transition to reflection. So in the child, we must say, there already is a consciousness of what it is in itself and what it is like, a consciousness that allows for a heightening to a higher level and a transition to reflection —albeit perhaps not before a higher stage of development—. On the other hand, consciousness of "own nature [*Art*]" does not guarantee that even adults can know it conceptually or describe it in language.

---

220   Children differ greatly, however, in how much their "depth" is involved in their actual living; we should sharply distinguish this involvement or non-involvement from the kind we are reflexively aware of. I daresay, though, that on average children also live "with their whole soul" more than adults do.

[Individuation and St. Thomas]

What the human soul gives qualities to —not soul as such nor even man's soul as such but *this* man's soul— and what streams forth from the soul as its distinctive aura obviously verges {178} on what we were calling the "core of the person." Insofar as the core is simple (in our earlier, qualified sense), it cannot be further analyzed nor grasped conceptually; it can at most receive a proper name. We said that the "spirit" of animals attaches to the species, or more precisely, that the species is what forms the animal and at the same time issues from it as its distinctive aura.

Now, when we take "soul" in the narrowest sense (wherein —according to H. Conrad-Martius— man alone has a soul) as the ground from which man's inner life wells up and which becomes actual and transparent in this inner life, albeit not altogether actual and transparent, are we dealing here with a species that can occur in a number of instances or with something individual?[221] We are speaking of *classes* of people and *types* of people, hence of "the worker's soul," "the artist's soul," or "the woman's soul," "the child's soul."

When speaking just now of the "aura" issuing from the pure soul of a child, we were also obviously referring to something specific. Conrad-Martius, too, says that "the world engulfs a woman's soul differently than it does a man's." On the other hand, in our relationship with someone else not only does his "specific" aura (in the sense of a general type) affect us but the aura of his *individual* distinctiveness. The wondrous attraction and repulsion among people that we call sympathy and antipathy obviously go back to our being affected by another's individual distinctiveness.

While we said of the animal soul that the "spirit" (in the sense of

---

[221]   Cf. p. 252f for distinguishing and equating "spirit" and "soul" in animals.

"idea") is individuated to the singular soul as the animal's form and as the midpoint of its life through its bond to a determined piece of matter, in man we must consider "spirit" itself to be already individual.[222] When we think we have now "really known" a man, we are facing something that can no longer be expressed in properties that we can grasp in general or by its belonging to a type. "What he is and what he is like in himself"— this is something absolutely unique. This is the "core" that gives his soul (as well his body) its qualities. Is the core synonymous with the soul itself, or is it something *in* the soul? And how is it related to the types of souls which are also found in people?

[The soul of the soul]

If we take soul in the general sense as a principle of form, {179}, the body will appear as what is informed by the soul, according to the Aristotelian-scholastic principle "*anima forma corporis* [the soul is the form of the body]." But if we consider the process of becoming of a be-ing having a soul, specifically of a man, then obviously <it> is not only the "outside" that is shaped and reshaped from within over time; the "interior [*inneres*]" is shaped along with it. The "development [*Entwicklung*]" is both of body and of soul.

Now, can we say that the soul forms the entire individual, itself and the body? Or should we see the principle of form within the "interior" that we called the "soul" as a "soul of the soul"? We suggested this when distinguishing an enduring and relatively unaltered core from a character that remains in constant change and is determined in its development by the core. Even our ordinary way of speaking attests to this distinction. When we simply refer to people as "souls" (or call someone a "dear soul" or a "faithful soul"), we obviously mean

---

222   This is obviously a departure from St. Thomas, for whom only angels are their own species. We must appraise his view but not disrupt the present discussion; cf. p. 394 below.

what is most proper to them, what makes the man a man. This is not his "interior" in the most general sense, I mean, everything belonging to him except his body, but his "innermost [*innerstes*]," that is, what in his soul (in the broader sense) is distinct as a human soul from the plant and animal soul and what is distinct as the soul of some particular man from any other human soul. This implies that it is at once "general" and something individual; more precisely still, it is something generic, something specific (or typical), and something individual.[223]

What distinguishes the human soul from the animal soul is the fact that the human soul is *spiritual* (in the specific and higher sense of "spirit"); that is, it is illumined and open (only it can be "engulfed by the world"), and it is its own master. The soul has typical qualities, such as a "woman's soul," a "child's soul," or souls of whatever other "type." And as individual the soul is "itself" in its inexpressible peculiarity. These are not all in the soul beside one another as separable parts; they are rather in one another as *realiter* [really] inseparable species and genus, for the genus can exist only as specified. This is why, unlike matter, which is composed and divisible, we may call the soul simple and indivisible, albeit the genus and species can be distinguished at different levels down to the "*species specialissima* [most specific species]" (the individual quality). {180}

§ 8
Essence, potencies, core of the soul.

[The soul in psychology]

Now, another problem is how this "core" of what is specifically human in the human soul is related to the soul as a whole (taken as

---

[223] Later we shall differentiate between genus, species, type, and individual, pp. 308ff, 324ff, 391f.

analogous to the plant and animal soul). May we say that the core (the soul as the "innermost") forms the soul (in the broader sense of the whole "interior") and that the soul forms the body? Or should we say rather that the core forms the entire organism of body and soul? In either case we would be claiming that the soul is formed.

It does not make sense to assume that in the plant soul, taken as the inner principle of form that shapes the organism, there is another principle of form that shapes the soul. But we must speak of an inner development in the animal soul as well as in the human soul insofar as it coincides with the animal soul— and *this* is the soul that empirical psychology is chiefly concerned with and is named after. In man and animal not only the body but also the soul assumes a different shape under the varying conditions of life. The soul's "shape [*Gestalt*]" is the entire habitual and actual being into which all its predispositions, that is, whatever potencies it is "endowed with," have unfolded.

[The soul's essence]

Thomas makes a sharp distinction between the entire potential, habitual, and actual stock of the soul and its "essence [*Wesen*]," which, we claimed, is the soul's inner principle of form.[224] For the soul's potency and essence cannot possibly be identical, since its essence is simple but its potencies are many, corresponding as they do to its acts. These potencies are not its essence itself but the natural properties grounded in the essence. St. Thomas says that only an fool could equate the soul's acts and habits with its essence[225] (obviously, since acts and habits come and go but the essence remains).

However, they may inhere essentially or accidentally. We may understand the relation of the soul to its potencies in a certain sense as

---

224   *De spiritualibus creaturis*, a. 11.
225   Loc. cit., a. 11, ad 1.

that of a whole to its parts. But this is not the relation of a *universal* [*universell*] whole (which inheres in each part— as genus in relation to its species), nor the relation of an *integral* whole (which does not inhere in its the parts either in its whole essence or in its whole power and hence cannot be predicated of any part— as the house in relation to the wall). The relation is rather that of a potential whole, which is in the parts with its whole essence but not with its whole power.[226] The potencies are not parts of the soul's {181} essence but of its power as a whole.[227] (We leave undecided here how we are taking "power [*Kraft*].")[228]

In his remarks St. Thomas obviously understands the soul as the whole "interior" and the essence as the principle of form inhering in this whole. He then adds[229] that the *whole soul* is the *form of the whole body* [*Körper*] through its essence, not through its potencies. The essence, he says, forms all organs as subjects of the corresponding potencies. Here he calls what forms the body [*Leib*] the soul's inner principle of form. However, the reason why he says that the *whole soul* is the form of the body may well be that the essence cannot be separated from the soul whose essence it is. We should not understand him as saying that the soul is formed first and then the body through the soul, but rather that the soul is formed through its essence and the body is formed along with it— in accordance with the soul and for the soul.

[Core, soul, and essence]

Do we have warrant then to equate core, essence, and soul (as the "innermost")? As the innermost principle of form, core and essence have an identical range of meaning. The words vary in use

---

[226] Loc. cit., a. 11, ad 2.

[227] Loc. cit., a. 11, ad 19.

[228] Cf. pp. 382ff.

[229] *De spiritualibus creaturis*, a. 11, ad 9.

since when we hear "the soul's essence" and "man's essence," we are inclined to think of what is general, what makes the soul a soul and man a man, whereas "core" is confined from the first to what the particular individual is in himself.

Even to the animal we must attribute an inner principle of form that shapes it in soul and body, but since in itself it is not characterized as individual absolutely, we shall not call it a "core." No more can we call what shapes the animal in body and soul "soul" (in the sense of the "innermost") since it is not shaped personally. It may be best to call it "species."

In man, however, we may equate core and soul since what makes up his individual being and shapes him inside and out is at the same time open in his inner life for himself and open for taking in the world spiritually. It is his distinctive human soul that makes man a spiritually personal be-ing, that makes him a person. The soul makes his entire organism of body and soul different from the animal's. For by such a spiritual, personal soul dwelling in them, body and soul are in a way spiritually open and free, and hence shaped personally. {182}

§ 9
Personally spiritual life.

First of all, "the life of the I [*Ichleben*]" properly speaking, I believe, is the free spiritual acts wherein the person takes in, or by doing shapes, something objective [*gegenständlich*] as well as the different states of the soul wherein the soul feels itself and its inner movements. At first we attributed only an animal-like, dull consciousness to sensations and rightly so when referring to pure sensations, like those proper to the soul of children before they awaken to spiritual life and those proper to adults who are in states of spiritual dullness and apathy.[230]

---

[230]   Cf. pp. 250ff.

[Through sensation to the object]

In the normal, wakeful life of the soul, however, sensations are interwoven with the intentional life of the spiritual I at the innermost, for an "animating [*beseelen*]" conception (as we are wont to say) passes through sensations, making them evincings [*Bekundung*] of what is objective [*Gegenständliches*]. In all external perceptions, the look [*Blick*] passes *through* the "sense material" to the things of the world outside. The entire fabric of the data of sensation and intentions comprised by an "act of perception" is known intellectually and can be made an object upon reflection.

Insofar as I perceive my own body not only as some external thing (through the agency of the data of sensation) but at the same time as unlike any external thing outside of it (through distinctive systems of sense data), and insofar as I characterize my body as the proper "bearer" of my sensations (by localizing the data of sensation), moreover, insofar as I experience my body in all my external doing as under my control and as the instrument of my activity (again, through special systems of sensations, sensations of movement), my body is also penetrated by my spirit and I am intellectually aware of it and can know it as "my body."

All this goes to show how man's body and soul are formed by his spiritually personal soul, how the distinctive human soul or, as we could also say, "*his spirit*," makes a man a man.

§ 10
"Soul of nature" and "soul of spirit."

[Conrad-Martius: the evolution of human nature]

So far the claims about the human soul in Conrad-Martius's *Metaphysische Gespräche* have been confirmed. Her distinction between "soul of nature" and "soul of spirit" also seems to be warranted. But we must look a bit further into {183} what this means. "Human nature" appears here as the highest stage in an evolutionary series starting from the lowest things of nature and continuing through the many different plant and animal species. This evolution

> presses... upwards from below, it grows completely and definitively on the ground of nature, longing to rise upwards, and as such brings itself to conclusion within nature.... For *nature...* *is* what is bodied, fixed, contained, and enclosed; it may well breathe out "spirit," but it may never, itself and personally, *become* spirit, for this means to issue personally in freedom, no longer merely to be shaped and contained in shape, but to be a free *self,* hence no longer "nature."[231]

But man *is* a free and personal *self;* he is at the same time "raised in himself beyond himself"[232] This elevation is possible only through a "birth from the spirit." Being a personal self means being an I.

> And thus this odd absurdity [*Unding*] of a "beginning," novel and free in a personally radical way. A self without selfhood, a beginning without content, a be-ing yet without being and for the first time, with all this emptiness and detachment and freedom, the personal *par excellence*!... For what can be a spirit personally and hence issue personally in a radically unselved way if not as such an "I"?... But is it not also so that such a beginning cannot be created or set or formed from nature and with nature? Is it not so that only the primal begetter can itself raise itself from itself from age to age from the abysmal, primal

---

231   H. Conrad-Martius, *Metaphysicische Gespräche,* op. cit., p. 233.

232   Ibid.

grounds of its nature to radical freedom, can engender itself to a free primal beginning in itself? And then whatever... as spirit is to issue and live, can do so only by personally taking part in this one substantial primal spirit and primal beginning?[233]

A finite thing, a creature, cannot stand and stay as beginning by itself alone in radical freedom, but only

by coming forth immediately from the primal I —not as created but as lastingly begotten or born thereof or dwelling therein— is it an I, otherwise it is impossible.[234]

[Conrad-Martius: Man's second birth]

She speaks of man's second birth in this way.

He is begotten and formed from the quality-giving bottomless, primal grounds of nature, yet at the same time he is born from the "spirit"— hence issuing personally from below and from above.[235]

Man as man dwells {184} on the one hand in his own spirit, that is, in the spirit of his essence that has qualities and is selfish, that is, in the spirit that goes forth from him as from a living natural be-ing [*Naturwesen*]. However, "he can dwell in his own spirit personally only by *formaliter* [formally] issuing in the 'primal I.'" As a free I he can only issue above himself and in his own spirit by —at first *formaliter*— "dwelling in God's" spirit."[236]

---

[233] Loc. cit., p. 234.

[234] Loc. cit., p235.

[235] Ibid.

[236] Loc. cit., p. 236.

"*Formaliter*" means that man, although *formaliter* fastened "on high"— taking therefrom the possibility of grasping and possessing himself as a person in radical freedom, elevatedness, and self-mastery toward himself —, nevertheless stems with his whole material essence from the deep and out of it is engendered.[237]

> Man *takes* himself totally up from below, but to be able to take himself from below as a person, he must take his freedom in the spirit from above. So not only his spirit but also his soul becomes his free personal property. Thus he is enabled to lead all that lives and drives in the dark of his soul up into the light and into freedom."[238]

[Critique]

There are problems here both with the "birth from the depths" and with the "birth from the heights." We must not imagine the contrast of nature and spirit as one of nature and *grace*. Conrad-Martius explicitly stresses that fallen man, too, dwells on high *formaliter*, but in turning away from God he is cut off from God's spirit which could fulfill him *materialiter* [materially]. But are we really warranted to say that man as a free personal I issues from God in a way different from all other creatures, that he is not created but engendered?[239] No finite, creaturely being is otherwise conceivable than as coming forth from original, uncreated being. We have met this point again and

---

[237]   Ibid.

[238]   Loc. cit., p. 237. [Some of the above passages were quoted earlier, pp. 243-6.]

[239]   Such language brings man precariously near to the Son of God— but this interpretation doubtless lies quite far from the author of the *Metaphysische Gespräche*. Our concluding critique is found on p. 406ff.

again. Everything that is owes to uncreated being that it is and what it is. In *what* it is, no earthly creature lies closer to uncreated being than man, none is "created in His image" to such a degree, since only man as a person, as an I, as a beginning, is an analogue of God's being. But must there be another origin besides this nearness to God in the form of object which man is, in his *what*, and in his mode of being? This I do not think we may say. Man, it is true, is created {185} as a be-ing [*Wesen*] that differs from all merely natural things (if we take "merely natural things" to mean things not shaped as persons), for his own nature of body and soul is given into his own hands, given to the spiritual person, as a free possession. But this structure [*Struktur*] is bestowed upon him; it is a part of his essence [*Wesen*] just as much as what is "of nature" in him and just as much as merely natural be-ings [*Naturwesen*] are given their own "nature."

§ 11
The problem of evolution.
Constitution "from below" and "from above."

[Conrad-Martius: evolution and essence]

We shall not be able to decide about Conrad-Martius's claim that the personal, spiritual be-ing [*Wesen*], unlike "nature," comes "from above" before understanding what she means by "up from below." This notion dominates her entire view of nature in the *Metaphysische Gespräche*, and it may find its most vivid expression in her description of "demons." (Some of the passages we have quoted may already have put off the reader; we have not commented on them because we wished to discuss them in their proper place.)

Underlying the diversity of be-ings of nature, she asserts, there is a general "drive [*Trieb*]" to *gain shape* in material existence,... a primeval [*urhaft*] striving to be embodied into essential existence.... Every material entity in this way becomes some specific and quite direct manifestation of this yearning to be shaped.[240]

In favor of such a general drive and

> over against the possibility that ever new self-contained primal qualities appear [*Ansetzbarkeit*]... bearing such shapings in themselves, as it were *a priori* and prescribed beforehand,

> there seems to speak

an essential something in nature— the endless transitions, the random shapings of all these appearances thronging ahead, past one another and upon one another, with their endless modifications.

> On the other hand

each shaping *bears* a unique and radical stamp of qualities. Both phenomena, which for the first time make nature into nature, must be traced and pursued.[241]

> The scholastic view of the world, she says, accounts for the "qualitative autonomy of each shape,"

> the substantiality of nature; that is, the fact that every natural thing harbors the source of its being in itself and stands upon its own roots that give it shape.

---

[240]   <Loc. cit., pp. 110f.>

[241]   Loc. cit., p. 112.

Creation is not thereby excluded.

God sets each thing into its substantial source {186} which, therefore, will nourish it henceforth, build it, preserve it *in itself.* He creates it and conserves it in its substantiality, but it is henceforth created and conserved in itself on its own ground.[242]

On the other hand,

when entities of nature are seen in isolation as essential qualities, when they are understood as a priori essentialities of shape,... then there is no longer any real room for any evolution [*evolutionär*], nor for transition, chance, for the *attempt*, the *experiment*, for *luck*, for what "succeeds" but halfway or not at all,.... In this view entities of nature in the fullness of their appearance lose that element of being a certain ultimate "indifference"; they lose that aspect of their shape as being the *more or less...* successful outcome of a single, vast life that yearns to be shaped.[243]

One has yet to understand nature who has not also understood all of this: the blind drives out of the primeval depth found in all shaping, the naked hunger for shaping and bodying in itself, "however" it may be, the dead ends over and over again, the muddles, the rough, grotesque endeavors and random outcomes that lead at one time to this species and at another to that species, and now —happily possessing *one* form of true bodying and issuing [*Wesung*]— over incalculable eons

---

[242]   Loc. cit., p. 113.

[243]   Loc. cit., pp. 113f.

reproduce and preserve themselves such as they have become. This is the indestructible groundwork for any evolutionary view, any "vital" view, of nature....[244]

And yet "the *Logos* stands over every shape, blessing it —just the way it is—," and "gives it its name, encloses its entire essence," nor "would any thing be without the begetting, bodying, and quickening power of the Godhead."[245] Conrad-Martius interprets life's chaotic driving as the "perfect nothingness [*Nichtigkeit*] and essencelessness of all being which, precisely, entails the burning hunger and draining restlessness."[246] This essencelessness should not be likened to the "essence [*Wesenheit*] that merely has *yet* to unfold but is already posited fully in potency; that is, to seminal essence.[247]

[Conrad-Martius: power and possibility]

When "potency" is used of either case, the word contains an ambiguity. Potency as "being able" (in power, force [*Kraft*]) does not lie in the "primal depth," but "possibility" (in content) does, "insofar as nothing [*nichts*] is here and nothing can become out of the possibility itself, {187}, rather everything can become *from* it."[248] This passage of the Conrad-Martius' work itself recalls "*materia prima* [prime matter]." It is not the matter [*Stoff*] that is already present as the "passive and patient material to be formed," but

---

[244] Loc. cit., pp. 179f.

[245] Loc. cit., p. 180.

[246] Loc. cit., p. 181.

[247] Ibid.

[248] Loc. cit., p. 182.

the hollow, the primal depth, the void, the very abyss.... It contains nothing, even but in potency, and it can become everything and anything. Yet in longing..., in hunger, craving, it does contain everything and anything. It is not lifeless material but nothingness [*Nichtigkeit*] alive— it is not fullness without quality but void driven about in all qualities.[249]

The problem now is how "what is impotent through and through..." is to "be raised to the potency of itself, how what lacks body and essence is to be raised to bodiliness and essentiality."

[Conrad-Martius: Godhead]

Power "to actualize [*Aktualisierung*] and bring to light what is vainly [*nichtig*] consuming itself in darkness" can come only through "powers of light" that "beget, body, quicken, that can but pity what lies powerless and shut up in darkness,"[250] through the "threefold power of light."[251]

Who but the Godhead, insofar as Godhead itself engenders itself from age to age and raises itself from itself, should lift and draw all things out of their essenceless nothingness— who but the Godhead, primal begetter and father of all being? Who but Godhead, insofar as it grasps and posits itself in the glorious fullness of itself, insofar as it becomes body and word in a mysterious gathering, should work in all things as power to gather, body, truly effect and shape? Who but Godhead, insofar as from its raised and gathered fullness it goes out from itself as

---

[249]   Ibid.

[250]   Loc. cit., p. 183.

[251]   <Loc. cit., p. 184.>

spirit in free power and radiant glory, should, even there where Father and Son are present and effective in things in their power, go out from them with and in the quality of the thing, making it breathe, issue, and live?[252]

She asks whether the Godhead itself dwells in the things of nature by giving them qualities, or whether it gives them,

in its threefold essence, only the power in which and through which the thing henceforth will give itself qualities, the power through which the thing glorifies itself and so only indirectly the Godhead wherefrom it creates itself.[253]

She emphasizes

that this power in its threefold effect must {188} really enter the thing, be assimilated, embodied by it, in order now... to work actually as the power proper to the thing itself, substantiated in itself by this power.... *God, Who Himself is and works all in all, withdraws so that the things be, and can be, themselves.*[254]

Yet God

withdraws without withdrawing—... For without Him they would be nothing. Neither would they be anything in His manifest, His mastering, splendor. They can only be what they are in and with His *serving* power.[255]

---

[252]   Ibid.

[253]   Loc. cit., p. 186.

[254]   <Loc. cit., pp. 186f.>

[255]   Loc. cit., p. 187.

[From darkness to light]

Now Conrad-Martius speaks of the transition from the darkness of chaos to existence in the light.

> When the power streams toward primal life in the powerlessness of its essencelessness buried within itself, to autonomous issuing and bodying, then all qualities vainly spiriting in it will surge and rush, hungering and craving, into "existence," into "daylight," into this possibility of shaping, bodying, and manifesting."[256]

But it does not seem conceivable

> that the natural cosmos, all realms of nature in its manifold shapes, can be founded from below in this driving and seeking.... It looks much more like a chaos leaping out than a cosmos. A chaos of fullness, just as before it was a chaos of emptiness.[257]

What we are more likely to imagine arising in this chaos is items of matter.

> For they are, after all, the immediately bodied expression of pure quality. Without any additional shaping.... Yet even the fullness of these items of matter, each, perhaps, yet to body separately, in its very own way, closed off, yet to be in some set form, rather... ceaselessly thrusting each other aside in tension and restlessness, hence all in all and nothing by itself.... Like a huge solution....[258]

---

[256]   Loc. cit., p. 188.

[257]   Ibid.

[258]   Loc. cit., pp. 188f.

[Conrad-Martius: from chaos to cosmos]

What this chaos lacks, in order to become cosmos, is sorting out, articulating, shaping.

Hence a kind of forming principle had to supervene, a principle that now locks each essence into its own bodied being, delimits it within itself and seals it into itself.[259]

What she called "bodying" in the Godhead, "interiorizing [*Innern*] itself in its fullness," is here divided

into two elements, so to speak: [1] spreading fullness or, as such, *gaining* fullness, and, in bodying, [2] withdrawing fullness and informing [*einformen*] the fullness into the self {189} that encloses and contains itself within itself.[260]

This "forming, the bodying interiorization [*Innerung*], the containment of self in definite form" is

quite properly the principle of Him... Whom we called the "Son" or the "Word."... Hence what turns chaos into cosmos and constantly renews it at each and every instant would be brought forth in the most proper sense through this "Word" that bodies, interiorizes, delimits, shapes.[261]

The thing takes the shaping and interiorizing power of the Word into itself in order now to raise itself up out of itself and from itself to a

---

[259]   Loc. cit., p. 190.

[260]   <Loc. cit., pp. 190f.>

[261]   Loc. cit., p. 191.

shaping of itself. And one may even say, it seems, that the Word itself bodies itself in the thing. Now it no longer appears

> as if all shapes are simply the mere blind, random outcome of striving after shape,

but that "an 'idea' stands over each shape effected," not, however, "a different idea over each plant species...." Rather there seem to be

> certain more general "guiding ideas.".. that, more or less perfectly realized in different species, are now more or less perfectly and purely bodied out [*ausleiben*].[262]

Then the possibility of the many often unhappy results of "luck" that she repeatedly speaks of could be thus understood:

> as if they all emulated a definite idea of form, to which, however, they can come up to only in quite different ways because of their different primal qualities and other, external, conditions.[263]

She did speak

> of a primal life passing through qualities [*durchqualifiziert*] which, precisely as such, forces its way to essentiality."

One should not imagine, she says, that a palm tree, for example, is shaped "as if the pattern of its shape had been elicited by a definite idea from a piece of matter indifferent to the content...." Rather

---

[262]   Loc. cit., p. 192.

[263]   Loc. cit., p. 193.

a definite primal quality, nourished by adequate natural powers, had struggled its way to this very shape,... drawn and led, it is true, by a most general shaping idea, without which not even the slightest elevation beyond mere matter would be possible.... Bodying alone, in separate delimitation and self-containment, can only lead to matter. It is, after all, the pure, the simply posited substantiation in form ever new, in luck ever new. Here the bodying potency is sufficient all by itself, and this bodying, precisely, *is* the "idea" that stands above this lowest dimension, or it is the *Logos* Who is at work {190} therein.[264]

On the other hand, the plant, "the be-ing of shape [*Gestaltswesen*] *par excellence*" is "shaped beyond pure bodying insofar as it grows up into a quite definite form, and its essence consists precisely in effecting and setting forth anew this definite form again and again.[265]

[Conrad-Martius: plants and the Logos]

But an "elevation" above the pure bodying of matter lies not only in the fact of the living shaping itself.

"The general kind of shaping that passes through all particular forms also expresses this elevation.... All the various forms are not strung together haphazardly, nor do they merely happen to be in fact here like this and there like that.... An idea can be found, as it were, toward which they rise, albeit with many movements across and athwart.[266]

---

[264]   <Loc. cit., pp. 193f.>

[265]   Loc. cit., p. 194.

[266]   Ibid.

We deem one plant higher (flowering plants, say, higher than seaweed) when its "essence appears to be altogether open and has attained purest manifestation."[267] And it is essential, it seems, for the plant

> to *ascend* and break open toward the light in the most dematerialized form possible.... To rise from the potentiality shut up in the bowels of the earth that harbors and conceals it, to the open actuality at the moment the radiant sky appears — as an eye opens toward its light.[268]

It is

> the true power and potency in... the plant... thus to ascend and unfold toward the light. The power, too,... of evolving from the lowest forms wherein it still wriggles in water and on land, to each higher form and to the highest forms that attain erect stature.[269]

In the plant, "a self-containment of its own" is added to the bodying potency of self-containment in the fullness that leads from primal life to matter." This self-containing is

> such that it takes effect only in and with the ascent to the light; it has in itself, as it were, this upwards "pull" to attain erect stature, to be opened and dematerialized, and ultimately it guides all attempts and risks, primitive as well as complex.[270]

---

[267]   \<Loc. cit., p. 195.\>

[268]   Loc. cit., pp. 195f.

[269]   \<Loc. cit., p. 196.\>

[270]   Loc. cit., pp. 197f.

The bodying potency that contains, delimits, shapes, *unifies*, was actually the potency of the *Logos*, of the Son, of the Word.... Here, then, this *Logos*, by becoming involved with His bodying power and {191} by plunging into primal life rising to existence, thus imparting to this life the possibility and power to delimit itself in ever newer shapes and, as it imparts it, bearing and securing these shapes— this *Logos* must at the same time take effect by raising, by guiding to the light! The potency streaming in ever afresh through the *Logos* must be burdened, as it were, with this striving and seeking as with an entelechy [*Entelechie*]![271]

[Conrad-Martius: shaping and the Logos]

Seen from this perspective,

the particular kinds of shapes contained within themselves in their essence and ever setting themselves forth afresh... are manifestations (more or less successful and achieved, here "faring well," there grotesque, here still at a preliminary stage, there already unfolded) of this one shaping idea that is vitally effective in the entelechy mastering it.[272]

In this view, one would have to speak of a *single* primal idea in every area of shaping, as here in the vegetative area. Each particular shaping would be

chance, condition, luck, course— occasioned by what gives it qualities precisely here from below..... But, wherever and

---

[271]   Loc. cit., p. 198.

[272]   Loc. cit., pp. 198f.

however,... the primal life has now found a possibility and a way to body into existence— *according to* that guiding idea, there... a true essence has come about, a whole, enclosed within itself and, as it exists, resting in its own particular measure of shaping. There... a manifestation *is* brought to pass, a symbol, something attesting to and expressing itself and, *through* itself, that primal idea.[273]

The "*Logos*, wherein God's infinite essence is set as one aglow" contains,

in essential and true shape, albeit unseparated and supratemporal, each and every possible shaping. And now, when a definite kind of shaping (in and with its issuing, bodying, and guiding power, in its seeking and driving, in its bestowing of quality and in its ascending, all blind in themselves) has singled itself out and posited itself bodily and essentially, does not something exist, set in its little creaturely and transitory place, *yet, precisely, truly and essentially as well*, something that has become body and life by that spirit that bodies and issues everything in inexhaustible splendor? And must not the *Logos*, which as an empowering and guiding star went before the shaping quest, now stop over this happy birth to bless it and seal it with a fitting name in that distinctive character that it has reached and found?[274] {192}

[Critique of the foundation of Conrad-Martius's view]

We should take these quotations from the *Metaphysische Gespräche* not as the result of strict analysis but as the author's attempt

---

[273] Loc. cit., p. 199.

[274] Loc. cit., pp. 200f.

to feel her way forward. It would be wrong, then, to seize upon each word and press it. We ought but to represent her words as faithfully as possible, thus allowing the general lines to emerge that relate to our purpose.

We asked what it means for man to be taken "up from below" and we have gone into the meaning of the phrase. We found a view of nature containing two tendencies already present in purely natural entities (I mean, not for the first time in man, who "is born of the Spirit"): something coming "from below" and something coming "from above." Whatever gives shape even in the lowest formed objects, that is, in an "item of matter," is "idea" from above, "objective spirit," sunk from original being into the matter, to its own substantial being.

In the end all that remains of "from below" is *prima materia.* What prime matter is, though, is still unclear in very many ways. Does it, too, have its origin in God (in accord with the scholastic view, as we sought to show earlier in this work)? Several passages in the *Gespräche* touch on the question, but give no definite answer. If *materia prima* were to be conceived as absolute nothing [*Nichts*], then of course the question of its origin from absolute being would not come up. But can we imagine this nothing as living, as driving greedily for being? Life is surely a kind of being. The life of earthly creatures is naturally not pure being; it is rather a constant transition from potentiality to actuality but from a potency that is not mere empty possibility.

When discussing evil, it is true, we also came upon the paradox of null [*nichtig*] being. But we took it as annihilation [*vernichten*] being maintained in its nullity [*Nichtigkeit*] by the absolute. That we should not think of it as the "dark abyss" wherefrom all natural things are supposed to be born is clear from Conrad-Martius' description of the "demons," the "hungering spirits" that personify the hunger for life. She expressly distinguishes them from the fallen angels who come from God and remain bound to the heavenly sphere even after falling from it. So this entire magnificent conception of nature rests upon an obscure foundation.

[Evolution and scholasticism]

If we set aside the question of whether the nonspiritual that enters into things of nature is or is not ultimately created by God, we do have a common basis, namely, *the fact* that precisely something nonspiritual, the opposite of all form, is included in these things and, contrasting with it, a hierarchy of forms. A decisive point is the distinction between "gaining fullness," the sheer bodying of matter [*Stoffleibung*] as it is present {193} in "lifeless nature," and evolution that strives upwards, drawn by a "guiding idea," which is characteristic of all living things.

The question whether we should assume a *single* guiding idea for any area of shaping, and the question whether we should take the great diversity of shapings, species, and "varieties" as unsuccessful or more or less perfect drafts of this idea, in my opinion, is independent from how we are eventually going to judge the material factor. What the "living form," the entelechy, takes into itself is not *prima materia* but an "item of matter," hence something already formed. I daresay we may imagine that the "guiding idea" leaves room for a number of more or less "faithful" implementations depending on the conditions imposed by the matter. Thus fitting the notion of evolution into the scholastic world view would not be ruled out.[275]

---

[275]   We shall discuss this possibility further below.

§ 12
The hierarchy of nature entities.
"Nonliving" and "living."
Act and potency, form and matter, in both.

[Thomas and the hierarchy of being]

In any case, "from on high" already has a new meaning here in contrast to "lifeless things." The living form has more of the divine in itself; the *analogia entis* reaches further in living forms than in material forms. Life as movement from within and actualization from within lies nearer the actuality of divine being. Analogously, "potency," too, now has new meaning.

Thomas is wont to equate the relation between form and matter with that between act and potency. Between "*actus purus*," divine being, and the absolute potentiality of *prima materia*, he sees a hierarchy of be-ings wherein each is act or form relative to the lower and each is matter or potency compared to the higher. Items of nonliving matter are formed matter. The material form which dwells in them and to which they owe their being *formed* matter has actual being, for the form *is* and imparts its being to the matter that it informs in such a way that the whole is called a "be-ing." The whole is potential at the same time, for at no moment of its being is it actually all that it can be. But it bears in itself what it *can* be actually as potency (that is, all its possibilities of appearing and working), and in turn it owes to its form the fact that it bears this potency in itself.

Must we now say that the form itself is potential too? This seems to turn everything upside down. Strictly speaking, the potency to {194} a determined actual being and working is not absolutely potential since after all it bears within itself the seed of the actual into which it can unfold. We should ascribe to form this positive aspect of potency, which, so to speak, is burdened with actuality. But the fact that what can become actual is *not yet* actual is due to the matter.

[Unity of living form]

The whole of form and matter, the "item of matter [*Stoff*]," is in turn matter [*Materie*] for a higher form, the "living form" or "soul," that gives it life and shapes it into an organism. Is the lower form also matter for the higher form? In the Aristotelian-Thomistic view of the unity of the substantial form, the answer is obviously no. It is always a *single* form that gives being to the be-ing and makes it what it is. Life is the being of the living thing, not something added on to its being. The soul forms the nonliving thing into an organism wherein each part is incorporated as a "member" or "organ" into the life of the whole.

To be sure, something material [*stofflich*] exists before life and the vital forming process from within begin, and something material remains behind after the life that was therein ceases to be. This is just the reason why we can indeed say that an already formed amount of matter [*Materie*] is in turn matter for this higher forming, that life "begins to bestir itself" in it and disappears from it when the organism "dies" while the lifeless thing continues to exist. Now it seems as if the living form were added on to the "material" form. But can we say that the same thing is lifeless at first, then alive, then dead?

[Before and after death]

We equivocate, says Thomas, when we speak of the "eye," "ear," etc. of a dead thing.[276] After the soul has left the body [*Leib*], it is no longer a body. A thing left behind, so to speak, by the body

---

[276]   *De anima*, a. 1.

does continue to exist. Death as transition from living to nonliving existence is not a change in a thing like the changes that occur in a living organism nor like the changes in a nonliving body [*Körper*]. Up until the moment of death, it is the organism that undergoes all the changes and lives in this process. From this moment on, the organism no longer exists. We may say that "at the moment of death" something happens "to it." After a certain moment the organism no longer exists, and something else exists "instead."

This of course does not mean that one thing is removed and something else (that looks just like it) is put in its place. Rather, a *metamorphosis* has occurred; what used to be an organism is now a lifeless thing. Something identical does exist. But *what* it is is no longer the same, for a new form has taken the place of the old one. What is identical? If we {195} take the material thing that existed before life began and the material thing that remains after life disappears, the two would not be recognizable as "the same thing" without the continuity of the changes occurring during life. And what exists after life has disappeared would not exist without this previous life that formed the body [*Körper*] as it is now.

[Continuity in change]

The very fact that the living form, the "living soul [*Lebensseele*]," confers not only life but, precisely together with life, being, speaks for the Thomistic view. Each organism, by being this organism, is also what it is as this material body. To be an organism means to be constructed as a living body, and this means being constructed as a material body. Another form, the "material" form, existed before life began, and had it remained as it was instead of giving way to the living form, something quite different would have happened to what the material form was informing. Then when life ceases, something quite different happens to the body [*Körper*] that was shaped by the living soul than would happen to it were it still alive. This is just why we must say that the living form has in turn given way to a material form.

When a substantial form gives way to the other form "in the same thing," is the unformed matter "the same"? This obviously will not do either. To be sure, it was a "piece of matter" (shaped by the material form) wherein the life began. But during its life the organism has constantly been taking on new material, "incorporating it" (the "living soul" is after all essentially a "nutritive soul"), and eliminating other material. It may be that by the end nothing more exists of the matter that first made it up. What, then, can still be "the same" if it is neither the substantial form nor the matter? What remains is the individual's form of object, the "this here," in a continuity of being although when the substantial form changes, the mode of being also changes, as well as in a continuity of changes (which include the addition and elimination of matter).

[Live and dead parts]

Another problem seems to be that the forming of matter by the living soul during its life is obviously not complete. The matter does not seem to be fully "organized down to the last detail." In our experience we deal with things that are organisms only in a part of their stock and are partially dead matter, for example, a dry leaf on the blossoming twig, a dead branch on the growing tree. These are material things formed by the organism, but they are no longer members of the organism; its life no longer stirs in them.

We must doubtless say that only what is encompassed by its life belongs to the organism, and what is not organized does not belong to this whole. Still, {196} the organism may form part of a material whole in space, where other parts no longer belong to it or do not yet belong to it. And in this spatial, material whole, unorganized parts may not only adhere to the organism on the outside (in the spatial sense), but they may also be found among the organized parts.

[Act and potency in the nonliving]

If the "living form" differs in principle from the material form, then its being and the being of the entire formed object must also be of a different sort; potency and act must mean something different in either case. In regard to both we should recall the twofold sense of potency and act that we have met several times; that is, they denote *what* is potential or actual but at the same time they denote potential or actual being itself. When we take form as act we mean both what has actual being and what the whole acquires being through. When we take matter as potency, we mean both *what* is potential and what can be led to actual being by the form.

When the whole is a nonliving thing, its potentiality, which is the characteristic being of the matter, is pure receptivity for the form. The actual being of the form, insofar as it is in the matter, is the forming of the matter, but working or being able to work —that is, in part actuality and in part potentiality— belongs to the being of the whole. *This* potentiality, however, already differs from the potentiality of sheer matter, for it is not pure receptivity, but it is "burdened with actuality"; it is power, "potential energy [*Energie*]." And the actuality connected with the potentiality, if it gets "free," is "activity." But it is "freed" *from outside*, and as free activity it is a working *outwards*. The transition from potentiality to actuality is a *causal occurrence*, I mean, a process in the *context of material nature*.

[The soul and evolution]

When we take "living soul" as an act of the organism, we are referring to what gives being to the organic object as a whole, indeed the characteristic being that we call "life." When analogously we take as "potency" what is "given life" by the soul, we are no longer referring to pure matter but to a material object already informed. For even if we understand the "living form" not as added on to the "material form" but as taking its place, what form preceded it does indeed matter, for it is *determined* matter that is ready to receive life, and for different living forms the matter is determined in a different way.

Act, understood as the actual being of the living soul, is life. This implies for one thing that the organism itself continues to be constructed; it takes in the matter it needs to build itself up (strictly speaking the living soul itself does not do this but the organs {197} that the soul has already formed and guides in their activity) and forms the matter it receives into the characteristic shape of the organism formed.

In the *Metaphysische Gespräche* more is implied; namely, "striving upwards toward the light" and striving beyond itself for ever higher forms, drawing ever closer to the "guiding idea." This first aspect, striving upwards toward the light, striving to become manifest, we may take for what drives the forming process itself; I mean, the "soul of the soul," for the forming *is* indeed a self-revelation, an unfolding into visibility. But this is at the same time the guiding idea expressing what is characteristic of the vegetative as such. This idea not only stands above whatever as such is shaped as living, but it is itself effective therein.

May we speak over and above this aspect —still in the proper sense, not in mere metaphorical paraphrase— of a striving beyond itself to higher forms (which would, strictly speaking, be the point of the theory of evolution)? It is quite obvious that the manifestation is more or less complete [*vollkommen*] in objects of different species as well as in individual instances of a species, and so the guiding idea will be more or less realized. It is a fact of experience that there are transitions from one type of shaping to another (brought about by a change in the external living conditions, by "interbreeding [*Kreuzung*]," etc.). But may we speak of one *form* passing over into another and of one form striving beyond itself for a higher form as something that pertains to the being of the form?

§ 13
The problem of generation.

[Propagation]

Reproduction supposes that the shaping process extends beyond the particular instance. It is commonly attributed to the instinct to "conserve the species," and this would be another interpretation of "striving higher." Our first task is to understand reproduction itself. When life is said to be the construction of an organism as the matter it needs is taken in and formed into a specific shape, are not nourishment and growth as well as reproduction all included therein? The reception and formation of matter are found in both. What distinguishes reproduction as a living function is that a *new* organism is formed. What is it that separates the producing organism from the organism produced in such wise that we must now speak no longer of *one* but of two individuals?

[Form and being]

It is clearly not essential that the two individuals be spatially disconnected. But whenever a new form exists we are always warranted and required to speak of two individuals. Bearing fruit is still {198} a function of the old organism, but when a new life begins to stir in the fruit on its own, a new organism has begun to exist whether it is spatially connected with the old organism or not. Ought we then to regard the new *form* as generated [*erzeugen*] by the old form?[277] This would clearly do away with the essence of form: both generating and being generated. For the form would no longer inform but create, that is, it <would> bring about being that differs from its own.

We might try to see the process as a division of being. One part of the organism would have been so far informed by the form inhering in the whole that it would be ready to receive a form of its own. But then the form would split into two; one form would take over this one part and the other form the rest of the organism. Right at this point the existence of a new organism would begin.

If a definite *measure of being* belongs to every created thing —indeed, through its form— dividing [*Teilung*] would have to mean dividing *up* [*Aufteilung*] this amount of being. On the one hand the being of the old organism would have to be diminished, hence consumed little by little in a series of generations [*Zeugung*] (certain facts of experience indeed seem to speak for this). On the other hand the being of the new organisms could never come up to the original measure of being of the organism that produced them or only in the limiting case where the organism perishes in a one-time generation and hence would deliver its entire being to the new organism. In this borderline case should we speak of a new form at all? Should we not

---

[277] The dogmatic question in regard to the human soul was answered in the negative. (Cf. <H.> Denzinger <and C. Bannwart>, *Enchiridion symbolorum definitionum <et declarationum de rebus fidei et morum* [handbook of creeds, definitions, and declarations on matters of faith and morals], Freiburg i. Br., 1928; first ed. Würzburg, 1865> 533 and 1910. The philosophical basis for this decision obviously lies deeper.

say rather that the *single* form has ousted or surrendered the greater part of the organism that it constructed in order to build a new organism out of the remainder?

But neither should we imagine a "split of being" as the emergence of new forms when being is divided up among a series of individuals but as a shaping of divided matter into several instances of the *one* form by this very same form. The unity of the species in the plurality of instances would be a numerical unity and at the same time a real, not an ideal, unity. And the whole shaped by the single form would have to be called an "individual" in the strict sense; only in their outer shape would the instances be seemingly selfsufficient parts. {199}

[Form in individual and descent]

We do not wish to ask now whether there are actual cases that correspond to this fiction. It is more important to consider other types of reproduction which cannot readily be understood in this way. First —if we continue to regard reproduction as coming from a single individual— a whole series of organisms may equal or even surpass in external development the organism that generates them, and the generating organism itself may to all appearances go on living in undiminished vigor. And when it finally does perish, we should attribute its demise to circumstances quite other than reproductive exhaustion (when a healthy tree is cut down or pests destroy a plant).

Then do we have here an increase in the measure of being that would not be explained on the basis of the one organism? This we cannot say without qualification. If the measure of being is revealed not only in the forming of the one individual but in that of its entire "descent [*Geschlecht*]," we could not gauge it until the entire descent comes into existence or until we could get some idea of how far the possible generations included in the measure of being extend. Hence we may still hold for the unity of the form in all individuals of the "descent."[278] Will this view remain tenable even when more than one individual is involved in the generating? And how is this compatible with the fact that each "instance" appears to have its *own* life?

[Whence and whither in the present]

The first question is relatively easy to answer. Were the whole genus as kind [*Gattung*] (or the species [*Art*]) to be seen as shaped as a *single* individual by a *single* form, then neither would male and female "instances" be selfsufficient individuals with their own inner form but members or organs of the single great organism, differently shaped and in tune with one another for the sake of a common function.

The second question proves more difficult. Throughout our previous analysis of the living thing, we took forming from within to be what essentially distinguishes the organism from nonliving but already formed matter. Each organism appears as a self-enclosed whole which is formed over time from its own interior in a process we call "life," or which opens its interior to outer visibility. If the organism must be viewed as part of a whole and if the form, understood as the shaping principle, is proper to the whole, is not the root of the organism's being shifted out of itself, and does this not do away with what seemed {200} to make up its being as an organism?

I hardly think so. The form of the entire organism is in each of its parts, and it shapes each from within. To regard the particular plant, say, as something fully selfsufficient is at bottom an abstraction that picks out its present stage, leaving out the questions of whence and whither that lie in the present stage itself. This procedure, permis-

---

[278]   The double meaning of "*genus* [*genus*]" as "kind [*Gattung*]" and as "descent [*Geschlecht*]" suggests that we start from genus as kind [*Gattung*], as a formal unity, and from this unity seek to understand the species [*Spezies*]. This we shall do below (pp. 294-6).

sible and suitable for certain purposes, is not the attitude of one who would press ahead to know the essential structure of being. Hence our consideration of the living thing must lead us to its genesis and thus to its *genus* and its *generations* (in the twofold sense of generating [*Zeugung*] and what is generated [*erzeugt*]).

§ 14
Genus, species, individual,
Instance in the organic area.

[Terms in an evolutionary context]

Thus our first question, restricted to the organic area, concerns the relationship of *genus*, *species* and *individual* or *instance*. (Whether the "or" here is exclusive or whether "individual" and "instance" are only different names for the same thing will have to be discussed in its own right.)[279] The meaning of these terms must be determined here solely in the context of our investigation without regard for their traditional logical or formally ontological meaning.[280]

[Phylogenetic genus]

The being of a living thing, as we described it when considering an individual plant, is not the persistence of something unchanged but a *becoming* in the sense of something shaping itself over time, and the word "evolution, development [*Entwicklung*]" implies this. Evolution, traced backwards, leads to the *origin* of this item from another item more or less "like" it and, traced forward, to the origin from this

---

[279]   Cf. p. 296f.

[280]   We can decide later how the two sets of meanings are interrelated (cf. pp. 324ff).

item of others more or less like it. The term "*genesis*" denotes the origin. The process within the living thing wherein another thing or several other living things come into existence is called "*generation* [*Generation* (*Zeugung*)*.*" The term is transferred to the totality of particular be-ings [*Einzelwesen*] that owe their existence to a *single* generation (that is, to one particular generative process).

The totality of generations going back to one ancestral organism (that is, whatever an ideally complete phylogenetic tree would include), may be {201} called a "*genus*" (= descent, lineage) [*Genus* (= *Geschlecht*, *Stamm*)]. The genus is a whole, enclosed within itself and unified by a series of generative processes. The whole is *finite* when the series of generations goes back to a single ancestral organism and forward to some latest generation. We must come to a single ancestor organism when we depart from a single living thing and try to identify its "family tree" (assuming of course that our search is not hindered by practical considerations or by limits in principle to our knowledge). Backwards the series cannot be infinite. But forwards we can conceive it as infinite in principle. In this case the whole would not be finite, but it would still be closed in the sense that any particular be-ing that can be traced back to the ancestor and to no other organism belongs to it.

[Genus and species as content; individual]

Thus we have taken genus first as *unity of origin*. But there is another unity. Something runs through all generations, propagated from the ancestral organism to the latest "offspring," I mean, that wherein they all resemble one another, genus as kind, stock of content [*Gattung, inhaltlicher Bestand*]. What *is* this content, and how should we understand its "reproduction"? The content is not *all that* the particular instance of the genus is, and conversely, what the particular instance is is more than what it is *as* an instance of the genus.

We said above that the instances are "more or less" alike. What they all resemble each other in is the stock of content of the genus. What they do not *all* resemble each other in may in turn be something wherein members of a narrower *group* do resemble each another or something that the *particular* has by itself alone. If we call the group wherein a part of the instances of a genus is united by a common stock as well as this common stock itself *"species* [*Spezies oder Art*]," it is easy to see that the word still embraces a diversity.[281] Within the genus we should imagine a series of species *ranged on the same level* whose only common content is the stock they share from the genus. If we call *"specific difference"* what the instances of a species share with one another but not with other instances, each coordinate species will possess such a specific difference and share nothing of this difference with the other species.

However, we can also think of other levels of generality, of *higher* and *lower species*, whose relationship is analogous to that of genus and species. I mean that all instances of the lower species are contained in the higher, but only a part of the instances of the higher is contained in {202} the lower (which is therefore less "general"). The stock of content of the higher species is contained in the stock of the lower, as is also the specific difference that is proper only to the lower species and distinguishes it from other species at the same level of generality. In principle there is no definite limit on the number of levels, but the differentiation cannot proceed *in infinitum* [to infinity] *realiter* but must stop at some *specialissima* [most special] species, at some lowest species. We are not saying that this lowest species can only contain a *single* instance. In principle we can imagine several instances that are completely alike. Where the *species specialissima* can exist [*existieren*] only in one instance, the specific difference should be called an *"individual"* difference and its instance an *"indi-*

---

[281]   This had already became apparent in our formal investigation (II, §§ 1 and 2).

vidual" (in a special sense different from the traditional one). *Genus* and *species specialissima* or individual represent the upper and lower limits of the differentiation or specification.

[Genus of origin and of content compared]

We took the unity of the genus first as a unity of origin and then as a unity of content [*Einheit des Inhalts*]. It is not immediately clear if they both have the same extension. In its unity of origin, the genus includes all instances issuing from a single ancestral organism. In its unity of content, it includes all instances sharing a stock of content. We could imagine in principle —at least so it seems — that not everything having a common stock stems from a single ancestor but from more than one. Consideration of this possibility leads us back to the question of how we should understand the "reproduction" of the stock of content within the genus.

We can, however, begin by considering the possibility apart from this question. Following St. Thomas, we would have to say that if two things have a common stock, either one must be the cause of the other or they both must go back to a common cause. This would also be true of two ancestral organisms alike in genus as kind. All we would have to ask is whether the causal relation between the two organisms or between them and their common cause could be different from the relation of generation to which the "lineages" that are generated by them and are separate (as we are supposing) owe their existence. If we cannot imagine any other kind of causal relation, then we would establish their connection through generation and discard the fiction of separate lineages. The unity of the genus in content and in origin would coincide in extension.

So the question is *whether* we can imagine a causal relation of another sort here. But first we must ask how Thomas's principle can be clarified. A thing is what it is through its form. {203} When it consists of form and matter, the matter (taken as *prima materia*) is actually nothing by itself, for it is first shaped into something by the form that it takes into itself. When two things share some content, it must be something formal. Matter does not possess its form of itself. Can matter receive form from some other thing that is formed matter?

§ 15
Initial informing of *prima materia*.
Elements, spatial motion, causality in nature.

[Elements and atoms]

Prima materia can receive the first form that gives it being only from the first being. First being is the *first cause*, and creation is the *first causality* [*Kausalität*] underlying all else. Earthly causality does not involve initial forming but only transforming. The lowest genus in the material [*materiell*] domain represents what is closest to *materia prima*: simple items of *matter* [*Stoff*], the *elements* [*Element*] *out of* which whatever else is material is made and emerges, but which do not themselves consist of or emerge from anything else. They hark back only to the initial forming not to any other. Every element is a species, more precisely a *species specialissima* allowing no further differentiation.

If we call the totality of elements the "the genus of the be-ing," we should ask if we are taking "genus [*Gattung*]" exactly as we did earlier, I mean, as a stock of content that is contained in the species and corresponds to the unity of origin, its emerging through the initial forming. In virtue of this forming, they are precisely what we call "elements," that is, spatial matter given qualities. These qualities are the content of their species, wherein a genus common to all and a specific difference cannot be distinguished. The elements occur not in instances but in "pieces," that is, in various quantities, spatial shapes, and positions, that are inessential to the element as such and do not differentiate it.

(When atomic physics sees the elements made up of the smallest parts and attributes the diversity of the elements to differences in the shape and position of the atoms, the "atoms" would be what specifies the "elements" in the sense that we have explained here, and the simple items of matter that we can experience would be pieces made up of the atomic elements. The diversity of atoms must then be a specific diversity, and their idea itself must indeed be what first allows us to understand the possibility of smallest parts which we cannot get from space or matter.)

[Space and the elements]

Whether we set out {204} from the atomic elements or from an amount of matter [*Stoffquantum*] as a whole, there is in either case another form besides the one giving qualities, namely, the *spatial* form (spatial in shape, size, and position). The element is constituted by the substantial form as a single element and as a whole, meaning an amount [*Quantum*] of matter. Being in space is essential to the element as such but not which part of space it occupies or whether it exists in combination or separately. Since being separate or combined is not essential, nor is the shape, size, and position of the pieces, they cannot be derived from the initial form but need another causal explanation.

(Assuming the atomic theory, we should say that the initial form accounts for the shape, position, and size of the "atomic elements," but we would have to seek a further cause of the atoms combining into the "pieces" of simpler matter that we experience.)

If we consider as static [*ruhend*] the *being* of such features of the thing as its being separate or combined, positioned and shaped in space, we could take them as something originally proper to the material —I mean, from the beginning of its existence— yet as something given to it over and above its initial, substantial, form, and as the result of an arranging action that accompanies the creating act and would be a second kind of effect of the first cause.

But if we take these features as *becoming*, I mean if we take them as alterations of an original state, then we should understand them as material processes entailing *spatial* motion. (In principle we can also imagine changes due to a spiritual arranging action; change through spatial motion is but the possibility favored by experience.)

None of these changes are based on the element's form; they are what befalls it from outside; they are *causal process*. How is it conceivable that something whose motion is not due to its form is set in motion from without?

[Motion]

The motion of one material thing can be brought about by that of another material thing. We say that a moving ball imparts motion to a stationary ball when it strikes it. To see if we are justified in speaking like this, we must be clear about our ontic understanding of motion (specifically, about the movement of material things in space that concerns us here). Motion *is* not the change of place wherein it reveals itself.[282] In regard {205} to the thing moved, motion is an *act*, that is, *second act*," activity [*Tätigkeitsakt*] in a sense that includes "passion" as well as "action," both undergoing and doing.[283] Motion is a mode

---

[282]   Cf. Adolf Reinach, "Über das Wesen der Bewegung [on the essence of motion]," in his complete works, Halle, 1921; <cf. the footnote on p. 68 above>.

[283]   Cf. *Des Hl. Thomas Untersuchungen über die Wahrheit* [St. Thomas's *De Veritate*], vol. 1, loc. cit. p. 329, footnote <new edition, p. 296>.

of being wherein the thing moved is found to be in a certain duration. In regard to the result (in this case possibly a change of place), we may call motion a transition from potency to act insofar as the possibility of reaching a certain place is actualized by the motion.

On the other hand, we may understand the motion itself as an act of a potency of movement inhering in the thing moved when it is at rest. The question is whether we should take this potency as active or passive. One thing that distinguishes living from nonliving things is that the latter have a passive, and the former an active, potency for motion, for actual motions are passions in the nonliving and actions in the living. When motion is taken as passion, the principle of the motion does not lie in the thing moved, at least not only in the thing moved. Insofar as it is act, motion cannot accrue to the material thing in virtue of its matter but only its form. However, that motion can only be a passion must lie in the matter as such.

[A rigid universe]

Matter is not determined, but determinable, in position, shape, and size (that is, spatially). It must be determined in order to come into existence. As *prima materia* it lends itself equally to any spatial determination; the one it does receive must be fixed by the first forming giving it existence. Were it *completely* fixed so that it could no longer be determined in any way, nature would be one rigid object with a fixed spatial arrangement. Each element would fit into it in a fixed amount (as a whole or in separate "pieces" among which "pieces" of other elements would be inserted). Each element would have its fixed place (or more than one place if divided) and its fixed shape (if divided into pieces, each would have its determined shape, which need not be like the shape of the other pieces of the element). In this case in material nature there would be no motion.

[Spatial indetermination]

The second possibility is that the initial forming does not confer complete spatial determination. The elements might exist in a certain spatial arrangement, not a necessary arrangement but one allowing them to be determined in different ways. Here there are several possibilities. (1) The spatial determination could be something added on to the element purely from without (since it must {206} have *some* determination or other) in such wise that it remains open to any determination whatsoever. (2) A certain *definite* spatial determination (not any whatsoever) could be essential for the element and through it a range of possible changes could be defined.

In the first case, different determinations would be caused purely from without and in the second case, partially from without and partially from within. The possibility of a change in determination allows for motion. Within material nature, we can imagine this happening only in connection with the whole, that is, as something affecting the whole. This means that if *something* is set in motion therein, then everything must move. This "if... then" is the basic form of *natural causality*. If the spatial determination of the whole as well as of each element were fully arbitrary, the change in determination would have to ensue through an impulse from without, that is, from something nonmaterial.

If a definite spatial determination were proper to each element and hence to the whole, we would in turn have several possibilities. A partial determination could include an order tending toward complete determination, that is, to a rigid final state. (This possibility obviously lies behind the view that ascribes to each thing a striving for "its place.") If this ordering lay in the elements themselves as a potency, we would have to imagine nature as a whole in motion from the beginning of its existence and the whole process of nature as many different motions intersecting and impacting on one another. (We could imagine here a order in these intersecting movements that must lead to the final state of rest. Again, a "striving" could be imparted only to each element, which would be intersected by others, so that everything would remain constantly in motion.)

[Principle of motion]

We have shown that all motion must have a standard principle. The possibility of a rigid stationary position of the elements shows that this principle must be added to the first forming, whether it is an external impulse from a spiritual originator [*Urheber*] of the motion or a potency for motion with which the elements are endowed. We could ask if in this second case the potency would have to be deemed active and the distinction between material and living motion would disappear. This second case would in no way obtain. Being in motion would be the natural state of each element —taken in isolation—, but its motion could be hindered by other elements, and the actual state of motion of each at any one time would result *with natural necessity* [*naturnotwendig*] from its potency and that of other elements working together.

The actual motion of living things, however, is not determined by the overall state of material nature, nor does it occur with natural necessity or mechanically; {207} rather, it is determined by its inner form (albeit not by this form alone), and —within certain limits— it is *free*. Insofar as the actualization of each element's potency for motion depends on the whole assemblage as we explained, this potency would remain passive; the actual motion itself that results from internal and external moving forces would be a mixture of action and passion.

§ 16
Mixed matter.
Supramundane and intramundane causality.

[Mixtures and compounds]

The motion of the elements would explain how they displace one another, how joined pieces are separated and separate pieces joined, how they are mixed [*Mischung*] and unmixed. All this would happen to them externally without affecting their substantial form. No new form would emerge, no form would be "reproduced" from one thing to another. The case seems to be different in what scholasticism called "mixed bodies," in chemical compounds.

Hydrogen and oxygen combine to make water. After a certain moment a new item of matter exists, and the former items no longer exist. Something new has arisen. It differs from a mixture wherein the old matter remains unaltered (<and wherein> there is something new at most in its outer look, I mean, in its overall appearance).[284] But it also differs from organic reproduction when a new individual of the same species emerges from one or two individuals. In the new material item, there is a form that differs from the form in each of the elements.

May we say that the forms of the elements have been attached to the form of the mixed body? Obviously not. The outer shape and the

---

[284]   Is it conceivable that compounds go back to mixtures and so to processes of motion? Obviously the atomic theory supposes that the atoms recombine when new matter emerges. There would only be a mixture of separate atomic elements, or a separation of elements previously joined, and this would alter the behavior and the outer shape of the concrete items of matter. Thus there would no longer be any difference in principle between mixture and compound; I mean, in a mixture the elements would survive, but in a compound they would not. But a formal principle must be assumed besides the motion principle to account for the specifically different ways of shaping and behaving when the same atomic elements are accumulated and when different elements are mixed.

causal behavior of the mixed body —and hence what the substantial form takes effect in and reveals itself in— may have nothing in common with the shape and behaviors of the elements. If the forms were actually preserved {208} in the new object, the actual accidents of both would show up in it. Thomas says that the elementary forms are not actual in mixed bodies but preserved virtually, meaning that the accidents of the elements survive in them "in a certain way."[285] That the new item of matter emerges from the old and the old is transformed into the new without the old being destroyed or the new created afresh is supported phenomenally by a certain continuity in the transition and by its regular recurrence under the same conditions, as well as by the irreversibility of the process, for the old items cannot be recovered from the new. Ontically, we would have to understand the emergence of the new item as a re-formation of the same matter that had previously had been otherwise formed.

[Forms and chemistry]

In view of the unity of *materia prima* and its indifference to all the forms it may receive, we could in principle imagine an order of nature wherein any item of matter could be transformed into any other. On the other hand, there may be an order wherein laws determine the transitions of natural forms. The laws would not only govern the combination and separation of elements (which could not be transformed into one another) but also so limit how every element may be combined that each elementary form has a potency for certain combinations (this is called "affinity").[286]

When Thomas speaks of a hierarchy of natural forms wherein we should see each lower form as matter for the higher, he does not

---

[285]   *De anima*, a. 9, ad 10.

[286]   Chemistry presupposes such a system of laws.

mean that one form is informed by another but that the informing of matter by the higher form presupposes that the matter is informed by the lower form. In our present case, the new formation of a compound presupposes the formation of its elements. What is informed here, as anywhere, would be *materia prima*, except that the new form would presuppose a previous forming. When compounds emerge from elements, we may say that new forms "emerge." Whenever we say this, the word has but the improper sense, that matter becomes informed. Forms as such do not come about or pass away.

We should understand the emergence of mixtures in terms of material motion. The emergence of compounds also supposes motion, but it supposes affinity as well. Their actualization is linked to elements "meeting" (hence to motion); it is also linked in turn —as motion itself— {209} to the entire assemblage within material nature wherein each process triggers others (for example, when the emergence of one compound dissolves another).

[Causality above and within the world]

We have thus met a number of different causalities, both "supramundane" and "intramundane." "Supramundane causality [*Kausalität*]" means the dependence [*Bedingtheit*] of created being and what occurs therein on uncreated being and "intramundane causality" the interdependence within created nature. As we saw, the first kind of supramundane causality is creation, which involves two aspects: creating [*Erschaffung*] and an initial informing of matter (the two are only conceptually separable since matter cannot come into existence without form). The second kind of supramundane causality is that presupposed to the origin of motion (either by giving an initial impulse or providing the elements with their own potency for motion). The third is the principle of the transformation of some items of matter into others.[287]

"Intramundane causality" includes the dependence [*Abhängigkeit*] relation of one process of motion upon others or upon the entire assemblage of movement as well as the dependence of material transformations upon the motions and upon one another.

We have yet to ask whether, in view of the several kinds of supramundane causality, the causal process runs "automatically," I mean, without renewed supramundane intervention in a particular process. We can in principle think of a supramundane intervention in every case, but we can also conceive —at least in motions— of things running their course in a purely mechanical way. (The phenomenal difference between regular natural events [*Naturgeschehen*] and miracles suggests that we take regular events as purely intramundane). The case when matter is transformed seems to be different, since new forms are coming into existence. May we take this —in view of the natural endowment of the elements— as a purely intramundane process? We may if we see in affinity not only a potency making the transition into another form *possible* under certain conditions, but a *determined* potency where, given certain conditions, the transition is bound to take place. {210}

---

[287]   Our objective distinction and classification of several kinds of supramundane causality says nothing about the temporal sequence or the actual way in which the world has emerged. We can think of a multiple forming in a simple act just as well as in a series of separate acts. (A plurality is inconsistent only with the simplicity of the divine essence.)

§ 17
The idea of material nature.
Genus, species, individual.
Instances within material natural Species
as content of appearance.
Emergence in the material area.

[Review of cosmology]

According to everything we have learned about coming about and passing away, we can take *material nature* to be the totality of everything that is informed matter and nothing else, as a unified whole, as a self-contained network wherein nothing new is created. We should think of *prima materia* as a determined amount that is neither increased nor decreased. It is present in certain basic forms and in forms derived from them, and there is an ordered transition from the one to the others. We should see the whole in constant movement going back to original impulses, and we may take it that no new impulses supervene and that the natural process is the sole effect of original motive impulses.

Whether the creation of matter began in time or is from eternity, whether the world was in motion from the beginning or was originally in a stationary state, whether only separate elements existed at first and later mixtures and compounds were produced through natural processes or all possible combinations were present from the start— these are all questions of fact that cannot be decided *a priori*.[288]

---

[288]   Some have been settled dogmatically, others have not.

[Various classifications]

May we speak of *genus*, *species*, and *individual* here? Clearly not in the sense of a network of generations [*Generationszusammenh ang*] such as we find within living nature. In material nature we ought to distinguish genus, species, and individual according to their characteristic origin. We could group together as *genus* whatever goes back to the same set of principles of origin (for example, all the elements together, insofar as they go back to the first forming alone). *Species* is whatever by itself is included within this genus and has distinctive qualities. (Accordingly, particular elements would be species of the genus "element," and particular "mixed bodies" would be species of the genus "mixed body.") If we take the items of matter themselves as species, then the species is constituted by matter and form. But insofar as the forms are what specify the matter, we can see why the term "species" is applied to the form.

We may say that genus and specific difference constitute a species insofar as the genus' stock of content, spatial matter with certain qualities, keeps a place-holder open for the species within these "qualities." But between this genus and its species there is no "necessary {211} connection" like that between color and the species of color. Moreover, different stocks of content need not correspond to genera of different origin. The mixed pieces of matter genetically constituted by more than one principle make up a common genus because of their unity of origin. There may be a narrower unity among the species of a genus: for example, all the compounds that a certain element can enter into. These unities would also be unities of origin. Hence we would also have to call them "genera," seeing them as genera on a lower level of generality.

On the other hand there is an even broader generality than that of the genus "element" and of the genus "compound," namely, the genus that includes any "formed matter" whatsoever. Here we have the most general genus, which denotes the stock of content common to genera of different origin. The genera "element," "mixture," "compound" fit into it and are subordinated to it, each arrayed side by side insofar as one does not include one or more of the others. On the other hand, they form a hierarchy insofar as each goes back to a different set of principles.

Within the genus "element" we could call the unities formed by each element with other elements to which it has affinity "narrower genera"; within the genus "compound" the narrower genera are the unities that belong together as compounds of an element. The genus "formed matter" *includes* only the incorporated genera without their species. The genera "element," "compound," include their subordinate genera and acquire a specific stock of content in the particular elements without a more generic and different stock being distinguished within the species.

Now in the relation of the narrower genera —we may call them "families" to distinguish them from the others— to their species, are these species constituted by the genus plus a difference? For all the compounds of hydrogen, we obviously cannot give any common stock of qualities that are different from their specific characteristics (as we do have in the relation of triangle to right-angled and oblique-angled triangles, or in the relation of living thing to the various animal species). On the other hand if we take a definite kind of matter, say, marble, and the different "varieties" it "comes in," like Italian or Silesian marble, we have something with a common content and a specific stock, related as a "*species universalior* [more universal species]" and a "*species specialior* [more specific species]." And here there are levels of differentiation down to the *species specialissima* [most specific species]." {212}

[A new approach: sensible appearance]

Clearly, this general and specific content stands out in the *sensi-*

ble appearance of the things, and considering this sensible appearance will give us a quite fresh approach to natural objects that differs from the "objective [*objektiv*]" approach we have taken thus far. Are we not overstepping our bounds here, or is this shift in viewpoint legitimate, even necessary? We cannot say whether our former approach is "objective" and our new one "subjective," nor can we say what "objective" and "subjective" mean, before making a final analysis of the meaning of being, whither our study of the genera of the be-ing and the ways of being must, after all, ultimately lead.

We were led to consider material objects because our purpose was to understand how organic things emerge by comparing their emergence with that of purely material things. We found similarities and differences in their origin, to which similarities and differences in their content were not directly parallel. Our attempt to identify these differences and similarities in content led us to "content [*Inhalt*]" in the sense of the "contents [*Gehalt*] of sensible appearance." We must now ask whether "content" as such can have yet another meaning in the material domain.

[Objective content and empirical inquiry]

The literal meaning of "species" already suggests "visibility." The elements, as well as the mixed items of matter, are different species (at least *also*) as various contents of appearance. They do not differ in principle in the content of their appearance; I mean, we could not distinguish the genera "element" and "compound" from the way they appear to us. We tell them apart both by examining their origin ontically, as we have just done, and by studying the causal behavior of the material objects empirically. (We need not consider here how these two approaches, which correspond to philosophy and to the natural sciences, are related in the theory of knowledge and the practice of acquiring it.)

An empirical inquiry can tell us that kinds of matter have in fact emerged and at the same time it can identify their "objective content," in the sense of a material [*stofflich*] stock of content. It can point out the constituents common to and different in various sorts of matter. We thus arrive empirically at elements and compounds as well as at their "families." But any empirical inquiry about the material world starts from what is perceived by the senses or from the species in the sense of the contents of appearance. The scientific analysis of these species will identify these "objective contents" and determine whether they {213} are simple or composed and how they are composed.

But no necessary relation between the "objective content" and the intuited [*anschaulich*] species can be established in this way. We cannot say that a particular intuitive species is possible or necessary only in virtue of this combination and no other. On the other hand, where we can bring out what is common and what is different in the content of appearance itself by intuitive [*intuitiv*] abstraction, we can find genera and species on various levels as well as the necessary connections among them.

[Genus, species, and the unity of origin]

When speaking hitherto of "species," however, we were not referring to the contents of appearance themselves, to the sensible species, but to the be-ing that shapes the contents of appearance, the form. When empirical inquiry shows that something which is simple for intuition is composed, it does not mean that the form is composed but that there is more than one forming principle. What is included in a unity of origin makes up a genus in the genetic sense. When the origin implies that what emerges is provided with a common stock, the stock itself may be called a genus. Otherwise the forms contained in a unity of origin should be called species, which, however, ought not to be taken as genuine specifications of a general stock.

Thus different contents are compatible with a single, common origin. Where there is a unity of content in the sense of an inner unity of a species, there must be a single principle giving the form, although this giving may presuppose other principles. Where there is a unity of content in the sense of a stock of content common to several species, the common stock will in turn hark back to a unity of origin in the sense of a principle that gives form.

[Likeness and causation in tokens of species]

We have thus come up with a meaning for Thomas's principle that likeness [*Gleichheit*] goes back to a common cause. The meaning is clear when "cause" is the *prima causa* [first cause], the principle that gives form ultimately, and when what is alike is a generic stock in a number of species. But it is still not clear in the case of a likeness of species in a number of instances, nor have we explained as yet the second half of the principle, that when two things are alike one must be the cause of the other (*or* both must go back to a common cause).

In our earlier study of matter we did not go into "instances" of the species and "things" at all. We touched only briefly on the question whether the pieces wherein matter "occurs" are instances and possibly individuals. "Pieces" are {214} spatial and spatially separate parts of a whole. We call the particular things that exemplify a species its instances. Is the whole, which is the total amount of matter, a species, and are the pieces instances of the whole?

We have called the item of matter "species," understanding thereby matter [*Materie*] with specific qualities or even the form itself that gives it its qualities. The whole is the entire amount of matter (whether or not we should think of it as limited). This idea of totality in extension is not contained in the idea of species; even if we include matter in the species, no particular amount of matter is included. The species leaves its stamp on each piece just as it does on the whole. The material item as an amount then is different from the species. The whole as an amount leaves no stamp on any piece, nor are the pieces instances of the whole.

May we say that the whole and the pieces of the whole are instances of the species (for example, are all the actual and possible pieces of gold instances of the species "gold")? In any case they are not instances of the species as whole *and* pieces because the whole does not exist *alongside* the pieces but *consists of* them. Hence only in them and through them could the whole be an instance or —when undivided— the only instance.

But when a species has but a single occurrence in principle, we call the individual itself the species. Moreover, this singleness in principle is not relevant to matter because matter is essentially divisible. All pieces can be further broken down, although not indefinitely.[289] Items of matter, as anything material, share in the divisibility of space and matter. However with them, divisibility goes further than in the case of other material things insofar as the whole is not affected by division.

The material whole is only an amount or quantity, not a definite shape. The whole, as any particular piece, must have some spatial shape, but *what* shape it has is "accidental," meaning that it does not follow on its species but is the result of what happens to it from outside. Where one particular spatial shape or even a limited number of possible shapes belongs to a material thing specifically, a spatial division may still be possible, but the whole, if divided, will be destroyed. This is the reason why we may call such a thing an "individual," something indivisible. And we speak properly of "instances" only

---

[289] Where these limits lie will shortly be indicated.

where there are individuals (in the sense given) wherein the species is instantiated.

[Crystals, instance and individual]

How can we speak, still within purely material nature, of what "else is material" besides items of matter? We may call a crystal, but not a piece of gold, an individual. The crystal's spatial shape, more precisely, its external contours, {215} is not accidental to the crystal but springs from its inner principle of form and is founded on the species. Pieces of matter that crystallize do not occur only in separate crystals, for there are pieces that consist of many crystals, and we can still "break up" the individual crystals. This does not affect the sum-total of the matter, but the crystal is destroyed when broken. The inner structure of the matter has preference for a certain kind of division that does it justice, but it does not make another kind of division impossible.

Crystalline and amorphous matter also have an inner makeup that is relevant to their fragmentation. Indeed, lacking specific contours, they cannot be broken down into individuals (in the sense given). But they do show a characteristic surface shape, nor do they come apart or shatter "arbitrarily," but in a specific way that reveals their own material structure. Here, too, they can be divided practically regardless of their inner limits; however, the actual outcome will always be determined by outside *as well as* inside factors.

So here, too, we have "characteristic" —albeit not specifically determined— contours. We may say that the crystal's shape is formed by its inner form, but more or less favorable external circumstances also affect how purely the specific shape leaves its stamp. In the case of other items of matter, "external chance factors" determine the shape of the pieces, but their material structure limits their possible effects. A block of stone of characteristic shape appears to us as an individual just as much as a crystal; in either case we have a unity of appearance that division would destroy. But the inner principle of form is different. A block of granite is not an instance of the species "granite" (it is at most an instance of the *type* [*Typus*] "block of granite").

The atomic view assigns a specific shape to the "smallest parts" (atoms or molecules) of each piece of matter. The differences in material structure, however, would not be eliminated thereby; they would become various principles of accumulation that in one case has led to a specific spatial shape and in another has not.

In answer to the question whether "instance" and "individual" mean the same thing, we may say that only an individual can be a instance of a species. But "instance" means something different than "individual," and the meaning of individuality that being an instance supposes is not its only possible meaning.

[The cause of being the same]

We may apply the principle that like [*Gleichheit*] things point to a like cause to the relation between species and individual. When {216} two things are alike they may owe their likeness to a *single* inner principle of form, they may be instances of the same material species. Also, a likeness that we intuit may result from several active factors and perhaps to an interplay of *different* factors at work in both. But there must be *one* dominant principle of form that causes the results to be alike.

The question of how one thing can be the cause of another thing (more precisely, of another thing like it) is related to another: whether one thing can owe its emergence to another thing. So far we have taken emergence as matter coming into existence and becoming formed. Matter comes into existence in the form of different species that occur as items or pieces of matter, individual material items. The "fortune" of all these material objects hinges on their interdependence in such wise that any *event* in the material world can be regarded as a *cause* of another. Moreover, the items of matter of which others are made up can be called "cause" (in another sense of the word), or more accurately, their inner form or nature, which is what is effective in them.

The nature of things and natural events —intramundane causes— presuppose the supramundane, the *prima causa* through which everything is what it is and through which *this* is what it is and can do [*wirken*] what it does. We can discover no causality by which one individual would bring another about [*hervorbringen*] within material nature. Genus may denote genetic connection, but in this case genesis is an ontic origin from a forming principle, not the emergence of an individual from what generates it.

§ 18
The new relation of form and matter
in the organism.
Entelechy.
Genus, species, individual, type.

[Crystals and living things]

Only living individuals are connected through generation. In material nature, emergence would mean either the initial forming of matter or the transforming [*Umformung*] of matter already formed into new kinds of matter wherein the re-forming cannot be attributed to the material constituents or to their forms. Material nature seems to come closest to organic nature in crystals, insofar as crystals are individuals of a specific spatial shape and are shaped from within.

But such individuals are not connected by generation. Where there is a completely novel effect, there must also be a different kind of being and a different kind of inner form behind it. Shaping from within seems to {217} be common to crystals and organisms. But if their forms are generically distinct, the shaping from inside, too, will differ generically. When a solution crystallizes, the matter undergoes a transformation in its material structure and for the first time comes actually to possess its "proper" structure as well as the specific spatial shape that belongs to it. It is a temporal process within the material object. It does not extend beyond itself nor is any new matter incorporated. And when crystallization is complete, the matter remains in the form it has received without anything else being done to it from the inside.

[Organization of the organism]

The self-constructing organism constantly reaches beyond itself, absorbs materials and "organizes" them. If in an object nothing is occurring any longer from the inside, if it remains in a rigid state or is subject only to outside forces, it has ceased to be an organism. In the particular living individual, then, the relation of form to matter already differs from the same relation in the purely material object closest to it. In material things being is the result of forming; in living things the forming itself is their distinctive being, their life; they form themselves for as long as they are. The organism constructs itself and incorporates materials into itself with the help of movements that themselves come from within. The organism first transforms the material items it takes in so they can enter the organism itself, become part of it. They are not "organized" until this takes place.

"Within" here obviously has two senses, parallel to the different levels of forming. First, taking in nourishment means only bringing food in from the outside in a spatial sense. The items of matter that are taken into the organism, as long as they remain what they are, are foreign bodies. They must first be transformed into the items that the organism itself is made of before they can formed into it; "digestion" is presupposed to "conservation" and "growth."

We have already discussed the transformation of items of matter in material nature. We described it as a new formation of the matter, as supramundane forming, not as an effect of the forms presupposed in the order of nature. The need for such transformation in the conservation and growth of living things shows that only certain kinds of matter can make up the living body; in Thomistic terms: reception by the soul presupposes certain dispositions of the matter, analogous to the way compounds presuppose elements.

[Entelechy]

Now, how are we to understand the transformation of properly disposed matter into an {218} organism; I mean, how is it *brought to life [Belebung]* and *organized*, in the sense that material items are shaped into an articulated whole? As soon as it comes to life, from the first moment of its existence, the living thing organizes itself, that is, it shapes itself progressively into an articulated whole. Organization is a *goal*-directed process; that is, it works toward a specific shaping of the individual, the shape wherein the individual unfolds fully, wherein the form is brought to effect purely.

This is why the living form merits the name "*entelechy* [*Entelechie*]." It takes effect as it moves to bring in needed materials and transforms and arranges them. The goal that the forming aims at is the whole which, in its entirety and in each of its parts, carries on the way of being of the forming principle, namely living, appropriate activity. "Organism," meaning an individual that lives and acts appropriately, a "living thing [*Lebewesen*]," denotes a *genus* in three senses. It is [1] an origin from a like principle, that is, from a living form, from an entelechy, [2] a stock of content, which is just what the word "organism" connotes, and [3] a domain of all individuals that emerge in this way and embody this stock of content.

Genus both as forming principle and as stock of content occurs only in specific forms. There is no organism as such, only organisms with specific qualities. Nor is there any entelechy that forms generically without forming specifically. Again, what is formed specifically in its totality is not an item of matter existing as a *single* material whole and allowing fragmentation that does not destroy the whole. It occurs rather in the form of individuals that are instances of the species. So it denotes at once a stock of content that includes the stock of the genus and a domain of individuals belonging to the domain of the genus. And each individual has its *own* entelechy.

[The lime tree]

We must now ask how the generic stock of content is related to the specific and individual stocks (if the individual does in fact denote a stock of content over and above its specific stock), and how the individuals of a genus and of a species are connected through generation. Thomas lays great stress on the fact that the individual owes what it is to a *single* substantial form and so he denies that a generic form, a specific form, and perhaps an individual form exist and work *side by side*.

This lime tree, just by being a "lime tree," is also a tree, a plant, an organism. And just by being an organism, it must belong to *one* species, for it must be *either* a lime *or* an oak, etc. (We ignore here the relation of the more or less universal and particular species.) Genus and species are formally constituted in their mutual relations, for specification {219}, as *genuine* specification, is independent of the matter that is formed. In this sense we can also say here that the likeness of species, the commonness of its generic stock, points to a unity of ontic origin.

[Difference due to outer and inner factors]

This lime tree here is not only numerically different from that one, nor is it different only because it stands in another place or in the place where the other stood before. Nor are they completely alike. The specific stock is common to the two trees, but this one, say, is a more imposing specimen. If we take species as sensible appearance, we may call an individual's full concrete stock of appearance a *species specialissima* and from it abstract its more general stocks. But we are not saying that a substantial form stands behind the concrete stocks as if it were a genuine specification of a generic stock. We are not saying, in other words, that the entelechy at work in the individual as a forming principle has as its τέλος [*telos*, end, goal, purpose] all that the individual is.

Two seeds from the same plant may be quite alike, yet one becomes a stately tree while the other tree is stunted. The reverse might be true if the seeds exchanged places. The "external circumstances" that led to different results are outside forming forces that together with the substantial form affected how the individual is shaped. Either the same building materials were not found in the two places, in which case the matter was not disposed in the same way for the forming from within, or else the natural direction of the growth was blocked by the spatial conditions, when a material obstacle hindered the substantial forming.

In this way we can understand the individual distinctiveness "*de ratione materiae* [by reason of the matter]." But must it be so under all circumstances? The differences in exterior conditions may hardly be noticeable yet the development may differ considerably. Must we then not seek the principle of the individual shaping on the inside, in the entelechy? Still, we may continue to seek the reason for the different results in the material constituents of the seeds. If the entire individual stock of the organism is *de ratione materiae*, then it is "accidental" to the substantial form; the "*species specialissima*" is not a genuine form nor a specification of the genus. Accordingly, as an instance of the species the organism should be described as a *telos* of the entelechy. The entelechy forms the organism into a whole whose activity aims not only at conserving the species in itself but at constructing new instances thereof. {220}

[Variation and species]

If true what is handed down from one individual to another, it seems, is the species. That the genus must be handed on along with the species is obvious from the relation of genus and species. We asked before if we should understand this transmission as an old form fashioning [*Bildung*] a new one. Everything we have said about forming [*Formung*] seems rule this out. Just as in material nature elements are combined into mixed items of matter by fashioning material items properly disposed for the new forming, so organisms produce new instances of their species by shaping the matter appropriate for a new entelechy without being able to give it this living form itself. If under the influence of external conditions not only instances of the species are shaped into individuals differing in content, but *types* emerge under like conditions, that is, groups of individuals with a common stock of content over and above the content of the species (or this stock itself emerges), then these types are no more specifications of the species than are the individuals; they are rather accidental to the species.

But how are we to know when the distinctive type is handed on and when new types emerge from the crossing of different individuals? Are we not obliged to say that the substantial form is transformed and that some forms are fashioned anew [*Neubildung*] by others? Where a typical character is reproduced (as well as a character that at first was individual but becomes typical of the "family" through reproduction), the following interpretation is possible. The disposition of the matter resulting from the external living conditions in instances of a type modifies in the same typical way the effect of the specific form in the individuals, both produced and producing, so that what is actually passed on would be the matter disposed in one way or another.

If a new variation emerges when different "breeds [*Rasse*]" are crossed, we should take it that the fertilizing process (analogous to the compounding of elements) creates a newly disposed matter. But what species is at work in this matter, the species of the producing individuals or a new species? Here we should no more say that species are combined into a new one than we should say, where the producing and produced individual are alike, that the old individual delivers the specific form to the new or that the specific form of a compound is made up of the forms of the elements. We must speak of a new "species" whose occurrence presupposes certain other species and the crossing of their instances. That a set order exists for a new species to appear {221} is implied by the fact that just any two individuals cannot interbreed.

[Theoretical possibilities]

The form of the individual marks the boundary between material and organic nature. Formal structure is already found in the lower area, but it finds richer fulfillment and a new mode of being in the higher. The material area attains this form only in its highest types.[290] This form is essential for the organic area; here nothing that is can exist otherwise than in this form. And the order of emergence in which organic individuals issue from one another corresponds thereto.

---

[290] Relevant here is the Pseudo-Dionysius's axiom, frequently quoted and applied by Thomas, that the end of one area touches the beginning of the next.

The genus emerges specified in individuals. Each individual bears its specific form in itself as a vitally effective entelechy shaping its matter. Not just any matter but one disposed in a definite way is presupposed to each species and to the genus as a whole.

In principle it is conceivable that all possible species were placed in existence through the initial (creative) forming. The other possibility is that a small number of species existed originally and new ones emerged in a definite order through interbreeding, moreover that each species left its stamp on different types under the influence of different external conditions. It is just as conceivable that each species at first existed in only one or two ancestral individuals and all others came from them through generation, as that most like individuals came into existence through the initial forming.[291]

§ 19
The general ontic meaning of genus, species, category. "Formed matter."

[Meanings of "genus"]

We are now able to weigh the several meanings of "*genus*" that have come up in several contexts and to sharpen our concepts in their regard. At first, in our material investigation, "genus" stood for what is connected *through generation* [*Generationszusammenhang*] ("generation [*Generation*]" taken as individuals producing [*Zeugung*] other individuals). Later "genus" {222} appeared as a *genetic* unity in another sense; indeed, in three senses: (1) a unity of *ontic origin*, that

---

[291]   The creation account in fact decides between these possibilities in principle for human beings only; for animals the flood account gives a —not quite unambiguous— hint (Gen. 6:19 and 7:2).

is, a unity of the forming principles, (2) the common stock of content in what these principles constitute, and (3) the totality of individuals of the same generic stock and origin. The individuals of a genus in this sense need not be connected by generation. Generation (as producing) is a specific kind of empirical emergence pertaining to a particular genus. Hence for what is connected through generation, it is better to use another term such as "lineage."

[Initial forming and empirical genesis]

The unity of principles may have still other senses. The *primum principium* [first principle] is the same for everything created, and so the original genesis from this principle, insofar as it gives being, does not result in any differentiation of genera within the be-ing. The initial differentiation comes from the first principle precisely insofar as it not only gives being but *form*, that is, as it gives the be-ing its substantial form. What comes into existence directly through this forming by the first principle is bound together in a narrower unity of origin, although the forming constitutes each as a different species. The genus of elements is characterized in this way.

In the case of what does not come into existence directly through the initial forming but has an *empirical genesis*, in addition to this genesis there is an order functioning as a generically uniting principle, for what emerges through the motion and combination of elements forms a genus. What is grouped together by such a unity of empirical genesis (that is, elements and compounds) is at the same time a *material* [*stofflich oder materiell*] unity. The initial forming, which at the same time is a placing in existence [*Setzung ins Dasein*], is an informing of matter. What is first informed and what emerges therefrom in empirical genesis results in the totality of what is constituted as *formed matter* and as such has a distinctive *mode of being*.

[Category]

What shares this mode of being constitutes a basic form of the be-ing, namely, a *category*. The category is not purely formal if we take "matter [*Materie*]" in the material [*material*] sense as matter that fills space. But "formed" in "formed matter" is an empty place-holder to be filled materially [*material*] by different substantial forms. If we also take "matter" formally, we come back to that formal category that includes every finite (= created) be-ing. But if we understand "formed" as well as "matter" materially [*material*], "formed matter" denotes a definite area of being. If we use "material form" as space-filling matter, then everything belonging to this category is connected by laws [*gesetzlich*] through the order of empirical origin in a network: in the {223} network of *material nature*. We have called "species" the substantial forms giving definite qualities as well as the unity of the matter and the form that gives it its specific qualities.

§ 20
The category "organic" or "living."
Form, matter, mode of being, order of origin.

[Life]

If we are to describe the *organic* or *living* as a new category, it must have a *new mode of being* over against what is material [*materiell*]. And this implies a new material [*material*] sense of "form" or "matter [*Materie*]," possibly of both, hence a new *relation of form and matter* and a *another kind of genesis* as well. All this is already in evidence.

It is characteristic of genesis that in a way ontic genesis is prolonged in empirical genesis: *forming* becomes *temporal process*, and at the same time the form becomes a vitally effective *entelechy* that not only forms the matter given together with it but constantly appropriates and organizes new matter. The mode of being becomes life as goal-directed development with all the motions, activities, transformations, etc. from within that living implies. On the basis of what marks off the organic area as a category, we must now clarify other organic features, namely the fact that the be-ing in this area is constituted as an individual, as an organism, and as a instance of a species.

[Entelechy and species]

That which gives being to the material thing, that *through* which it is, is its substantial form. Since what gives being must itself be actual, we call the form the "*act*" of the matter and we call "*potency*" the matter that comes into existence only through act, that is, it comes to share in the being of the form. Just as the potentiality of matter is so to speak overcome by the actuality of the form, so the form in the matter takes on something of the matter's rigidity and potentiality. Its actuality is not pure actuality. The form is not in the matter through itself but through the creative act of the One Who is pure act. The form is in the matter, as it were, as an imprint [*Abdruck*] of this creative act, and its being is a *persisting* [*Beharren*] without being inwardly alive.

The *entelechy* is the substantial form of living matter. It is the act of the matter which it enters and to which it gives being, that distinctive mode of being that we call "life." In the order of ontic origin, the entelechy enters matter that is already formed and therein takes the place of the form that gave it purely material being. This matter is no longer purely potential, and so it is not unlimitedly receptive; it is open {224} to new forming only within certain limits and to an actualization of definite possibilities. Nor is the entelechy purely actual. It, too, owes its being in the matter to the creative act. But it is not in matter merely as a rigid imprint, nor is its being a mere persisting; it is *living power* [*Kraft*], as if something of the creating breath were left behind in it, and its being is a living working.

This power is limited; it aims at a finite goal [*Ziel*] and hence its direction is determined; its aim is to organize a definite amount of matter with definite qualities into a definite shape. This delimitation of its being, of its task, of its matter, results in the "gathering [*Sammlung*]" of this matter into the form of the individual and into the individuality of the entelechy itself. The unity of ontic origin and the unity of the mode of being that it brings about, for which mode of being the kind of material bond is essential, makes possible a number of like entelechies in a number of like amounts of matter with like qualities and hence a number of like individuals. The unity of the mode of being groups all individuals sharing in it under the *category of living matter*, the category of the *organic* or *living*. The unity of ontic origin, that is, the unity of the creative impulse that "distributes" a definite amount of matter with definite qualities among the many entelechies, unites these individuals into a *genus* in the sense of ontic genesis.

The distinctiveness of the entelechy as such and of its *telos*, the organism, results in the genus taken as the same stock of content in all the individuals that belong to it. On the other hand, the genus taken as the unity of origin and content marks off the domain of the individuals belonging to it. The possibility that the entelechy is differentiated in its qualities, in other words that its *telos* is differentiated within the framework of the stock of content that we call "entelechy" and "organism," enables the genus to disperse into different species whose stock of qualities includes a common generic stock and a separate specific one, and at the same time it enables individuals that are generically the same [*Gleichheit*] to be separated, each of which is held together in itself by a specific likeness.

[Theories of evolution]

We may think of the specification of the genus purely in terms of ontic genesis, that is, as an original difference [*Differenz*] of entelechies. But we may also see it linked to a course of empirical genesis. A number of like entelechies could be distributed among amounts of matter whose qualities are only partially alike. The formation by the entelechies would then result in different variations of the one *telos*, or different degrees of "approximation" to the *telos*.

We may also include generation in the order of {225} empirical genesis. We have taken generation to be a disposition of the matter for receiving a new entelechy through the forming power of an already existing entelechy. Here we should see the new entelechy as specifically like <unto> the old one. But the matter to be disposed could be varied by the effects of other formative forces that the matter underlies besides the forming by the entelechy. Because of this variation the new organism would also deviate from the old one despite the entelechy being alike. Finally, the interbreeding of individuals having different qualities (whether different instances of the same species or instances of different species), according to the order of empirical genesis, can cause a new species to arise. (These possibilities form the ontological basis for several biological theories of evolution.)

§ 21
Constitution of the living
"from below" and "from above."

[Critique of Conrad-Martius]

Our foregoing study suggests answers to some of the questions raised by the view of nature that Hedwig Conrad-Martius describes in her *Metaphysische Gespräche*. She spoke of a dark, formless drive for being and shaping, of guiding "ideas" and of the guiding "*logos*" that give this drive its goal and direction and enable it to shape. We can now understand her contrast of "from below" and "from above" in a certain way. All that is, is through the one single principle of all being, even what is nothing but pure receptivity for being and form, that is, *matter*. But matter, since it lies outside this principle and is opposed to it, is posited as it were as a second principle, and the play of the forms and forces put into the matter is left to itself or better, to the laws that govern it. In this "lower" world set outside the spirit, in this world of material nature, *life* awakens as something awoken in turn "from above," immersed in the matter disposed for it.

We need not see "life" as a dark, formless drive to be posited absolutely nor living nature as demonic. Life for us is the being of the living thing. What makes a living thing alive is a form and force or power, individually constituted and determined in its direction; better still, it is a *formed power*. This implies, as we shall argue in greater detail, that we should distinguish two factors, one formal (giving qualities) and the other "material [*materiell*]" (in itself formless), in the entelechy itself and analogously {226} in its being.[292] We may also see living nature as a "lower world" insofar as it, too, is released from the spirit and left to a definitely ordered course of becoming.

According to the *Gespräche* a single guiding idea active in the entelechy may be assumed for every area of shaping (such as the idea of plants), and the diverse shapings were seen as more or less successful "drafts" of the idea. But this, I daresay, leaves too much to "chance." Our attempt to understand the meaning of "genus" and "species" led us to ascribe a definite direction to the entelechy. This

---

[292]   Cf. pp. 238-9 and 382ff.

direction, however, is not one that determines what it forms down to the last detail, since the outcome, the fully determined *what* of the individuals, is determined not only by the entelechy but also by the lower material forms and forces that it presupposes. Thus the individual peculiarity and the typical variations of the species are accidental outcomes from the standpoint of the entelechy, but from the standpoint of the *Logos* they are foreseen as possibility founded on the ordered interplay of the forces.[293]

[Ascending and descending evolution]

Our study of reproduction showed us how one individual arises from others and how the "species [*Art*]" are both conserved and varied therein. The possibility of an ascending evolution also became understandable as an origin wherein certain species are presupposed to the emergence of others and the later species have a higher mode of being than the former.

On the other hand, we may understand "degeneration [*Degeneration*]" insofar as the entelechy is not only a form but a shaping power which, though extending beyond the individual and perhaps through a lengthy series of individuals over a whole "descent," exhausts itself in its attainments.[294]

---

[293]   This recalls the distinction in Thomistic theology between predetermining and permissive divine providence.

[294]   Of course the particular factors working together in generation and their interplay must be further studied in order to understand better the possible contributions of the entelechy, its scope and limits.

§ 22
The animal in contrast to the purely organic.
Body and soul.
Substance, potency, and act of the soul.
Power of the soul.
Subjectivity.
Species and individual.
Constitution from below and from above.

[Plant and animal species]

Wherever there is a characteristic mode of being and, what amounts to the same thing, a special material [*material*] meaning and a distinctive relationship of form and matter, of act and potency, we have a particular category. This is the way we have distinguished material and living nature. Do we also have such a radical split between the plant and animal kingdom? Is the "animal soul" a form generically distinct from the "plant soul"? The animal soul, too, is entelechy; it is what it forms (I mean that it is the result of its forming); it is an individual, an organism, an instance of a species. The order of empirical origin is analogous in plant and animal and so is their ontic origin.

May we then see animal and plant as species of the genus "organism" or "living thing"? We would find different levels of generality among the species within the genus since the particular plant and animal species do not simply stand side by side but some lie closer to one another and further from others. This is why the order of origin, too, is not *the same* but *analogous.* Some plant species are presupposed to other plant species and some animal species are presupposed to other animal species. However, some plant species are not presupposed to animal species nor are plant species as a whole presupposed to animal species as a whole in the way that material nature is presupposed to living nature, to the plant world and the animal world. No transition from the one to the other is possible.

[The wounded animal and the loyal dog]

What we found to be essentially new in the animal compared to the plant is the appearance of an "interior." The being of an animal's substantial form is not only life, shaping lifeless matter into an organism, but inner life. It feels itself in its body and controls its body in a "free" movement which does more than immediately form the organism. Here "life" acquires a quite new meaning (as indeed the word "*Lebewesen*" is used sometimes in the wider sense of "organism" and sometimes for *animalia*). Life is being that is immaterial [*immateriell*] in still another sense, in a sense different from the way in which the forms of nonliving and living matter are immaterial. Even material form and entelechy are not material (in the sense of matter filling space) but are ordered to matter as what gives matter form and manifests itself in matter.

No doubt life that is specific to the animal soul also develops bound to matter, but it does so as meaningful in itself and independent {228} of matter in its meaning. The pain gazing from the eyes of a wounded animal belongs to another world far from the whole of its animal body [*Leib*] (even when we see it not as mere body [*Körper*] but precisely as a living body [*Leib*] formed from within). And the devotion that binds a dog to its master, the alertness with which it awaits his signal, the readiness with which it obeys his command also belong to this other world.

We use words taken from the life of the human soul to describe what takes place in the animal soul. The two cases are certainly not the same, yet just as certainly we are not merely equivocating, or sentimentally reading something in or using metaphors (as when we give a psychic interpretation to shapes and movements in the plant kingdom). Rather, a genuine analogy forms the objective basis for our way of speaking. The animal soul then is clearly more than the mere form of a body; it is something that manifests itself not only in shaping the body but in a life that is *its own*, albeit its life in turn becomes apparent only through characteristic outward shapings of the body. The sensible shapings through which this takes place speak a symbolic language of their own and form a network that stands out from the overall network of sensible appearances of the body.

[The spiritualness of the animal]

When we call this life within the soul immaterial being, this is but a negative description. When we call it spiritual, we must ask what we mean by "spiritual." In one sense, in that of objective spirit, the being of the material form and of the entelechy is also spiritual insofar as each, form and entelechy, is actual being and a likeness of the highest actually spiritual being, pure personal act. The entelechy is a likeness of original being in a higher degree, insofar as it is alive and moves other things as well as itself by itself [*von sich aus*].

The animal soul is not yet spiritual in the personal sense —it is not its own master nor is it illumined for itself [*für sich selbst durchleuchtet*] —, but it comes closer than entelechy as such to this higher form of the spiritual. It "*senses*" itself and what takes place within itself; this sensing is like a previous stage [*Vorstufe*] to being illumined intellectually. It is *sensitive* to what befalls it from without; this sensitivity is like a stage previous to being open intellectually. It *reacts* with body and soul to what befalls it; this reacting that is like a stage previous to acting freely and personally mastering the body. If the stages of spiritualness are identical to the degrees of actuality, then we must see the being of the animal, too, as a distinctive mode of actuality or as a distinctive relation of act and potency.

[Soul and body of the animal, "reaction"]

The animal's body and soul are not bound up {229} with one another in the same way that a material form (or an entelechy) is bound up with its matter. The animal soul, insofar as it is entelechy, forms the matter that it forms into a body into an organism. But insofar as the soul is something more than entelechy, it forms the organism into what it is as a body and uses it in a typical way. The soul so to speak moves its body away from itself—the distinction between "outer" and "inner" comes about in just this way— and turns it into a handy tool it can freely move in space. The soul has a sphere of activity beyond the piece of matter that belongs to the soul as to the form of its own body. The possible effectiveness of the soul extends to the surrounding material nature that it reaches through the movements of its body; such is the soul's surrounding world, its *material environment* [*Umwelt*]. It also extends to the *organic* and *living world* of its surroundings; indeed, for each of these worlds and for the different species within each there is a particular possible effectiveness. This entire environment is "matter" for the forming power of the animal soul.

The body is but the piece of matter that is most thoroughly subject to the soul, being closest to it and inseparable from it. The body is at the same time what the soul needs to mediate all its activity beyond the body. We may say that the soul's total environment is in potency to the effects that the animal's soul can bring about therein, and that the soul itself is the act that corresponds to this potency (its act on the other hand is the actual being into which the animal's soul shifts the potential being subject to it in the outside world).

But neither is the soul pure act. It actually is and does at any one time only a small part of what it is and what it can do; the rest is potential in the soul and the soul is potential to it. Nor does the soul have the power to actualize what is potential in it. What is potential is bound to outside influences, so that the soul's own specific being can become actual only through an actual being that is not its own. All the actions of the soul in the outside world as well as all its inner movements are *reactions*; they are actualizations of its own being in contact with what is foreign to it. And any such contact, which we call innerly perceived "sensation," is mediated by the body.

Thus the soul is an act that is relative not only to the potency of the body's matter but to an entire wealth of potencies in its environment. And it also possesses potencies which, in order to pass into their specific act, depend upon forming acts coming from the environment. The soul fits into a greater whole which is a unity of forming powers and of matter to be formed. The soul is the center of action in this whole. The soul is spatially in this whole through its body, and in its body the soul is and does whatever it is actually and potentially, whatever it does and can do. {230} It has no life outside the body, yet forming the body is not the sum total of its life.

[Threefold structure of the soul, substance]

We have come then to a division of act and potency within the realm of the soul itself. This raises several new issues. Is the soul the form of the body as a whole or only through what it is actually? Is what the soul is actually act and form relative to what it is potentially? And should we see what the soul is potentially as matter for this form (or perhaps for another form)?

To answer these questions we must keep a distinction in the soul's structure in mind among [1] what makes up the soul's essence, what the soul must be enduringly if it is not to cease to be, [2] what it has as an enduring property that does not belong to its essence itself, and [3] what involves the possibility of passing over into something else, into the various states that we call "acts" after their mode of being. These three levels in the soul's structure we call *substance*, *potency*, and *act*.

The substance of the soul is that which constitutes the soul in its being, that through which the soul is (it corresponds to what the substantial form is in material objects). Filling time is characteristic of it, and hence it is something that endures and fills its duration with a stock of qualities that persists throughout changes. The changes are modifications in the qualities of the persisting stock, but change in the mode of being runs parallel to change in the stock of qualities. What persists is enduringly actual, but it defines a set of possibilities for the changing qualitative modes in such wise that a stock of potencies also belongs essentially to what persists actually.

But since what persists can be actual only in one of the changing qualitative modes, at least one of the potencies that belong to it must always be actualized throughout the duration of its being, and we call this actual qualitative mode an *act of the soul*. Accordingly, the substantial form or essence [*Wesen*] of the soul is the persisting stock of qualities that gives qualities to an amount, that is, to the power [*Kraft*] of a soul,[295] and it is the formal structure that binds the persisting stock to the stock of potencies and changing acts of the soul. What potencies and changing acts are possible to the soul are defined by its substance, and so substance may be called form and act relative to the changing stock.

But which potency of the stock is actualized at any one time does not depend on the substantial form alone. We said that the changing acts of the animal's soul are reactions to what is happening to it from without. Hence what the soul is potentially must be {231} actualized by its own substantial form but also by forms that come to it from

---

[295]   Cf. pp. 238-9 and 382ff.

outside. To understand how the soul is formed from without we must be clearer about what we are calling its persisting and changing stock of qualities.

[Lions and foxes, accidents and substance]

The lion, the fox, the bear, etc. are not only different animal species in their bodily nature but they also have a their own specific kind of soul. What specifically characterizes the soul of the lion, the fox, etc. is what persists actually in them. But this lives in what comes and goes in them, in their hunger, in their anger, in their pain, etc. These terms denote species of acts of the soul, and the corresponding potencies of the soul are specified parallel to them. The species of the acts of the soul make up the many diverse qualitative modes in whose changes the substance of the soul can be actual.

This diversity forms a new category of a be-ing that can be actual only in something else (namely in a substance). What species of accidents are possible in the substance depends upon the substance. Not all the species of acts in the human soul are possible to the animal's soul. And not all animal species have the same species of acts. Some acts of the soul are found in all *animalia*, and others are characteristic only of certain species. But even those acts proper to most animal species show specific modifications in particular species that correspond to their substantial form.

The diversity in all the species of the soul's acts is in a way analogous to the diversity of sensible qualities, that is, to the qualities of material things. Just as these qualities characterize the matter formed into things by their substantial forms, so something analogous to matter is formed by what souls are actually in an enduring way. Just as the matter of bodies and their accidents pass from potentiality to actual being only through a connection with a substantial form, so also do the accidents of the soul and this "matter [*Materie*] of souls" pass to actual being. The contents of the acts of the soul can come into existence only when a subject having a soul carries them out in its living. Each act given qualities by a species is "a piece of the soul's life."

[Matter of the soul]

Is not this the "matter of the soul [*seelische Materie*]" that we have been seeking, the analogue of corporeal matter? Just as in corporeal matter a definite amount of matter belongs to each substantial form, so a definite amount of "life power or force [*Lebenskraft*]" belongs to each soul.[296] Just as corporeal matter fills {232) space with its qualities, so the life of the soul fills time with its qualities. Just as the soul as entelechy causes living matter to gather into the form of the individual, into a self-contained organism, so too it gathers its "life" into an individual unity. Its life cannot be broken up into separate durations among which a life of a soul having other substantial qualities could intrude, as pieces of different kinds of matter are "jumbled together."

The individual unity of the life of the soul is conditioned on the one hand by the fact that the soul is entelechy not only for the body but also for itself —I mean that the soul bears a *telos* in itself that its living strives after— and on the other hand by the fact that the soul constructs itself as an "organism," that is, as a whole wherein all the parts work together according to a fixed order. The unity, however, has yet another pole wherein the soul's entire life comes together or, better, wherefrom it departs.

---

[296]   I borrowed the expression from Theodore Lipps in my former works (cf. *Beiträge zur philosophischen Begründung der Psychologie und der Gesiteswissenschaften,* loc. cit.).

[Breakthrough to subjectivity and instinct]

The life of a soul is the life of the subject that has the soul. The breakthrough into the interior that distinguishes the animal soul from the plant soul is a breakthrough into subjectivity. This is the "self-"sensing [*"Sich"-Spüren*] that pertains to the being of *animalia*. The subject lives a life that can be lived only as "formed matter," only as having qualities. And it gets these qualities both from without and from within. How should we understand it that an individual living whole is divided into specifically different acts?

The answer is relatively easy when the acts of the soul —as in man— have the form of intentionality. We can then say with Thomas that acts are specified by their objects [*Objekt*], and this is at least *one* principle of differentiation, although we must also ask if it is the only principle. We should not, however, ascribe to animal life the same intentionality we ascribe to human life. In its acts, the animal is not turned toward objects with the open eye of the mind. The animal does not "know, realize [*erkennen*]," it does not "perceive, become aware [*wahrnehmen*]." It is only "affected [*affizieren*]," it only "reacts" in actual and habitual stances, even attaining therein a lower stage previous to intellectual realizing [*Erkennen*] and knowing [*Wissen*].

The animal lies in wait for its prey, pounces on it savagely, greedily devours it. These are not purely objective [*objektiv*] causal processes, as when one stone falls on another and smashes it. As processes of the soul, these animal processes, although they no doubt allow an objectively causal [*objektiv-causal*] interpretation, are to be understood from within. In all of {233} this, the animal is in contact with something outside of itself. There is a tension here between subject and object, a tending toward and a being drawn, a taking possession and a getting satisfied, etc.

The animal is constantly being pushed and pulled, its living means being inwardly affected, acted upon. The entelechy feature of the soul's substance, the form of becoming of its being, gives rise to an urge and a drive from within toward what the organism must appropriate in order to construct itself. This urge and drive already varies, since it must aim at different things at different times. Encountering what promises to satisfy its drives —"encountering" and "promising" are but dully felt— gives aim and direction to the drives that were previously undetermined and leads to further differentiation and acquisition of other qualities.

Encountering means becoming one in a certain sense. When the animal is attracted by its prey, it suffers a break in the flow of its life and it reaches out beyond the sphere of its own life, not only in its body, by appropriating and incorporating the prey as nourishment, but also in its soul, by hankering after its prey, fighting for it, relishing it. And in all this actual being of its soul, the animal is bound to something other than itself. (We should not of course suppose any consciousness in the animal analogous to human consciousness whereby it could disjoin itself as a self from the other as other.) Just as material things are inserted into a causal network of material nature and can unfold what they are only in the network of causal events, so every being having life and soul, every animal, is placed in a network of effects coming from its environment, I mean that it is placed in whatever can fall upon its senses thereby affecting its soul and then in whatever it can reach by its own actions motivated by what affects it.

[Oneness of body and soul]

This "falling upon its senses" brings up a whole new set of issues. Here we can only consider what is indispensable for understanding the animal's specific being, that is, the fact that its senses are organs of its body and of its soul. Through them and in them the

organism of body and soul is open to the influences of the environment. *Through* the body and *in* the body or *at* the body the animal's
soul encounters all that it encounters. And whatever takes place in the
soul affects the body.

Although we may say that the being of the animal's soul is a
becoming, a process of development toward a telos, *analogous* to
the body's *telos*, we should not think that the soul's development is
going on *alongside* the body's development, nor that the soul has its
own *telos* apart from the body's *telos* since the animal organism and
its whole being are a thing of body and soul. This now enables us to
answer the questions concerning {234} the being of the soul and the
relation between soul and body.[297] Is the soul the form of the body as
a whole or only through what it is actually?

[The soul form of body and individuality]

Our preceding inquiry has given us two senses of "what the soul
is actually." What the soul is actually *in an enduring manner* must be
distinguished from its changing acts. What is actual enduringly, the
substantial form, makes soul and body into what they are. The potencies as well as the changing acts are at once of soul and body; they
are grounded in the substance as in their *single* root. But insofar as
the entire stock of potencies and acts of body and soul at any one time
determine the condition and behavior of the material body [*Körper*],
which, for having a soul, is a living body [*Leib*] (especially its spatial
shape and motion), the soul as a whole can be called the form of this
living material body [*Leibkörper*]. The substantial form, along with
what intervenes from outside by forming, causes the potencies to be
actualized and the soul's living to be formed into acts of various specific qualities.

---

[297]   Cf. p. 336-7.

The entire organism of body and soul should be called an individual, a unit that cannot be broken at will without being destroyed. What is it here that individuates [*individuieren*], divides one organism from another? To each organism belongs its *own* "piece of matter" and to each its *own* life power as the "matter" of the being of its soul, and each is separate from all the others through the form of subjectivity. Are individuals also separate in their qualities? We have called what gives acts their qualities "species," and we have also called "species" the substantial forms that differ in qualities and give qualities, as in the different animal species such as fox, lion, etc. All animals of the same species receive like qualities yet as instances of the same species they are not fully alike.

What is this diversity of qualities in individuals based upon? It may have its basis in the diversity of the matter which, in this and that individual, can be more or less suitable for being formed by the species. (We should recall that in the organic area the reception of the entelechy presupposes in the order of origin a matter that is already formed.) Influences are involved here that during generation already affect the matter of the organism that is becoming and dispose it more or less favorably. Differences in the external living conditions are also involved, in the environmental forces wherein the individual develops. Individuals of a species that are fully alike are conceivable in principle. Consequently we ought not to understand the quality of substantial forms as an individual quality. {235}

[Form above and potential below]

Our review of the makeup and emergence of entities of nature was prompted by the *Metaphysische Gespräche*, wherein Conrad-Martius views man as constituted "from above" and "from below." We sought to clarify what "from above" and "from below" mean. In a way, all being is "from above," in that nothing is that has not received its being and what it is from the highest being. This is true even of what is diametrically opposed to the highest being, what is lowest in the area of the be-ing, what —considered by itself — still "is" not, is not yet "something," but is rather pure receptivity for the being and the *what* that it acquires through a substantial form. This pure potentiality we met in two shapes: as *matter* filling space and as *life* that presses forward into time and through time.

We may call the substantial forms immersed in the absolutely potential that gives it being and content "from above" relative to what is potential, and we may call the potential "from below" relative to the forms. The substantial forms parallel to the two kinds of "matter" differ as "material forms" and "living forms." The organic form in a way lies in between the material and animal form, since on the one hand it is attached to the matter according to the kind of material form, and on the other it shapes the matter, that is, it shapes it organically according to the kind of animal form.

[Plants, animals, and man]

We have grouped under the heading "category" what is set apart and united through its own mode of being, and under the heading "genus" what has a unity of genesis. The organic, we said, constitutes its own category distinct from what is merely material. We might wish to see *animalia* as species of the genus "organism" insofar as animals are organisms whose specific difference, unlike plants, is the capacity to sense and to move about freely in space.

But this would not do justice to the radical division between plants and animals. As organisms, animal species must be classified with plant species. But as be-ings endowed with senses and soul, as open inwards and outwards, they form a new category. The life of the soul, as inward life and as life reaching out by its forming power beyond the matter of the organism, has its own mode of being and is closer to personal spiritual being. We must now ask whether we can find something in man's makeup that we ought to call "from above" in a radically new sense. {236}

<h1 style="text-align:center">§ 23
Man.</h1>

a.
Personhood as free, conscious spiritual being.
Differences from the life of the animal soul and from pure being.

[Dullness and freedom]

In the Aristotelian-Thomistic view, man is a species of the genus "animal." Like plants and animals he is an organism, and like animals he has sensation and reaches beyond himself in actions that are reactions to impressions from without. But man's inwardness is not limited to that of the animal. The human soul is opened up on the inside and opened up to the outside in a new sense. For man not only senses himself and his own being as well as his contact with other things in animal dullness; his soul is rather conscious, with intellectual clarity, of itself and of being contained in itself as well as of all other things as other. Here, too, we have three levels in man's makeup: [1] substance, which forms from within and is enduringly actual, [2] potencies, which are caused by what is enduringly actual and cause the fluctuating actuality, and [3] acts, the actuality that fluctuates and changes in its specific qualities.

Human acts *can* have the mode of animal dullness (in the life of the soul during early childhood and in states of diminished consciousness). But not *all* human acts can be in this mode, and for those that can, a transition into freely personal being is possible. Specifically, the human acts that cannot be in animal dullness are those that are *free* and *deliberate*, often simply termed "acts" in psychology: acts of the will and acts initiated and directed by the will.

[Consciousness and freedom]

If we recall that acts are the soul's specific being that is actual and has qualities, the phrase "deliberate act" already points to the distinctive character of the being that is present in them. It is a being that wants, wills [*wollen*] itself and is through itself. I want, let us say, to solve a problem (I mean, I want to start at once and if possible go on until I find the solution). By this will act, the I that wills to solve it sets itself in motion spiritually in a definite direction. In this act, it must keep hold [*gefasst halten*] of itself, of the goal it aims at, and of the movement leading to the goal.

To "keep hold of itself," the I must have itself, and in several senses. It must be aware of itself, have itself *intellectually*— only an I that is *conscious of itself* can will. And it must be *in control* of itself— only an I that is *free* can will. And it must be conscious of its control over itself, of its being able to will— only an I that is *consciously free* [*bewußt-frei*] can will.

The I {237} that wills keeps hold of its goal in several ways. It does so in the sense that it has the goal intellectually. Having a goal, however, in the sense of having something objective differs specifically from having oneself. Having objectively <means> turning the attention to something that is closer or farther away (the objective thing — in our example, the solution— is not well enough known; it is uncertain). It means there is something that I can set about practically, something that lies within my reach.

And in just this way the I keeps hold of the movement leading to the goal; it means that I am familiar with it [*Kennen*] and am able to achieve it. The will act is the decision to set out for a goal. (We can decide at once to start and follow through or we one can decide later and then follow through or not.)

[Freedom and actuality]

Deliberate acts are movements toward a goal. They differ specifically according to their goal but agree with one another and with the will act itself in that the freely active subject is conscious therein of itself, of its goal, of its being free, and of its being able. It is just this clarity and freedom which is the distinctive feature of spiritual being in the personal sense and which animal dullness cannot attain. It comes closer to the pure actuality of divine being than anything we have hitherto called "actual being." It is not only something which itself is and through which what is other than itself is (such as substantial forms), but something that is certain of itself and of other being and is in a certain way through itself.

However, it is not pure actuality nor is it what lies closest to pure actuality. (*N. B.* [*nota bene*, note well]: the degrees of approximation go on *in infinitum* [to infinity], hence no degree can be said to lie "closest." But even among those degrees that we can perceive, free acts are not the closest approach to pure being, at any rate not absolutely.) Human acts begin and cease. We said that they are being through itself "in a certain way"; we must now ask in what sense they are so and in what sense they are not.

[Ascending to freedom]

Human acts are the subject's being, the being that is actual in subjects. But these acts are not the subject's *entire* being, which is not enduringly actual *in them*. Strictly speaking, human acts are not through themselves; rather it is the subject that is in them through itself. The subject decides on this or that act and thus determines its own actual being. But it determines it in *this* way only for a fleeting duration, and this fleetingness is radically different from the eternity of pure being. In comparison to the fleetingness of the particular act, the subject's overall duration in being is closer to eternal being. But it has the mode of being of a free act in this duration only temporarily.

Free acts arise from one mode of being of the subject and end in another. {238} Again, it is the subject that raises "itself." And *raising* itself means that it ascends from a lower to a higher actuality. And free acts represent a closer approach to pure being than this lesser, lower, being. The subject can rouse itself from dull brooding to think freely or to act practically. Then it is in the higher mode of being through itself. But it may also happen that it is roused to act from without, and, although it is free to remain in the new mode of being or fall back into the previous mode, this freedom in any case has its limits. The possibility to pass into the higher actuality is given in the lower actuality. At this stage the subject is at once actual and potential.

b.
Substance.
Formation of the life of the soul from within and from without.

[Freedom and co-determination]

The subject does not have the possibility of passing to a higher mode of being nor of doing so by itself although the possibility is rooted in the subject's essence, or better, *because* the possibility is rooted in its essence. For the subject after all *is* not through itself, but it *receives* being and essence and therein the freedom to *share* in determining [*mitbestimmen*] its changing actuality.

I say to *share* in the determination because even in freely passing from one mode of being to another the subject is not the only determining factor. All of its actual and potential being is materially fulfilled: it is ever *something* that is and that is of this or that kind. Each act has some content (it is an act of knowing or of willing, etc. and in turn it is an act of knowing this or that object, willing this or that goal). Nor can the subject itself give its contents to itself; all it can do is give itself over with its being to this or to that content, possibly in a free choice.

In man as well as in the animal, the acts of the soul have specific qualities, for the life of the soul, both its lower and higher life, is formed by species. And in either case specific acts are differentiated through the substantial form; the life of the human soul, too, is formed from within and from without. We have discussed often and at length the substantial form that shapes the "person's core" from the inside out: *what* the personal subject is in itself and what defines the range of its changing actuality.

[Personhood and freedom]

What is the "material [*Material*]" that is formed by the inner form, the potential that is brought to actuality? It is first of all the person's own inner life that is only as formed actual being. It receives qualities through the quality of the substance itself and through the accidental species that successively determine its actuality. The life power is the "matter" that belongs inseparably to the substantial form; the forming {239} of this matter is the very being of the form.

Do the substance of the human soul and its relation to the body that it shapes represent something new over and above the animal soul? The form of personhood is radically new, for the substance can be freely conscious [*frei bewußt*] of itself. This "*can*" should be stressed, because the soul does not have this kind of being throughout its entire duration; it *awakens* to it after a previous duration of duller being, and after awakening it can also sink back into dullness.

Freedom implies first of all the possibility to pass by oneself from the lower to the higher mode of being (this possibility does not apply to the awakening, nor is it given even after the awakening under all, but only under certain, circumstances). Secondly, freedom implies the possibility of passing from the original form of consciousness wherein consciousness belongs to the person's momentary being, to another form, to a proper act of reflection wherein the person comes to face himself and his act. Finally, freedom implies that it is possible to enter into the changing actuality with more or less of one's own substance and to determine this actuality by choosing among the possible accidental species themselves. Based on all this is the fact that the formation of life here can be *free self-shaping.*

[Freedom and potencies]

To better understand this free shaping of the inner life we must discuss forming through accidental species. But to understand this *forming*, it will be good first to revisit the area of potentiality relevant to the substantial form. In the human soul, and in the soul of animals as well, substance defines the area of possible changing acts, but it does this by defining a stock of potencies that differ from one another in the species of their acts.

Freely deciding among different possible acts implies at the same time deciding what potencies are to be actualized. Hence this decision does not only regard the person's momentary actual being since actualizing the potencies brings the person enduringly into a new kind of being that we have called the being of *habitus.* So we may say that the potencies of the soul are more "matter" to be formed from within where the enduring shaping of the soul, "character" formation as we called it, is inseparably linked to forming the actuality of living.

c.

Formation of the body.

[Inwardness, body, touch]

Anima forma corporis [the soul is form of the body]— the phrase applies to the human as well as to the animal soul. Here we first come upon the relation of the substantial form to the matter [*Materie*] in the usual sense of the word. Just as are plants and the bodies of animals, {240} the human body [*Körper*], too, is shaped by an inner form into an organism. Just as the animal's body [*Körper*] becomes a *living body* [*Leib*] because in it ("in" here has no spatial sense) the soul has its own inner life and is able not only to form the body but to manage it once formed in external activity, so too the living human body is as it were the scene in which and around which the life of the soul unfolds as well as the tool that extends its effectiveness beyond itself.

But the new form of inwardness also requires the body to be formed in a different way. The animal soul is completely attached to the body wherein it is immersed or dispersed. The personally formed human soul animates the body and controls it from a center wherein it is gathered into itself and leads its own life that does not affect the body at all or rather only in a quite secondary way. Man's personally spiritual life, however, does rise upon the foundation of his sensible life which, like his animal life, is attached to the body. Nonetheless it is formed in a different way owing to its connection with a higher life.

The animal soul is defined specifically as a sensible soul. Sense data are that wherein body and soul, and at the same time the world within and the world without, come into contact and wherein they are one in a distinctive way. The bond is not the same for all the senses; it is the strongest in touch, the "most sensuous" of them all. Pressing, pushing, pulling, etc. are sensed by the soul, but at the body and in the body. In just this way the subject having a soul senses its body as belonging to it or senses itself as bodily [*leiblich*]. In such "impressions," a contact with something outside is perceived at the same time. We should think of animal sensing as dull feeling wherein the body is not apart from the soul nor is the inside apart from the outside. The self-conscious, personally spiritual soul perceives this bodiliness given in sensation as a covering that is closely bound to it, wraps it around, and marks off its own area of being, and the soul perceives the particular data as contact with something outside that it notices precisely in and through this contact.

[Freely shaping the body]

The body is formed then as the scene of what plays in the soul and as the organ for engaging the outside world. It is so first of all through a forming that is not carried out any more freely or consciously than in plants or in the body of animals. But man can *freely take charge* of his body in a way that the animal cannot. The animal can also move its body in this way and that, to this place and that, thereby prompting a definite series of sensations. Its body [*Leib*], depending on how it is used, is also shaped as an external body [*Körper*] in different ways so that its actual activity shares in the forming of the matter. In this sense, we could call {241} the soul as a whole the form of the body and the act of its potency.

Now, the activity of the animal is reactivity; it does not choose among possible reactions or between reacting and not reacting. This is why its living body is not matter for free shaping. But man is not altogether given over to the reactions of his body; he is rather their *master* (albeit not without restriction). He can repress reactions begun involuntarily, he can bring his body into play as he pleases in this way or that, and thus shape his body itself. This is true of the body as the "scene" of sensation and as the organ of movements and outer perceptions, and it is true of the body as the tool of activity reaching into the world outside. This is just how forming activity extends to matter far beyond the individual's own existence to the entire environment within its reach. This activity, although mediated by the body, is personally spiritual and freely conscious [*frei-bewußt*], and it can shape the environment at the individual's pleasure, that is, knowingly and willingly; and body and soul are shaped in turn through a feedback effect.

In yet another way the body is subject to free shaping. The inner life of the soul leaves its mark on the body. We spoke of the symbolic language of certain shapings of the body that express things of the soul. Again, what in the animal is not subject to choice can in man be influenced voluntarily [*willkürlich*] in two ways. First, since he is the master of his body, he can curb expressive movements or cause them at will [*willkürlich*], thereby impeding, possibly distorting, the natural language of expression. Second, insofar as the actual and habitual being of his soul depends on his freedom, he can indirectly influence the expressive shapings of the body it causes.

[The spirituality of the soul]

The possible free behavior toward the body that is proper to the personally spiritual soul shows that the soul's bond to the body is much looser than the connection of soul and body in the animal. Although the soul is bound up with the body and cannot cast it off, it can nonetheless move it away from itself spiritually as it were— in order to consider it and handle it freely, make free use of it. And the soul can carry out an activity wherein the body no longer seems to play any role at all, when the soul is not concerned with the body itself nor through it with the sensible world but with purely spiritual objects.

Thomas is wont to describe the difference between the higher, spiritual potencies and the lower, sensible ones, by pointing out that the former are not bound to bodily organs and in them the soul leads a life independent of the body. As a purely factual [*tatsächlich*] statement this would be rejected today in view of the significance of brain activity which was little known and studied in his time. On the other hand, despite these {242} factual connections (indeed even today very little is understood about them), the relation to the body is quite different for spiritual acts than for the sensibility. The bond to the body does not form part of the proper content of spiritual acts as it does form part of the content of sense data. For this reason the connection does not appear to be essential but accidental and dispensable, and the soul itself, which is capable of such an actuality, appears to be a purely spiritual substance.

d.
Formation of the actual life of the soul
by *species sensibiles* and *intelligibiles*.

[Species and intentions]

Man's spiritual substance, we claimed, forms its own actual life as its initial forming, but this forming is done with the help of accidental forms, with the species of the changing acts. Traditionally the *species* are divided into *sensibiles* and *intelligibles* [sensible and intelligible]. We examined their ontic meaning earlier, in particular the meaning of intelligible species.[298] Several senses of "species" have emerged. Acts are specified first by their particular direction, by their *intention*. So we may say that spiritual living is formed by acts determined by changing intentions and distinguished from one another when one follows another and perhaps also when one occurs beside another. Such is the noetic sense of "*species intelligibiles*."

But every act inevitably has an *object* [*Objekt*] to which it is directed or to which the subject living in the act is directed. And the act refers to, means, intends [*meinen*], the object, by being directed to it in a definite (or more or less definite) *meaning* [*Sinn*], or it conceives it as something. The meaning or noematic content of the act seeks to get at what the thing itself is. What it seeks to get at is the species in the objective sense, the thing's substantial form. We saw that the "meaning" of the act had several aspects. [1] The noematic content that cannot be separated from it —we also called it the "subjective idea"— and may tally to a greater or lesser extent with what the thing is in itself. [2] The "objective idea," meaning the identical core in several acts of the same subject or even of different subjects that are considering the same object, which also may tally more or less with what the object itself is. [3] Finally, the "ideal idea" that would agree completely with the *what* of the object. The noematic content is not an object [*Gegenstand*] in the natural direction of the act to the object because the intention goes through it. It can, however, be made into an object through reflection. {243}

[Ideas and motivation]

We may call these contents or ideas forms of knowledge in the noematic sense, both subjective and objective (these, too, being only relatively objective). They are not *in* the mind, strictly speak-

---

[298]   Pp. 134ff.

ing —only intentions are in the mind— but they belong to the mind and make up its possessions. Insofar as they are inseparable from the intentions, ideas determine the species of the acts— hence in this sense they "form" them.

Now, ideas form spiritual living in yet another sense, namely, insofar as they determine the transitions from one act to another, thus determining the advance of spiritual living. The term "*motive* [*Motif*]" applies to them in this sense. But they motivate in virtue of their own inner make up. The subject seeks to get to the object toward which it is turned and to what it is. Its intention can get to the object's entire *what*, and it then harbors a fullness of partial intentions in itself. It can also live specifically in a partial intention. The noema of the whole intention is measured by the makeup of the object, but it may be more or less fulfilled or empty. Thing, for example, is grasped definitely only according to its category of "material thing"; it is so vague to us that its species is undetermined. But the direction to a species is contained in the overall intention, and this "empty" intention prompts the subject to act so as to bring it to fulfillment.

[Thing and appearance]

Noemata may be intuitive or unintuitive. But "intuitiveness [*Anschaulichkeit*]" and "unintuitiveness" may have different meanings. "Intuitiveness" may be *sensible*, and sensible intuition can in turn be either perceiving things present or making things present. When an object lies before us clearly and distinctly in sense perception, we apprehend it as determined in species, even when the species lying intuitively before us is unknown or unanalyzed.

The naive [*naiv*] way of thinking does not distinguish between the thing itself and the "aspect" in which it stands before our eyes in perception, say, its appearance from a certain perspective, the shading of its color, etc. But reflective analysis distinguishes the thing itself from its aspect or appearance. I mean, it makes it clear that the thing is something different from the appearance wherein it shows itself to me and that this appearance is conditioned not only by the thing itself but also by its relations to other things (for example, by the lighting conditions) and to myself who am perceiving it (by its distance from me, by the keenness of my eyesight, etc.).

In subsequent analysis we can apply this distinction to the content of the perception, but in the normal course of perception we cannot make out any separation between the thing and its appearance, as if the appearance {244} were an "image" making a thing present to me which itself is not present. In the conception that we have in our unreflective perception and clarify by reflection, it is the thing itself that appears in this way or that. The thing in its own nature [*Natur*] is what appears under such conditions to such a subject oriented to the thing in such a way. The thing tells me what it is in its changing appearances, and insofar as its appearances are conditioned by my position, which I can change in various ways as I freely move about, I can look at it in these various appearances and thus come to know it better. I do this also, as far as I can, by altering other conditions under which it appears. The conception of the thing as such includes the possibility of making headway in the network of appearance; it harbors within itself relevant unfulfilled intentions and with them the drive to fulfillment leading to progress.

[Coincidence of object and subject]

The appearance of a thing is what of it is present in an intuitively fulfilled way. And here we have a first meaning for "*species sensibilis* [sensible species]"; namely, what of the thing "falls upon the senses" at some time. (We should further distinguish between the joint appearance involving all the senses and what falls upon a particular sense.) Thus understood, what falls upon the senses is something that belongs to the thing itself, not detached from it. Yet at the same time it is something that belongs to me, who am perceiving it; it is the thing as it appears here and now to me, the perceiver.

In the *species sensibilis* (in this first sense of the word), sensible object [*Objekt*] and sensibly perceiving subject in a way coincide. The object is more than what happens to fall upon the subject's senses, and the subject is more than what happens to fall upon its senses from an object. The species, however, is something that belongs to both. The actual being of the species is the actualization of the thing's potencies to fall upon the senses, and it is the actualization of the subject's potency to be sensibly fulfilled. As an accidental form the species forms the being of the object as well as the actual life of the subject.

[The sensible]

The *species sensibilis* is not a pure *sensibile* [what can be sensed] (sense datum). It is a sensible *shape*, but the *sensibile* is unshaped. The sensible species is the thing insofar as its form as a thing [*Dingform*] is fulfilled by sensible material, or it is *sense qualities* insofar as they fulfill the form as thing. The "*sensibile*" can be interpreted in two ways: objectively as a sensible quality, detached from the form of thing (in this sense it need not concern us), and subjectively as a *datum of sensation*, detached from the context of the perception. Data of sensation can fulfill the actuality of the subject's life successively. The data are distinct in their qualities (this is why we can {245} speak of a succession of sensations), and consequently the *senses* are differentiated as *potencies* for sensations having these or those qualities. We should describe the senses as localized in the body or bound to certain parts of the body in a particular way; for this reason the word "sense" is transferred to the bodily organs associated with them. As such, a merely sentient subject is not spiritual (in the sense of having a free and conscious spiritual life). Such a subject has changing sensations and feels them; it is also stimulated by them to react in certain ways. But in its sensations it is not open to a sensible world. A spiritual, sensible subject, too, has sensations and feels them. But "along with them" it perceives both the outside world and its own body. Sensations, since the subject lives spiritually awake in them, are formed into sensible shapes, into the appearances of things.

One mode of being switches over into another; for example, when first only cold is felt but then, because of this sensation, a cold object is perceived touching the body. Through such switching the spiritual life awakens (when the previous mode of being was dull perception) and is formed into a definite perceptive intention, or the spiritual subject (when it is already awake) passes from one intention into another.

All perception of sensible things is built upon "material of sensation." We can think of these sense data in terms of what Thomas calls a "*phantasma*."[299] Insofar as the pure data of sensation initiate a movement of the spirit that "animates [*beseelen*]" them or puts them to use in knowledge, we may call them "motives" (in the widest sense of the word). We should call them "*stimuli*" to distinguish them from *those* motives which determine the forward movement as something grasped objectively within the network of spiritual acts. *Before* it enters into an intuitive network, the phantasm is still not a *species sensibilis*; it *becomes* one through "the animating conception [*beseelende Auffassung*]." {246}

---

[299]   The linguistic connection between "phantasm" and its cognates "fancy" or "fantasy" suggests we restrict the word to sensible material shaped by imaginative intuition. But this restriction, it seems to me, is not found in Thomas. On the other hand he uses the term not only for unformed, but also for objectively formed sense data.

Excursus on transcendental idealism

[Husserl and idealism]

It is of the utmost philosophical importance to interpret this transformation correctly, for this is the point where "idealism" and "realism" part company.

The "throng of sensations" is taken into the forms of the sensibility and of the understanding— in this way the spirit constructs the world that appears. Such is Kant's interpretation of the "animating conception." And while Kant clings to a "thing in itself" as the basis —real yet in itself unknown— of transcendental forming and of the world of appearance, the idealistic interpretation that Husserl gives his own teaching on the transcendental constitution of the objective world seems radically to do away with this last vestige of "naive realism."

For Husserl, "thing [*Ding*]" and "the world of things [*dinglich*]" is now nothing more than a label for networks of acts wherein a spiritual subject (or, on a higher level, an intersubjective community of "monads" in communication with one another), advancing from act to act according to fixed laws of motivation, gives meaning to the material of sensation —given beforehand but in itself meaningless— thus constructing intentional objects. Hence to speak of a thing which appears, something of which falls upon the senses, becomes a pure "*façon de parler* [way of speaking]"

If, in the phenomenological reduction, we pursue the forms and functions [*Leistung*] of the transcendental synthesis, at certain points we shall be again and again inclined to this idealistic interpretation. On the other hand, what just as often gives us pause is not only the conception of thing and being that lies in the original approach here, but the fact that this transcendental idealism itself ends up with a leftover —unsolved, unsolvable, and totally irrational—, I mean, the material of sensation presupposed to all constitution and the fact of the constitutive function. Here all spiritual living —which amounts to all being since spiritual living is the only absolute being— appears to dissolve into a meaningless game [*Spiel*].

It is therefore essential to come to understand the relation of the material of sensation to subject and object, as well as the mind's forming activity. Any attempt to do this will tell against transcendental-phenomenological arguments only if the attempt itself is made in a phenomenological reduction —as far as it is actually admissible—, indeed as we did in our effort to clarify the "*species sensibiles*" as a phenomenological analysis of perception.

[Stimulus from without]

When a stimulus of light makes me glance up and I notice that a street lamp has just come on outside, the first thing we find {247} upon reflection when we analyze this inner sequence of events is the stimulus. We are taking "stimulus" here in the immanent sense we have just seen, as a datum of sensation that triggers a movement of the subject, not as something existing outside the subject that affects it causally. The datum of sensation occurs as something claiming and fulfilling the actuality of my living and yet in a certain way it is independent from me. It comes unbidden, enters into the context of my life, perhaps breaking a train of thought wherein I was living. I lack the freedom to evoke or expel it by means of my purely spiritual activity. I can guard against it by closing my eyes and covering them with my hand, or I can expose myself to it by opening my eyes.

My consciousness that I am able to do this presupposes the experience that the light stimulus comes from without and that it has something to do with my eye. This does not first lie in the original sensation; the sensation occurs as something besetting me, coming to me from outside. "From outside" still need not mean from a world outside. It can be taken in contrast to what is "inner" in the most proper sense, that is, in contrast to my life as a subject [*Subjektleben*]. The data of sensation are not my life (I mean, they are not what my actual living is formed into at different times). Hence what comes "from outside" becomes a content of my life and in this sense penetrates into me; still, something "immanently transcendent [*immanent transzendent*]" remains there. In this way we may interpret what lies in the pure sensation.

[Instinctive vs. free and conscious]

The light stimulus "makes me glance up." These words can mean that it motivates certain corporeal movements like lifting my head, raising my eyes, and turning in a certain direction. This can happen "instinctively," as a "reaction," not in free activity nor with consciousness of the connection between stimulus and reaction. But for a subject spiritually awake the connections between stimuli and reactions, that is, between sensations and movements of the body, between them and bodily organs, come to consciousness in these involuntary reactions. At the same time the subject is consciously aware of "being able," that is, of its voluntary control over its bodily organs and movements and so —within certain limits— over its sensations. And because by virtue of such "experiences" (that belong to the transcendental constitution of the body and of the spiritual-bodily subject), the phrase "makes me glance up" can also refer to the motivation for a freely conscious doing. This implies, however, that "from outside" has now gotten another meaning.

[Space]

Coming to know the body and its movements means coming to know space at the same time, for all movements have a definite spatial direction and are carried out into space and in space. "Outside" now means outside spatially, {248} more precisely, outside the body. With the constitution of the body the data of sensation undergo spatial localization, some in or on the body, others outside in space.

Now, it is proper to certain stimuli to come from without. Since light and color data, for example, always appear at a certain distance from me but emerge, vanish, and vary according to the orientation of my body, the connections are established that I experience between these data and the movements of my body, especially of my eyes, as well as the connections between these and other data of sensation, sensations of organs, pain in the them, etc.

[Intentions]

A merely sentient subject does not get beyond sensing the data and reacting "unconsciously." An I that is awake spiritually, by virtue of such connections of experience, is prepared for the data of sensation in a definite way. Through each datum intentions are awakened that it interprets objectively and fits into the context of bodiliness or of the world outside. These intentions are the "forms" of the sensibility and of the understanding ("noetic" forms). The actual formation [*Vollzug*] of intentions is not voluntary, but neither is it entirely bereft of freedom.

With some data two intentions are possible. I can take coldness as the cold of my hand or as the cold of the object touching my hand, blackness as the "black before my eyes" or as the color of a thing outside. There is a voluntary shuttling from one intention to another.

Sometimes one intention is just as possible as the other, one does not "commend itself" any more than the other. In most cases, however, a firm intention readily becomes apparent that excludes all the others or makes them seem like a mere game that does not correspond to reality. It is the nature of the material itself, its clarity, definiteness, its inner structure, that motivates one conception and the corresponding sequences of acts without allowing for any choice, whereas material of another kind will admit of more than one interpretation.

[Constituting the world]

The opening of a spiritual subject to a world of objects is constitutive; spiritual life *is* intentional, and this intentionality is not altogether undetermined but formed from the outset —I mean, as soon as the I awaken to spiritual life— in certain general basic features (as we showed when discussing "principles"). The material, depending on its structure of this or that form, is fitted into these "categories of consciousness" thus actualizing this one or that.

It is in keeping with the basic form of intentionality —the tension between subject and object— that the objective [*gegenständlich*] categories into which the sensible material is formed correspond to the categories of consciousness, and definite "things of experience" correspond to definitely fulfilled intentions. Since the original general forms are fulfilled {249} with definite contents, the intention becomes specified in a specific direction, and it remains in the subject as a habitual attitude. In this way, more and more "acquired" forms gradually accrue to the original general forms of consciousness. A fixed system of laws governs the course of intentional living and the construction (the "constitution") carried out therein of a world of objects for the subject.

[Belief in things]

How are we to understand that the sequences of acts constituting the thing ascribes to the world of things a being independent from the sequences themselves? Can we give reasons to warrant this belief in a world of things existing in itself that lives in perception and experience, or ought we to reinterpret the meaning [*Sinn*] given to the existence of the world of experience by a consciousness where experience is naive? According to the naive belief regarding perception, what the perceiver has before his eyes is the thing itself, even though it cannot fall upon his senses as a whole. Every intention in perception goes beyond the appearance to the thing itself; at the same time it goes into further sequences of appearances as well, but only in order to come to know the thing better through them.

The words "it falls upon the senses" imply that the thing *was* present outside before it fell upon my senses and it will go on existing [*fortbestehen*] when I turn away from it or move so far away that it can no longer reach my senses. I can try to get a perception, and I can elude it, but by so doing I cannot call the thing into existence or destroy it.

[Recalling the girl she was]

Over against this world of perception there stands another world of objects that I control with much greater freedom. In *remembrance* I can to a large extent "picture, make present again [*vergegenwärtigen*]" things at will, and I can even "make up" things in free fancy.

I am picturing a room in a faraway city that was "my" room for a long time. "In my mind" I can transpose myself into a particular spatial situation that I was in. I am seated at my desk, and I see the pictures on the wall in front of me and to the side; I can "recall" what was in the room, one thing after another. I am actually sitting at my desk *here* and not there. In a way, by displacing myself there, I leave my body and its present situation— but without my body ceasing to exist for me.

The way I am there whither I am displacing myself in my mind, is quite different from the way I am here. My way of being at the distant place, and my intuition of what is visible from that place has the earmark of making present what is "not real [*wirklich*] now." In this representing I *intend, mean* [*meinen*] the things themselves and the place itself which are far from me now but which I perceived {250} before. But they are not falling upon my senses now. I can transport myself there, and if I do I am there in a way, but not really; I look at things in a way, but not really. I can also call the things over to me here; they hover before my mind here, but they are not really here in this space, for what hovers before me is not the things but their "image [*Bild*]."

The image of a girl I saw there now hovers before my mind. I neither see her there in that space nor here in my actual spatial surroundings. This is just what "having in mind" implies; what I intuitively have before me is rooted nowhere. I do not believe I have the girl herself before me. What hovers before me is but a memory, an "image in my memory," facial features with a quite definite familiar expression — not the shape, not the spatial surroundings, even the head lacks well defined contours.

This hazy, sketchy image places the person before me whom I have seen in various situations (without recalling any of them now) and who now is not here but elsewhere. The image may be clearer, more distinct and complete, it may include more background— but as long as it has the character of being made present, it is not the person herself I have before me, even though my intention (in my unreflective remembrance) aims at her and not at her image.

[Image in memory, intention, thing]

A "memory": this is a new meaning for "*species sensibilis*." Not the thing insofar as it falls upon my senses but what I have kept of the thing in my memory and am now bringing back. What I keep in my memory is not the thing itself. In myself (in the strict sense) only the intention toward this thing remains behind, the intention referring to the thing itself. And the totality of all intentions directed at real [*wirklich*] things that I habitually retain in myself at any one time makes up my world of experience. These intentions can be "empty," without anything that would mediate turned toward the things themselves and find fulfillment only in a renewed perception of their objects.

But something else besides the intentions may remain behind. I take "up into myself" what I have grasped of the thing; I mean, I hold on to it so that I do not lose it, and in a way I disengage it from the thing itself. This is a first degree of *abstraction*: the image that I have of the thing but that differs from the thing itself. The image that comes up in recall need not agree completely with the image that I have gotten in perception. It may be (as we said) sketchy, hazy, etc. With our intentions, we hold a world of experience, coherent in itself, made up of things sharply distinct from one another and related to one another. Moreover {251} we have a wealth of memories at our disposal whereby we can bring near now this thing and now that out of this world of experience.

We also retain memories through habitual intentions. These intentions and those directed immediately toward things do not automatically coincide, yet they are connected. At first the intention may aim at the thing itself meant in an empty way, and then a memory image may surface that gives the empty intention intuitive, but not "real [*eigentlich*]," fulfillment. Here the remembrance goes to the thing itself, possibly to the thing itself as it was once perceived, *through* its image, specifically through the particular features that make it intuitively present. It may also happen that the image comes up first and then the referring intention goes through it to the thing[300] itself; or the action of remembering can call the image up first *in order* to bring the thing near through it.

[Freedom in memory]

We have greater freedom toward our memory world than toward the real world. I mean that it is easier for us to turn to things we know mentally and to picture them than actually to set them before our eyes. They may be difficult to reach with our perceptions and at times they may be quite out of reach (when they are destroyed or have become something else).

However even in remembering we are not completely free. In the first place, our voluntary [*willkürlich*] memory needs a motive. Either "something comes to mind" that I once saw or experienced (without knowing why it is occurring to me now), or else something in my present situation reminds me of an earlier situation (or of a particular thing that I have perceived before). My freedom of memory consists in my ability to turn to the thing that comes to mind, to concern myself with it in an intention that makes it present and in a whole series of intentions that go with it and pass into one another as they are motivated.

But what is intuitive in the object that I am concerned with in my remembrance does not depend on my free choice. It may happen that the whole remembrance proceeds unintuitively, in empty intentions. The memory may have gaps, and it may show features that hover before my mind intuitively but in my consciousness do not correspond to the thing that I intend. What hovers before my mind intuitively does not

---

[300]   [Reading *"Ding"* for *"Bild."*]

fulfill the intention but appears as a stopgap standing in for the fulfillment that is really intended. Hence the memory is oriented to the thing
as I once came to know it; it is further conditioned by the material in
my imaginings and the involuntary course my mental life has taken. (A
{252} full phenomenological theory of association would be required
for a thorough treatment of remembrance and perception.)

[Freedom in imagining]

The area of freedom is broader in imagination; that is, a part of
the requirements for remembering no longer applies. I freely "create"
things, events, situations in my imagination. I am not bound to what
I once perceived and experienced; in other words, my intentions do
not seek fulfillment in something definite and particular that I once
experienced nor in the way that I experienced it.

But neither is my freedom complete here. Again, only intentions
lie in my power, but not phantasms, nor therefore the intuitiveness of
what I construct with my intentions. (We may be deceived about this
because in the case of an especially lively *imaginatio* [imagining] the
intentional turning is immediately followed by the emergence of the
"image" so that it would seem as if we could call up the images themselves at pleasure.)

The onset and course of a creative process also show that free
choice and an involuntary "play of the imagination" work in consort.
An imaginary idea may come to me while I am absorbed in a difficult
train of thought. I can dismiss it by force of will and go on working,
and then it may go away. But it is also possible that the idea keeps
spinning away in the background beside my thinking process, or that I
deliberately interrupt my train of thought and give myself to the intentions of the imaginative process. But the free activity always operates
on an undercurrent of processes running involuntarily.

[Unlionlike lions]

Finally, there is one more bond. Imagining is not oriented to the things of experience as remembering is. It is not its purpose to recall some single thing that was once experienced. The imagination can devise a world where the sky is green and trees are blue, where things fall up instead of down, rivers run backwards, etc. I mean that imagination may alter not only the concrete existence of particular things, but also the general types of experiences and the laws of nature. This free variation, however, has its limits. I can lend a thing any color I wish but it must have *some* color or other. I can constantly vary its shape but I cannot imagine it without any shape— otherwise it would no longer be a "thing." No more can I imagine a lion that is too unlionlike without it ceasing to be a lion.

The essence of things, what they are in themselves and what follows therefrom, sets bounds for the imagination (just as on the other hand the free variation of the world of experience leads to knowledge of its essential structure). Thus all intentional life, insofar as it constructs {253} a world of things, turns out to be objectively bound. We should now ask what this "objectivity [*Objektivität*]" entails and whether its meaning differs when the bonds differ.

[Objectivity of the laws of consciousness]

We spoke of firm laws regulating the course of the intentional life;[301] we may call them laws of motivation. The subject itself does not make these laws for itself. It *lives* in accordance with them, nor is it free to deviate from them (the laws themselves mark the boundary of its freedom). The subject comes upon these laws when it reflects on its own living and analyzes it in reflection.

---

[301]   P. 364-5.

The existence of laws regulating the life of consciousness is *objective* [*objektiv*] *being*, that is, it is independent of the subject, and because it is presupposed to consciousness, it is *a priori*. The fact that a world of objects is constructed for the subject through its intentional life is grounded in the laws [*Gesetzlichkeit*] of consciousness that are disclosed in reflection. We must now to ask what kind of being applies to the objects so constituted [*konstituieren*].

[The idealistic view]

Figments of the imagination have the characteristic of being created by me. Memories have the characteristic of belonging to me and being accessible to me through my previous experience but existing independently of me. Objects of perception have the characteristic of falling upon my senses now and existing independently of me. For the thing intuited or thought in the imagination, "being" means nothing other than being constituted and hovering before the subject's mind. The thing intended in memory (perhaps made present intuitively) and the thing perceived lay claim to objective being, that is, to a being independent from the subject that the things stand over against and from its acts. The meaning of our belief in regard to perceiving [*Wahrnehmungsglaube*] and remembering [*Erinnerungsglaube*] is that the thing was before it fell upon my senses and goes on existing when it no longer falls upon my senses, regardless of whether I do or do not retain it in memory.

Can this objectivity [*Objektivität*], the independence from my actual life, be reduced to the objectivity of the laws regulating my life of consciousness? Could we say this: the objective being of the world of experience means that where certain data of sensation occur as immanently transcendent data for a subject of a certain structure, acts are motivated that set before its eyes a world of objects having the phenomenal character of selfsufficiency in their being [*Seinsselbständigkeit*]?

One would attempt to attribute the fact that this character is attached to what is given in perception but not to what hovers in imagination to differences in the underlying material of perception. That is, it would be attributed to the fact that in imagination the vagueness of the material allows {254} it to be treated in more than one way, thereby leaving room for voluntarily forming. One could support this view by pointing out that where imagination is very lively, the boundaries marking it off from perception disappear and that (in illusion and hallucination) figments of the imagination are thought to be real. Illusions and hallucinations can be shown to be "deceptions," one would then explain, because they do not jibe with further experience and because we do agree with one another about it.

One can explain that our belief in regard to experience is inherent in memory, which according to the sensible material ought not to be distinguished from imagination, on the basis of the immanent structure of intentional life. For this life does not disappear when it has run its course but remains behind and holds its place in the continuum of life elapsed, so that the actual remembrance is a re-actualization of an experience that continues to exist potentially and as such is called "intentional."

So it does seem as if the different possible ways wherein the world of intuition is given ought not to be interpreted ontically; rather it is enough to interpret them on the basis of the laws of the construction of spiritual living. Is this "idealistic" interpretation so compelling that we cannot escape it? Or is there something that can be warranted objectively [*sachlich*] in what balks at this interpretation?

[Challenging Husserl's "objectivity"]

The picture of the world, as Husserl represented it in *Cartesian*

Meditations, the most compact and forceful summary of his constitution theory to date, claims "monads" to be the only "absolute being." Each I has its own life as a subject given as a first original sphere of its (transcendental) experience, and then it has as given the immanently transcendent data and the "transcendent" world that is constituted as "its" world. In this world, objects [*Gegenstand*] occur whose corporeal appearance matches my kind of body and which I therefore conceive as the body of another I, of a subject like myself with an inner life analogous to my own (but not directly accessible to me) and an outer world analogous to my own. The possibility of coming to an agreement with other subjects allows the worlds of each monad to become evidence of an *intersubjective world*.

Now, does "intersubjectivity" mean what naive belief in regard to experience means by objectivity [*Objektivität*]? does this "same thing" that I and others perceive —besides the fact that it appears to each of us in a different orientation and with other modifications in appearance— have existence [*Bestand*] in itself? Or is what is given here but a rule governing the course of synthetic acts, a rule that extends beyond the particular individual to the community of all individuals in communication?

It {255} is undeniable that the "objective world" is constituted intersubjectively and that there are objective items related in a specific way to a community. But doubts arise as soon as we give this fact the twist that the being of something objectively transcendent [*objektiv-transzendent*] has no meaning at all other than an intersubjective one, namely, being constituted for a community of monads. With what warrant is "absolute being" ascribed to subjects but not to material things? And what does this absolute being mean in the first place? does it mean that the transcendental I is "unconditioned," in the sense that it presupposes nothing else and itself conditions whatever else is?

["Absolute" in two senses]

The monad does not have the character of unconditioned or *first* being. The wakeful I finds itself "in existence [*im Dasein*]," and its existence as a fact cannot be detached from it although it can imagine the possibility of its nonbeing. (It differs from other empirical being because in the latter the existence of the perception and the existence of what is perceived are separable. I can perceive something, but it may later turn out that what I thought I perceived does not exist. However, it is not conceivable that my subsequent experience will show that I did not exist, nor that the consciousness of my existence will turn out to be a deception.)

This is why the existence of the I can be called absolute [*absolut*] as a fact [*Faktizität*]. And this factualness extends beyond the present moment. The I that is awake always finds itself already in existence and finds its present existence as an ongoing continuation of the existence that has run its course. (This is true of the *human* kind of conscious life, but not of all possible types, for we can imagine subjects whose entire life is wakeful and conscious and who can trace their life back to its origin or subjects who are eternally present to themselves.)

The I has a certain amount of freedom to determine its present and future life, but this freedom rises upon a ground of unfreedom [*Unfreiheit*]. For it finds itself "placed in existence [*ins Dasein gesetzt*]," not existing through itself, and it finds itself bound in two ways in its activity: by what is given to it previously and by the laws regulating its own activity. With this entire structure, the I points to something that[302] is absolute [*absolut*] in a sense other than that wherein it itself is absolute, for it points to a *principle* [*Prinzip*], that is, to what is original and unconditioned. Thus the I transcends itself in a direction toward something wherein the I itself has the reason for its being (hence toward

---

302   [Reading "*das*" for "*daß*."]

a transcendence opposite to that of transcendental idealism).

In its activity that forms the previously given material, the I transcends itself outwards into a "world" of things. The phrase "into a world of things" has two meanings: the I looks into this world as a world facing it (by knowing it) and it finds itself already in it (by acting and undergoing). This needs further clarification. First we need only establish {256} that the absolute factualness of the I's own existence does not apply to this world as a whole (as our consideration of doubt shows), much less that the absoluteness of the first principle applies to it.

[The existence of other bodies and things]

We find other "monads" in this world. What gives their existence precedence over the existence of the other things in the world? The fact that I conceive them as analogues of myself. The thing that is their body becomes evidence for me of a life of a subject that is analogous to my own life; it motivates in me the belief in an existence that is just as much an absolute fact [*Factum*] *for others* as mine is for me.

But *for me* their existence does not have this absolute factualness; rather it can just as much be doubted as the existence of material things. For what I took to be a living man may in my subsequent experience turn out to be a dummy, and if so I must delete everything from my experience that I thought I found to be the life of a subject. And even the give-and-take of lively communication is no absolute guarantee since it may all turn out to be a dream or delirium.

Now if we deem it reasonable, despite this possibility of being deceived, to maintain belief in the existence of other subjects independent of my own, and if this belief or the conception of other subjects is motivated by the givenness of their body analogous to my own that falls upon my senses— what then prevents me from also ascribing existence independent of my own to this body as well as to all other things that fall upon my senses, as does naive belief in regard to perception and experience?

[A world beyond appearing]

Admittedly, transcendental idealism does not say (as solipsism does) that the world of things is dependent on a particular individual subject; it only claims that such a world is relative to individuals having a certain structure through whose intentional life this world can be constituted. Nor indeed can I assume with indubitable certainty that the other subject exists; but *in case* it does, it needs no other subject to prove its existence. A material thing, or whatever else may be that is without being conscious of itself, cannot prove its existence by itself but needs something else for this, a spiritual subject, (perhaps several subjects interacting).

Does this impossibility of evincing itself mean that it is impossible for the thing to exist [*existieren*]? It is surely absurd to be speaking of being that cannot be experienced in principle. But it is absurd not because "being" means no more than being experienced or at least being able to be experienced but because what is not spiritual cannot be from itself (as our earlier inquiries have shown) but can be only as created. What is personally spiritual, however, by being, is conscious of itself and, by creating {257} what is other than itself, knows of this other.

For this reason, it may be correct to say that the world as it appears to us depends upon subjects of our own kind in order to evince itself in such courses of appearance. But it is not absurd to say that the world's being is not identical in meaning to such appearing, nor that another way to know [*wissen*] the world is conceivable as well as the existence of the material world in God's sight before there were living creatures upon whose senses the world could fall. And being created means being set outside God and having being other than being in the divine spirit.

Thus our inquiry into the functions of the intentional life of the spirit does not oblige us to abandon that view of the being of things as interpreted in the creation account and church teaching even if it does show that much that naïve belief in experience takes as absolute is relative to a particular sensible-intelligible [*sinnlich-geistig*] structure of the experiencing individuals.

[Spontaneous sensation and the world outside]

To make it clear that the theory about the constitution of the thing is consistent with a being of things independent of the assemblages of acts constituting them, we need another illustration of what "falling upon the senses" means. All constituting acts have as their foundation sensible material that makes complexes of things appear before us according to their kind, things present or made present, clear or vague, intuited more or less completely. We have already shown that the emergence of "phantasms" is largely even if not entirely beyond our free choice.

Something comes suddenly and unexpectedly before my eyes; I see it "without having anything to do with it." And even before I could recognize what it was, it vanished, and I could not hold on to it. But at another time it remains close so that I can take my time to consider it. It is a blossom blown by the wind that fell to the ground beside me. The entry of something in my field of vision makes me glance up "involuntarily," follow it with my eyes, perhaps go after it or bring it closer to see what it is.

In involuntary movements like these an experiential knowledge forms about the connections between the position, posture, and movements of my body on the one hand and a givenness of the things in perception on the other. My body, indissolubly attached to my life of sensation since all I sense I sense in, at, and through my body, is a unique thing through this solidarity, but it is at the same time a thing like the things of the world outside, woven into their own complexes and weaving myself into them.

The emergence of sense data as immanently transcendent data of consciousness, which in purely immanent reflection remains a quite irrational fact, becomes, {258} by virtue of the apperception of the subject, that is, by virtue of something psycho-physical, evidence for "being affected" from "*physis* [nature]," from bodiliness and from the world outside. There are two ways of being affected. Some kinds only evince a stimulation of the body, but others have an "objective [*objektiv*]" function, meaning that they actualize the specific knowledge function of the senses. In some cases, we hesitate between these two interpretations, and here deception is possible; progress in experience will bring more information and settle the matter.

It is certainly as reasonable to give credence to that conception of subjects having the same mode of being as my own which is included in the apperception of others' bodies as it is to retain that belief concerning perception and experience which ascribes to the outside world a being independent from experience as long as inconsistencies in further experience do not cancel this belief in regard to certain particulars.

* * *

[Species at once sensible and intelligible]

The dependence of the data of sensation, hence of the *species sensibiles*, on the outside world allows us to speak of external things forming the subject's actual living. We have already seen several senses of "*species sensibilis*": (1) the thing insofar as it falls upon the senses, (2) the "image" of the thing detached by the subject from the thing and appropriated as its own possession, that is, the "memory" or the appearance of the thing as modified when emerging in remembrance. (This modification and emergence are problems that we cannot go into here.)

Our entire investigation of the *species sensibilis* has shown that the *species* is not purely a *species* <u>*sensibilis*</u> [*sensible* species]. That the subject does not merely sense, but when perceiving, remembering, and imagining sees things before it in a sensible and intuitive way, is based upon the fact that the subject is "open" in its own structure, directed to objects— and it is so as an *intellectual* subject. Thus no intuition is simply sensible; intuition is a function of the understanding as well. Whatever stands or hovers intuitively before the subject is at bottom a *species sensibilis-intelligibilis* [sensible-intelligible species]. Sensible material appears as filling a formal structure, the form of thing to which certain forms of act correspond.

The subject can disregard the sensible material through the activity of its understanding (through the *intellectus agens in actu* [agent intellect in act]) and highlight the form. This is the twofold —negative and positive— role of *abstraction* in a second sense. In contrast to sensible abstraction, which detaches the image of intuition, we may call {259} it "the abstraction of the understanding" (we should not, however, think of sensible abstraction either without the function of the understanding). And since it abstracts from the material, we may call it "formal abstraction of the understanding."

The *species intelligibilis* isolated in this process is twofold. In the original direction of the spirit it is the noematic-ontic form of the thing, and for our reflective regard it is the form of the act, the noetic form. A further abstractive function of the understanding, generalizing abstraction, can highlight forms of greater and lesser generality on the side of the subject as well as on the side of the object.

e.

Activity and insight of the understanding.
Generic division of the actual life of the spirit.
Spirit and sensibility.

[Divine and human understanding]

The pure activity of the understanding, whereby the subject rises above sensible material and advances to pure items of knowledge in the understanding, is free activity in a higher degree than that bound to the senses. We have seen that this activity is in a certain respect the highest mode of being to which man can aspire, and in the consciousness and freedom that this activity involves, it draws near to pure being. What distinguishes the activity of the understanding from pure, eternally immutable being (apart from the numerous constraints on its[303] freedom) is the fact that it fluctuates and presses on toward a goal.

The goal that this activity strives after (unlike pure being, which ever possesses it already attained) is the insight of the understanding, the *actu intelligere* [to understand in act]. This is why the actual insight of the understanding at rest in its goal is, in a certain respect, a higher mode of being of the intellectual subject than the activity of the understanding that prepares for it and why it lies closer to pure being.

However, it is higher only "in a certain respect" for several reasons. First, because the insight of the understanding is the result of the voluntary work of the understanding, and without this preparation it is not (as a rule) to be had. Second, resting in the goal is never more than a transitory state since it is always but a partial insight that presses for activity that would lead it further on. Finally, the insight is inferior in freedom to the inquiring activity of the understanding. The inquiring understanding can move toward the goal, but it remains ever uncertain

---

[303]   [Reading "*ihre*" for "*seine*" and in the following sentence "*sie*" for "*es*."]

whether the fulfilling insight is attained. Even where the insight has been acquired, it has the mark of a "gift" received in a kind of passivity. Thus we earlier explained the *actu intelligere* by the *intellectus agens* [agent intellect] and the *possibilis* [possible (intellect)] working together. The simple actuality of divine *intelligere* is distended in our own into an actuality of seeking and finding, separate in time and quality. {260}

[Understanding, will, sense appetite]

But the actuality of the understanding, even when we regard it in its entirety, does not represent the closest approach to pure being in every respect. The hallmark of pure being is that *esse* [being] and *essentia* are one, that God is all that He is in an enduringly actual way. Not everything that the human person himself is enters into each of his changing acts, and what he is enters into specific, different acts to a greater or lesser degree. But the acts of the understanding are not those that what he is enters in the highest measure.

We learn of the "depths of the soul [*Tiefen der Seele*]" in what we are calling the appetitive life [*Gemütsleben*], that is, in our pain and joy, in our love and longing, etc. And these "emotions" are moving forces that determine our willing and acting, even the activity of our understanding. On the other hand, our emotional life itself is conditioned by our intellectual life, since our emotional life is largely, albeit not entirely, a stance on what the intellect discloses to it. Thus man's personally spiritual living is divided into three generically different actualities: that of the understanding, of the sense appetite, and of the will. In the intellectual life, it opens itself up to an outside world and is open to being formed from without. The actuality of the will enables the subject to determine and shape itself and the outside world. Emotional life is the strongest and purest effect of the inner form. This threefold activity, however, does not take place as threefold being but as a *single* life in its varied interconnections.

All of spiritual living in a way is intellectually illumined. I mean that it is conscious of itself and turned toward what is objective [*Gegenständliches*], and through the self-consciousness that "goes with it," it can be reflected upon and analyzed by the understanding. Moreover, all spiritual living is subject in a way to the control of the will. All specific "doing," even intellectual activity, is free and deliberate, and the emotions that stir involuntarily admit of control by the will which, by approving or rejecting them, allows them free reign or curbs them. Finally, all spiritual living is "driven" by these appetitive movements and through them retains its specifically personal qualities. This entire three-pronged spiritual actuality rests upon the foundation of the sensibility; further study may show an analogous diversity in its contents.

f.
Unity of the soul.
Life power.
Structure of the personal core.

[The poles]

We could call this whole articulated structure [*Aufbau*] the general form of the human soul. The soul is rooted in the body and shaped into it through the sensibility. Must we really continue to see the soul in its two functions, {261} namely as the form of the body and as the form of spiritual living, as a unity?

In animals, forming the body and its activity is primary in comparison to the "opening inward" in its life of sensation and instinct. In man, during the course of his development, the relation is reversed.

For at first forming the body is primary (in the fetus and the infant before its spiritual life awakens), but later spiritual living is what matters and the body is at its service. Between these two poles there are various intermediate stages. Not everyone reaches the highest level. The highest a particular man can go depends on his distinctive individuality. Nor does everybody stay on the highest level he has reached throughout his whole life; rather, even at maturity there are marked variations in his living. The body does not stop being formed after the soul's life has awakened spiritually; the body continues to grow and shape itself until it has reached —more or less completely— the shape that is the *telos* of bodily development. At the same time the soul develops in its actual spiritual living and forms therein the spiritual shape of the person, his character; this development usually reaches its goal much later than bodily development.

[Reviewing the life power]

The two processes do not run their course in complete isolation from one other. Actual living and the habitual shaping of the soul leaves its mark on the body. And the overall development of the body, the formation of its organs, seems to be ordained to serve the purposes of the soul. On the other hand, the course taken by actual spiritual living seems to depend upon the state the body is in at the time.

In a former work,[304] I sought to identify a distinctive "psychic causality" wherein all psychic processes depend upon what I called a "life power or force." We can see this power, or a greater or lesser amount of it, in such phenomena as vitality and weariness. They affect the way the spiritual life is lived, for example, effortless and lively, brisk,

---

[304] "Psychische Kausalität [Psychic causality]" <*Beiträge zur philosophischen Begründung der Psychologie und der Geisteswissenschaften*, I, op. cit.>.

intense, or toilsome and dull, idle, sluggish. In the present work, too, I had several times to speak of the power of the soul as a natural endowment, more precisely of a certain amount of power. We distinguished a "matter" in spiritual being that we called "life" and forms that, at work both from within and without, specified the matter to determined acts.

The life power {262}, we explained in our former work, is split into a bodily-sensible power and a spiritual power. The bodily-sensible life power is the overall bodily-sensible states of the vitality and weariness that influence the entire course of bodily-sensible living, of the body's movements and organic functions, and of sensations and instincts. The course of personally spiritual living depends upon the state of the spiritual life power, while this state itself appears to be conditioned by the state of the bodily-sensible power as well as by what is disclosed to the soul through its spiritual living and penetrates into it from the world disclosed to it, I mean from the world of spiritual persons and the world of objective spirit.

(To show this dependency, we took our cue from such phenomena as the "enlivening" of spiritual activity through joy in a beautiful thing or in a wish come true, the impairment of spiritual activity caused by things like grief at loss, and the support of spiritual activity though the power of other persons, etc.)

[Unity of sense and spirit]

The unity of the sensible and spiritual life power that lies behind their relative separateness, and hence the unity of the soul, is evident from the fact that spiritual living depends on the bodily-sensible state and possibly on the feedback affecting this bodily-sensible state from an "enlivening" of the spirit that comes from the world of the spirit open to it. Is this unity a combination of selfsufficient parts? To answer this question we must consider first how form and power and then the bodily-sensible and the spiritual are related.

Just as the soul's being, as we described it, is "formed matter" (life having qualities and specified for acts), its substance (whose being is life given qualities) is also formed matter = power having qualities. The soul's power without form does not have actual being any more than space-filling matter in the sense of *materia prima* without form has being. But neither could the form, if it lacked power, have actual being since *this* form is formal in the sense of an empty form and the first formed power is substance.

Through this empty form, the soul is open in three ways: it is sensibly receptive, intellectually directed to objects, and innerly open to spiritual contents. This last openness, the one "proper" to the soul, means that it can be formed by accidents, that is, by species coming to it from without. The power formed substantially and accidentally is the first thing that "is" in the sense of actual living. The form of the soul also has motivational connections between its sensible and spiritual activity and among its generically different spiritual acts as well as those that are generically alike but differ specifically. Finally, the form of the soul has the possibility {263} of being free to determine its own activity deliberately as well as the possibility, owing to this freedom, to intervene deliberately in the outside world and in its own development.

The empty form thus includes both sensible and spiritual life. And just as this form itself is indivisible and its life is *one* in such wise that in a *single* temporal act, say in a perception, sensible material and spiritual activity are united and cannot be separated *realiter* [really] but only through abstraction when analyzed reflexively, so the power that is formed by this *single* form and unfolds in *one* life must also be *one*.

[The need for matter and energy]

One reason why we must distinguish between the spiritual and sensible life power is that the sources nourishing the single power in a bodily-sensible-spiritual be-ing [*Wesen*] are different. Another is that there may be *other* forms that require the power to unfold either in a purely bodily-sensible life (the form of the animal soul) or a purely spiritual life (the form of finite pure spirits). These distinct sources that nourish the power are the material and the spiritual world. The soul is closely bound up with both. It organizes space-filling matter into a body that, thanks to the soul, is a living body and is able to take what it needs to maintain itself from the material world into which it is woven as a material body [*Körper*] and to form it into itself,.

All this activity of body and soul uses up matter and power and both must be replenished through further assimilation. (It should be shown in particular that incorporating matter requires an increase in power and why this is so.) When the assimilating and organizing process is disturbed and the supply drops, the power may be reduced and entirely consumed if not replaced from elsewhere. In its spiritual activity, the soul has a life of its own beyond forming the body. This life *as* activity also uses power, but at the same time it makes it possible to gain more power from the spiritual world. This is possible only where spiritual activity not only engages things intellectually but takes them into the interior of the soul.

g.
Communication among persons.
Community.

[The unity of living things]

Both the meaning of "taking into the interior of the soul" and the increase or decrease in power that it occasions may be clearest in our relationship with other persons. We mentioned briefly, speaking of Husserl's constitution theory, how the apperception of another's body as analogous to our own body implies that we should also see the other's inner life as analogous to our own inner life. But what takes place within us when we are {264} in a living relationship with others differs essentially from how we understand and interpret what lies before us on the basis of our senses. Such understanding and interpreting may form part of a "general impression," but as a rule it is quite secondary in our consciousness to an *impression* in a specific sense; I mean that it takes second place to being inwardly affected.

When we meet a living soul, we feel inwardly affected in a quite different way than when we meet lifeless things. Even when an animal is in the room (a "higher" animal, since we generally do not have such contact [*Kontakt*] with "lower" animals), the atmosphere is quite different than when no animals are about. And the general impression of our surroundings "switches over" when we suddenly realize that we "are not alone." We are "alone" as long as there is nothing near at hand (as far as we can tell) that can touch us inwardly or that we can touch inwardly. At times we realize for the first time that we are not alone when we are inwardly affected in this way.

What does "not alone" mean? I sense contact with something like myself and what is more with something whose life is *one* with my own. I sense along with it, "so to speak," what befalls it, what threatens it. Moreover, I may "scent" something hostile or friendly in it— and I may scent this in myself. I automatically notice its attitude to me —timid, trusting, or indifferent, ready to attack or to flee— and I adopt corresponding attitudes in myself. Even in my dealings with animals there may be a "sympathy" or "antipathy" —on my part or theirs— quite apart from whether I or they look friendly or unfriendly; this sympathy and antipathy may regard the species or the individual.

The unity of life, however, lies above all these conflicting impressions, attitudes, stances. I know that I am one with all living things but not with lifeless things. And I know them not only as I see them as analogues of myself; I know them in such a way that with them I have more "power," for their mere presence strengthens me. (However, this strengthening that comes from the life of living things may be offset, even more than offset, by mutual stances and behaviors.)

[The soul sensing itself]

This inner unity in the center of life is already found in animals in their dull sensing and being affected, and it is at the same time a mutual contact in the interior of the soul. For in fear or trust, with a friendly or unfriendly attitude, in sympathy or antipathy, the soul senses "itself"; it senses the modes of its own inner being even as it is directed to what is causing {265} them. (It would lead us too far afield to ask how far stances toward lifeless things are possible and how they vary.)

All these inner movements of the soul have a curious relation to its power. On the one hand, every act consumes power, and the greater the power the more the soul is involved. On the other hand, the emotions are marked by a polarity in their specific content that divides them into "negative" and "positive" emotions. These are not only stances for or against something approaching from outside, but also contrary kinds of feedback affecting the soul's very being, increasing or decreasing its own power. Anger, annoyance, grief, etc. sap the soul, while enthusiasm, joy, etc. enhance its life.

[Sharing in human openness]

Souls already engage one another, as we had need to explain, on the "animal" level intermediate between material and personally spiritual being, and as they do so the life power of each varies. But can we find another kind of *inner* openness of the soul on the higher level of intellectual openness and with it another kind of influence on its being? In the first place, intellectual openness enables us to follow and *understand* —not just be affected by— the life of the soul of others disclosed to us. It is not merely life as such that is united here but to a much greater degree a specific life; I am referring to the spiritual activity involved in sharing one other's thoughts, feelings etc. and in thinking, feeling, willing together.

And it is just in this acting together wherein we see phenomena such as finding support in another's power, perhaps with a curious combination of different effects. For example, a more energetic person may support a weaker one in performing some task for which the latter would not take the initiative, and by "getting dragged along" he may expend more energy than if he were acting alone. But because the other is "more gifted," he can do things with his help that he would never have achieved by himself. And joy in success can be so "stimulate" them that both gain in energy and their activity together continues "on its own." By entering into the world of objects a much greater diversity of positive as well as negative stances becomes possible within the soul and hence a greater diversity of movement in the increase and decrease of energy.

[People as objects]

The dependence of several {266} persons upon one another and their life in common, because of their personal *freedom*, is essentially different from the lower animals. The lower animals are defenseless against impressions from without, including those coming from "their fellows," as well as against their own reactions to these impressions. Free persons can keep themselves open to impressions (this is actually the "natural thing" for them to do) or shut them out and then again open up to them.

Moreover, a change of attitude may block the "natural" effect of relationships, and this may happen "involuntarily [*unwillkürlich*]" without any express action of the will— yet with a spontaneity [*Unwillkürlichkeit*] possible only in free persons. In someone inclined to be absorbed in the actuality of speculative knowledge, a "theoretical attitude" easily becomes a habit that relegates all objects, even people, to the remoteness of "objects" [*des Gegenstands, des Objekts*]." And the vital bond that in natural deportment is tied at the first encounter, if not cut, at least will remain without effect.

The case is similar to those who size up everything they meet to see whether and how much they can use it as a means to their ends.[305] They watch anyone they meet to see what he is like and what he can do, as well as what they can do with him and how they must handle him. For these persons, spontaneously [*unwillkürlich*] uniting their life with others and being inwardly affected by them is secondary; they may not sever their bond at the root, but it will remain largely ineffective.

[Value]

But by living in this way, they not only stay aloof from others, but they seal off the depths of their very soul, cut themselves off from their own depths, isolate their depths from the actuality of their life. Here we once again meet the question about whether the human soul has its own inner openness that differs from that of the lower animals (perhaps different from its own openness on the animal level).

Having depths in the sense just mentioned, we claimed, is the hallmark of the human soul. By depths I mean what the soul itself is

---

[305]   Cf. my work on "individual and community" <*Beiträge zur philosophischen Bergündung der Psychologie und der Geisteswissenschaften*, II, op. cit.>, p. 229, loosely following F. Tönnes and M. Scheler on "social attitude."

most properly and inwardly yet enters into the changing actuality of life to a greater or lesser degree. We also saw that the soul is open to something only at the depth where it can be suitably received— neither by the senses nor by the intellect (how far it is accessible to sense and intellect and how its reception through sense and {267} intellect relates to this "reception at depth [*Tiefen-Aufnahme*]" are important issues in their own right).

There are a great many kinds of "*something*," and this variety corresponds to the various locations in the depths of the soul that the something can and should fittingly reach. This is what scholasticism has called "*bonum* [the good]" and modern philosophy "value [*Wert*]." "Reception" into the soul means more than "knowledge" (the soul can also "know" the *bonum* only with the help of the intellect, but the intellect cannot know it without the depths of the soul). It also implies a reception into our own being that heightens it (or "diminishes" it in the case of a "*malum* [evil]"). The "entry into the spirit" that we had to reject in regard to the objects of the senses and of the intellect —in the strict sense of a "being *in* the spirit"— take place here *realiter* [really]. And it is a personally spiritual act, indeed in the proper sense, since only persons can live thus and "be nourished by the spirit." On the lower animal level only being affecting and reacting to the contact are possible, not openness and reception.

h.
Personal distinctiveness.
The genus, species, individuality of man.

[Man as "genus"]

We should assign the depths, as they are open to fulfillment from without, to the "empty form" of the soul of which we spoke.

But something else belongs to this empty form besides the depths and also besides the power that makes up its "matter," namely, what gives it qualities from within. This empty form is man's specific form, it is what gives him qualities as *man*. But it is not only fulfilled by the matter belonging to it and by the accidental species that successively inform this matter; it is also fulfilled by the individual person's own *quale*. The *quale* can be separated from the empty form of the soul and from its power only by abstraction; the soul, in the sense of what the soul is in itself, that is, the core, is the power having such qualities and forms, and it is the essence [*Wesen*] of *this* man, of the individual, or it is his substantial form. Now, is this substantial form a genus, a species, or is it itself an individual?

We took "genus" to mean a unity of origin (in the ontic and possibly in the genetic sense) or a stock of meaning harking back to a unity of origin and the domain of individuals sharing this stock. We took "species" in the stricter sense as the differentiation of a generic stock appearing in different species, I mean being differentiated = being specified. We may call what the word "man" entails a species of the genus "animal" insofar as man is an animal, having whatever belongs to this genus and at the same time differing in qualities from the other species of the genus, that is, from other animal species.

However, what marks {268} man as *man* (not as a species of animal) is his free, conscious, personal spiritualness (which means "endowed with reason" as well, insofar as "being conscious" is taken as "being open" = able to *become aware of* [*vernehmenkönnen*], and freedom connotes the possibility of following up on what one is "aware of"). But this distinction is not just one specific difference alongside those of other animal species; it rather makes "man's essence" a selfsufficient ontic shaping principle; that is, it makes it a genus. Men are differentiated into the species "man" and "woman," which we shall not discuss further here. They are also differentiated into a number of types (race, people, position, family, and suchlike) —we should ask here whether these are genuine species— and into individuals— where our problem in turn is to determine what kind of individuality they have.

[Human evolution]

When discussing the meaning of "genus," "species," and "individual" in reference to organic things,[306] we considered one possible order of ontic origin. In this view, a smaller number of species appears at first and gradually increases when the matter is disposed to receive new species by the interbreeding of individuals of different species or even of individuals of the same species that under the influence of different external living conditions in their development have brought the species to a different character or expression [*Ausprägung*].

In the case of the crossing of different individuals of the same species, we saw another possible interpretation. In this view, the matter of the new individual, disposed by the crossing, could lead to a character different from the individuals that generated it, and in this way "types" that would not be genuine species could emerge through generation.

We have analogous possibilities for the evolution of mankind. I mean that we could imagine a differentiation (even one that was original in time) into different species. This is in fact ruled out by revelation that avers an empirical origin from one human pair. Hence we should consider the other possible order of origin wherein the interbreeding of individuals would be a precondition for the emergence of a new species; that is, crossing the individuals would result in the relevant disposition of the matter for receiving a new species.

All types could be interpreted as such genuine species, even if linked to determined conditions in their emergence. But we could

---

[306]   Pp. 308ff (especially 323f).

also see some of them, all of them for that matter —the third possibility—, as "chance formations [*Zufallsbildung*]," that is, as a different
expression of the *one* form through different dispositions of the matter.
{269} (We must leave undecided for now if one of these possibilities
is preferable.)

[The human individual in St. Thomas]

We have taken individual living things below man to be instances of their genus and species, and we have seen their entelechy as the
substantial form that forms the particular piece of matter belonging to
it into an instance of the species, into a more or less perfect expression [*Ausprägung*] of it, depending on how favorably the matter is
disposed. Individuality —in its literal sense— we took first as the
unity of the singular whole brought about by the substantial form, the
unity that makes the singular whole something *indivisible* in the sense
that it cannot be further divided without being destroyed. Uniqueness
[*Singularität*] belongs to individuality, but it is based here on the matter that is formed into an individual not on the form which allows a
plurality of instances.

Thomas says that man's individuality, too, is *de ratione materiae*
[pertains to the matter]. He of course does not mean that all instances
of the "species man" are *alike*. Should we take him to mean that they
are more or less "successful" instances of the same species or at any
rate different expressions of it?

In Thomas's account of the relation of body and soul, found for
example in his *Quaestio de anima* [disputed question on the soul], it
is the kind of human knowledge —I mean the role that the sensibility
plays in knowledge— that requires the soul to be bound to a body and
so to a piece of matter. This bond makes it possible for there to be
many instances of the species man, whereas in pure spirits this is not

the case, and for this reason each species must be by itself in the sense that in them species and individual coincide.

Thus considered, a plurality of instances of the species man that are fully alike would be possible. The actually existing differences could be explained by different dispositions of the matter. To be sure, matter must have a certain disposition in order to receive any substantial form at all, but within certain limits there is room for much diversity. These differences need not simply be taken as degrees of nearness to the pure idea of the species, hence as grades of perfection. For one individual could express [*ausprägen*] the species better in one way and another individual in another way, and hence a number of instances differing in kind would be possible without differing in value (or at least in the same measure).

However, this whole approach, though plausible as an abstract consideration of possibilities, cannot be satisfactory, for it does not do justice to the concrete phenomenon of human individuality, and there may be other possibilities that do it more justice.

[Clones?]

In our natural view of man, the concept we {270} have of ourselves and of others in our unreflective living, individuality means something else to us. Without being theoretically clear about it, we take it that every one of us, every individual, is unique in kind, I mean, each of us is our own species— the claim Thomas made for the angels. Even someone who holds a different view will feel his human dignity injured if he is treated as a mere "number," a mere "instance of his type."

Behind all our longing to be "understood" and all our complaining about "not being appreciated," lies the desire to be seen as an individual with our own specific peculiarity which is unique. There is something dreadful, unnatural, about the idea of a "double

[*Doppelgänger*]" (though it does suggest that having a double is not completely impossible or absurd). Will this basic outlook and attitude of mind, which is anterior to all our theories, prove to be unfounded?

[Each human soul a species]

Let us first set another theory beside the one Thomas espouses. Although bonding to material bodies makes a plurality of instances of the same species possible, it does not make it *necessary*. There is another possibility, namely, to take every human soul as a species that forms for itself the matter at its disposal into *its* body. I mean that the soul shapes its body not only into an organism of the human kind but into an expression [*Ausdruck*] of its own individual distinctiveness and into a tool for its specific (= individual) spiritual working, although it does shape it more or less perfectly depending on the disposition of the matter (and on other circumstances that we mentioned earlier when discussing "self-shaping").[307]

This interpretation seems to accord with an unreflective outlook on life, but not with the average *theoretical* conception of individuality. The theoretical view takes distinctiveness as the "intersection" of different types (age, sex, position, people, etc.), and it takes man as a product of heredity and environment. All this does, of course, is reduce one unknown to many others. We have just left undecided how these "types" should be interpreted (whether as genuine species or chance results of individuals interbreeding). We touched on the problem of heredity when discussing how, in the case of new individuals emerging through generation, we are to understand the relation of the new form to the form of the generating individuals. We mentioned the problem of environmental influences when speaking of taking up "spiritual building material" into the inner soul. The {271} key to

---

[307]   Pp. 180ff.

solving all these problems, it seems to me, is first to get a proper view of individuality.

[The basis of character]

How are we to think about this "intersection of different types"? The soul as a mix of different substantial forms? Everything we have said so far rules this out. Naturally we no longer find the words "soul" and "substantial form" among the ideas and terms usual in popular science (as it has developed from modern philosophy and psychology). One prefers to speak of "character," of inherited character predispositions and traits acquired throughout life under the influence of various environmental factors. A man's hereditary dispositions gives him the traits "typical" of his communities like family, people, and race, and should he remain under their influence, these traits become more and more pronounced throughout his lifetime. When he enters other communities (a profession, for example) he falls under their influence and acquires their typical traits. The end result is an "individual character," one that is not in fact identical to any other, although it is similar to many; that is, it has certain features in common with them. Diversity of character is explained by the diversity of conditions under which characters have been formed.

The little we have said about molding character,[308] shows that all character formation harks back to the original being of the soul, to what it itself is in itself, or to its core— to what determines actual living and hence the formation of habitual "traits," from within. This is precisely what we have been asking about all along: is it man's generic essence [*Wesen*], is it a species into which this generic essence is differentiated but which occurs in a plurality of instances (say, a type of community), or is it an "individual" species?

---

[308]   Pp. 180ff.

[Individuality not due to matter]

The substantial form that shapes the individual man as an organism of body and soul cannot be uniformly alike in all men, since this organism of body and soul as a whole as well as its actual living have an individual stamp of qualities. It will not do to derive this stamp from the matter. (1) My first reason for saying this, from a purely phenomenal viewpoint, is that actual spiritual living and habitual, spiritual shaping, as well as a man's original being revealed in both, are what progressively shape and reshape the material body and stamp it "in its image." (2) My second reason, from a general, ontological viewpoint, is that matter is {272} what is potential, what receives being and form, but the spiritual is what is actual, what gives being and form. The individual stamp could be explained by the matter only if it should be seen as deviating from the intended (general) species, as a flaw or lack [*Mangel*] (as something "abnormal" and "degenerate [*entartet*]").

But this will obviously not do. The individual stamp of the person —of his organism of body and soul as a whole, of his actual living and of all its effects— is heightened together with the intensity of his spiritual being. And if a certain one-sidedness is connected with this, if spiritual living is linked to some forms of activity while others take second place, with the result that some "sides" of a person's character are cultivated at the expense of others, I daresay we ought to blame this lack —relative to an ideal image of mankind— on the "matter." I mean, we should blame it on the limitation of the power that prevents a well-rounded development of spiritual activity. Now, the principle behind positive development, spiritual activity, must be spiritual and it cannot be material. (How far the deviation from that ideal of mankind should be seen as a deviation from human nature or see human nature itself as one-sided and how we could, say, reasonably aspire to be well-rounded are all questions needing further discussion.)

Moreover, a one-sided development in actual living and in habitual shaping may go back not only to a limited power but also to a limited openness since openness in finite spirits is not universal. But individual spirits should be characterized positively, by what they are open to, not by what they are not open to. (Since in the Thomistic theory differences between higher and lower angels are differences in openness, we cannot understand their differences as *de ratione materiae* from this viewpoint— at least if "matter" means space-filling matter.) This means that openness belongs to spirit as such; to the infinite spirit belongs universal openness, and to the finite spirit (hence to man, too) belongs an openness of a particular kind and pointed in a particular direction; in *which* direction depends on how the particular spirits are determined specifically. What generically distinguishes spirits bound to bodies and bodiless spirits is not their kind of openness but the *kind of access* that they have to what they are open to.

[Substantial form and the *quale*]

We have described man's substantial form as a unity: [1] of the measure of power at his disposal (and each man has *his own* measure that differs from that of others as a *quantum* [amount], not as a *quale*; in principle we can conceive of individuals that have the same measure of power), [2] of an empty form,[309] that is, an openness to contents (which varies in individuals {273} but not as if a number of individuals all alike were inconceivable), and [3] of a *quale* filling this empty form from within and adhering to the entire being of the substance. This *quale* in a number of individuals cannot be compared because there is no measure for it. Nor, I daresay, can the power be measured in a quantifiable fashion; yet it may be assessed in its "accomplishments," in the actuality of its living. Analogously, openness is

---

309   [Reading "einer" for "eine."]

revealed —albeit inadequately— in the environment constructed for and through the individual and makes itself known to others through what the individual expresses.

But that *quale* is only "sensed" as such by each in how he "feels about himself"; <it denotes> not a transitory mode of his being (the "mood" he is in at the time) but the specific mode of his being: *as he himself is as himself.* And we sense this *quale* in another man. We do not come to know his *quale* better as we acquire more experience in the same way that we gradually learn about his particular properties and his overall character. We are more or less forcibly affected by it inwardly, indeed more often than not in our first encounter with the man. He addresses us through what we are calling his expressive phenomena, not through what reveals the changing actuality of his life nor what reflects his enduring character traits —both occur in a general, typical expressive language — but in an individual stamp of these typical expressive phenomena, which, however, does not come to the fore in everyone with the same intensity.

Our response to this "personal impression" that we receive from a man is a spontaneous attitude of our own being toward him: an attitude of sympathy and antipathy or, in their most intense forms, love and hate. Both are as diverse as the peculiarity of the persons to whom they apply and as the peculiarity of the person himself who loves or hates. We may perceive "resemblance," "kinship," between one such *quale* and another, but we cannot attribute it to a same common stock nor for this reason can we measure it.

[Arguments from faith for human uniqueness]

(It cannot be proven rationally that there cannot be two men alike. But arguments can be given from faith. If each angel represents its own species, its specific (= individual) distinctiveness should obviously be seen as a *bonum* [good]. Various reasons can be given for this, but the primary one is that angels are created in God's image— as are all creatures, but they in a privileged way. But *as* creatures they can resemble [*nachbilden*] not the whole of divine being but only a ray thereof. This is why a diversity of specifically different creatures can reflect *more* of the divine being than a plurality of like creatures. Now if —according to a certain theological view[310]— {274} the elect are called upon to replace the number of fallen angels in heavenly glory, they would also have to replace the missing qualitative diversity, and so, like those fallen angels, each would have to represent its own species.

The privileged way in which man was created in God's image, stressed in the creation account, also suggests man's distinction, that every man in his peculiarity was to reflect a ray of the divine essence, that his personal distinctiveness —now in its full sense as *quale*, openness, and power — is the special "talent" that God gave each particular man to take with him into his life.

This also explains why there is something eerie and unnatural about a double, for one of them or even both would be robbed of this special personal gift from God. This gift represents man's highest nobility— higher still than his general privilege of being endowed with reason, since this gift brings each man into a quite personal relationship with God, the natural basis for the gift of grace of being a child of God.)

[Unity, development, and being touched by another]

It is the *single* substance of the soul from which power, openness, and *quale* are abstracted. Not only are they really [*real*] inseparable, they are also one analogously in such wise that each *quale* will have its *own* specific openness and power. Hence if one element is

---
[310]   [Cf. Boethius, *De fide Catholica*, 70ff, 274]

absolutely unique, the others will also be unique.

But we should remember here that this substance, or the person's core, is entelechy. Its core has the task of constructing the entire organism of body and soul in a process of ongoing development. And this means not only progressively forming from within a given matter into which it is immersed but also appropriating the matter it needs for its *telos*, which is the fully developed individual. This matter includes first of all the space-filling matter the body needs for its conservation and growth, but it also includes the "matter to construct" the soul.

We have shown that the originally existing power is not a set, invariable amount; rather it is both consumed in actual living and replenished in part from the body and in part by being immediately received into the soul. As the body can fall short of its *telos* and diverge from it for want of the matter it needs for its construction, so too the soul. If the soul lacks power, it cannot unfold the actuality that its "nature would allow," nor can it receive the corresponding habitual stamp. In that case it cannot build its "own" world as its openness would demand, and so in turn it cannot gain access to whatever it could take into itself for nourishment. And where the relevant possibilities of actualization are wanting, neither can the individual {275} *quale* emerge as it could of itself. But it may also happen that the spiritual environment wherein a man comes into existence and spends his life does not offer him what his original power and openness would allow him to take into himself, and so he falls short of his *telos*.

This inner reception may supply power, but it may do more. The soul can only take into itself what it is originally open to. But what it is open to has qualities, just as the soul itself and what it receives is not pure energy but energy that has qualities. When the soul is affected by the distinctiveness of another man, it can take this distinctiveness into itself in a certain way and grow by so doing. By "in a certain way" I mean that the soul receives the other's *quale* in its *own* way and receives it *into itself.* I do not mean that the soul thereby becomes a mere copy of the other (albeit it does become like him) nor that its *quale* and the other's *quale* are added together. Through such receiving the soul's openness, too, can, and generally will, grow.

(The following related points need examination. 1. How far can freely opening oneself up and shutting oneself off help or hinder this reception? 2. How far can power, openness, and the wealth of qualities grow *independently* of one another? 3. How should we understand the analogous growth of the soul as it takes in what is spiritual in the nonpersonal [*nicht-personal*] sense?)

[Growth and pseudo-growth]

Any reception into the inner soul involves the growth and unfolding of the soul itself, not what we called "development [*Entwicklung*]," not, that is, the habitual stamp advancing throughout the actuality of life. The soul's unfolding, the increase in its inner wealth, has an effect on the ensuing actuality of its life and on its habitual stamp (and so on its development). The full unfolding is prescribed beforehand as *telos* in the entelechy, in the person's original core. Reaching this goal hinges on the soul's finding what it is open to. On the other hand nothing that it is not open to can enter its interior.

(Growing inwardly in consort with others is quite different from becoming like them outwardly. By using his personal freedom a man can copy others' behavior in the actuality of his own life, and by so doing he may also come by a certain stamp that resembles them. There may be something like this in spontaneous imitation. In either case, the development is not based on any inner unfolding; it is pseudo-growth.) {276}

i.

A spiritual cosmos.

Human development and the evolution of mankind.

[Two cosmic scenarios]

Man, through the entelechy characteristic of his soul, is put into a cosmos where he interacts with his fellows who are like him yet unlike him. All men are specifications of the "nature" they share, but they open to one another in what is specific in each in such wise that they can take the other's specificness into themselves and grow thereby. It is conceivable in theory that mankind came into existence as an already constituted cosmos, full of individual persons fully developed (as the angels), each in accord with his own *telos* and at the same time in possession of all others.

Experience tells of the other possibility, namely, an unfolding and development over time that makes possible, yet presupposes, a progressive opening to one another. And in such an order of becoming, we cannot imagine an entelechy unfolding in isolation from others like it unless in place of this connection with other men there were an analogous relationship with higher spirits or directly with God Himself, Who out of the infinite fullness of His being could place in the interior of each soul whatever it needs to unfold. (Something like this takes place when a gift of mystical grace replaces the natural order whereas the "normal way" of the redemptive order is nature and grace in consort.)

In regard to the first possibility (the being of spiritual persons is not a becoming), the life of these persons would be a universal community wherein all live together and understand one another. Viewed from the other side, the being of the "spiritual cosmos" would at the same time be individual living, mutual understanding, and community of life for the persons making up the cosmos. Community life and individual life would be equally original. Communities would no more grow than individuals would develop.

Smaller communities within the universal community would not be completely ruled out (they could exist in virtue of a kinship of the species), but they would not exist necessarily (since such kinship is possible but not necessary). Nor for that reason would there be any need for types of communities— as general "species" between the genus "finite person" and the *"species specialissimae,"* individual persons.

The mere fact that human being is linked to a process of development and that man's soul is bound to his body, his way of knowing is bound to his sensibility, and so his access to other persons is tied to spatial proximity requires that an actual human community involves development and narrows it to determined groups. What we see {277} in our daily experience and throughout history is always human individuals and communities that are what they are potentially, habitually, and actually (in the sense of changing actuality) thanks to a development whereby they condition and influence each other.

[Comparisons]

If we ask about the ontic relation between the individual and community, we again meet the several possibilities that we mentioned before. We could imagine an original differentiation of mankind into species marking off smaller groups within a general human nature but further specified to individuals. Where spatial proximity enables individuals of the same species to live together actually, the species would become a type of community— or more correctly a *basis* for a type of community, which itself would be the result of development. The individuals would bear the species in themselves as an original predisposition.

On the other hand, the species would confront them in the other individuals of the community and would influence their behavior from without (through involuntary and voluntary imitation). But the species would be specified in each to an individual distinctiveness; hence the individual species would come to unfold the general species, and insofar as it is an inner growth in contact with others, it would lead to a genuine mutual resemblance. Besides this genuine resemblance, there would also be one that is not so when the individual distinctiveness of others is imitated externally. All this would lead to a typical stamp in the individuals and in their whole community that could diverge considerably from the original general species.

We may also conceive of such a formation of types without assuming an original differentiation into general species. Actual communities, thanks to general human nature and the mutual influence of individuals with their peculiarities living together, would suffice to form types. Finally, we should consider another possibility, namely that we need not assume any *temporally* original differentiation into general species (in fact excluded by the creation account), but on the other hand we should not see the types of community as pure chance results of mutual influence but as genuine species whose emergence is bound only to a determined course of generation and process of development. Accordingly, we would have to regard not only individuals but all of mankind, including the smaller communities into which it is divided, as formed by their own inner forms, entelechies with their own *telos* (the view of the order of nature and grace that accords with faith). {278}

j.
Summary account of human being.

[Man as animal and angel]

Our lengthy discussions on man's nature has arrived at the age-old conclusion that man is at once animal and angel. Man is an animal species when we regard his bodily organism and those functions of his soul that belong to him inseparably as a body. When we consider the soul in itself and the body as formed by the soul, each individual man is his own species, that is, each man is a spiritual person of specific distinctiveness. Yet he is no double be-ing [*Doppelwesen*]; rather, the *one* man through *one* soul is both.

In this sense Hedwig Conrad-Martius's claim in her *Metaphysische Gespräche* is confirmed: a split between a "soul of nature" and a "soul of spirit" does indeed run through man's soul. We should not think of "two souls," however, but of man's "soul of spirit" taking over what the animal's "soul of nature" does. Also confirmed is her claim that what is "constituted from above" —true of all creatures— acquires another, special, meaning for men; that is, in his freely conscious personal being as such he draws near to pure being, and furthermore his being is privileged to be an individual species.

[The personal I and nonpersonal creatures]

Is that other claim of Conrad-Martius also confirmed, that this highest mode of being of a finite be-ing —personal being— is possible only as "sharing [*Teinahme*]" in God's being? To answer this question we must be clear about what we mean by "sharing." She said first that man, insofar as he is raised above himself in personal freedom, is born from the spirit, from the "primal I."[311] Now, this of course is true of all finite be-ings, as we have repeatedly shown, if we take "born" not in the strict sense as opposed to "created" but in a sense that includes both; that is, "placed in existence by first being." However, she says, we ought not to take it in this way. "Birth" for her denotes a special kind of being placed into existence [*Ins-Dasein-gesetzt-Werden*]. This is necessary, she claims, because

---

[311]   <H. Conrad-Martius,> *Metaphysische Gespräche*, <loc. cit.,> pp. 234f.

man as a personal spirit is an "I," that is "a self without selfhood, a beginning without content," and so in his finiteness he "cannot stand and stay by himself in radical freedom." This is why he must come forth from the primal I— "not as created but as lastingly begotten or born thereof or dwelling therein...."[312]

According to our foregoing study of personal being, this description of the I brings out only an abstract element of personhood. Considered *in concreto*, the personal I is not a {279} "self without selfhood" nor a "beginning without content" but a be-ing already materially fulfilled in itself, a "be-ing having a core [*kernhaft*]." Nor is it, in the way it is, placed into existence "all by itself [*für sich allein*]"; it is rather put into a world from which it can gain content and life owing to the openness that belongs to its very own being.

So the I is set outside original being in an analogous sense, just as any created thing. However it differs from all nonpersonal be-ings in that even what it is lies in its power. This implies that it is "free" and raised above all being "of nature." What it is is in part something "of nature" or of "matter" which it can and ought to shape, and it is in part something belonging to its personally spiritual being which does not lie in its power to shape but is rather given to it as the form *through* which it can and ought to shape its matter or, insofar as openness belongs to this form, through which it can and ought to *let* its matter to be shaped by what comes from without.

"Can" is inseparable from the idea of freedom, and "can fail to" belongs to both just as inseparably. And "ought" presupposes all of this. The "can freely" and the "ought" allied with it is inseparable from openness, and "can shut oneself off" also belongs to this openness, as openness is free.

---

[312]   <Loc. cit., pp. 234f.>

[Willingness to stay open]

Man's spirit awakens to his freedom and openness; more precisely, man awakens as free and open. He does not awaken by himself, nor is he *originally* free and open by himself. But once awakened, once having his original freedom and openness, it is up to him to keep himself free and open. At the same time, it is possible for him to lose both. If he does not "keep himself on high," he can fall back into the being of nature from which he has awakened to personally spiritual being.

A specific action of the will is by no means the only way to "keep himself on high." The person "keeps himself" on the higher level —by his own power and by what he is open to— to a large extent by merely "letting it happen," by not deliberately [*willensmäßig*] stopping it, and to this extent it is voluntary [*freiwillig*]. Only when his power fails, possibly when a strong pull from below leads it down into an activity of nature withdrawing it from higher activity, need he deliberately withstand the pull and keep himself on the higher level.

He also needs an act of will when his openness leads him to an awareness of an "ought" that demands a certain activity. He may be required to open himself deliberately to something that enhances his inner power and his inner wealth; I mean to open himself to a *bonum* [good]. He may also be required deliberately to shut himself to something that would sap his energy and diminish his inner wealth, that is, to {280} a *malum* [evil].

[Opening to God]

Finally, the person may be called upon to open himself deliberately to the *summum bonum* [highest good], pure being. The reason is that the elevation of his personally spiritual being above all being of nature finds completion in the fact that his being, as free and open, not only bears an analogy to the divine being, an analogy surpassing all other earthly things, but through its openness his being is open even to divine being itself, yet by its freedom it can actively either open up to divine being or shut itself off therefrom.

This openness makes it possible for the divine spirit to enter directly into the human spirit. In the words that Conrad-Martius applied to the constitution of the I, openness is the "open gate that God's spirit can freely pass through."[313] God's spirit "*can*" pass through it, for it is a matter of *divine freedom*. God's passing through is not automatically given from the moment when the I is constituted along with its openness nor when a man freely opens himself— the opening to which this passing through binds itself. Only by God entering and "passing through" —theology calls what enters "*grace*"— is man "born of the spirit" after having already been created by God as a personally spiritual be-ing [*Wesen*].

[St. Theresa Benedicta's view]

At this point our own inquiry has led us to a view of man that differs from that found in the *Metaphysische Gespräche*. Man, together with all creatures, is placed in existence and hence set outside divine being as a be-ing by itself. By his origin man, along with all creatures, has his being "from above." Because he is given a nature that in some sense is left up to him and to the totality of be-ings that his nature is woven into, he, along with all creatures, has a being "from below." But since he is given an analogy with divine being that sets him apart from all nonpersonal creatures, he is "from above" in a way different from all nonpersonal creatures.

And in virtue of this higher being, which is his personally spiritual being, a "being born of the Spirit" (a life of grace) is possible for

---

[313]   *Metaphysische Gespräche*, p. 238.

him. It is possible simply because of his original openness, and it may come to his share by his merely "allowing" it, indeed even if he does not actively allow it but just fails to resist it. But it may also be associated with certain demands which a man may become aware of by virtue of his openness and with which he must actively comply through his freedom in order for the divine life to enter into him.

He can refuse to act to meet these demands, and he can even shut himself against learning of them. In either case, he bars his access to the divine life, {281} more radically in the second way than in the first. He thereby isolates himself from the infinite source from which power and inner wealth would inexhaustibly flow to him (it should be shown how this may or even must lead him to cut himself off even from the other sources of spiritual living, that is, "created goods"). In this activity against God, he lives from his own power and, if he persists in being in this way, he must in the end exhaust his power. His actual being must lead to nonbeing, that is, to that empty, powerless, *null* being of which we spoke earlier: the being that will continue to be maintained without its own substance and potency.

Conclusion:
Being and Nonbeing, Spirit and Matter, Act and Potency

[Being]

The null being of the spirit that lacks substance must be sharply distinguished from the sheer potentiality of pure matter that we have also called "nonbeing." There are two different poles opposed to pure being. All being and nonbeing, every be-ing, as far as it is to be grasped at all, is to be grasped only from the vantage of pure being, although we, who are finite and limited, can find access to pure being only from the vantage of finite and limited being —from our own being and from that of other be-ings near at hand— by removing bounds [*Entschränkung*].

Pure being, which has nothing of nonbeing in itself, is in such wise eternally infinite that no nonbeing is before it or after it, and it contains in itself all that is and can be. This being is all that it is in the highest measure of being, or more correctly, it is measureless (it is the very measure by which all else is to be measured)— it is *pure act*. In it nothing is shut, nothing remains unfolded; it is rather in absolute openness, illumined in itself and through itself; that is, it is light itself— it is *pure spirit*.

If anything is other than pure spirit, it can be only through pure spirit. Whatever is other than pure being can be set off from it only by having bounds [*Einschränkung*], by being *something* yet not everything, by *being* yet without being in full measure— by being as an *analogue of pure being*, I mean by being like pure being yet more unlike it.

That it is something but not everything implies that what it is is meted out to it, that it has its own stock of content for being, a bounded *essence* [*Essenz*] or *substance*. That it *is* not in full measure implies that it is not actually all that it is. This is possible only if it is *extended in time* [*sich zeitlich strecken*] ("*zeitig*" is Heidegger's term) and only if now this of what it is and now that, in temporal succession, is actual or potential.

[Matter]

It is possible for being to be limited to something (which is not everything) and to a measure (which is not pure actuality) only because it is bound to something that cannot be by itself alone, I mean to something formless and limitless in itself that receives form and limitation, content and being, by what it is bound by and by what is called its form and its act because it gives it form and being. This absolutely potential something that is necessary for a thing to be able to be without being {283} pure act we call "*matter* [*Materie*]." Matter stands to form as what is unformed, to act as what is potential, and to spirit as what is unopened [*unerschlossen*].

Matter may have these features without filling space. Every limited be-ing must have matter, even the so-called "pure spirits" insofar as they are finite spirits. (If Thomas was somewhat vacillating on whether matter should be ascribed to created pure spirits, the reason may be that he had yet to separate the purely formal idea of matter from the material [*material*] qualifier "filling space.") We shall have to claim, I believe, that corresponding to every measure of being and to every category of be-ings that is marked off by a characteristic measure of being there is a kind of matter proper to it.

[Persons]

The highest category of be-ings, having, of all finite be-ings, the highest measure of being, is that of finite spirits or persons. Persons, too, have their matter (what we called their "life power") as well as their essence which forms this matter, and they need all this for their full being. But they have something else in their personal structure: the fact that each person is an *I*, and with this I each yet lies beyond what it is substantially as formed matter. And this being an I [*Ichsein*] can, when detached from the substance, continue to be maintained as null being, as a negative counterpart [*Gegenbild*], as it were, to divine pure being, to the fullness of being. But it is at the same time, as fully dematerialized being, a counterpart to matter. We should think of it only as being which is "eked out [*gefristen*]" from pure being and which is not the being of any be-ing nor the actualization of any potency.

All finite substantial be-ings are found among these poles: [1] pure being, which is pure spirit and pure act, [2] "*materia prima* [prime matter]," which is pure potency and of itself lacks spirit [*geist-los*:], and [3] the null being of dematerialized [*entmaterialisiert*] finite spirits. Each finite substantial be-ing is a something that is partially actual and partially potential; each is matter, formed and thereby filled with spirit. Yet they all differ from one another in the measure of being lent to them, and so they differ in how act and potency are related in them as well as in what "spirit" and "matter" signify in them.

SUPPLEMENT I

(To page 54)[314]

[Real being]

Here we are to consider the fact that when we speak of finite individuals, "actual [*aktuell*] being" does not signify the peak of being [*Seinshöhe*] of fully unfolded being, but *real* [*wirklich*] being, to whose duration succeeding peak-phases belong. To this rose its own color —say, bright red— is proper, its characteristic scent, etc. It is still the real rose even when its color fades and its fragrance wears off. But it was not yet real while it remained in the bud, and after its leaves have fallen off it is no more. Before it acquired its characteristic color and scent, these properties, which belong to it essentially, were only in it as possibilities yet to be actualized. Both properties may reach their peak of being at the same time or at different moments. And both may have already passed away by the time the rose comes to its full growth. Thus finite things are never actual (in the sense both of reality and of peak of being) in their full stock of being but remain ever partially actual and partly potential.

[Ideal being]

"Potentiality," as it is taken in this example, denotes a lower level of being destined to pass over into the higher level —into reality and full development— *within* this individual. This potential being has

---

[314]   [This text also appears in *Knowledge and Faith*, part iii, "Actual and Ideal Being, Species, Type and Likeness," pp. 75-79 (*Erkenntnis und Glaube*, 57 61).]

the substance of the rose as the basis of its being. But there is another potentiality that we should identify here. The bright red of the rose can be taken as a species, that is, not as the property of this rose but as a particular shade of red that could be actualized elsewhere as well. The possibility of being actualized in any individuals whatsoever characterizes a species as such. While actualized in *one* individual, it retains the possibility of being actualized in others. And this potentiality that belongs to the species is irrelevant to the individual's overall state of reality, whereas this does share in determining its state of reality if the property in question has yet to be actualized.

In a corresponding way, the property, even with its potential being, is rooted in the substance of the thing whereas the species has a being independent of this thing. The{286} possibility of the species becoming actualized in *other* things is not grounded in *this* thing nor in the being of any other things at all but in itself. Its potentiality as possibility to be actualized rests on its own being, which is not some lower level of the reality of things. It is the being characteristic of "ideal objects" and hence can best be called "*ideal being.*" We should claim that this ideal being —the being of "pure" (that is, not of things) colors, pure tones, pure geometrical forms—, considered in itself is something actual. It even stands closer to pure being than does the reality of things, since it is not flowing being but one exempt from time and from change through time and remains at rest at the same peak.

[Plato]

Hence we can see why Plato viewed the world of coming to be and passing away as something less than the "world of ideas." All the same, we would hesitate to attribute actuality [*Aktualität*] to his "ideas." One of the chief objections against this Platonic doctrine has always been that his ideas are something rigid and dead. However, we should take "actuality" not only as being real and being unfolded but as being effective [*Wirksamsein*], being active, as well

This objection is closely bound up with another: how are we to understand the relationship of the ideas to things and their properties? Plato described the ideas as the types of things and explained the being of things in terms of their "sharing" in the being of the ideas. But he did not fully clarify what "sharing" means. Should the ideas be conceived not only as archetypes or proto-*images* [*Urbild*] but as proto-*causes* [*Ursache*] at work [*wirksam*] in the coming to be and passing away of things and in shaping them into what they are?

[Ideal being, God, and the being of things]

Dealing with this question would take us beyond the formal focus to which we wished to confine ourselves for the present. We note only, first, that besides the divine Being, which is Pure Act, and the being of things, wherein actuality and potentiality are characteristically present, there is a third kind of being that we called "ideal." It differs in one way from the divine being in that its being is not boundless but fixed to a definite "what." It further differs in that it is not *actus purus* [pure act]; it has a relation to the being of things that gives it the character of unfulfilled possibility.

On the other hand, the being of things has a relation —whose content we have yet to define— to ideal being. The relation of individual objects to the "ideas" attaches to "what" they are and what they are "like." The broadest answer to the question "what is the thing?" is: "the lowest species," which is the "archetype" of the concrete individual (e.g., the name of a completely determined variety of rose). The answer to the question "what is it like?" is: "a quality" in a species (such as a determined shade of red). {287}

Now, what distinguishes the concrete individual from the species that it matches feature by feature? What distinguishes the property in the thing from the pure quality of color that it actualizes? This question is very closely connected with another: what distinguishes the being of the thing from ideal being? Is it the concrete individual's form that the lowest species enters? And, correspondingly, is the form a property of the thing?

This is obviously no solution. The thing is not composed of a general species, which of itself allows a plurality of several actualizations plus the empty form of the individual. This form is rather proper to the individual because it is itself not anything general but individual through and through. It has a characteristic fullness and weight [*Schwere*] which the species lacks and which cannot be reduced either to an assignable content or to an empty form. It is just this fullness and weight that characterizes the being of a thing in contrast to ideal being.

[Matter and individuation]

Traditionally, this aspect of the thing's makeup [*Aufbau*] that cannot be grasped qualitatively is called "matter [*Materie oder Stoff*]." We shall examine it now not in regard to what it is in its being but will focus instead —again, only from the formal viewpoint— on what grounds the distinction of the thing from the lowest species, the distinction of the thing's being from ideal being, and on what makes it possible for a species to "occur" in a plurality of individuals.

Two further questions come up at this point. (1) Is matter in all cases the *principium individuationis* [individuation principle]? I mean, is matter what makes the thing an individual —this one and no other—, or are there objects that are individuals in their "what"? (2) When we ascribe actual being (in the sense of real being) to the concrete individual, to what does it owe this being? Does it attach to the form of the individual, to the species that determines its "what," or to the matter that gives it its characteristic fullness and weight of real being?

The first question has previously (<see above> p. 39) been mentioned briefly and answered to the effect that there are individuals for which matter is not the principle of individuation. The question about what they owe their being to must be asked specifically in their regard (<see above> p. 60f).

Material things, we must say, cannot have the being that is characteristically actual to them by virtue of the form of the individual, since only an unselfsufficient [*unselbständig*] and hence potential being characterizes this form inasmuch as it is empty. Matter, we said, gives the thing's being its characteristic fullness and weight, but the being of the thing cannot be due to matter either, since matter cannot exist by itself but, again, has only potential being. To come into existence, matter needs forming of two sorts: it must be formed by the species that determines the thing to its content (the form of *essence* [*Wesensform*] {288}, to be distinguished from the empty form) and by the form of the individual, into which the matter, as formed by the species, enters.

Is it then the species to which the thing owes its being-real? If we take the species as "pure idea," this, too, does not seem to be free of problems. Can something whose being is said to be "ideal" ground the thing's being? The *bearer* of a thing's being is obviously the *whole* whose component parts we are now considering separately: the matter formed into the concrete individual. We would not need to bother to reduce the being of this whole to anything else if it had always existed [*bestehen*] as a whole, if the parts therein connected belong together indissolubly. We need not now discuss whether such indissoluble connectedness is conceivable at all, or whether the fundamental separability of its parts does not correspond instead to the composedness of a whole.

However it may be, there *are* at any rate some things that intuitively demonstrate a material thing being formed. This we can observe with particular clarity in *artistic shapes* and *organic becoming*. When an artist forms the shape of a boy in marble, the finished work of art is the concrete individual standing before us as the result of the "forming." "This thing here" is the form of the concrete individual. The shape of the boy in its characteristic beauty is the species that makes this thing into what it is. Before it was actualized, the artist "had the idea in mind."

SUPPLEMENT II

(To page 73)[315]

[St. Thomas on Platonic ideas]

Is this contradicted by St. Thomas's words:

whatness [*Washeit*] is said to be created because before having
being it is nothing save in the Creator's mind, where it is not as
creature but as creative essence [*Wesenheit*]"?[316]

If we rightly understand what Thomas means by "idea" and "whatness," the passage actually confirms our view. The *whatness* is what
a thing is formed into, *what* it is, "a part of the composed whole." He
also calls it a "form" (in the sense of the form of essence).

However, the whatness of the thing is usually not called its
idea, for the word "idea" seems to mean a form that is separated
from what it is a form of. [...It] is that "*according to which* it
is formed; and this is the exemplary form into whose likeness
[*Abbild*] something is shaped...."[317]

---

[315]   [This text also appears in *Knowledge and Faith*, pp. 79-80 (*Erkenntnis und
Glaube*, 61-62).]

[316]   Quidditas creati dicitur: quia antequam esse habeat, nihil est nisi forte in
intellectu creantis, ubi non est creatura, sed creatrix essentia, *De potentia*, q.
3, a. 5, ad 2).

[317]   [Et quamvis forma, quae est pars compositi, vere dicatur esse illius forma,
non tamen consuevit dici ejus "idea" quia videtur hoc nomen "idea"
significare formam separatam ab eo cujus est forma. Tertio modo dicitur
forma alicujus illud ad quod aliquid formatur; et haec est forma exemplaris

Furthermore, the intention to give a particular form to the thing is proper to the relation between archetype or original [*Urbild*] and likeness or copy [*Abbild*]. Where there is only a chance resemblance we cannot speak of copying [*abbilden*] or imitating [*nachbilden*]. In the end, the agent to which the forming is ascribed must set itself the goal of fashioning something according to a archetype as an artist does.

So this seems to be the notion of 'idea': the idea is a form that something imitates in virtue of the intention of some agent...."[318]

For natural things God is the "creating artist."

But since it is unfitting to suppose that God acts for a goal other than Himself or receives from elsewhere the wherewithal to act, we cannot place the ideas outside God, but only in the divine mind."[319]

Consequently Thomas rejects {290} an independently existing world of objective ideas. He admits created "forms": the forms of essence that have their being in things, and he admits ideas different from them as eternal archetypes of things in the divine mind.

---

ad cujus similitudinem aliquid constituitur.] *De veritate*, q. 3, a. 1 corpus (*Untersuchungen über die Wahrheit*, vol. 1, <op./ loc. cit.,> p. 93 <*Edith Steins Werke*, vol.3, p. 89ff.>.).

[318]   [Haec ergo videtur esse ratio ideae: quod idea sit forma quam aliquid imitatur ex intentione agentis qui determinat sibi finem]. Ibid. p. 94.

[319]   [Non est autem conveniens ponere Deum agere propter finem alium a se et accipere aliunde unde sit sufficiens ad agendum; ideo non possmus ponere ideas esse extra Deum, sed in mente divina tantum.] Op. cit., p. 95.

{291}   **Works cited by Edith Stein**

Augustine, Aurelius. *De Trinitate.*

Conrad-Martius, Hedwig. *Metaphysische Gespräche*, Halle, 1921.

———. "Die Zeit," *Philosophischer Anzeiger*, 2 (1927 and 1928), pp. 143-182 and 354-390; reprinted in *Schriften zur Philosophie*, vol. 1, ed. E. Avé-Lalemant, Munich, 1963, pp. 101-184.

Denziger, Heinrich and Clemens Bannwart. *Enchiridion symbolorum definitionum et declarationum de rebus fidei et morum*, Freiburg i. Br., 1928; first edition by H. Denziger, Würzburg, 1865.

Heidegger, Martin. *Sein und Zeit,* Neomarius Verlag, Tübingen, 1927. English translation by John Macquarrie and Edward Robinson, Harper and Roe, New York and Evanston, 1962, and Joan Stanbaugh, State University of New York Press, Albany, 1996.

Husserl, Edmund. *Logische Untersuchungen*, first edition, Halle a. d. S., 1900-1901; critical edition, *Husserliana*, vol. xix/1, ed. U. Panzer, The Hague, Boston, and Lancaster, 1984.

———. *Ideen zu einer reinen Phämenologie und phänomenologischen Philosophie*, first book 1, Halle a. d. S., 1913; critical edition, *Husserliana*, vol. III/1, ed. K. Schuhmann, The Hague, 1976.

———. "Vorlesungen zur Phänomenologie des inneren Zeitbewußtseins," *Jahrbuch für Philosophie und phänomenologische Forschung*, IX (1928), pp. 367-498; critical edition, *Zur Phänomenologie des inneren Zeitbewußtseins (1893-1917)* (*Husserliana*, vol. X), ed. R. Boehm, The Hague, 1966.

——. *Formale und transzendentale Logik*, Halle a. d. S., 1929; critical edition, *Husserliana*, vol. XVII, ed. P. Janssen, The Hague, 1974.

——. *Méditations Cartésiennes*, Paris, 1931; critical edition, *Cartesianische Meditationen und Pariser Vorträge* (*Husserliana*, vol. I), ed. St. Strasser, The Hague, 1951.

——. *Vorlesungen über Ethik und Wertlehre*, 1908-1914 (*Husserliana*, vol. XXVIII), ed. Ullrich Melle, Dordrecht, Boston, and London, 1988.

Manser, Gallus. "Das Wesen des Thomismus," *Divus Thomas/ Jahrbuch für Philosophie und spekulative Theologie*, [Freiburg i. Ü.], 38 (1924).

Plato. *Theaetetus, Philebus, Republic, Timaeus*.

Reinach, Adolf. "Über das Wesen der Bewegung," *Gesammelte Schriften*, Halle, 1921, pp. 406-461; critical edition, *Sämtliche Werke*, ed. K. Schuhmann and B. Smith, Munich, Hamden, Vienna, 1989, pp. 551-588.

Stein, Edith. *Zum Problem der Einfühlung*, Halle a. d. S., 1917; reprint, Munich, 1980 [*On the Problem of Empathy*, tr. Waltraut Stein, third revised edition, *The Collected Works of Edith Stein*, vol. III, *Washington*, D. C., 1989].

——. "Beiträge zur philosophischen Begründung der Psychologie und der Geisteswissenschaften" (I. Psychische Kausalität, II. Individuum und Gemeinschaft), *Jahrbuch für Philosophie und phänomenologische Forschung*, V (1922), pp. 1-283; reprint, Tübingen, 1970.

——. "Husserls Phänomenologie und die Philosophie des hl. Thomas v. Aquino," *Jahrbuch für Philosophie und phänomenologische*

Forschung, Ergänzungsband [Festschrift zu Husserls 70. Geburtstag], Halle a. d. S., 1929, pp. 315-338; reprint {292}, *Husserl* (*Wege der Forschung*, vol. XL), ed. H. Noack, Darmstadt, 1973, pp. 61-86 ["Husserl and Aquinas: A Comparison" (original ms version included), *Knowledge and Faith*, tr. W. Redmond, *The Collected Works of Edith Stein*, vol. VIII, Washington D. C., 2000].

Thomas Aquinas. *Quaestiones disputatae de anima.*

———. *Quaestiones disputatae de homine.*

———. *Quaestiones disputatae de potentia.*

———. *Quaestiones disputatae de spiritualibus creaturis.*

———. *Quaestiones disputatae de veritate. Des Hl. Thomas von Aquino Untersuchungen über die Wahrheit*, tr. E. Stein, 2 vols., Breslau, 1931 and 1932; new edition *ESW*, vols. III and IV, Freiburg and Louvain, 1952 and 1955; *Lateinisch-deutsches Wörterverzeichnis*, Breslau, 1935.

Index of Persons[320]

A

Aristotle, *xliii,* 15, 23, 27, 63, 68, 76, 88, 90.

Augustine, Aurelius, *viii,* 7, 9, 106, 111, 115, 138.

Ave-Lallemant, Eberhard, 291f.

B

Bannwart, Clemens, 291f, 425.

Boehm, Rudolf, 14f, 425.

C

Conrad-Martius, Hedwig, *viif, xxii-xxv, xxvii, xxxviiif, xlii, xlvi-xlviii,* 229, 231, 235-239, 241,244, 254, 257, 259, 265, 266f-269, 272, 275-276, 278, 281,284, 329, 343, 407.

D

Denzinger, Heinrich, 291f.

Descartes, Rene, 4, 23.

E

Euclid, 88.

G

Gerl-Falkowitz, *xlif.*

Goethe, J.W., 88.

---

[320]   Page numbers marked by an asterisk refer to persons mentioned by the German editor in the footnotes to his biographical study.

Index of German expressions[321]

A

Abbild: likeness, image, copy, 60, 115, 423-424. Contrast: *Urbild*.

abbilden: copy, imitate (*imitari*, p. 73, footnote 112, 423f). Cf.*nachbilden*, 60, 424.

Abkehr: turning away, 212. Parallel: *aversio*, 212. Contrast: *Hinwendung*, 212.

Ablehmung: rejection, disapproval, 177. Contrast: *Zustimmung*, 177.

Abstraktion: abstraction, Cf. 29

Absendung: turning away, 215-217. Cf. *Abkehr*. Contrast: *Zuwendung*

Affekt: emotion.[322] Cf. 198: x, 176, 179-180, 182, 190, 195, 198

Affektion: being affected, affecting. Cf. 142, 378.

Affektiv: affective, emotional, 216. Cf. 216-217.

Aktion: action, 173-174, 300. Contrast: *Passion*, 300.

aktiv: active, 132. Parallel: *tätig*.

Aktivität: activity, 7, 13, 122. Parallel: *Tatigkeit, Betätigung.*

aktualisieren: actualize, 8, 42, 67, 71, 73, 74, 102, 105, 117, 129, 160, 171, 175, 180, 183, 195, 200-202, 211 Cf. *verwirklichen.*

Aktualisierung: actualize. 8, 42, 67, 71, 73, 74, 102, 105, 117, 129, 160, 171, 175, 180, 183, 195, 200-202, 211. Cf. *verwirklichen.*

Aktualität: actuality, 13, 122, 418. Contrast: *Potentialitat, Möglichkeit.*

aktuell: actual, actually, in act, 52, 159, 417. Parallel to *wirklich*, 159. Contrast: *pontentiell, möglich.*

---

321 Translations are those found in *Potency and Act*. Words used by Hedwig Conrad-Martius are marked "C-M."

322 St. Theresa Benedicta translates *affectus* as "activity of the *Gemüt*" in the vocabulary of her translation of St. Thomas' *De veritate.*

Akzidens: accident, 36. Cf. *zufallig*.

allgemein: general, universal, 141. Cf. *Universal, universell*.

Allegemeinheit: generality, universality, 13.

Analogie: analogy. (1) *des Seins*, 128.

angeboren: innate, 158. Cf. *eingeboren*.

Angst: dread, 216.

Anlage: (pre)dispositions, 15, 202, 262. Cf. *Disposition*, 15, 202.

anrühren: touch, strike, 161, 167, 187-188, 282. Cf. *Berührung, Kontakt*, 15, 163, 187-188, 387,

anschauen: intuit, 84. Contrast: *denken*, 79.

Anschauung: intuition, 79-80, 82, 86, 92, 97, 108, 130, 136, 138, 232 Parallel: *Intuition*, 79-80.

anschaulich: intuitive, intuited, 143-147, 150, 312. Parallel: *intuif*, 312.

Anspannung: intensity, 167-168, 220 Parallel: *Intensität*, 167.

Apperzeption: apperception, 79.

Art: kind species, 252, 258, 296, 351.

Aufbau: makeup, structure, construction, 384.

aufbauen: makeup, constitute, construct, 379. Parallel, *konstruieren*, 371.

aufgeschlossen: open, 264. Parallel: *geöffnet*, 264.

Aufgeschlossenheit: openness, 385.

aufnehmen: receive, take in, 170. Parallel: *empfangen*, 170.

Aufnahme: reception, taking in, 391.

ausatmen (C-M): breathe out, exhale, 237, 328.

Ausdrucksphänomen: expressive phenomenon, 396.

Auseinander: from one another, 191, 220. Two senses: 130, 189. Cf. *Nacheinander, Nebeneinander*, 130, 189.

ausleiben (C-M): body out, 277.

Aussage: proposition, 33. Cf. *Behauptung, Satz*, 89.

Außenwelt: the world without, 22, 25, 98-99, 106, 145, 147, 172, 330. Contrast: *Innewelt, Überwelt*, 22, 25.

[323] This word translates *operatio* in the *De veritate* vocabulary.

Bild: image, picture, 103, 142, 366. Parallel: *similitudo*, 73, footnote, 112.

Bildung: forming, fashioning, 322.

Blick: look, regard, (the mind's) eye, 265.

Böse (das) evil; *der Bose* the Evil One, 207, 210, 213.

C

Charakter:
  (1) character, mark, kind, 10, 146, 181f, 393-394, Cf. 181.
  (2) character, "personality." *ii*, 224.

D

Dasein: existence, xxiv, 17, 35, 101, 117. Cf. *Existenz, Bestand für-sich-Dasein*: existing by itself. xxiv, 17, 35, 101, 117.

Für-sich-selbst-Dasein: (also without hyphens): existing for itself, 98, 222. Cf. *Hypostase* of the person, 221. Contrast: *für-ein-geistiges Subjekt dasein,* 123.

Ins-Dasein-Rufen: calling into existence, 60.

Ins-Dasein-setzen: place in existence, 325.

Ins-Dasein-Treten: coming into existence, 60.

(das) Daß: (the) *that (it is)*: 97, 178, 284, 287-288, 292, 295-297, 300. Contrast: (the) *what* (it is), 178.

Denken: think, 79. Contrast: *Anschauung,* 79.

Denkend-Sein: being of thinking, 15.

Differenzierung: differentiation, variation, difference, 16, 31, 71,88, 91, 96, 107, 125, 156-157, 213, 224, 226, 322-323, 329, 331. Cf. 31.

Ding an sich: thing in itself, 360.

Dingform: form of thing, 358.

Disposition: disposition, 64, 220, 224-225, 228. Cf. *Anlage.* 64

Dumpfheit: dullness, 255

empfinden: sense, feel, 250.

empfindend: sentient, sending, 250

Emprindung: sensation, 77, 264-265, 336, 345.

Empfindungsdatum: sense datum, datum of sensation, 185, 189, 194, 208.

Empirisch: empirical, 11, 311. Contrast: *ontisch,* 311.

Entelechie: entelechy, 62, 280. 319, 327.

entfalten: unfold, 212. Cf. *entwickeln, erwachsen.*

Engfaltung: unfolding, 209, 220. Contrast: *Engwicklung,* 203, 409.

Entgegennahme: engagement, 189-190.

entgegennehmen: engage, 141.

entgeisten (C-M) unspirit, 121.

entmaterialisiert: dematerialized, 415.

Entschränkung: removing bounds, 6. Contrast: *Einschränkung,* 413.

entselbsten (C-M): unselve, 242.

Entselbstung (C-M) unselving, 242

entstehen: emerge, come about, 57-60.

Entstehung: emergence. Cf. 57, 317.

Entsubstanzialisiert (C-M): unsubstantialized, 240. Contrast:
    Substanzialisierung.

entwickelein: develop, evolve, 25, 62, 151, 156, 189, 212, 219, 224
    Cf. *enfalten, erwachsen,* 25, 189, 212.

Entwicklung: development, evolution, 15, 209, 260, 294, 403.

Erfahrung: experience, 28, 15, 116, 184, 186, 198, 220, 228. Cf.
    Erlebni

Erfüllung — fulfillment, 22.

Erhebung: elevation, 204.

Erinnerungsbild: memory, image in memory, 184, 196.

Erkanntwerden: become or be known, 223. Parallel:
    Durchsichtigwerden, 222.

erkennen: know, recognize, realize, xi, 153, 223, 340. *von sich selbst*
    erkannt: known by Himself (God) 113.

F

Fähigkeit: ability, capability, capacity, power, 51. Cf. *Vermögen*.

Faktizität: factualness, 374.

Fixiertheit (C-M): fixedness, 30-31.

Form: form, kind, ii, 105, 173, 222.

formal: formal 13, 52, 58, 61, 76, 100, 103, 222, 289 Contrast: *Material*, 27.

formal-ontologisch: formally ontological, of formal ontology, 24. Contrast: *material-ontologisch*, ii, 24.

Formbegriff: concept of form, 76, 78, 90, 102, 105, 123, 137, 139, 344.

formen: form, inform, 40. Cf. *enformen, hineinformen*.

Formprinzip: principle of form, 13.

formsein: being of form, 65, 67, 82, 88, 91, 94, 115, 147, 150, 155, 163, 168, 256, 333.

Frei: free, 205.

frei-bewußt (also without hyphen): freely conscious, 350, 353.

Fülle: fullness, 22.

Fühlen: feel, 178.

Fühlung: contact, 221. Cf. *Berührung, Kontakt*.

G

Gattung: genus, 31, 85, 92-93f, 295, 298. Parallel: *genus*, 31, 92, 293. footnote, 278.

Gebilde: object, item, 29-30, 57-58, 61, 65-66, 88, 91-93, 97, 99-100, 105-107, 110, 113, 116, 121, 123-124, 126, 132, 135, 140-141, 145-149, 151-153, 158, 160, 162-163, 169, 173, 179, 194, 282, 231, 290, 301, 311, 318, 337, 340, 355, 358, Cf. *Stoffe, Stücke von Stoffen, individuelle stoffliche Gebilde*, 316.

Gebot: command, commandment, 204-206. Cf. *Befehl*.

Gegenstand: object, 28-30, 34, 44, 100, 126, 136, 140, 221, 253, 355, 373, Parallel: *Objek*: 390. Cf. *Etwas*, 91.

Geschaffensein: being created (state), 60-61.

Geschaffenwerden: being created (act). 71.

Geschehen: occurence, happening, process, 250. Parallel: *Vorgang,* 288

Geschlecht: descent, 5-9, 212-213, 292-293f, 295

Geschöpf: creature, 5-9, 60-61, 65, 71. 165, 212-213, 240, 245

Gestalt: shape, form, 262.

gestalten: shape, 27, 173-175.

Gestaltwesen: (C-M): be-ing of shape, 378.

Gestaltswesenheit: (C-M): essentiality of shape, 238, 240.

Gestaltung: shaping, 174-175, 180-182.

Gestimmt: in (a) mood, 178.

Glaube: faith, belief, 21. Cf. 21. footnote, 99, 423f.

Gotteserkenntnis: knowledge of God, viii, ix, xi.

Gotteskindschaft: being a child of God. 211-212.

Gottesleugnung: denial of God, 213-216.

Gottverbundenheit: union with God, 21-23, 190-191, 201, 206.

Grundform: basic form, 24, 50-51, 56, 58.

Grundgerüst: basic framework, 69.

Grundkategorie: basic category, 88-90, 91, 92, 98, 118, 152.

Grundsatz: principle, 151. Parallel: *Prinzip,* 151.

Gut: good, thing of value, 94. Parallel: *bonum,* 94. footnote, 125.

H

Habe: belongings, holdings, property, 182, 232, 239. Cf. *Habitus,* 232.

Habitualität: habituality, 61, 63, 65, 170, 225, 226, Cf. 225.

Habitus: habit, 182, 350.

habituell: habitual, in habits, 180.

Halt: upholding, support, 21.

   Halt geben: uphold, 20-21.

halten: uphold, 14, 20.

Hauch: (also C-M): aura, 237.

immateriell: immaterial, 66, 223, 333. Contrast: *materiell.*

Individuation: individuation, 27, 32, 54.

individuieren: individuate, individualize, 55, 116, 343.

Individuum: individual, xxxiv, 29-31, 52-125, 178, 183, 188, 191, 193
    Cf. 221. *Exemplar,* 183f, 199f, 294, 296.

Inhalt: content, 311. Parallel to *Gehalt,* 311.

Innenwelt: the world within, 22, 25, 98, 160, 161, 172. Contrast:
    Außenwelt, Überwelt. 22, 25.

Inneres: interior, 102, 260.

innern (C-M) : to interiorize, 276.

Innerstes: innermost, 261.

Innerung: (C-M): interiorization, 276.

Innesein: awareness, 9, 250.

innewohnen: inhere in, be in, befit, be proper to, 34, 252 .Parallel:
    "inesse", 34.

In-sich-Geschlossensein: being closed in itself, 99. Cf. *Nach-außen-*
    Geöffnetseins, 99.

Intellekt: Intellect, 169, 255.

intelligibel: intelligible, 99, 133. Parallel: *durchsichtig,* 99, 133.

Intensität: intensity, 16. Parallel: *Anspannung,* 167.

Intention: intention, 146.

intentional: intentional, 187.

Intentionalität: intentionality, 186.

intramundan: intramundane, 317. Contrast. *supramundan,* 317.

Intuition: intuition, 83.

intuitif: intuitive. Parallel: *anschaulich,* 317.

irgendwas: some *was* (or other), whatever, 36. Contrast: *irgendwie,* 36.

irgendwie: some *wie* (or other), however, 36. Contrast: *irgendwas,* 36.

K

Kausalität: causality, 298, 306.

kennen: know, recognize, realize, 347. Cf *er-kennen,* 159.

Kenntnis: knowledge, *viii, ix,* 9-11, 22, 25, 82, 153, 159, 172-178, 194, 256, 340, 347, 376, Cf. *Erkennen,* 159.

Kenntnis: knowledge. Cf. *erkennen,* 159.

Kern: core, 132.

kernhaft: having a core, 408.

Körper: body (as material), the human body, *xii, x,* 230, 263, 286-287, 230, 263, 286-287, 306, 333, 342, 351-352. Nonliving and living 285f. Contrast: *Leib.*

körperlich: corporeal Contrast: *seelisch,* 338f.

Konkretion: concreteness, concretion, " growing together," 100, Cf. 28, 42.

Koexistent: coexistent, 118.

konstruieren: construct, 371. Parallel: *aufbauen,* 371.

Kontakt: contact, 387. Cf. *anrühren, Berührung,* 387.

Kraft: power, force, 27, 263, 272, 328, 337. Parallel: *Energie,* 288.

Kreuzung: crossing, interbreeding, 290.

L

leben: live, experience, 15.

Leben: life, living, 149.

Lebenskraft: life-power, 337, 339.

Lebenwesen: living thing, animal. Cf., 248-250, 294f, 319, 332f-333.

Leerform: empty form, 28.

Leerformal: empty, formal, empty and formal, 22

Leib: body (as living), *xl,* 174, 230-231, 263, 285, 333, 342, 351-352. Contrast: *Körper.*

leiben: (C-M): to body, 237.

leibhaft: (C-M): as body, *x, xi,* 27, 74, 93, 114, 230-231, 263, 285, 333, 342, 351-352.

Leibhaftigkeit: (C-M): bodiliness, 180, 196, 235, 237, 251.

Leibkörper: living material body, 342.

Leiblich: bodily, 352.

leiblich-geistig: of body and spirit, 125, 154, 166, 235

Leiblichkeit: bodiliness, 180.

Leiblich-seelisch: of body and soul, 229, 235, 255-257, 260

Leistungsgebilde: (Husserl) produced formations, *xxxii*

Logisch: logical. Contrast, 89. *ontisch, 89, ontologisch*, 123.

Logos (C-M): logos, 111-112, 276, 278, 280-281, 330-331.

Lust: liking, 177. Contrast: *Unlust*, 177.

M

Macht: power, 6.

Makel: staom. 204. Parallel: *Befleckung*, 204.

manifestwerden: become manifest, 274, 289, 334.

Manifestation: (C-M): manifestation, 113, 270, 279, 281, 289.

material (adjective): material, having fullness or content (not to be confused with *materiell*), 223, 43, 67, 74-75, 93, 101, 118, 125, 414. *nhaltlich erfulltes*, 27. Contrast: *formal*, 96.

Material (noun): material, *ii, xi, xxix,* 9, 22, 27, 54, 56, 75, 77, 79, 82, 85-86, 90, 106, 173-175,332,, 349.

Materialisierung: materializing, 117. Contrast: *Vergeistigung*, 117.

Materialität: materialness, 29.

material-ontologisch: material ontological, of material ontology, iim 24, 96. Contrast: *formal-ontologisch*, 24.

Materie: matter, piece of matter, 8, (285; as *Stück Materie*), 24, 27, 32, 39, 60, 67, 75-78, 115-117, 124, 229, 253, 285, 313, 326, 339, 351, 414. "Space-filling" matter is the "usual sense" (229) but said of spirits (414), Parallel: *Stoff,* 60, 76, 101, 116, 298, 420. (*Materie oder Stoff* 420) . See Translator's Note

materiell: material of matter, *xi, xxix, xxxv,* 13, 27, 30, 96, 76, 100-102, 115, 118, 224, 226. Parallel: *stofflich (stofflich oder mate-*

P

Passion: passion, 300-301, 303. Contrast: *Aktion,* 300.

peripher: peripheral, Contrast: *zentral.*

Peripherie: periphery. Contrast: *Zentrum,* 196.

personal-geistig: personally spiritus, 258.

Personalität: personhood, 121, 129, 345-346

Personlichkeit: personalness.

Personsein: being a person, xxii, 176-177, 179-180, 182-186, 188-192.

Phantasie: imagination, 77.

Phantasiegebilde: figment of the imagination, 41

Phantasma: phantasm, 359.

Potentialität: potentiality, 8-12, 15-21, 184, 192-193, 200-201.
Contrast: *Aktualität.*

potenziell: potential, in potency, 14, 16-20, 52, 56-58, 82, 192-193, 210, 262-263, 284-288, 336, 344

Potenz: potency, lv, 214.

potenziell: potential, 5, 14, 16-20, 52, 58, 63, 71, 97, 101-102, 104-105, 115, 131-132, 135, 139, 169-170, 182, 192-193, 210, 284, 343

Prinzip: principle, 151, 374. Parallel: *Grundsatz,* 151. Cf. 224.

Priorität: priority, Parallel: *früher*, 37.

protentional: (Husserl): protentional, 14.

Q

Quale (plural: *qualia*): *quale,* 17, 35-37, 48, 82-84, 90, 219, 253, 399, 400-403. Contrast: *quod quid est, quid, Wie, Qualität,* 28f, 101. *Seinsmodus, Wie,* 182., *Quantum,* 399. Two senses, 35f.

Qualifikation: qualities, 27, 173-175, 190-192.

qualifizierend: giving qualities, quality-giving.49,

qualifiziert: having, given qualities, 22, 27, 50, 101-102, 107, 129, 261, 344-345. Defined: "fulfilled in content or material,", 22, 27, 179.

Quantum: amount, quantity, unit, 299, 399. Contrast: *Quale,* 399.
Quid quid. Cf. 35f, 35-39, 213.

R

räumlich-materiell: spatially material, material in the spatial sense, ix,
13, 27, 173-175, 200.
Raumefüllend: space-filling, 101, 326, 333, 344.
real: real, 22, 108, 151, 185, 401. Cf. 108, 112. Cf. *wirklich,* 33, 257.
realisteren: realize, make real, 54, 56, 62, 108, 125, 142-143, 148-155.
Cf. *verwirklichen,* 54-56.
Realität: reality, 21, 69. Cf. *Wirklichkeit.* Contrast: *Idealität,* 69.
Idee, 21.
Rechtfertigung: warrant, justification (also religious sense), 23-24, 182.
Rechiktion: (phenomenological) reduction. viii, x, xxi-xv, xxilif, xxv,
xxx, xxxvii.
Regung: stirring, 13.
Relation: relation, 97, 262-263, 297, 312, 316, 332, 335 Cf.
Beziehung, Verhälinis, 6-8, 24, 86, 191, 207, 209.
retentional (Husserl): retentional, 14, 202.

S

Sache: thing, matter, *xxx*
Sachgehalt: content, ix, 185-186, 311.
sachlich: objective, 43, 99, 125, 153, 176, 255, 372.
Sachlichkeit: objectivety, 48.
Sachverhalt: state of affairs, 107.
Satz: sentence, statement, 34, 107, 154. Cf. *Sachverhalt,* 107.
schaffen: create. Cf. *erschaffen,* 306.
schaffend: creating, 173-174.
Schauen: contemplation. Cf. 21f-22.
Schöpfer: Creator, 59-60.

---

[324] Latin-German vocabulary of *De veritate* translation.

stofflich: material, 285, 312. Parallel: *imateriell (stofflich oder materiell,* 325). See Translator's Note.

Stoffogigkeit: matterlessness, 29, 115, 130.

Stoffquantum: amount of matter, 299.

Stück: piece, 106. (1) *materie,* 106.

Subjekt: subject, 34, 73, 98, 123, 177, 182, 185, 188-189, 191, 194-195, 214, 318, 340 Cf. 37. Contrast: *Objekt,* 34f.

subjektbedingt: dependent upon a subject, 98, 150.

subjektiv-geistig: subjectively spiritual, 175.

Sibstamz: substance, 164, 414. Parallel: *Wesen, Essenz,* 164, 413f.

Substanzialsterung: (C-M) substantialization, 239. Contrast: *Entsubstanzialisieren.*

substanzlos: lacking substance. 208, 398.

supramundan: supermundane, 317. Contrast: *intramundan,* 317.

T

tätig: active, 13, 102. Parallel: *aktiv.*

Tätigkeit: activity, 6, 102, 121. Parallel: *Aktivität, Betätigung, operatio.*[325]

Tätigkeitsakt: activity, 22. Cf. 300.

Tat: deed, act, 74.

Telos: goal, end, purpose, 321, 329, 342, 383, 402, 404. Parallel: *Ziel*: 328.

Tiefe: depth(s): 5, 67, 179, 192, 203, 205, 211, 237, 243, 247, 249. Contrast: *Oberflache*: 5,102, 203, 205. 179.

Tiefen der Seele: depths of the soul, 381.

Tiefen-Aufnahme: reception at depth, 391.

Tiefenlage: depth levels, 186.

Träger: bearer, 124. Parallel: subjectum, ὑπόστασις, 123f.

---

[325]   Latin-German vocabulary of *De veritate* translation.

Ursache proto-*cause,* 419.

Ur-Sache: primal cause, 135

Ursprung: origin, 70 Parallel: *Genesis,* 317. Contrast: *Entstehung,* 317.

Ursprunghetrachtung: consideration of origins, 295.

Ursprungsordnung: order of origin, 295.

Ursprungsrelation: relation of origin, 11.

Ursprunglichkeit: originalness, Cf. 232.

urstanden: (C-M): revive, 240.

urzeuger: (C-M): primal begetter, 245.

V

Variation: variation, 16, 25, 71, 88, 91, 107, 157, 322-323, 329, 331. Cf. *Generalization, Spezifkation,* 88.

Verbindung: union, compound, 304. Contrast: Mischung, 304.

vereinzeln: instantiate, 38.

vergegenständlichen: objectify

Vergegenständlichung: objectification, 14, 177, 365.

vergegenwärtigen: make present, represent, picture, imagine, visualize, recall, 365.

Vergegenwärtigung: picturing, imagining, making present, 141, 177, 365.

Vergeistigung: spiritualizing, 117. Contrast: *Materializierung,* 117.

Verhältnis: relation, conditions, proportion, 6-8, 11, 24, 186, 191, 207, 209. Parallel: *proportio,* 73, footnote, 112. Cf. *Beziehnung, Bezogenheit.*

vernehmenkönnen: being able to perceive, become aware, 392.

vernichten: annihilate, destroy, 179, 204, 210, 213.

vernichtung: annihilation: 204, 206-207, 214-215.

Vernunft: reason, 22

  natürliche Vernunft: natural reason, *viii,* 112, 119, 133-134, 158, 167, 172, 193, 199

Wertsskala: scale of values.

Wertspecies: species of value

wertvall: of value, 94

wesen: (C-M) issue, 164, 238-240.

Wesen: *x*, 84, 177, 235, 247-249, 252, 256-257, 262, 269, 337, 386, 392, 397, 410.

(1) essence: Parallel to *Washeit, Was, essentia, quidditas*, 84, 131. *(Substanz oder Essenz*, 164. *Wesen* = substance or *Essenz)*, 233.

Wesensattribut: essential attribute, 169.

Wesenseigentümlichkeit: essential property, 152-154

Wesenseingung: union of essence, 138.

Wesenform: form of essence, 57, 421.

Wesengemeinsamkeit: commonness of essence, 138.

Wesensgleichkeit: sameness in essence, 99.

(2) be-ing, *xii, xxxiv*, 12-14, 24-29, 51-52, 58, 248, 176, 178-179, 192, 194, 210, 213,

wesenhalt: essential. Parallel: *seine*: *Natur nach*, 164.

Wesenhaltigkeit: (C-M): essentiality, 238.

Wesenheit: essence, 272, 423. Parallel: *essentia*, 423.

wesentlich: essential, 164-174, 196.

Wesung: (C-M): issuing, 271.

Widerspruch: (Husserl): contradiction. 151. Contrast: *widerstreit*, 151.

Widerstreit: (C-M): "contraposition," conflict, 151. Contrast: *Widerspruch*, 151.

(das) Wie: (the) *what it is like*, (the) *how*: 35, 37, 177, 232. Distinguished as *Seinsmodus* and *Quale*, 182. and as *Seinsmodus* and *Qualität des Seienden*, 232, footnote, 182.

Wille: will, *x*, 14, 176, 190, 224,

Willensbestimmtheit: determination by the will, 94, 214-215, 345.

Willensleistung: work of the will, 190.

willensmäßig: voluntary, deliberate, 61, 407. Contrast: *unwillkürlich*, 61.

---

[326] One translation of *operatio* in the Latin-German vocabulary.

[327] Cf. J. Macquarrie and E. Robinson, translators of Heidegger's *Being and Time* (New York and Evanston, 1962), p. 962.

Index of Latin expressions

A

a posteriori: a posteriori, 81-82, 87

a priori: a priori, 81, 82, 84, 109, 308, 371

a se: from, by another, 131

a se esse: being from, by, itself (God), 129.

a se, non ab alio esse: from itself, not from another (God). Parallel: to be through itself or from itself, 127

ab alio: from, by, another, 127

*abstrahere:*to abstract, 29

accidens: accidens, 48.

actu: in act, 219

*actu ens:*being in act, 219

*actu intelligere:*to understand in act, 170-171, 380-381

*actu intelligible:*understandable in act, 103, 135

actus: act, 122

actus purus: pure act (God), *xxxiv-xxxvii, xlii,* 6, 8, 13, 19, 52, 171, 176, 201, 219, 225, 284, 419.

*agens:*acting, active, agent, *xi*

*agere:*to do, act; doing , acting, 117.

agere intellectus: acting of the intellect, 171

agere sequitur esse: acting follows being, 213

aliquid: something (the transcendental). Parallel: *Etwas, xxxiv,* 28, 90, 93

liud quid:"another what" compared to "aliquid," 93z

*analogia entis:*analogy of being, *xlii,* 6, 11, 24, 219, 284

anima: soul. Contrast: *mens,* 256, *xlii,* 256

*anima forma corporis:*the soul is the form os the body, 260, 351

animal: animal. 345

aseitas: being from itself (God), 128

aversio: turning away. Parallel: *Abkehr,* 212

B

bonun: good, value (also the transcendental). Parallel. *Wert,* 94 and
footnote 91, 93, 125, 179, 391, 401

C

concretum: concrete, 34, 46, 84

creatrix essentia: creative essence. 424, note.

D

De ente et essentia: On Being and Essence (work of St. Thomas), *xliii*

*De potentia: Disputed Question On Power (*work of St. Thomas), 70f.

de ratione materiae: by reason of the matter, 321, 394, 399

De spiritualibus creaturis: Disputed Question On Spiritual Creatures:
(*work of St. Thomas). 90, 131f, 262f, 263f.

De trinitate: On the Trinity (work of St. Augustine). 7

De veritate: Disputed Question On Truth (work of St. Thomas). 73f, 90,
107, 122f, 130f, 159f, 300f, 423f, 424f.

dissimilitudo: unlikeness, 129, 219. Contrast: *similitudo.*

E

*ens:*be-ing (also the transcendental). Parallel: *Seiendes,* x, 28, 179, 91f.

ens primum: the first be-ing, 232.

eo ipso: by this very fact, 234.

esse: to be, being, *x,* 28, 213, 331.

esse in individuo: being in an individual. 34, 42.

esse in intellectu sive in memoria: being in the understanding or in the

in individuo: in the individual, 38, 55, 63, 68.

in infinitum: to infinity, 296, 347.

*in potentia illorum intelligibilium:*in potency toward those intelligibles, 157

*in ratione materiae:*by reason of the matter, 220.

*in se esse:*being in itself, 127.

in se, non in alio esse: being in itself, not in another. Parallel: to be by itself, 127.

in specie: in the species, 59, 68, 83, 90.

in statu termini: in the state of life after death, 218.

in statu viae: in the state of earthly life, 219.

indere: put into. Parallel: *hineingeben,* 115.

inditus, inditae (indere): put into. Parallel: *hineingeben,* 139.

individuum: individual, 54

*inesse:*being in, inhering in, being proper to. Parallel: *innewohnen,* 34, 116-117.

*innatus (innatae):*inborn, innate. Parallel: *eingeboren,* 139.

*intellectum:*what is understood, 153.

intellectus: the understanding or intellect. Parallel: *Verstand,* 152.
    Contract: *mens,* 152-153, 170-171, 256.

intellectus agens: agent intellect. Parallel: *tätiger Verstand,* 103, 136-137, 161f, 169f, 170-172, 195, 381.

*intellectus possibilis:*possible (passive) intellect. Parallel: *mögliche Einsicht,* 135, 161, 169-171, 195.

intellectus purus: pure understanding, 171.

intelligens esse: to be understanding, 153.

intelligere: to understand, understanding, 129, 153, 171, 381.

intelligere posse: be able to understand, 153, 157.

intelligibile: intelligible, *v.*

intelligibilia: intelligibles. Parallel: objects of knowledge, *(Erkenntnisgegenstände)* 157.

intelligibilitas: intelligibility. Parallel: being illumined.

Q

qua: as

Quaestio de anima: Disputed Question on the Soul (work of St. Thomas), 394.

*Quaestiones disputatae: Disputed Questions (*work of St. Thomas) *xliii,* 2

quale, (the) *quale,*what (it is) like *(Wie),* 17, 35-37, 82, 190, 219, 253, 392, 399-402.

quantum: amount, quality, 299, 399.

quid: (the) , *quid, what (Was),* 36-39, 213.

quidditas: whatness. Parallel: *Washeit,* essence *(essentia, Wesen),* 39, 84.

quod quid est: (the) what it is, *xxxiv,* 28, 35, 39.

R

ratio: notion, reason, 79.

realis: real, 149, 151, 401.

realiter: really, 20, 36, 125, 184-185, 261, 325, 391.

res: thing, 117.

S

sensibile: sensible. Parallel: sense datum *(Sinnesdatum), xxxiv,* 354, 358.

sensibilis-intelligibilis: sensible-intelligible; parallel: *Sinnlich-geistig,* 377.

similitudo: likeness. Contrast: *dissimilitudo,* 129, 219.

species: species, 31f, 49, 51, 54, 59, 86-90, 222, 261, 293-296, 309, 311-313, 317, 322-324, 326-327, 329-330, 343, 349, 354-355, 419-420.

species in individuo: species in the individual, 34, 39.

species intelligibilis: intelligible species, *xxxvii,* 379.

species sensibilis: sensible species, *xxxviii,* 357-358, 361, 367, 378-379.

species sensibilis-intelligibilis: sensible-intelligible species, *xxxvii.*

species specialior: more specific (lower) species, 310.

species specialissima: most specific (lowest) species, 261, 298, 310, 321-322, 405.

Index of Greek expressions[328]

---

[328] Words are given in the alphabet used by St. Theresa Benedicta.

logos: Word, Logos; reason. 111-113, 280-281, 330-331.

noēma (Husserl): noema. 147.

noēsis (Husserl): noesis. 147.

organon: instrument. 5, 23.

Physis: nature. 378.

πρώτη φιλοσοφία (prōtē philosophia): first philosophy, 26.

synteresis [synderesis]: synderesis (also Latin), 208.

telos and τέλος: end, goal, 321, 329, 334, 342, 346-347, 349,383, 402, 404, 406.

Parallel: *Zeil,* 328.

ti: what, something. Cf. 92.

ὑποκείμενον (hypokeimenon): *subjectum*, subject, matter. . Cf. 87zzz, 123-124.

ὑπόστασις: hypostasis, 221-222.

Index of English expressions

A

ability, capability, capacity: *Fähigkeit, Vermögen,* 51, 78, 104, 157, 172, 224.

able: 104-108, 114-115, 140-141, 165.

a priori., 81-84, 86, 371.

a posteriori, 31, 82.

absolute(ly): *absolut, schlechthin*: 11, 21f, 52, 54, 58-61, 64, 67-68, 70, 71, 73-75, 100-101, 104-105, 107-108, 115, 131f, 136, 206, 211-218, 222-223, 225 374-375.

abstract: *Abstrakt;* 29, 70, 105.

abstract: *abheben*: 85.

abstraction: *Abstraktion*: 28-29, 146, 157, 159, 232, 379.

generalizing abstraction: *verailgemeinernd,* 33, 88.

ideating abstraction: *ideieremd*: 81-82.

accident: *Akzidens,* 7, 39, 59, 74, 90-92, 96, 132, 164.

act: *einwirken, wirken, tun,* 6, 102, 104, 121, 182, 214, 223, 317.

act: *Akt, v, xxviii-xxiv, xxix,* 10-13, 15, 23-24, 50, 65, 71, 74, 96, 108-110, 115, 118, 121-122, 175-176, 180, 184-187, 189-190, 192-194, 204- 206, 219, 224.

acts one after another: *Nacheinander,* 15-20, 27, 57, 60, 64, 117, 127-129, 130, 131, 136, 139, 147, 154, 157-160, 163-165, 169-171, 210, 214, 401, 424.

acts one beside another: *Nebeneinander,* 130, 184.

acts one from another: *Auseinander*: 103-104, 130, 149, 152-153, 191, 220.

assemblage of acts: *Aktgefuge*: 14, 112, 122, 128, 176, 189, 209.

second act, 102, 134.

sequence (s) of acts: *Akgefuge*:

action: *Aktion, Tun,* 62-63, 125, 134, 167, 171-174, 195, 208f, 308.

fullness of being: *seinsfulle*: 11, 22, 55, 60-61, 97, 123, 126.
heightening of being: *seinssteigerung*: 129-130, 132, 164, 211, 333.
human being: *menschlisches sein*: 28, 66, 139, 150-151, 214, 405-406.
ideal being: *ideales sein*: 106, 109-110, 115, 128, 417, 419-420.
imparting being: *seinsmitteihlung*: 60.
impulse to being: *Seinsanstoß*; 64.
measure of being: *seinsmaß*, 92, 97, 165, 110, 121, 164-165, 414.
mode of being: *seinsmodus*, 8, 52, 57, 67-68, 83, 96, 99, 154, 182, 211, 388.
null being: *nichtiges sein*, 215, 415.
pitch of being: *seinshöhe*, 51, 417.
rank of being: *seinsrang*, 112, 132.
real being: *eigentliches sein*, 112, 117, 193, 420-421.
region of being: *seinsregion*, 24, 233.
self-sufficiency in being: *seinsselbstsandigkeit*, 52, 372.
share in being: *seinsanteil*, 8, 14, 344.
special being: *sondersein*, 93, 124, 131, 138, 155, 165.
being stretched: *ausgestanntsein*, 121.
be (this being): *das "dies sein" (haecceitas of John Duns Scotus)*.
way of being: *seinsweise*, 153, 210, 233, 235.
be-ing: 93-94, 216, 218-219, 223-224, 228, 233, 237-238, 240, 242, 243, 249-253, 260, 407-408, 413-414.
(noun) *seiendes, wesen, xxxiv*, 12-14, 24, 27-29, 51-52, 58, 66-67, 89, -93, 97-100, 105, 112, 118, 124, 127, 154, 156, 164, 176, 178-179, 192, 194, 210, 213-215, 221, 224, 235-236, 240, 248, 250-251, 253, 255, 385,
(participle) *seiend*, Cf. 58, 91.
belief (the English word, 21, footnote 99), 21f, 210, 217, 235.
belongings: *Habe*, 106, 132, 138, 149. 182, 232-233, 239.

bid, bidding: *Anrufung, Appell,* 162-163, 166.
bodiliness: *leiblichkeit, leibhaftigkeit,* (C-M), 180, 196, 235, 237, 251, 352.
bodily: *leiblich,* 239, 249, 352
    bodily sensible: *leiblich-sinnlich,* 385.
body: *körper,leib, x-xi,* 174, 230-231, 235, 242, 263, 285, 333, 342, 351-352, 383-384.
    of body and soul: *leiblich-seelisch,* 239, 235.
    of body, soul, and spirit: *leiblich-seelisch-geistig,* 255-257, 260, 402.
    of body and spirit: *leiblich-geistig:* 125, 154, 166, 235.
body (verb), (C-M): *leiben,* 236-239, 242, 252, 254-255, 260, 278, 376-377, 398.
body out (C-M): *ausleiben,* 277.
Born: 221-222, 246, 408.
    born of nature (C-M), 157, 240.
    born of spirit (C-M): 240, 243.
bounds: *einschränkung:* 35, 116-117, 135, 144, 413.
    removing bounds: *entschränkung:* 7, 282, 413.
breathe in, inhale, (C-M): *einatmen:* 328.
breathe out, exhale (C-M): *ausatmen:* 257, 328.
buried talent: 96, 203-204.

C

capacity, capability, ability, 14, 51, 102, 192.
category: *ix,* 7, 15, 29, 96, 100.
    basic category: *Grundkategorie:* 88-92, 118, 152, 198.
Catholic: *viii,* 202, 207.
causal: *kausal, Kausal,* 227.
    objectively causal, *objektiv-kausal,* 64.
causality: *Kausalität,* 296, 306.

energy: 167, 385.

engage: *entgegennehmen,* 191, 236, 254.

engagement: *entgegennahme,* 189-190.

engender: (C-M): *erzeugen,* 291, 294.

enlighten: *erleuchtung:* 133-134, 155, 168, 171.

enlightenment: *erleuchtung:* 133-134, 138.

entelechy: 62, 76, 321-322.

essence: *wesen, essenz, wesenheit, x,* 5f, 73, 84, 99, 177, 121, 181, 213, 217-249, 252, 272, 370, 392, 397, 410, 414-415, 423.

commonness of essence, 131-132, 138, 164-169, 392.

form of essence: *wensensform,* 57, 82, 84, 87, 107-108, 121, 134-135, 139, 140, 156-157.

sameness of essence: *wesens, gleichheit,* 99, 130-131, 135-137.

union of essence: *wesenseinigung:* 122, 132, 138.

essential: *wesentlich, wesenhaft,* 24, 64, 118, 164, 174, 196, 213, 240, 246, 253.

essential attribute: *wesensattribut,* 169.

essential property: *wesenseigentümlichkeit,* 152-154.

essentiality: (C-M): *wesemhaftigkeit,* 238, 240.

eternal: *xxvif, xxvii,* 2, 10f, 27, 67, 71, 107, 109-110, 122, 128, 154, 172, 191, 211, 227.

eternity: 6, 14, 22, 67, 70f, 73, 107, 109, 114, 122, 128-129, 171-172, 201-202, 204, 207, 210-211, 219.

event: *geschehen:* 184, 288.

evidence: *zeugnis:* 179.

evil: 207, 210, 213.

the Evil One, 207, 213.

evince: *bekunden,* 151, 376, 378.

evincing: *bekundung,* 179, 265.

evolution: *entwicklung, ix,* 209, 260, 294, 403 .

course of evolution: *entwicklungsgan.,*

(living, lived) experience: *erlebnis*, 81, 87, 147, 149.

experiential knowing: *erfahrungswissen*:

expression: *x*, 111, 114, 130, 139, 142, 147, 169, 190, 253, 260, 394, 396.

expressive phenomenon: *ausdrucksphänomen*: 81, 108.

F

fact: *factum, tatsache*, 11-12, 23, 65, 108, 110, 112, 114, 127, 149, 135, 131, 142, 186, 221, 232, 255, 315, 375.

factor: *faktor*: 63, 185, 190.

   active factor: *wirkfaktor*, 65.

factual: *tatsächlich*, 354.

factualness: *faktizität*, 374.

feel: *empfinden, fuhlen*, 178, 180-181, 186, 250, 252.

feeling: *gefuhlfuhlen*, 157, 178, 186, 190, 246, 247.

   feeling of being alive: *lebensgefühl*, 212, 254.

fill: 50, 92, 110, 126, 156, 164, 168, 223.

filling: 30, 69, 149, 414.

finite: *xxvif-xxvii*, 8, 24, 58, 88, 122-123, 127-128, 153-154, 191, 201, 210, 213, 215-217, 222, 224-225, 227, 399, 414, 417.

fix: *fixieren*: 133, 339.

fixedness: *fixiertheit*, 30-31, 106.

flight of ideas: 162.

flaw, lack: *mangel*, 398.

flawed, missing: *mangelhaft*, 210.

the flower: 62.

force, power: *kraft*, 27, 56, 63-64, 168, 263, 272, 328, 368.

forgiveness, 212.

form: *bilden, formen, gestalten*, 40, 62-64, 66, 70, 174.

form: *ix*, 22, 27, 31, 52, 88, 89, 93, 105, 139, 173, 191, 214, 227-228, 247-249, 255, 260, 364, 379, 381, 384-385, 394, 398, 421.

basic form: *grundform,* 29, 50-51, 56, 58, 138, 152, 222.

being of form: *formsein:* 82, 88, 91, 94, 115-116, 123, 131-132, 150, 152, 155, 163, 165, 168, 333, 420.

empty form: *seinsform,* 28-31, 50, 53, 69, 92-93, 96, 100, 126, 385, 392, 399, 420-421.

form of essence: *wesensform,* 57, 123, 131, 137, 421, 423.

form of object: *gegenstandsform,* 30, 56, 91, 123,126, 137, 145, 246, 253.

form of thing: *dingform,* 3, 50, 60, 91, 102, 114,117, 136, 122-123, 135-136, 157, 318, 352, 358, 379, 420, 424.

form of the what (it is): *was-form,* 47, 59, 100, 104, 222-223, 246.

principle of form: *formprinzip:* 224-225, 253, 260, 124-126, 135, 166, 316, 345.

formal: *formal:* 13, 52, 58, 61, 76, 100, 103, 222, 289, 379.

formal category: 80, 92-94, 110, 124.

formal cause: 57, 67, 73, 95f, 97, 100.

formal ontology: 51, 91-92, 94-97, 131, 230.

making formal: *formalizierung,* 78, 91, 93, 96.

formalization: *formalisation, formalizierung,* 85, 220.

formalness: *formalität,* 29.

formation: *formung,* 59, 115, 220, 241, 394.

produced formation, (Husserl): *leistungsgebilde,* xxxiii.

forming: *formung, bildung,* 62, 65-67, 77, 115, 202,227, 318, 322, 360.

frail: *hinfällig:* 21.

frailty: 10f-11, 21-22.

framework: 92.

basic framework: *grundgerüst:* 69, 108-109.

free: 66, 171, 204, 211, 214, 216, 223, 225, 242, 246, 254, 257, 370.

consciously free: *bewußt-frei,* 146.

free, conscious, personal: *frei-bewußt-personal,* 129, 153, 205.

freely conscious: *frei-bewußt,* 134, 138, 163, 180, 195.

human being: *menschliches sein*: *xxii,* 166-167, 192, 202, 208, 221, 236.

human nature: *menschennatur,* 209, 398, 406.

human soul: *menschenseele,* 257, 259, 396.

human spirit: *menschengeist*: 99-100, 230.

knowing human nature: *menschenerkenntnis*: 114.

hypostasis: 221-222.

I

(the) I: *Ich, xlivf,* 9-10, 15-16, 177-179, 181, 187, 415.

activity of the I: *ichtatigkeit.*

birth of the I: (C-M): *ichkonstitugaon*: 125-126.

constitution of the I: *ichkonstitution*: 125-126.

depths of the I: *ichtiefe,* 186.

foreign to the I: *ichfrend,* 186.

life of the I: *ichleben,* 123, 126, 264.

primal I: (C-M): *ur-ich,* 125, 246.

proper to the I, *ichlich*: 186.

idea: *idee, ix, xxxvii,* 7, 27-28, 46, 51-52, 56, 60-61, 81, 103, 105-108, 110-113, 115, 117, 139-147, 151-152, 159, 162, 172-176, 222, 226, 254, 260, 369, 418-419, 424.

world of ideas: *ideen, welt,* 88, 96, 109, 114, 129-130, 140, 151, 418.

ideal, *xxxiv,* 53, 59, 92, 105-108, 110, 114-118, 146, 181, 423.

idealism: *xli,* 360.

ideating: *ideierend*: 82-83, 232.

ideation: 88.

illumine: *durchleuchten, drleuchten,* 154.

illumined: *durchleuchtet*: 154.

being illumined, transperent: *durchleuchtetsein, Erleuchtetsein,* 154, 177, 227, 254.

nymphs: (C-M):

O

object: *objekt, gegenstand, gebilde,* 28-30, 52-53, 57-58, 61, 65-66, 88, 91-92, 97-100, 105-107, 110, 113, 116, 121, 123-124, 126, 132, 135, 140-141, 145-149, 151, 158, 160, 162-163, 169, 173, 179, 194, 231, 282, 290, 301, 311, 318, 337, 340, 355,-358, 363, 368, 371, 373, 420.

ideal object: *vergegenstandlichung, xxxiv-xxxvi,* 15, 25, 27-28, 73, 110, 118, 190, 193, 196-197, 305, 418.

objectification: *vergegenständlichung,* 141, 177, 365.

objectify: *vergegenständlichen.*

objective: *gegenstandlichkeit, objektvitat, ix, xxxi,* 39, 41, 43, 99-100, 121, 123, 125, 130, 137, 139-140, 143-147, 153, 158, 160, 168, 175-176, 185-186, 190, 192, 203, 231, 255, 265, 307f, 311-312, 340, 346, 355, 358, 371-373, 378, 381, 384.

objectivity: *gegenständlichkeit, objektvität, sachlichkett,* 43, 146, 160, 175, 370-373.

occurence: 52, 68, 100, 107, 130, 135-136, 147, 156, 288, 314, 323.

ontic: *xxxi,* 11, 89, 92, 108, 118, 300, 317, 320, 324, 326-329, 354, 392, 405.

ontological: 294, 394, 398.

formally ontological: (ontological in the formal sense): *formal-ontologisch,* 21f, 24-26, 70-71, 75, 89, 93, 122-123, 127, 151.

materially ontological (ontological in the material sense): *material-ontologisch, xxxi,* 9, 24, 81, 89, 92, 99, 204.

ontology:

formal ontology: *xxxi, xxxiii,-xxxiv,* 9, 26-29, 51, 55, 91-92, 94, 96-97, 311.

material ontology: 70, 85, 87-89, 92, 94, 99, 103.

ontology of spirit: 115, 118.